A GENTLE WIND
of GOD

Don Jacobs

A GENTLE WIND
of GOD
The Influence of the East Africa Revival

Richard K. MacMaster

with Donald R. Jacobs

Herald Press
Scottdale, Pennsylvania
Waterloo, Ontario

Library of Congress Cataloging-in-Publication Data

MacMaster, Richard K. (Richard Kerwin), 1935–
 A gentle wind of God : the influence of the East Africa revival / by Richard
K. MacMaster with Donald R. Jacobs.
    p. cm.
 Includes bibliographical references and index.
 ISBN 0-8361-9318-0 (pbk. : alk. paper)
 1. Revivals—Africa, East. 2. Africa, East—Church history.
 3. Mennonites—Missions.
I. Jacobs, Donald R. II. Title.
 BV3777.A42M33 2006
 289.7—dc22
                                                    2006006570

A GENTLE WIND OF GOD
Copyright © 2006 by Herald Press, Scottdale, PA 15683
  Published simultaneously in Canada by Herald Press,
  Waterloo, Ont. N2L 6H7. All rights reserved
Library of Congress Catalog Card Number: 2006006570
International Standard Book Number: 0-8361-9318-0
Printed in the United States of America
Book design by Sandra Johnson
Cover by Greg Yoder

12 11 10 09 08 07 06   10 9 8 7 6 5 4 3 2 1

To order or request information, please call
1-800-759-4447 (individuals); 1-800-245-7894 (trade).
Web site: www.heraldpress.com

To Eve

Abbreviations and Name Changes

AE	African Enterprise
AEE	African Evangelistic Enterprise
AIM	Africa Inland Mission, founded in 1895
CLC	Christian Literature Crusade, founded in 1941
CMS	Church Missionary Society, founded by the Anglican Church in 1799
EMBMC	Eastern Mennonite Board of Missions and Charities, founded in 1914
EMM	Eastern Mennonite Missions, after name change from EMBMC in 1993
PCEA	Presbyterian Church in East Africa
Ruanda	name changed to Rwanda in 1962
Tanganyika	united with Zanzibar under the name Tanzania in October 1964
Urundi	name changed to Burundi in 1962
WEC	Worldwide Evangelization Crusade in 1919 succeeded the Heart of Africa Mission, founded in 1910–1913 by C. T. Studd

Contents

Foreword

The first wave of the modern missionary movement crested in the 1840s. By that time Christian missions had gained a footing in India. With the cure for malaria still several decades in the future, the continent of Africa was widely regarded as the "graveyard of missions." China continued to fend off all foreigners. Only a few determined missionaries managed to get a toehold in coastal trading centers. Add to this the fact that in 1840 and 1841 the world economy was in crisis. Yet this was the moment when a few mission leaders began to speak of the "blessed reflex." They foretold the day when missionaries from Africa, Asia, and other parts of the world would bring a fresh word from God to Europe and North America. Christendom was in trouble. Secularization and nominality were relentlessly doing their work. The vital signs indicated that Western Christianity was in decline and becoming spiritually sterile.

In the twentieth century the East Africa Revival became an important expression of this "blessed reflex." *A Gentle Wind of God* recounts the origins and main developments of the East Africa Revival, starting in 1929, and shows that God's servants were soon taking the revival "message" to other continents. This book traces the means by which the East Africa Revival came to North America and the people who gave it leadership.

Authentic revival is never a program; it is a movement of the Holy Spirit. It emerges in situations where faith has grown cold and spiritual vitality is at a low ebb. Although we want to establish the precise origins and key leaders of a new movement, real revival typically defies such easy analysis. In the popular imagination the Pentecostal movement started at Azusa Street in Los Angeles, California, in 1906. In reality, in the early 1900s "Pentecostal manifestations" were cropping up on all continents without any central leadership. We cannot predict when such a fresh stirring of God's Spirit will take place; we can only step into the stream of God's movement and transformation. Revival movements have consistently caused controversy, for they always upset the status quo.

The East Africa Revival started among people greatly burdened about the nominal Christianity they observed around them. On the one hand, it was becoming popular to "join the church," and so the churches were growing; but on the other hand, for many people this meant merely exchanging an old religion for the new. This kind of Christianity lacked depth and did not result in Christian discipleship.

When revival came, it addressed this condition directly. The Holy Spirit led people into a deepening relationship with God in Jesus Christ and, second, a new awareness of the unity that ought to characterize the people of God. This experience was marked by immediacy, intimacy, and consecration: walking daily in close and transparent relationship with Jesus and in the company of God's people. The compelling concern was that believers should experience continual cleansing from all sin, to live in the freedom of forgiven people and in the presence of Jesus.

The East Africa Revival was not a missionary-led movement. From the beginning both Africans and Europeans teamed up to carry the revival message into the churches. This was true both in East Africa and internationally. Early on, African leaders in the revival found opportunity to travel to Europe and North America. The face of the East Africa Revival was multiethnic. In the light of the work of Jesus on the cross, the church had to repent and be cleansed of racism. African church leaders and missionaries carried the leaven of revival to North America. It continued to be replenished and shared through correspondence, prayer letters, and extensive itineration.

Mennonites were not present in East Africa when the revival started in 1929. In 1934 the Eastern Mennonite Board of Missions—now Eastern Mennonite Missions—established a mission in Tanzania—then Tanganyika; it was several years before Mennonites came into contact with the revival. Richard MacMaster, together with Don Jacobs, traces the steps by which Mennonite and other missionaries serving in East Africa begin to share their own experience of revival with friends and churches in North America. The revival was an important source of renewal for Mennonites after World War II.

As happened in other revivals, the one in East Africa challenged traditional patterns of hierarchy and gender-based roles. From the beginning women played an important role. The witness of Anglican missionary teacher Mabel Ensor, burdened by the widespread nominal faith among Christians in East Africa, helped ignite the fires of revival in the late 1920s. For many years Mennonite laywoman Erma Maust held up the torch of revival from Lancaster County. Using her home as a base, Maust was a networker par excellence.

A Gentle Wind of God is an engaging account of a movement that has exerted remarkable influence on several continents over the past seventy-five years. It reminds us that the renewing and transforming work of the Holy Spirit is never finished.

Wilbert R. Shenk
Fuller Theological Seminary
May 2006

Preface

This book began fifteen years ago, although I didn't know it at the time. Like many North Americans, I knew nothing of the East Africa Revival. I was then teaching history at a small college related to the General Conference Mennonite Church, and African history was one of my subjects, so I had less excuse for ignorance of this determinative Christian awakening in East Africa. I was certainly aware that revival is a constant theme in the history of the Christian Church. Just as the Great Awakening and other revivals shaped the churches on this continent, the younger churches also experienced periods of renewal. I had heard stories of a great revival in Indonesia, for instance, but no one had ever told me about a revival in East Africa. That there had been a revival there seemed likely, but it could not have been important. Or so I thought.

My first acquaintance with a revival in East Africa came indirectly. I was reading the letters and reports of Mennonite mission workers in New York City, preparing to write about their work there. In 1960 one of the pastors in the South Bronx complained about "the new ideas that Erma Maust is bringing into the church." I knew that Herbert and Erma Maust helped with the vacation Bible school program at the Seventh Avenue Mennonite Church in Harlem every summer, but I had no clue about what "new ideas" they might be introducing there. It was a puzzle. I asked some of my informants who had been part of the Mennonite city missions; to my surprise, they pointed to something called the East Africa Revival.

Missionaries from Africa, home on furlough in the 1940s, told about what the Lord was doing in the East African colonies of Tanganyika (Tanzania from 1964), Kenya, Uganda, and Ruanda-Urundi (Rwanda and Burundi from 1962). Erma Maust learned of the message of revival from them. She evidently brought it to the churches in Manhattan and the Bronx. But it was still a puzzle.

Erma was never an ordained minister, much less an evangelist bringing thousands to make a decision for Christ. A traditional Mennonite woman, she wore the conservative clothes and devotional covering prescribed by her church. With her husband and children, she attended Marietta Mennonite Church in Lancaster County, Pennsylvania. Herbert and Erma Maust understood their ministry as one of helping, doing a sick neighbor's housework, or encouraging a despondent friend. The veteran New York City mission workers spoke of the encouragement they drew from letters and visits, and of regular fellowship meetings for prayer and for sharing frankly their victories and their failures. They talked about repenting and walking in the light. If this was what the East Africa Revival meant to them, it was a different kind of revival from what I understood by the term.

I associated revival with services held twice a year in many churches, when a visiting pastor preaches every night for a week, or with crusades that brought a well-known evangelist to town for a series of meetings sponsored by churches in the community. When Erma Maust was telling Bible stories to small children or helping prepare their snacks, Billy Graham was filling Yankee Stadium and delivering powerful messages every night in his first New York City crusade. In their crusades Graham and his team challenged thousands with the claims of Christ and reached many thousands more through radio. Through the centuries revivals were always associated with Spirit-filled preaching by great evangelists. What sort of a revival could there be without preachers?

The East Africa Revival intrigued me. I asked people who had lived in East Africa what it meant, and I read everything I could find on the subject. There was not a great deal in print. Writers on church history and missions gave only glancing attention to the revival, dismissing it in a few sentences, if they mentioned it at all. Jocelyn Murray of London, author of a history of the Church Missionary Society, where I found the fullest treatment of the East Africa Revival, kindly sent me a list of books and articles, many in hard-to-locate journals. Later, Wilbert Shenk, now teaching missiology at Fuller Theological Seminary, added other titles.

One of the first things I read made a lasting impression on me. David W. Shenk wrote in *Peace and Reconciliation in Africa:*

> The revivalists were a people who "walked in the light" and who lived in "brokenness" in their relationships with one another. They challenged one another to live in complete transparency and humility. They lived in the joy of precious fellowship. This fellowship is the only community in East Africa which authentically transcends ethnic, racial, denominational, economic, or national barriers. It really is a new peoplehood.[1]

Other revivals changed individuals. This movement went further, molding them into an altogether new community.

The revival broke down barriers between African and Westerner as well as tribal and national rivalry. Public confession of sin and weakness characterized the regular group meetings of the renewed ones. This frank acknowledgment of failure brought each one to the same level at the foot of the cross. Reconciliation is the heart of the gospel message. In East Africa observers could identify this new people of God by their love one for another, which broke down artificial barriers of race and nation and gave a new freedom to the oppressed and the powerful, a new equality to men and women.

The testimony of all those touched by the revival was that Jesus had met each one at the point where he or she was broken. Each person could testify to the moment when God's grace touched his or her life. But at that same moment they became part of his people. When revival came, one Tanzanian pastor explained, "The Holy Spirit gave us the insight that both the missionaries and the Africans were all lost from that one true village, the new village of God our Father." Everyone who migrated to God's village, he discovered, became part of God's new people. "The Holy Spirit showed us that Jesus' sacrifice made it possible for all of us to be brothers and sisters in the same village."[2]

This emphasis on Christian community and a new peoplehood founded on Jesus Christ contrasted sharply with prevailing Western notions of individualism. One African Christian "expressed surprise that Westerners ever took to Christianity or the New Testament, whose implications for society seemed to him alien to Western attitudes and much closer to African attitudes." The revival message was thus an important corrective to ideas introduced into the Christian church by the eighteenth-century Enlightenment in Europe and America.[3]

The East Africa Revival brought sincere believers together—whether Anglicans, Free Methodists, Quakers, Lutherans, Mennonites, Presbyterians, or Seventh-Day Adventists—into a new peoplehood; it encouraged them to remain faithful members of their own churches. With few exceptions, the Christians who found a new beginning in the revival did not withdraw from their denominations to find a pure, awakened church where all shared their experience or followed their particular rules. Nor did the revival fellowships hive off to form new denominations. They were determined to learn brokenness in their own denominations and also to be salt and light in the church and in the world.

The revival fellowships did not emphasize signs and wonders, nor did they put great store in techniques or rules. They believed in the necessity of a personal, close walk with Jesus Christ on a daily basis, but they shied away from the spectacular, preferring rather to point to Jesus. They were careful lest anything eclipse the glory and worth of Jesus Christ. Festo Kivengere's biographer summed up their attitude: "Festo would challenge people who spoke of *having had* a revival, those who believed that when the miraculous manifestations subsided, that was it. As always, his insistence was, 'But real revival is Jesus Christ himself!'"[4]

The more I read about the East Africa Revival, the more I wanted to know. But I knew about it only from books and articles. I had not shared their experience or talked with anyone who had met the Lord in a new way in East Africa.

That changed when my wife and I moved to Lancaster County, Pennsylvania, late in 1994. I had had a series of health crises, among them a heart attack and cancer surgery, and my last year of teaching had been quite difficult. On our first Sunday in our new church, Paul and Lydia Kurtz invited us to dinner. They also invited Pastor Wayne Lawton and his wife, Mary Lou. In response to a question about current research or writing projects, I said something about the East Africa Revival. I discovered that the Lawtons were part of the Revival Fellowship in Pennsylvania since 1959 and knew many of the revival brothers and sisters in Africa and North America. From that first meeting, Wayne encouraged me to write a book on the influence of the East Africa Revival. He told me that his daughter and son-in-law, Ruth and Paul Stewart, urged him to make sure that someone collected the many revival stories while quite a few of the pioneers were still alive. Wayne had a burden for this but did not know how it would be accomplished. When I appeared on the scene, he believed that he saw the answer to his prayers!

I began to meet returned missionaries who had begun a closer walk with the Lord in East Africa, brothers and sisters from Kenya, Uganda, and Tanzania, and men and women who heard the message of the East Africa Revival on this side of the Atlantic. All of them had found Jesus Christ sufficient. Their joy and love of the Lord was evident. It was evident that there was power and conviction in what they said. I met others, no longer living, through their diaries and letters. The Spirit of Jesus Christ shone through them on every page.

We soon had a committee of oversight for this project. Don Jacobs has served as chair, and Catharine Leatherman, Paul and Bertha Miller, David Shenk, Janice Hess, James Maust, Wayne Lawton, and Nathan Hege each gave freely of their time and their wisdom. As the book progressed, it became evident that we could enhance the storytelling if a person of long standing in the revival would join with me. Don Jacobs consented to do that, and he added many additional insights, which readers will appreciate. In addition to several interpretative sections of the book, he contributed heavily to the opening sections and wrote the final chapters. All of the sections written in the first person singular, however, refer to me, Richard MacMaster.

Early in the project, we agreed to try to tell this story as much as possible in the words of the men and women who experienced revival in their own lives. I have tried not to let my voice intrude too much on their narrative. This is also the explanation for the endnotes, which some readers may find distracting. We insert them not as part of the scholarly apparatus for a doctoral dissertation or an article in an academic journal, but simply to let the reader know the origin of a particular quote. Since I never knew Elam Stauffer or William Nagenda, for example, I think the reader is entitled to know where I learned what I say about them.

I regret that during the writing of the book Paul Miller and Catharine Leatherman went on to glory. Before their deaths, however, they made significant contributions. Catharine was especially helpful because much of the story involves the unique ministry that she and her husband, John, had in encouraging the flow of revival blessings in both East Africa and North America.

I also want to acknowledge the excellent advice we received from Herbert Osborn, who is an active member of the Revival Fellowship in England and author of several books on revival. Each member of the book committee made valuable contributions. Nathan Hege did the index, Wayne Lawton gave valuable time to the project and was the chief fundraiser. Janice Hess and James Maust gave many hours to ensure that the material in the book was accurate.

—Richard MacMaster

Introduction

In speaking to the Jewish theologian Nicodemus, Jesus described how the Spirit of God works. "The wind blows wherever it pleases. You hear its sound, but you cannot tell where it comes from or where it is going. So it is with everyone born of the Spirit." "How can this be?" Nicodemus asked (John 3:8-9 NIV). Indeed, it is a mystery. Every move of God's Holy Spirit defies explanation. Yet the effects are always the same. Ordinary people bow as the winds blow, like reeds in a pond, as God touches their lives with grace and truth, found supremely in Jesus Christ.

Where does this wind come from? Students of revival seek to find its common keys, the prerequisites for the pouring out of God's blessing. Behind the search is the assumption that if we do the right thing in the right way, then the winds of revival will blow. To be sure, zealous prayer, a crying out to God for revival, precedes all authentic Christian revivals. Yet not all such agonizing prayer eventuates in a great revival. Revival does not come from human effort; it is the work of God's grace alone.

What happens when the winds blow? People are born of the Spirit. They are fundamentally changed by the power of the atoning work of Jesus Christ. They confess their sins, make Jesus Christ Lord of their lives, and then seek to live according to the teachings of Jesus, in close fellowship with others who are experiencing the transforming power of Jesus Christ.

Where is it going? Who knows? Who would have predicted the long-term effects when a small group of missionaries and Ugandans bowed at the foot of the cross and found peace with God and one another? It happened in the mountains of remote Ruanda, where a small fellowship felt the first stirrings of the wind of God. Thousands in East Africa and lands beyond are still feeling that wind of revival.

It is the purpose of this book to tell the story of how this mighty wind of God stirred and blew with great force across East Africa, and how it impacted lives in Europe, England, and North America. Imbedded in the story is the message of God's redeeming and sanctifying power. The story describes the mystery. It is a mystery of God's grace. It is the mystery revealed in every authentic movement of God's Spirit in the world.

The story is biographical

The East Africa Revival story is best told by concentrating on a few people who represent the thousands. It is impossible to speak of revival in the abstract. Revival comes to life in revived people. So we tell this story by walking alongside some of the people God chose to embody and communicate the way of the gospel.

They are not the only ones or even the most important proponents of revival. But they do represent people who went beyond where others were to extend the rule of Christ. Our story includes people like Simeon Nsibambi, "Joe" (John Edward) Church, William Nagenda, Roy Hession, Festo Kivengere, Erma Maust, John Leatherman, and Dorothy Smoker because of their role in opening new vistas for the saving grace of Jesus. Unnumbered thousands are not even mentioned even though there were energetic firebrands for Jesus Christ. Thousands of quite ordinary people embodied this movement of God's Spirit. As the apostle John said, trying to describe Jesus would take more books than the world can hold (John 21:25). Yet telling the story of a few highlighted people should not distract from the understanding that all of the "saved ones" burned with an uncommon zeal for their blessed Lord and Savior, Jesus Christ.

Defining revival

God sent special seasons of refreshing throughout the history of the church. We call such times revivals. This book is the story of but one such movement, which began in East Africa in the late 1920s, when Christianity was experiencing phenomenal growth in that region. Across the land churches had sprung up like mushrooms. Many people were pleased to call themselves Christians. As the churches grew, however, so did nominal Christianity. Many people had accepted Christianity as a "religion" without experiencing a close and intimate daily walk with Jesus Christ. This book describes how a mighty wind of revival swept across East Africa, beginning more than seventy years ago. The Holy Spirit moved with power, bringing men and women into a love relationship with Jesus and with other believers. They rediscovered the grace of God in Jesus Christ, the common theme of all authentic revivals.

What was the essence of that movement of God's Spirit? The report of International Revival Conference held in Les Diablerets, Switzerland, in

1991 gave a fair description of East Africa Revival and the Spirit's work within it:

> In the early 1930s a few spiritually hungry Africans and Europeans received a new vision of the cross of Jesus Christ in the small East African nation of Rwanda. When they saw the Lamb of God, crucified and raised from the dead, they then saw the sinfulness of their own hearts. Consequently they fled to Calvary for cleansing. There at the cross they not only received forgiveness for their sins and a new in-rushing of the Holy Spirit; they also discovered another delightful gift, a completely new family which knew no color, denomination, or station in life. All those who fell at the feet of the Crucified One loved one another with a compelling love. These Christians who had formerly known Jesus Christ only as an historical figure or a passing acquaintance found to their amazement and joy that Jesus wanted to relate to them as a living presence constantly. This was an exhilarating discovery.

From those humble hearts the message of revival spread throughout East Africa and ultimately around the world. Through the life and testimony of those who were touched by what has come to be called the East Africa Revival, Jesus Christ has set free literally tens of thousands of people. The word "revival" was a word which "outsiders" used to describe what was happening. The brothers and sisters themselves talked only of Jesus. Jesus Christ was for them the New Life. Jesus Christ is revival![1]

The message

If one were to try to summarize the message of so-called revival, it would be something like this. Come to Jesus with your sins; repent and be cleansed by the blood of Jesus Christ; live in the immediacy of the presence of Jesus, and walk in open fellowship with the brothers and sisters; absorb yourself in the Word of God by life-changing Bible study; allow Jesus Christ to do good deeds through you by the enabling of the Holy Spirit; and witness with word, life, and action that Jesus Christ is the head of the individual and of the body of believers.

The 1991 conference, held in the magnificent Swiss Alps, chose as their theme hymn the song written by Revel Hession, Roy Hession's first wife. The Hessions were enthusiastic carriers of the revival message literally around the world.

He left his father's home for Calvary.
He walked this earth alone to Calvary.
His eyes with tears were wet
As o'er our sins he wept.
Daily his face was set for Calvary.

His face was deeply marred at Calvary.
His hands and feet were scarred at Calvary.
He bowed his head and died
As from his wounded side
A fountain opened wide at Calvary.

No diadem adorns at Calvary.
He wore a crown of thorns at Calvary.
Dear Lord, make us to see,
We nailed thee to the tree.
We caused thy agony at Calvary.

Come, let our footsteps wend to Calvary.
Our proud, stiff necks will bend at Calvary.[2]

These lines contain the essence and the way of the East Africa Revival. One can find a fuller version in a small booklet, now a classic, written by Roy Hession, *The Calvary Road.*[3]

Some terms used in this book

This book uses the word "revival" to embrace the totality of God's work in the human heart, as described above. In East Africa people did not usually refer to themselves as "the revived ones," but as "the saved ones." They used the term "saved" in a much broader way than theologians would. For them, to be saved was to move into a living, vital relationship with Jesus Christ and with other believers. The saved ones had a testimony of newness of life in Christ, which included receiving Jesus as personal Savior and Lord and walking with him constantly in the company of others. Some of the nominal Christians continued to dabble in the occult and in ancestral veneration, but not the saved ones. They committed themselves to follow the teachings of Jesus, so they worked out in ethics what they were experiencing in their relationship with Jesus every day. This book refers to those who embraced Jesus Christ in revival way as "the saved ones." In actual fact, they referred to one another simply as brothers and sisters in the Lord Jesus. They saw themselves as an intimate and responsible family. They discovered that in this new family of faith, cultural background is irrelevant. "The ground is level at the foot of the cross," they declared.

When the saved ones met people whom they did not know, it would not go long, normally, until they said, "I am saved; are you?" In the East African context, no further explanation is required. It may put off some Christians to be asked, "Are you saved?" What is really meant is, "Have you been born again, and are you walking with Jesus in a life-giving way? Have you left the world to walk as 'children of light'?" It implies not only conversion but also walking with Jesus in obedience to him. In the East African context it includes walking in love and transparency with brothers and sisters.

The revival did blow across East Africa first, but it moved beyond, to other lands. For this reason we will refer to it as the East Africa Revival, but it is as universal as the gospel itself.

The wind of the Spirit of God blows where it will. We cannot determine where it came from nor where it is going, but we know that it is the sovereign work of almighty God. We also know that it always has the same effect, no matter where it blows. It blows sinners to the foot of the cross where they find their sins forgiven; and it blows them to the empty tomb, where Jesus stands alive and well, full of grace and truth. It also blows them into intimate, loving fellowships. Those who have been touched by this eternal wind are never the same again.

As you read this story, may you also experience the stirring of the wind of God, the Holy Spirit, who makes Jesus more real than the morning sun.

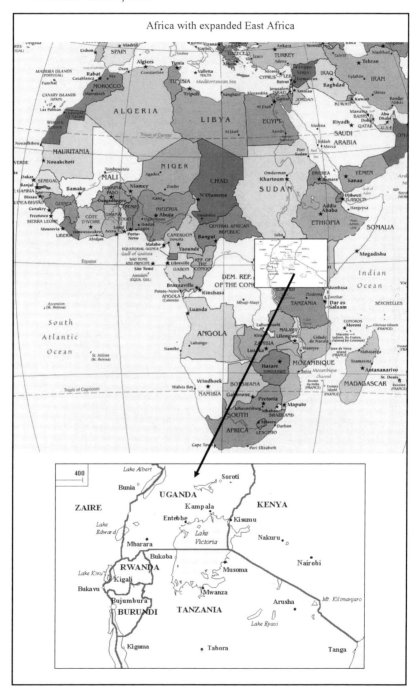

—1—

Praying for Revival
1929–1932

Revival is not just history

Are the winds of God still blowing today in East Africa and around the world? I found the answer to that question when I was in Ireland recently, involved in academic research. One Sunday I was having lunch in a Church of Ireland rectory in Belfast, with the rector, his family, and two visitors from Kenya. They had come to Northern Ireland for medical studies at Queen's University. We talked of many things. They told us about their work and how they would use their specialized studies in combating disease at home. We discussed our churches and talked about clergy teams from Kenya and Rwanda who were teaching Christians in Northern Ireland and in England about evangelism. It was a wonderful example of the younger "mission" churches bringing new life to the older churches that once evangelized them.

After a while I mentioned my interest in the history of the East Africa Revival and asked if they could tell me about it. They had both experienced the revival in their churches and felt that it had shaped them as they grew in Christ. But the history—that was a different matter. It had its beginnings a long time ago, to be sure. It seemed more important to them that it was continuing today.

Early stirrings of revival breezes in East Africa before 1929

How did the revival in East Africa begin? It is difficult to find anyone willing to assign a where and when, although everyone agrees that the mission hospital at Gahini in Ruanda[1] was one of the places where the Holy Spirit began working in the hearts of believers. I soon discovered that such questions did not much interest men and women who met the Lord through the East Africa Revival. "It began at Calvary," some would say.

25

When Yohana Omari, the Anglican bishop of Tanzania, a clear voice for revival, attended his first Lambeth Conference of Anglican bishops, the Archbishop of Canterbury asked him when the revival started. Without hesitation, Omari said, "It must have been about two thousand years ago, when Jesus hung on the cross for my sins." They were more interested in what God was doing today than in what happened sixty or seventy years ago.[2]

The wind of the Holy Spirit blows on two cultures

Two names did recur as being there at the beginning: Simeon Nsibambi from Uganda and Joe Church from England. Church and Nsibambi met on the hillside in front of the Anglican cathedral at Kampala, Uganda, on September 23, 1929. They both had concerns about their church and had been praying for God to renew its fervor. Below them the city of Kampala was set amid the beauty of flowering trees, yellow cassias, scarlet flame trees, and blue jacarandas. The massive cathedral itself stood at the crest of Namirembe Hill, overlooking the city, and its dome, much like the dome of St. Paul's in London, could be seen for miles. The Church Missionary Society had its headquarters nearby, and the bishop's residence, church offices, and schools for boys and girls surrounded the cathedral. Mengo Hospital was on the slopes of Namirembe Hill, just below the great cathedral.[3]

Like Rome, Kampala was built on seven hills, a few miles from the vast inland sea known as Lake Victoria. Hills and deep valleys rose up from the lakeshore, leveling off to a high plateau stretching over much of the country. The climate was mild and rainfall plentiful, especially in spring and fall, so crops were abundant. Covering the countryside around the capital and for miles beyond were small farms, where bananas, coffee, and cotton grow almost without cultivation, and also some larger commercial tea and coffee estates. Further west were broad plains, best-suited for grazing cattle, and beyond them high mountain ranges on the borders of Congo and Ruanda, the famous Mountains of the Moon.

Joe Church, British missionary

Joe and Decie Church, missionaries to Ruanda.

Joe Church was a young British medical doctor, full of idealism and energy. His closely cropped mustache and distinctly English varsity bearing set him apart. Joe excelled not only in his academic studies but was also an excellent cricket player and hard to beat on the tennis court. He was the product of the best of English education and culture. Instead of settling into a medical career in England, he dedicated his life to the Lord as a missionary doctor. Here he was in Ruanda, in East Central Africa, doing his best to provide assistance to a famine-stricken land. He had been busy for months organizing famine relief for drought-stricken Ruanda. In early 1928 the rains in northern and eastern Ruanda had failed, and by June people were widely feeling the effects of drought.[4] When the normal dry season began, famine gripped the country. Starving families fled across the border into Uganda to find work and food. By November a thousand hungry refugees paused every day at Gahini Hospital on their way to Uganda. "They crawl to us from miles round, and by the time they arrive, have scarcely sufficient strength in their shrunken, shriveled bodies to hold out their hands," Church reported. In addition to his hospital duties, he worked with Bishop James J. Willis to let the world know what was happening and to set up a famine relief appeal. By September 1929 the famine was over, and he went to Kampala for a few days of rest.[5]

On that Sunday morning, Church joined a stream of Africans going up the hill for the morning service.

> I walked through the old sun-dried brick archway at the top of the hill and there, opposite the entrance to the Synod hall, was a man in a dark suit standing beside his motor bike. He spotted me and ran out to greet me. It was Simeon Nsibambi, whom I had met in March when I spoke to Miss Ensor's Bible class. He said he had enjoyed that time and asked if I had any more to tell them. I said that I was looking for a new infilling of the Holy Spirit and the victorious life. He warmed to this as we talked.[6]

In a letter to a friend in England, Church told about their meeting:

> Yesterday a rich *muganda*⁷ in government service rushed up to me
> at Namirembe and said he had heard me speaking at a small meet-
> ing run by Miss Ensor. I had spoken about surrendering all and
> coming out for Jesus. He said he had done so, and had great joy
> in the Lord, and had wanted to see me ever since. And then he said
> in his own words that he knew something was missing in the
> Uganda church and in himself; what was it? Then I had the great
> joy of telling him about the filling of the Spirit and the Victorious
> Life.

Nsibambi and a friend of his visited with Church the next day. "We
have talked together, going over Scofield's notes on the Holy Spirit, and
both have kneeled in my room with me, deciding before God to quit all sin
in faith, and have claimed the Victorious Life." All three men shared a
desire for renewal in the Anglican churches in Ruanda and in Uganda and
committed themselves to regularly pray for revival.⁸

Simeon Nsibambi, Uganda's chief health officer

Eva and Simeon Nsibambi, pioneers in revival.

In some ways
Simeon Nsibambi was
like the rich young man
in Mark's Gospel
(10:17-22). He had
kept the command-
ments from his youth,
but he had this gnaw-
ing question about
something more. The
Lord was leading him
step by step, and his
personal pilgrimage taught him lessons that he could later share with others in the revival fellowship.

As chief health officer, Nsibambi had a responsible job in the public
health department of the Uganda civil service when he experienced God's
call to him. The son of a Christian chief in Busiro and a large landowner
in his own right, Nsibambi was indeed a rich young man and dressed in the
latest British styles for gentlemen. Like Church, he was an outstanding

product of a culture that honored education and civility. He lived with his wife, Eva, and their children in a large house on Namirembe Hill, one of the seven hills of Kampala, Uganda's capital city. Simeon and Eva devoted themselves to the work of the Good Samaritan Society, helping poor people in Kampala. He sang in the cathedral choir. In 1926 Bishop J. J. Willis asked him to lead a weekly prayer meeting at the cathedral and then a Bible study. Although Nsibambi was not a good public speaker, the bishop asked him to speak at the golden jubilee celebration of the Church of Uganda in 1927, marking fifty years since the first Christian missionaries arrived in the country.[9]

Born in 1897, Simeon Nsibambi was baptized at the nearby Anglican cathedral and attended services there every Sunday. His father sent him to the Church Missionary Society schools at Kampala, and to King's College, Budo, which modeled classes, games, and student life exactly on Eton and other British public schools. At King's College he was a natural leader and excelled as a singer, footballer, artist, crack shot, and in his last year the head prefect.[10]

As with so many other European and African boys, Nsibambi's schooling was interrupted by World War I. He served as sergeant in the African Native Medical Corps and went by ship to Zanzibar. He had a lot of worry in his heart, but God taught him something. Nsibambi saw that the ship was on a big ocean but had a captain who guided it. He saw that he too needed a captain to guide him in life. God showed him that the captain he needed was Jesus.[11]

Nsibambi's new walk with Jesus

That was the beginning. Conversion, a new way of thinking and living, came later. He returned to King's College after the war and resumed his studies. Zebuloni Kabaza, a young contemporary, heard Nsibambi say that he bitterly resented the selection of a classmate for advanced study overseas. He thought he should have been chosen. Nsibambi later testified that he was overcome with envy by the snub. He acknowledged that salvation was of greater value than any material advantage from a British university degree.[12]

A reading from the gospel brought Simeon to the next step, as God reached out to him. "In 1922, God, through the words, 'Seek ye first the kingdom of God and all these things shall be added to you,' spoke to his heart and brought him to acknowledge his sin. He determined to seek the kingdom of God with all his heart." He pointed to that day as a turning point in his life. At that time there were no "saved people" in the sense of being touched by the later revival in Uganda. No one showed him the way, but he knew that he had to follow Jesus.[13]

In 1925 Eva, the eldest daughter of Erasto Bakaluba, became Simeon Nsibambi's wife. It was a happy marriage. "He loved his wife very much and was absolutely loyal to her." Her father was the first African teacher on the faculty of King's College, and Eva and her sisters were educated in the best schools. More important, she shared her husband's commitment to follow Jesus.[14]

Theirs was an unusual marriage by any standard. Simeon and Eva were partners. They shared in the nurture and education of their children, who later remembered that their parents worked as a team, never struck them, and "never forced their religion on us." Eva made decisions regarding finances. Their son John recalled: "He had inherited lands and money and all this was entrusted to my mother."[15]

On October 3, 1927, Simeon Nsibambi wrote of a new conviction: "As from today I desire to be genuinely holy and never intentionally to do anything unguided by Jesus."[16] He was still seeking to walk in this way when he met Joe Church in Mabel Ensor's Bible class. And then they renewed their acquaintance in front of the cathedral almost two years later.

Neither man had any idea of what God was about to do among his people or that he would use them in that work. But both cared deeply for the followers of Jesus Christ in Uganda.

Once burning with zeal, coldness settles over Uganda's churches

Christians in Uganda had a long and eventful history since the first missionaries came among them in 1877. The main people of Uganda were Baganda. The name of their country, Buganda, means the territory of the Baganda or Ganda people. When the missionaries arrived, their kingdom on the west shore of Lake Victoria, was well-organized and prosperous, already a nation-state under the rule of its *kabaka*, or king. The earliest Baganda converts came from the governing elite. These powerful people gladly accepted the gospel message and embraced costly discipleship with enthusiasm. Some of them went joyfully to their death as Christian martyrs during a time of persecution in 1885. The blood of these martyrs proved again to be the seed of the church.[17]

After that, the church grew rapidly in Uganda, and excited believers almost at once carried the gospel message beyond the borders of their own kingdom. On the crest of that enthusiasm, in 1893 they sent 260 evangelists at their own expense to 85 preaching stations. The mission church rapidly became their own "Church of Uganda." The first African deacons were ordained in 1893 and the first priests in 1896. By 1909 the Native Anglican Church of Uganda had "over 100,000 adherents, including 70,000 baptized converts, and not only the whole Bible translated and circulated by tens of thousands, but [also] an extensive religious literature." The Church of Uganda was governed by its own synod, "in which European missionaries were to participate on equal terms with their African converts." This church synod was "the only constitutional body in Uganda which successfully cut across tribal boundaries."[18]

Unlike other African countries where the gospel was slow to take root, the Protestant church in Uganda was "unique in the speed, scale, and sheer enthusiasm of its early missionary movement and in the production of an ordained clergy by 1900." They provided many of the personnel for the expansion of Christian missions in Kenya, Tanganyika, and Ruanda-Urundi.[19]

The Church of Uganda had an important legacy. Bishop Alfred Tucker, who served there from 1893 to 1911, "envisaged a Church in which African and foreigner would work together in true brotherhood, and on a basis of genuine equality." Although only a part of Tucker's vision could be realized during his time as Bishop of Uganda, "for him the vision never faded, and he was able to communicate it to others."[20] The great revival that followed two decades later brought to fruition the vision that God had given Bishop Tucker.

Christians were still only a third of the people of Uganda, but they had a disproportionate share of social, economic, and political power and dominated the government. All the members of the governing council (*lukiko*) and nearly all the chiefs were Christians.[21]

Prosperity brought problems. The Church of Uganda, comparatively rich and definitely part of the establishment, had much in common with Protestant churches in the British Isles and North America. Like them, it was a church in need of revival. Albert Cook, director of Anglican Mengo Hospital, located in Kampala, Uganda, wrote in 1931, "Missionaries had lost their fire and African Christians were being pulled away by growing wealth, racial feelings and bad habits."[22]

A fresh voice

Mabel Ensor, a Church Missionary Society teacher and evangelist, saw the Church of Uganda as "backslidden," with baptized Christians returning to polygamy, witchcraft, and false worship. She had come to Kampala as a nurse in Mengo Hospital, but church leaders recognized her gifts for teaching the Bible and assigned her to this wider ministry.

Ensor became the center of a group of earnest Christians praying for revival and renewal in Uganda. Simeon Nsibambi joined her Bible class in November 1927, and others, like Joe Church, attended whenever they were in Kampala. But Ensor grew impatient. Matters came to a head in 1928, when she publicly accused an African clergyman of sin and resigned from the Church Missionary Society. Nsibambi and others in the Bible class shared her views about the need for revival, but they hesitated to go with her when she left to found an independent congregation. Nsibambi told her, "Our church needs reviving; stay with it."[23]

The Mengo Gospel Church Ensor founded lasted only a few years. Nsibambi always spoke highly of her, but he remained convinced of the need of revival within the church. "As she was equipped with all these wonderful gifts," he said, "I am sure she would have revolutionized the whole Church of Uganda. I and many others broke away from her movement because she had introduced such things as rebaptism of her followers, and the celebration of the Holy Communion by anybody at any place, and intended to form a new church other than the Native Anglican Church."[24]

Simeon stayed with his church, writing at the time: "Those who are corrupt in this church that I am in are my brothers, and if I leave they will not hear me, so I cannot leave." He devoted much of his free time to work as a lay evangelist and was effective in this new calling. The Bishop of Uganda gave him permission to conduct Bible classes in the cathedral in Kampala, and he frequently visited the bishop to point out abuses within the church.[25]

What happened to Nsibambi?

Before he left Kampala to return to his own station at Gahini in Ruanda, Joe Church met a missionary who asked him: "'What have you done to [Simeon] Nsibambi?' 'Why, what's the matter,' I asked. 'Oh, he's gone mad and is going round everywhere asking people if they are saved. He's just left my gardener.'" The missionary was not pleased. She thought that "Africans were not ready for this teaching about sanctification and the Holy Spirit."[26]

Nsibambi was certainly in earnest about beginning a new life. He had always dressed in fashionable clothes, but he gave up wearing shoes in favor of going barefoot like the poor. The *kanzu*, a long white robe, now replaced his British-tailored suits. He sold many of his possessions and gave away the proceeds. He quit his post in the health department on November 30, 1929, and "began a life of daily personal witness in the streets, shops, and hospitals" of Kampala.[27]

This was not an easy decision. Nsibambi later recalled: In 1929 "God asked me to be ready to go everywhere he would send me." He feared for the future but finally obeyed. Leaving his work in the Uganda government, "he began to talk to people in their homes and in the streets." They thought he was crazy, but he didn't mind.[28]

He became a familiar figure in Kampala, speaking to people near the cathedral and in the market. He also met with refugees from the Ruanda famine who had settled in Kampala, helping them in different ways.[29]

Every Friday afternoon Nsibambi and thirty or forty eager Christians met in the Synod Hall of the cathedral for prayer and Bible study. Joe Church commented on his "very practical and thoughtful" teaching. "He spent much time in prayer and Bible study, and God gave him great discernment."[30]

Nsibambi was not a university man, but he read widely and had a profound knowledge of the Bible. His familiarity with Scripture made him a gifted Bible teacher. He read other books and before long asked a missionary friend for a book on revival. Canon Grace, then headmaster at King's College, Budo, gave him a copy of Charles G. Finney's *Lectures on Revivals*. This book became a favorite of his, and he often quoted from it and encouraged others to read it. He frequently affirmed Finney's declaration that any kind of manipulation or human effort to bring about revival would fail.[31]

Finney's ideas were certainly congruent with what Simeon Nsibambi and Joe Church experienced. Finney believed that a permanent stage of higher spiritual life was possible for anyone who sought it wholeheartedly. Finney, an American evangelist and president of Oberlin College, published *Lectures on Revival* in 1835. The book influenced the later Holiness and Keswick movements, which in turn shaped the Anglican evangelicals of the Ruanda Mission.[32]

East Africans have understood "revival" to mean a *renewed* life in Christ sometime after accepting Jesus as Lord and Savior. Many of the newly saved ones had long professed faith in Jesus Christ and were often already leaders in the church; hence, Nsibambi and his associates used familiar terms in a way that sounded strange to many ears. When they asked if people were saved, they meant, "Are you living a victorious life in

Christ?" Even today African friends speak of being Christians for many years before they were saved. One man said, "I've been a Christian for so long, it's time I got saved."

Students of revival have recognized that people never referred to Nsibambi as the "founder" of revival, even though he was a mighty pillar among the brothers and sisters for many years. Additionally, when he gave his heart to the Lord, he gave away most of what he had and, as we noted, abandoned Western-style clothing. One might have imagined that others would have done the same, in order to emulate him. That was not the case. Nsibambi would have objected to that because it would have distracted from the central issue: abandoning all to follow Jesus. The brothers and sisters did not adopt a particular dress pattern or lifestyle. They allowed the Holy Spirit to speak to people in different cultures to conform to the image of Christ as they understood it.

Fellowship groups and teams form

Two small groups, one in Uganda and the other in Ruanda, soon discovered what abandonment to Jesus Christ meant in their own lives. Nsibambi's Bible study at Kampala grew into a team, an approach he favored as a way to discern God's purpose. These teams would go preaching on weekends, especially in the markets or wherever people were willing to listen. They did not force themselves on strangers. Observers have remembered Nsibambi as a calm man, humble, polite, always ready to apologize, and his ministry was most effective on a one-to-one basis. People began to come to him at his house, to ask advice, and to ask him to pray with them.

Another team assembled at the Gahini station of the Ruanda Mission. Joe Church teamed up with an Anglican minister named Lawrence Barham and two African teachers, Blasio Kigozi (Simeon Nsibambi's younger brother)[33] and Yosiya Kinuka. All shared Simeon Nsibambi's vision for renewal.

Yosiya Kinuka came to Gahini in 1928 as head of staff at the mission hospital with his wife, Dorokasi. Working closely together in the hospital and in evangelism, Kigozi and Kinuka experienced tensions and strains. In 1930 Kinuka decided to go back to Ankole, in western Uganda, where he was offered a post as subcounty chief (*gombolola*, district officer), but the others convinced him to go to Kampala. He did not know that it was to prepare him for a ministry in the school of the Spirit.

In a letter he wrote four years later, Kinuka told what happened:

There were many troubles and "judgments" in the hospital in those days. About that time a Muganda Christian named Blasio Kigozi came to Gahini to work, but I did not like him. I wanted to go to Uganda, so I asked him to take me and he agreed. Dr. Church also wanted me to go and paid my fare. I arrived at Kampala and lodged with Simeon Nsibambi, the elder brother of Blasio. I had never seen such a fervent Christian before. We kept talking about the subject of being born again. Simeon had heard that the spirit of the hospital was bad and he asked me the reason. When I began to tell him he turned to me and said it was because of sin in my own heart, and that that was the reason why the others on the staff were bad. I agreed with him that my heart was not right, and he taught me many more things, but my heart was still unchanged. [34]

Kinuka returned to Gahini and thought about everything Nsibambi had said. "On the road back to Gahini, I kept pondering over these things, and before I got back I was deeply convicted. My sins became like a burden on my back, and I yielded to Christ." Back in Gahini, he was a different man. "I repented openly of stealing and began to make Kinuka's restitution." He broke with old companions. One man was so angry at Kinuka that he threatened to burn down his house. "But a wonderful thing happened to him; he was truly converted too and is now one of my greatest friends." [35]

Joe Church never forgot the afternoon Kinuka returned from Kampala: He "came walking up the hill to my house. People gathered round him and one came running up to our veranda and said, 'Have you seen Yosiya's face?'" Kinuka's conversion was a turning point, Church recalled. Thereafter Yosiya Kinuka and Blasio Kigozi were a real team together.

Dorkasi and Yosiya Kinuka of early revival teams.

William and Sala Nagenda, destined to play a major role in spreading the revival message.

Fresh winds blow in the workplace

Algernon Stanley Smith, the Anglican missionary in charge of the Kabale Hospital in southwestern Uganda, observed the change at Gahini:

> A new spirit came into the hospital staff, and one by one they became out and out for God. Those young Christians were characterized by the same zeal as that first seen in Simeon Nsibambi. There grew in them, too, a new spirit of prayer.[36]

The hospital staff prayed together for an hour or two before dawn. They prayed for their wives and families; before long they too confessed their sins and began to live in a new way.[37]

Joe Church acknowledged that there were still problems at Gahini. Not everyone appreciated the zeal of new converts, who challenged others to repent and come to the cross. "We were outwardly a united station, but we were divided over the enthusiasm of the newly saved and their methods sometimes of 'tackling' those who were not yet saved, especially their seniors."[38]

The wind of the Spirit and the church

Bishop Willis, however, continued to be quite supportive of the renewal. In September 1931, for instance, Joe Church and Simeon Nsibambi jointly led a two-day retreat for students at Bishop Tucker Theological College, founded in 1913 in Mukono, not too far from Kampala. They also held meetings at the Synod Hall of the Anglican Namirembe Cathedral in Kampala and met with the Makerere College Students' Christian Union. The Church of Uganda stood ready to accept the revival blessings.[39]

Erica Sabiti, clergyman shaped by revival, and wife Geraldine.

Revival came to East Africa in ways like this, in hidden sins confessed, in restitution made for thefts or injuries, in the coming together of two and three and four seeking to know and do God's will.

Lawrence Barham was the only clergyman

among the first team in Ruanda. The revival winds blew irrespective of position in the church. As a result of their common experience of the amazing atoning work of Jesus Christ, clergy and laity found themselves as true brothers and sisters in Christ.

The first people to be touched by the Spirit of God in revival were well-placed and gifted people. Kigozi was a natural leader, Joe Church was a highly trained medical doctor, and Kinuka was a high-ranking medical officer in his own right. People recognized Barham for his scholarship. Simeon Nsibambi was the son of a wealthy, influential landowner.

While revival does not depend on people, it is evident that God does call out certain persons to provide leadership. If those called-out ones embody and teach the gospel of Jesus Christ, then the movement goes forward. It is certainly true that revival is the sovereign work of the Holy Spirit, but the Holy Spirit always works through people. If leaders falter in their obedience, all suffer, to some degree.

—2—

Blasio Kigozi: Beginnings in Ruanda and Uganda 1932–1936

A surprising feature of the revival was its spontaneity. As it spread from community to community, each fellowship shouldered its responsibility to deepen the understanding of the gospel. Each person and each fellowship felt equal partners in the new life that was spreading. The fellowships were tied together by frequent visits from other saved ones and by regular district meetings. They did not look to a central authority to aid them in their walk. They just did what the Holy Spirit directed them to do. Each group saw itself as a part of the family of the saved ones, which meant that they opened their doors to one another. As brothers and sisters moved about, whether in ministry or on private matters, they invariably linked with the fellowship groups wherever they went. This marked the saved ones as special: they loved one another in spite of all barriers. Even in the earliest stages of the revival, the hallmarks of the gospel were clearly visible in the dynamic fellowships of light.

Revival spreads through teams, house groups, and large conventions

Three characteristics emerged in the early days of the revival and mark it even today. First was the spontaneous emergence of teams of local saved persons who went out to neighboring homes and villages, sharing what God had done for them. Second, small groups gathered in each place for regular fellowship meetings in which they were accountable to one another, much like the weekly class meetings of John Wesley and the early Methodists. Third, as the movement grew it seemed good to bring saved people together in large conventions. A team united in prayer and discernment would determine the speakers and texts assigned to each one.

No one set these goals or encouraged revival brothers and sisters to follow this particular pattern. They simply followed where they believed God was leading them. In this way, they met the needs of others around them.

Neville Langford-Smith, Anglican bishop of Nakuru, Kenya, recalled the spontaneity and lack of formal organization in the revival movement. The news of dramatically changed lives traveled from village to village, and new Christians shared their testimony with neighbors. He later reported:

> There was never any planned and organized campaign for spread-ing revival. The movement spread as groups of revived Christians were burdened with the need of some particular place and went there. . . . It spread also as Christians from other parts came, hungry to know more of the power of the cross, and went home with a new witness in life and word.[1]

Teams emerge

Joe Church recalled that by 1933, in the early days of revival, it was the custom at Gahini "to send out parties of evangelists into the district, especially on Sunday, and for the weekend to more distant places." Blasio Kigozi and Yosiya Kinuka had become the leaders: "They had their own special meeting on Saturday afternoon at which those who were to go on these evangelistic efforts were chosen."[2]

Church leaders and other missionaries were certain they had never taught such methods of evangelism, but mostly they did not discourage the effort when it emerged. A local fellowship would decide who should go on a preaching mission. When the team arrived its members would prayerful-ly determine who was to speak and what text they would use. Teams were soon fanning out from Gahini and other centers of revival. "They traveled widely, camping on hillsides or in the homes of Christians, preaching wher-ever they could collect an audience." They also held their first large fellow-ship meetings at Gahini in 1932 and 1933, with a great number of sponta-neous confessions and testimonies.[3]

In 1933 Joe Church observed: "God was preparing the teams in the hard school of experience and of working together in the light, all learning brokenness."[4]

Lawrence Barham, the Anglican missionary who taught at Kigezi High School in the district's largest town, Kabale, was one of those touched in the revival at Gahini. He arranged a four-day meeting in September 1933.

This was the first teaching convention, something that was also to be an important part of the revival. Kosiya Shalita, from Gahini, and Algernon Stanley Smith, one of the founders of the Ruanda Mission, were the speakers. Of these conventions Stanley Smith wrote, "There had often been meetings for deeper instruction when people came in for baptism, confirmation, and church councils, but it was something new for people to be brought together for no other purpose than to get a fresh vision of God and of their own hearts."[5]

The evangelistic appeal of changed lives

The appeal of the revival was always in changed lives. Strangers could see that something had happened to the men and women who came to tell them more of Jesus. The change was always in the way they lived. Freedom to confess hidden sins had marked the first stirrings of revival. Joe Church wrote of the first convention at Gahini in December 1933:

> While everyone was bowed in prayer one of the African Christians got up and began confessing some sin he had committed, and then all sat up. It seemed as though a barrier of reserve had been rolled away. A wave of conviction swept through them all and for two and a half hours it continued.[6]

A real breakthrough came when two missionaries asked for forgiveness from African Christians for their own sins and bad attitudes. Africans were not used to Westerners acknowledging any kind of wrongdoing.[7]

One immediate result was "a deeper oneness and fellowship between the missionaries and the born-again Africans." British medical staff like Joe Church had a tendency to be "reserved and stand-offish with the African hospital staff." They discovered a new way. "We found that when once we had repented and in some cases asked forgiveness for our prejudice and white superiority, a new realm in relationships was entered into which altered the character of all our work."[8]

As time went on, this willingness to admit hidden faults and make restitution for wrongdoing became an integral part of coming to Christ in the revival. Government clerks and laborers confessed to stealing the property of others. Respected church leaders acknowledged sins of lust. Employers admitted cheating those who worked for them. Public confession stripped away all pretense and revealed each one as a sinner in need of the cleansing blood of Jesus Christ.

God uses key firebrands

Blasio Kigozi, Simeon Nsibambi's younger brother, became a key member of the Gahini team and had a major role in spreading the message of revival. He was weak, his brother said, until "God enlarged his heart and filled him with grace" in 1925. He volunteered as a missionary to Belgian Congo, but authorities there would not accept mission workers from British-controlled Uganda. Instead, he trained at the Mukono seminary to be a teacher in a church school. Graduating at the top of his class in 1928, he came to Gahini the following year. He taught school at Gahini, became headmaster of the normal school, and prepared to dedicate his life to evangelizing the people of Ruanda.[9]

Kigozi returned to the Mukono seminary in 1932 at the bishop's invitation to study for ordained ministry in the Church of Uganda. Bishop Willis himself taught a special group of seven students he had recruited, including Kigozi and Erica Sabiti. Kigozi was ordained in 1934 as pastor of Gahini parish church. His return to Gahini brought new problems. He was responsible for teaching teams of evangelists. But, as Algernon Stanley Smith later recalled:

> The Evangelists' Training School at Gahini was a heart-breaking job for Blasio Kigozi; the men were dull and unresponsive and the term ended with a strike [by the students]. Blasio realized his powerlessness and asked for leave of absence for a week; he gave himself to prayer and Bible study with fasting, pleading with God for the induement of the power of the Holy Ghost. It was his spiritual "wilderness" and he came out a new man. No one could help being struck by his radiant personality.[10]

Eriya Kanyamubari, then one of his students, remembered how Kigozi emerged from a week of prayer and fasting, "a different person from what he usually was, confessing to the students that he had been the cause of the trouble in the school." A few days later, their response to his questions caused him to "cry like a child," and several students were convicted of their own failings and converted.[11]

His influence at Gahini extended to every section of the work there. As Joe Church remembered:

> Sin loomed large in his preaching, and he was more than ever urging repentance and a coming to Jesus Christ for release from the

burden. There was much conviction, and in May 1935 there were many conversions at Gahini. The preaching of sin is never palatable to the natural man, so this renewed zeal and aggressiveness on the part of Blasio caused a fresh outbreak of opposition to him.[12]

One of the newly converted Gahini hospital workers went home to Kabale in southwestern Uganda "and caused surprise by going round to all his old friends and telling them of his new life, and that he could no longer go and drink with them as he used to." This came at a moment when Lawrence Barham was praying about how to deal with the apparent spiritual deadness at Kabale.[13]

Revival spreads to hospitals, schools, markets, and homes

Lawrence Barham invited Nsibambi and a team from Gahini—including Blasio Kigozi, Yosiya Kinuka, and Joe Church—to come to Kabale in September 1935 for a week. At that time one of the students at Kigezi High School was a young man named Festo Kivengere, who was related to the royal family. He recalled:

> Our attention was riveted by the shining faces of these men who obviously had spiritual freedom, were in love with God, and at peace with one another. We listened, wide-eyed, to what they had to say. Nothing big happened during those meetings, though one or two were set free. It was too new and startling for most people. But a spiritual bomb had been planted.[14]

The timing of revival did not depend on anything that the team could do or say. Festo recalled:

> Within a month, people began to weep unexpectedly, dream dreams of Heaven, or cry out under conviction until they came to know Christ personally. My boarding school was one of the places that was shaken up. That was when I first made the start which I subsequently abandoned. I suppose I was about fourteen years old.[15]

Students at Kigezi High School began to talk about knowing the Lord and gathered in small groups for prayer. Philip Tribe, another teacher, was an evangelical with a personal relationship with the Lord, but he was "bemused by all the repenting and weeping and talk of brokenness" among his students. Festo Kivengere was part of one group who met in a storeroom for prayer. "There was no weeping, no hysteria. But I knew immediately something had changed within me." Kigezi High School students spent their weekends preaching in Kabale and neighboring towns and villages.[16]

Teams went out in all directions from every place reached by revival; "wherever the message of sin, repentance, turning to Christ, and confession was preached, results were seen." There were reports of "whole congregations praying, trembling, and crying out all night." There was also restitution of stolen money and goods, restored relationships, and changed lives.

Meetings for prayer and praise often went on for hours, far into the night, and sometimes right on to the early morning. And there was always that strong, heart-felt singing. Men and women were saved, and children, sometimes crying out with tears at these gatherings.[17] At all hours one could expect a song to burst out, announcing a new victory for Jesus. "Glory, glory, hallelujah, / Glory, glory to the Lamb, / For the blood of Christ has reached me. / Glory, glory to the Lamb."

It was in the boarding schools and hospitals that manifestations of revival presented most difficulties. "Missionary head teachers and hospital sisters found their entire institutions disrupted while . . . singing and praying went on all night." They sometimes complained about this emotionalism to church authorities. But no missionary could deny that, after the emotion passed, revival left "a love and zeal that glowed and burned and must testify."[18]

Zabuloni (Zeb) Kabaza was a fifteen-year-old student at Mbarara High School when revival began in southwestern Uganda in 1935. He said it was the first time he had seen people publicly confessing their sins. He was a good student and well-behaved. When he compared himself with other boys, he believed he was better than they were. "I was blind to my own sinful heart," he recalled. On January 24, 1936, he was saved. "The Lord showed me the lusts of my heart, and I saw my own sinfulness. I had an intellectual belief; I believed what I was taught, but I had no heart." He doubted he could live wholly for Christ. "I feared. Can I really follow this way? I may not keep it up. Couldn't I enjoy the world for a time? But I knew God wanted my life there and then. I stood up and told the school assembly what God had done for me."[19]

Typically, saved ones of all ages found ways to make restitution for the wrongs they had done, and this teenage boy was no exception. "God sort-ed me out and showed me the areas that needed to be put right." He remembered an incident in 1932 when a student supervising an exam in the absence of the teacher gave the answers to the class. Zeb Kabaza met the teacher in Kampala years later and apologized for his part in the incident. He undid the lies he had told and asked forgiveness of boys to whom he had shown hatred. He paid for another boy's pencil that he had broken. That was costly but he found this was easier than dealing with his sins of attitude, grumbling, greed, lust, and anger, which other people did not notice. "If I wanted to walk properly with Him, I had to take them seriously. There is no differentiation between big and small sins, but the blood of Jesus can cleanse away all sins."[20]

Blasio Kigozi dies

Anglicans were approaching the sixtieth anniversary of their first missions in Uganda, and Bishop Cyril E. Stuart, who followed Bishop Willis, planned renewal meetings across the country to mark this jubilee. Blasio Kigozi entered into this project with enthusiasm and called for prayer and repentance, inviting Christians in Uganda to confess their failures and make a new beginning.

In January 1936 the bishop invited Kigozi to address the clergy in a weekend retreat before the biennial meeting of the Church of Uganda's synod. He preached at the retreat and then collapsed the next day. Bishop Stuart came to his bedside in Mengo Hospital at the moment he died. "As soon as it was clear he was going, Katharine [his wife] and Nsibambi started to sing hymns, and when I got there they were just finishing. They felt quite truly that he had gone straight to be with his Savior."

He was buried next to the cathedral on Namirembe hill in Kampala, beside the pioneer missionaries and martyrs who had begun the Church of Uganda. On his stone they carved "*Zukuka!*" (Awake!)

He died before he could address questions he had put on the synod's agenda: What causes coldness and deadness in the Church of Uganda? Why are people living in open sin allowed to come to the Lord's table? What must be done to bring revival to the church?

But in life and in death Kigozi awakened the Church of Uganda to its need for renewal. The Church Missionary Society published *Awake! The Story of Blasio Kigozi and His Vision of Revival* in both English and Luganda versions later in 1936.[21]

Kigozi's death had a profound effect on his brother-in-law, William Nagenda, husband of Sala, the sister of Kigozi's wife. Both Nagenda and

Kigozi had good educations for their day. Nagenda had earned a diploma from Makerere College and held a good post working for the government. He was a truly saved man but he did not have the vision and zeal of his brother-in-law.[22]

Others move on in revival

Others took up the challenge. Large teams carried the revival to the remote countryside. Revival prayer fellowships formed to support them. Bishop Stuart met with revival brethren all over the country, joining in fellowship and walking in the light. At the same time, fellowship meetings had begun to break down the barriers between Europeans and Africans, between rich and poor, and to challenge the complacency of the church. "Tribal distinctions are being swept away," observers reported. Thus, revival in Ruanda and Uganda in the 1930s created a new community that made identification with God's people more important than being Bachiga, Batutsi, English, or American.[23]

Radiating from Gahini in Ruanda, and from Kabale in southern Uganda, witness teams traveled, sometimes on foot, to other stations in Ruanda and Burundi. From these centers, teams visited outlying schools. Hundreds of ordinary people experienced the convicting and saving power of God in their lives. Most of the teams included ordinary men and women whose distinguishing features were a dynamic experience of a living Jesus Christ, a burning desire to share with others the truths that had become so real to them, and a power in communicating those truths that brought conviction to their hearers.[24]

In the next few years the revival spread rapidly, crossing the barriers of denomination as well as of tribe and nation. During the 1930s the revival reached most of the areas served by the Ruanda Mission and the Church Missionary Society, which was active in Uganda. These mission stations provided personnel to carry the revival message to new areas.

Renewal continued within the Church of Uganda and the stations of the Ruanda Mission in southwestern Uganda, Ruanda, and Urundi, all Anglican missions. The way was opening for the revival to reach other Protestant missions in East Africa.

Revival fires reach Urundi

Uganda was a unique nation in East Africa in that the only Protestant church of any consequence was one planted by Anglican missionaries. It was vitally important, therefore, that in Uganda the Anglican Church place its stamp of approval on the revival. To a large degree, they did so. But things were much different in Urundi.

The Danish Baptist missions had been the only Protestant mission at work in Urundi for several years. They realized that they needed to invite other mission societies to share in the work there, so they invited the American Quakers, also called Friends, to take over one of their stations in 1933. Arthur Chilson, his wife, and daughter were the pioneers. Then John Wesley Haley, a veteran missionary of the Free Methodist Church in South Africa, began a mission in 1934. Before the end of that year, A. C. Stanley Smith, Bill Church, and Kosiya Shalita left Gahini to accept the Danish Baptists' invitation to begin work of the Ruanda Mission in Urundi.[25]

Both the Free Methodists and the Friends were in the Holiness tradition, believing that "sanctification could be experienced at a definite moment in a person's life, subsequent to and separate from the experience of conversion."[26]

A mixed response from Ruanda and Urundi mission societies

In 1935 the Ruanda Mission took the lead in forming the Alliance of Protestant Missions in Ruanda-Urundi with Danish Baptists, Friends, Free Methodists, and the Church Missionary Society. They intended "to coordinate all efforts for the spread of the gospel, to harmonize all standards of church membership and discipline, and to aim at the ideal of forming one united church of Christ." They agreed that organizational details were secondary to spiritual unity. "To that end united missionary and African conventions began to be held, and the blessings of revival to be shared with other missions."[27]

When representatives of the five Protestant missions met to consider this closer relationship, discussion brought to light wide differences in aims and outlooks, especially on matters of church discipline. Archdeacon Arthur Pitt-Pitts of the Ruanda Mission observed: "No longer is the battle today fought over the matter of views on inspiration or baptism, but questions of what to us appear minor points such as smoking of tobacco. . . . On the first day, our conference leader stated that any European or African who used tobacco in any form or for any purpose would, in their church, be excommunicated from the Lord's table." Pipe-smoking Anglican missionaries did not share the Holiness prohibition of tobacco. The use of alcohol was also a source of differences in church discipline. "On this occasion, a deeply spiritual missionary of the Free Methodist mission, Rev. John Wesley Haley, brought the conference back to repentance and prayer." The issues which had dominated the conference did not disappear but "the spiritual oneness of the missionaries was sufficient to keep alive the aim of a united, evangelical, indigenous church in Ruanda-Urundi."[28]

For many of these missionaries, regardless of denomination, some of the happenings they observed in the revival were difficult to fit into their evangelical understanding of things.[29]

Carriers of revival: Ordinary people obeying God

But revival never depended on missionaries. Stanley Smith, of the Ruanda Mission, wrote, "Missionaries as a body played only a very minor part in the revival, at least until they too had passed through a time of conviction." African Christians carried the message of renewal to new places and organized daily or weekly fellowship meetings to provide a community of support for new believers. The support of individual missionaries and Bishop Cyril E. Stuart's tolerant attitude to what he sometimes perceived as the excessive zeal of revival Christians was nonetheless crucial. Simeon Nsibambi and others always insisted on renewal of the existing church and rejected calls to form a new one, even though their church could have cast them out.[30]

The East Africa Revival did not depend on missionaries or on ordained church leaders either. Higher authorities could silence church leaders. Sprinkled through the fellowships were clergymen, certainly, but the revival movement was, if not a lay movement, at least an egalitarian one in which all shared a common experience of cleansing and renewal in the atoning work of Christ. Fellowships came into being and spontaneously reached out to other Christians in love. They desired communion because they had experienced a oneness in Christ. They encouraged each other to stay in their denominations if at all possible, but to continue in meaningful, ongoing fellowship with one another as born-again brothers and sisters.

Revival spreads among the churches

Even though some in the mission churches remained critical or even hostile to the movement, teams of men and women went out to preach without waiting for official permission. Revival continued to spread. It had no central headquarters, but in those early days links between the Anglican mission stations kept fellowships and teams in contact with one another.

Little was said about physical healing in the early days of revival. The emphasis was clearly on the healing of the heart. This becomes noteworthy because miraculous physical healing figured prominently in almost all of

the African-founded independent churches in the second half of the twentieth century. It is not surprising that African-founded churches usually
placed greater emphasis on healing and exorcism. A central concern of traditional African religions was prosperity and fertility, and people assumed
that the ancestors had much to do with one's welfare.

The East Africa revivalists did not place much emphasis on God's
power to heal and to bless in a material way. They elevated reconciliation
with God and people as the center of concern. For them the marvel of
Christ's redemption was salvation in its broadest sense, including being
able to withstand the fierce attacks of Satan. The saved ones did not run to
the traditional healers when they grew sick or faced an insurmountable
problem, as many nominal believers did. That does not imply that they did
not experience healings and deliverances. They healed and were healed in
the name of Jesus. But physical healing was always in the background,
experienced as a serendipitous overflow of salvation, and the saved ones
were reluctant to make a big thing of physical healing, probably because
they wanted nothing to distract from the life-transforming atoning work of
Jesus Christ.

Nor did they emphasize the need to evangelize. Evangelism was the
natural overflow of the fellowship they were enjoying with their Lord and
with one another.

—3—

Expansion and Opposition 1937–1942

As the revival spread into each of the East African nations, God called forth gifted brothers and sisters who provided Spirit-directed leadership. We will look at each nation separately to see how this happened.

Uganda

Revival movements are the sovereign work of the Lord. He chooses messengers who live the gospel and share the good news with immediacy, clarity, and grace. As we have seen, the Lord called and enabled Simeon Nsibambi, Blasio Kigozi, and Yosiah Kinuka to lay the groundwork for the great movement that was to follow. However, the time had come for God to call out many more "firebrands" to take the freeing message of the grace of Jesus Christ to the next village and the neighboring nations. He did it in unexpected ways.

William Nagenda

The revival fellowships flourished. As they did, they encouraged a new generation to volunteer for pastoral ministry. Bishop Cyril Stuart of Uganda reported, "Ten [government] clerks at Entebbe have banded themselves together to resist sin and to spend whole weekends preaching around the countryside. Four of them have come to me saying they want to read for orders." (In the Anglican Church men could prepare for ordination by following a course of study under the direction of the church, "reading for orders," or taking seminary classes.) One of these young men who began studying for the ordained ministry was William Nagenda. He was to become one of the best-known evangelists of the East Africa Revival and often visited Europe and North America.[1]

William Nagenda was the son of an important chief and a graduate of

Makerere College in Uganda. Early in the twentieth century his father had been a regent, ruling the kingdom of Buganda in his sovereign's name. Like Nsibambi and Kigozi, his family home was on Namirembe Hill in Kampala. While serving in the government of Uganda, a scandal over discrepancies in his accounts brought the young Nagenda to a moral crisis. Simeon Nsibambi was instrumental in his conversion. Soon after meeting the Lord, Nagenda resigned from government service and prepared for Christian service.[2]

Bishop Stuart sent him to serve as chaplain at the Gahini Hospital in Rwanda. Joe Church recalled:

> He was unknown to any of us but when we were asked by the bishop which station would like to have him, my hand went up because I knew that he was a convert of Nsibambi. God was answering our prayer for one to take Blasio's place. I set off on Tuesday, January 5, 1937, to drive to Kampala with William, the first of many thousands of miles we were to travel together. He spoke very good English as he had gone through the best secondary school, King's School, Budo, and Makerere College.[3]

Nagenda was aware that at Gahini he was walking in Blasio Kigozi's footsteps and that some people expected him to be a spiritual giant like his brother-in-law. He decided to visit Nsibambi, share his fears and concerns, and ask his advice. "Don't try to 'do' things, William," Nsibambi counseled him. He urged him to repent of trying to copy Kigozi and simply to be what he was as William.[4]

In a sermon he delivered at the Urbana (Illinois) Missions Conference in 1954, years later, Nagenda told how he felt called to take Blasio Kigozi's place. He said he went to Rwanda "to be a wonderful missionary" and "to do something greater than what that man had done." He learned that this was "trying to build up one's own name and become a great man." Then he recalled Nsibambi telling him, "As you are going to this mission field, don't look for anything but the kingdom of God and His righteousness. When you are tempted, do not try to hide sin. Whenever there are temptations, deal with them, and repent."[5]

Nagenda discovers daily cleansing

Soon after William Nagenda came to Gahini, Yona Kanamuzeyi, a young Ruandan evangelist and schoolteacher, a Tutsi by tribe, came to him for help. This encounter led William to a major emphasis in the East Africa Revival.

One evening as Nagenda was returning home from school prayers, Yona came running after him in tears. They sat down together in Nagenda's house, and Kanamuzeyi told him that he was defeated by secret sin. Nagenda was taken aback because he knew that he himself had not yet learned the secret of victory. He said, "Yona, I am defeated, too; we are in this together." That evening Nagenda could not eat but went alone to pray. He asked God to show him clearly the way of victory, and God led him to 1 John 1:7: "If we walk in the light, as he is in the light, we have fellowship one with another, and the blood of Jesus Christ his Son cleanseth us from all sin." His eyes were opened to see that Christ himself is the light and that to walk in the light is to be open to its searching rays, "bringing to light the hidden things of darkness" that are in us. He also saw that the blood of Christ cleanses what the light reveals. "Walking in the light" thus means constant repentance of even the beginnings of sin and constant cleansing in Christ's blood. Nagenda saw this to be God's way of deliverance from sin.

When Yona Kanamuzeyi came to him the next evening, Nagenda was praising God and said, "Yona, I have found the way. There is victory for those who walk in the light and let the precious blood of Christ keep cleansing them." This wonderful verse, which the Holy Spirit thus illuminated to Nagenda as a result of Yona's torment of soul, has led countless defeated Christians into the experience of walking with God in fellowship one with another, through daily repentance and daily cleansing in that fountain opened for sin and for uncleanness.[6]

Having had a father who was a national figure, Nagenda often felt inadequate and at times doubted his self-worth. Later in life he shared an early dream that had helped him tremendously. In it he saw a shepherd, looking after his father's sheep. One night as he brought the flock to the pen, the shepherd discovered that he had only ninety-nine. William, a troublesome sheep, was missing. In desperation he begged his father to give him permission to go out and look for William. His father reminded him of the perils of the night but could not dissuade his heartbroken son. "I must find William," he insisted. Early in the morning the father saw his son, the shepherd, coming from a distance. His clothing was torn and he was bleeding. Obviously, it had been a difficult night. As the son approached, his father heard him shout, "Father, I have found William!" Seeing the sheep across his son's shoulders, the father replied, "Was he hard to find, Son?" The son said, "Yes, Father, but he is worth it." William Nagenda could never get over the wonder of Jesus dying for him. And he was humbled with the thought that he was "worth" all that Jesus did for him. That helped him to overcome any feelings of lack of self-worth.[7]

Nagenda and the Bible college incident

William Nagenda believed that his ministry would be more effective if he were ordained, so in 1939 he entered Anglican training at the Bishop Tucker Theological College, Mukono, Uganda. Many of the young candidates for the ministry had come to Christ in a fresh way through the revival. Joining them were many more mature saved people like Nagenda, thus forming a strong fellowship. They offended some of the more traditional faculty by their extended prayer meetings and evangelistic campaigns in the countryside.[8]

Their leaders, notably Nagenda and Eliezar Mugimba, were much better educated and came from a higher social class than the other students. Mugimba was the son of a county chief in Ankole and eventually prepared for a teaching career at prestigious Ugandan institutions, Budo and Makerere. He later studied at Oxford in England. This was rare at the time. As for Nagenda:

"Totally at ease in the company of Europeans, fluent in English, sophisticated and with a boundless self-confidence, he did not fit easily into the usual type of Mukono ordained." The faculty were used to docile and deferential African students, not to students who questioned their interpretation of Scripture. The *balokole* (saved) students challenged one of their teachers on his understanding of the Bible, encouraging others to refuse to take notes in his lectures. They took a militant stand against what they saw as a departure from evangelical teaching and conducted an aggressive campaign against the evils of sin, theft, and immorality, which they discovered in the college.[9]

Bill Butler, a young missionary with the Church Missionary Society (CMS) had already served in Uganda for two years. He was rather hastily ordained in November 1940 and sent to Mukono to teach. This was his first introduction to twentieth-century theology, and he was bewildered by much of what he was supposed to be teaching. "My previous reading had been confined to the Scriptures . . . and a few standard evangelical textbooks." He felt challenged by the *balokole*, especially William Nagenda, who had voiced concern about his compromise with modern thought and growing coldness. Butler explained his resentment of these saved Africans to a missionary from Ruanda. Bill did not report what the missionary said. But Bill met the Lord. He broke in repentance before God and came away a new person. The next day Butler went to ask forgiveness of Nagenda. He drove to the house where William Nagenda and his wife, Sala, were staying.

> Before I could say a word William took one look at my face, and with an indescribable look of joy greeted me, "Praise the Lord, Brother!" My prepared speech, like that of the penitent prodigal, was brushed aside, as William hugged me as I had never been hugged before, in an African embrace. For the first time in two years I knew myself one with an African! Never before had I known such readiness to forgive or such warmth of love—God's love, Calvary love—as met me then.[10]

Thereafter Butler was one with the revival brethren and joined Simeon Nsibambi, William Nagenda, and Benoni Kagwa, chaplain at Mukono Seminary, as a team preaching in western Uganda during seminary vacations.[11]

Some church leaders saw revival as divisive, setting up *balokole* as the only true Christians and making their experience normative for all. The seminary faculty and administration nearly all held this view and had little sympathy with the aggressive evangelism of the students influenced by "the Ruanda revival." The authorities forbade the "revivalists" early morning prayer meetings. "To stamp out our prayer meetings is rather like stamping out *balokole*," Nagenda wrote to a friend. They refused to be stamped out and held their prayer meetings as usual. The prolonged crisis at Mukono ended in October 1941 with the transfer of Bill Butler, and Benoni Kagwa, an African teacher who was sympathetic to the revival, and the expulsion of twenty-six students tainted with the East Africa Revival. William Nagenda and eight other students accepted their dismissal from Mukono as a call to unordained ministry as free evangelists, rather than as parish clergymen. Eliezar Mugimba and others returned to teaching.[12]

The seminary authorities saw the issue as primarily one of discipline and the refusal of Nagenda and the others to obey simple regulations about daily routine. The revival brothers believed much more was at stake. They saw the issues as defense of the gospel against modern theological trends and the need for renewal of the church in Uganda. In December 1941 they met with Joe Church and others from the Ruanda Mission and adopted a statement of their struggle against a modern viewpoint that "minimizes sin, and the substitutionary death of Christ on the cross, and mocks at the ideal of separation from the world to a holy and victorious life." Leslie Lea-Wilson, an English tea planter in Uganda, had the statement printed at his own expense and gave it wide circulation.

In the view of the influential Bishop Stuart, it was allowing "a little domestic difficulty" to develop into a crisis "which threatened to split the whole Church."[13] Bishop Stuart personally favored the revival and sought to be a mediator in the crisis. "I always remember," he wrote, "that St. Francis must have been an awful nuisance to the church authorities of his day, but they had the sense to keep him in the church, to its great advantage; whereas we in England drove out the Wesleyans, to our great loss." Stuart's influence and his "unshakeable patience" helped avoid a schism.[14]

When William Nagenda was expelled from seminary, his father decided not to give him the house on Namirembe Hill in Kampala, as he had promised. William and Sala stayed for a time with Simeon Nsibambi and his family. Then Leslie Lea-Wilson "felt it right to give William a house and garden at Namutamba if he wants to make it his headquarters." The Lea-Wilsons had developed Namutamba into a prosperous tea plantation. William and Sala accepted Lea-Wilson's invitation. At Namutamba in November 1942, convicted of "the need of so many all over Uganda and my inability to help them," William asked God "to fill me with the Holy Spirit of power" for the work ahead.[15]

Erica Sabiti

All of these early revival leaders were laypersons. That gave them a certain freedom. They could move around without hierarchical permission, preaching and teaching the message of God's grace in Jesus Christ. They submitted to ecclesiastical authority but were not employed by the church. One of the earliest clergymen to experience the freedom of Christ was Erica Sabiti. After him followed many clergymen who pursued their pastoral vocations while walking in fellowship with the revived brothers and sisters. In their fellowship meetings the clergy were just like everyone else. Being ordained did not give them any privilege. All in the fellowship knew that. As the saved ones met together, they closed the gap between clergy and laity. All were one at the foot of the cross, they asserted. But God was about to bring a prominent Ugandan clergyman into fellowship with the brethren.

In February 1937 William Nagenda, Simeon Nsibambi, Yosiya Kinuka, and others went as a team to preach at Bweranyangi in the kingdom of Ankole in western Uganda, where God had been blessing a number of people. Erica Sabiti, then a young Ugandan clergyman, was in charge of that large parish. He had been a seminary classmate of Blasio Kigozi and was also ordained in 1934. In 1936 a keen Ugandan, Eliezar Mugimba, witnessed to Sabiti while on a team visit.[16] Sabiti was impressed, deeply moved, and welcomed the revival teams that visited his parish. "I found that all over the parish people started getting saved," he said later, "and I praised the Lord for that." But Sabiti did not yet feel led to follow their example. His wife, Geraldine, first rejected the testimony of the team, then repented; Sabiti stood at a distance from the revival, even though the teams stayed in his house.[17]

In 1939 the Bishop of Uganda invited Sabiti to accompany him on a visit to the churches in Ruanda and Urundi. There Sabiti met Christians who, though less educated than he was, were experiencing a reality of which he knew nothing.[18]

> People thought I was a wonderful Christian, very devout and help-
> ful. Bishop Cyril Stuart invited me to go on a visit with him to
> Ruanda and Urundi, and so we traveled together to those coun-
> tries. He also invited William Nagenda to go with him. William
> had been touched by this wind of God's Holy Spirit. At that time
> he was working in Rwanda. William talked to Bishop Stuart and
> explained to him that many of the clergy under him were not
> saved. Bishop Stuart smiled and said that he knew that there were
> clergy who were not saved, but he commented that some were
> good and others not so good! He loved me and counted me as one
> of his "good" clergy, and gave me as an example of a "good"
> ordained man, but I was a big hypocrite and a man-pleaser, and I
> went along with the bishop, and approved of his remarks about
> me being "a good Christian."[19]

At Gahini they found Christians "who were not dressed as well as we were, and who were not so well educated, but they had peace." While he was reflecting on this, Sabiti "was invited to preach, and I preached about the blood of Jesus." After the service, one of the congregation told him bluntly, "I do not think you have really experienced it in your life." When Sabiti returned to his home, he repented and began a new life in Christ.[20] He realized that the blood of Jesus was not just a topic to preach about; instead, when applied to a life, the blood of Christ Jesus changes everything.

Later Erica Sabiti was archbishop of Uganda, Ruanda, and Urundi.

Kosiya Shalita

No less significant was the choice of Kosiya Shalita, an Anglican clergyman from Ruanda. Shalita, later bishop of Ankole, belonged to a family who fled Ruanda and found refuge in Ankole. Bishop Willis sent him to King's College at Budo. "He left Budo just when he was needed for the work in Ruanda, equipped with the best education Uganda could afford, with a sound knowledge of English, and with a heart steadily fixed on the ideal of being a missionary to his own people." Shalita worked briefly in Kigezi, Uganda, before joining the missionaries in Ruanda. He was one of the Gahini team from the beginning of revival there.

Kenya

Breaking down barriers in Kenya

Revival was rapidly spreading from Gahini to new territories. The first contact with Kenya was in April 1937, when Nsibambi and a team from Ruanda visited Kabete, near Nairobi.[21] Obadiah Kariuki, later bishop of Mount Kenya, was then interim rector of the church and headmaster of the primary school at Kabete. He later recalled, "They shared their 'revival' experience of walking in the light of Jesus Christ. Other Kenyans joined me in confessing their sins, being forgiven, and becoming new witnesses of Christ. Many received Him into their lives for the first time."[22]

Nsibambi stayed with Kariuki and his wife. Each morning they met at the mission church for prayer and confession. Kariuki testified:

> I received an entirely new and clear understanding of Christ as personal light and savior from Nsibambi, the result of our close interaction both at my house and at the revival meetings themselves. It was also through him that my wife experienced the wonderful light of Christ and became his witness, although I recall that she was never very enthusiastic about the daily confession of sins that everyone was partaking in.[23]

Because the central message of the revival was brokenness at the foot of the cross and an honest confession of personal sin, another essential teaching of the movement emerged quite early: oneness in Christ Jesus. The cross brought reconciliation, the equality of African and European, and a rejection of every form of racism, as Joe Church reported:

We insisted on African and European leaders sitting with us and joining in the planning. I wrote in *Ruanda Notes*: "I stress this because I believe here lies the secret of blessing and revival in Kenya: mistrust between European and African must be broken down." . . .

A searching remark was made by one Kikuyu: "I have never before seen any white man admit that he had any sins."[24]

Neville Langford-Smith, later bishop of Nakuru in Kenya, was part of the revival from the 1930s. He wrote later:

At the very heart of revival is the atonement, the message of reconciliation of man to God and man to man through Christ crucified, and outstanding among its fruits has been the reconciliation of races and tribes. We tend to underestimate the hatred of the European that is so widespread among Africans in Kenya, and it is a humbling and moving experience to be approached by an African brother who comes to apologize for having had this hatred, from which the Lord has now cleansed him. It is no less a victory of the Spirit when Kikuyu and Jaluo and Masai find that they are brothers, made one by the blood of Christ. No less a victory when a smiling African, introducing his wife, says to you: "This is my sister, my wife" raised to equality, but more, to oneness, in the cross.[25]

Breaking down racial barriers was especially important in Kenya, where colonial development followed a different pattern than in Uganda. To have easy access to prosperous Uganda, the British had assumed control of the territory between its eastern boundary and the Indian Ocean. They proclaimed this area the East Africa Protectorate, called Kenya by 1895. The real beginnings of Kenya colony, however, had come with the building of the Uganda railway from the seaport of Mombasa to Kisumu on Lake Victoria in 1902. The future city of Nairobi began with railroad repair shops and warehouses. The railroad wound through miles of fertile uplands, elevated enough to have a cool climate. Europeans could settle in these highlands and raise crops on a large scale. The newcomers conveniently believed that neither Kikuyu nor Masai had any claim to these lands. Within a few years, European settlers covered the White Highlands with plantations and hired Kikuyu laborers to do their work. Unlike

Uganda, where British colonial administrators relied on "indirect rule" through Africans, they developed Kenya as a British colony, which to some meant "a white man's country."[26]

Development of Kenya as a colony directly under British rule proceeded steadily through the 1920s. As the Kikuyu people of central Kenya developed in the next two decades, they required more land and thus cast their eye on what they considered to be their ancestral homeland, now occupied by white people. As they perceived the history, the more radical Kikuyu leaders blamed missionaries for collaborating in the land grab. Racial tension led to hostility and finally open violence, which came to a head in the Mau Mau uprising, flourishing in 1949–56 and leading to the independence of Kenya in 1963.

Ethnic animosity

Transfer of land to European planters was not in itself responsible for Kikuyu overcrowding, but at the point in time when the growing Kikuyu population needed more land, they pushed into what had become known as the "white highlands." The white settlers resisted the movement and believed that they had absolute right to that land. This situation fed Kikuyu resentment.[27] Hostility toward missionaries on the part of some African Christians came to the surface in Kenya. "Conflicts between missions and the mass of the Kikuyu population became open during the 1920s, missions being accused of wishing to destroy Kikuyu culture and to acquire Kikuyu land."[28] When Anglicans, Presbyterians, and the Africa Inland Mission took a stand against female circumcision in 1928, many Kikuyu left the mission churches for African independent churches.[29]

In Nyanza Province on Lake Victoria in western Kenya, on the other hand, there was no transfer of land to Europeans, and Luhya, Luo, and Kuria farmers were the richest producers of corn and cotton in Kenya. But ill feeling between different tribes needed to be overcome. Hostility between Luo and Luhya continued unabated in the 1930s; they could not unite even to press the colonial government for better schools and split into two groups with the same purpose. When revival came, however, people from these hostile communities did join in the revival fellowships.[30]

Kenya's first revival convention

In September 1938 more than two hundred Christians "from all over Kenya, drawn from many different missions and representing some twenty different tribes," came to the Alliance High School in the town of Kikuyu near Nairobi. This was the "largest African convention that had ever been held in Kenya" till then. The team included Church Missionary Society and Africa Inland Mission missionaries and six Africans. Joe Church commented: "It was a big team and rather unwieldy, but I think a new thing was seen in Kenya—team fellowship with Africans." William Nagenda spoke on the words "Jesus wept" and "Jesus died." Simeon Nsibambi and Yosiya Kinuka also preached. At the time Joe Church reported:

> I have never known the messages to go home with such tremendous force. We decided to avoid all holding up of hands so as to leave the results entirely to God. This was a big decision, pressed by the wise counsel of William and the African team members who felt at this stage we should check emotionalism, and even make it difficult.[31]

The evidence of changed lives at Kabete did not convince everyone that revival was a gift from God. Bishop Obadiah Kariuki recorded:

> Some of our church leaders opposed this "new teaching." When the revival message spread through the Kabete area, almost the whole council of elders felt the church was threatened by the "Followers of Ruanda." Some sneeringly dubbed them "Obadiah's Group." We were summoned before church courts and our meetings were banned from church buildings. We felt no resentment and enjoyed our fellowship under the trees.[32]

Simeon Nsibambi, Joe Church, and others met with the Kabete elders on their way to the Kikuyu convention. They heard familiar arguments: "These people think they are better than us." Yet they praised God when Nsibambi in his humble way "dealt sympathetically but firmly with these things, and then there seemed to be joy and laughter again."[33]

Revival overspreads Kenya

African evangelists took the lead in spreading the revival through Kenya in 1937 and 1938. Evangelistic teams gave ample scope for Africans to exercise leadership, and the revival nurtured many future leaders for the churches of East Africa. While the obvious leaders of the fellowship groups were usually men, there were exceptions in which women took the leading role. That does not mean that the women were quiet; they were completely involved in every aspect of life together in fellowship. Whether a woman or a man spoke made little difference; the important thing was the authenticity of the word that was shared.

Don Jacobs well remembers the time when, after he had shared something, a widow challenged him in a fellowship meeting: "Did Jesus tell you that or Satan?" Don examined his heart and had to admit that what he had spoken was not entirely free of selfish desires. In the intensity of listening to the Holy Spirit, there was truly neither male nor female.[34]

Tanganyika

There were other stirrings of revival by 1939, particularly on the cattle-grazing plains in the southern parts of Uganda and in southern Sudan, where William Nagenda went as a team with Joe Church and his wife. They also ministered in the eastern Congo in the mission stations of the Africa Inland Mission.

That same year, Lionel Bakewell welcomed the first revival team to the Teacher Training College at Katoke, located in northwestern Tanganyika, not too far from Ruanda and Uganda. His overseer, Bishop George Alexander Chambers, the Anglican bishop of Central Tanganyika, had invited the team into that country. Nsibambi, Erisifati Matovu, and Joe Church preached, but without any apparent impact on the students. Bakewell reported: "The team went away feeling that they had done all they could, and by the last day they were rather discouraged." After they left, the confessions began.

Extraordinary outbreak of signs in Tanganyika

The Katoke revival continued for many months. In October 1939 Bakewell wrote, "Katoke has now received the baptism of the Holy Spirit and Jesus' name has been most wonderfully glorified." Bakewell himself "had an experience after repenting deeply to the Africans of white superiority and of despising the Africans and had asked their forgiveness."[35]

Other places in western Tanganyika had similar outpourings of the Spirit in 1939 and 1940. By April 1940, the signs and wonders at Katoke led Bishop Chambers to order an end to these fellowship meetings and the protracted church services. Bakewell obeyed and reflected: "Last year, before we began seeking for the Holy Spirit with outward physical signs, revival was really going ahead. We were constantly seeing people converted and the 'revived' had real fellowship with one another in Christ Jesus."

The East Africa Revival was well aware of the Pentecostal expressions thereafter. They neither encouraged nor discouraged them.[36] A veteran of the Ruanda Mission, Herbert Osborn, explained the attitude of the revival to such "signs and wonders":

> There were many remarkable dreams, in many of which people were pointed to passages in Scripture which particularly applied to them or to some sin they were concealing. On occasions, people would fall to the ground in a seemingly trance-like condition. These more unusual expressions of revival were not condemned nor repressed, as some have claimed, but they were not considered as important compared with the expressions of conviction of sin, assurance of forgiveness, and power to witness boldly.[37]

Bishop Stuart of Uganda counseled patience to Chambers, his brother bishop. Stuart expressed his doubts as to whether there could be revival without some excesses "and certainly in Ruanda and Uganda we have found that they do get through these outward signs and go on to real deep faith and changed lives."[38]

Kenneth Moynagh, a missionary doctor in Uganda, clarified the position of those experiencing revival in this poem, which he wrote in light of the attraction of signs and wonders:

> When different winds of doctrine blow,
> Then set their sails who will,
> But as for me, content I go
> To Calvary's lonely hill.
>
> Let others cry for greater power
> And marvelous gifts declare,
> But all I ask is every hour
> My Christ to know, my Christ to share.
>
> Let others tell of mighty signs
> And miracles they've seen,
> But keep me, Lord, in light that shines
> And shows where I'm unclean.

May grace be given to bring the sin,
Contrite to Calvary;
My only goal be Christ to win,
My only good be He.

From Calvary there flows God's love,
The love of Christ to me;
No wind of doctrine shall remove
Me from that fruitful tree.

I need not fear—I have within
The friendly Paraclete;
He shows me Christ,
He shows me sin,
He shows the Mercy Seat.

So worthy Lamb, I join the song
That the redeemed will sing,
A member of that blood-washed throng
who gather round their King.

By this time the revival had spread to other areas of Tanganyika, especially in the region west of Lake Victoria. Revival, for instance, reached the Lutheran churches in northwestern Tanganyika in 1939. Shortly after that, incidentally, the first winds of revival moved across the Mennonite churches on the eastern shores of Lake Victoria.

Urundi

In 1941 revival reached the Free Methodist mission at Muyebe in Urundi. Belgian colonials were amazed when servants returned things taken from their kitchens and begged to pay for stolen food. Observers were astounded to hear Protestant Christians who were harassed by chiefs or colonial authorities refusing to return evil for evil and replying simply, "I will pray to God for you."

The Free Methodists of Urundi hosted a convention in May 1942 and invited William Nagenda, Erica Sabiti, and Joe Church to bring a team. More than sixty missionaries from all the Protestant missions and about three thousand Africans participated. "The convention opened with a scene of tumultuous welcome of the African brethren coming from the different CMS stations." They greeted one another by singing choruses of the hymn already identified with revival:

> Tukutendereza, Yesu, Yesu, / Omwana gw'endiga,
> Omusaigwo gunaziza; / Nkwebaza, Omulokozi.
> We praise you, Jesus, Jesus, / Lamb of God.
> Your blood has cleansed me; / I praise you, Savior.

Joe Church wrote in his diary, "The final breaking of bread [presided over] by a Free Methodist, a Baptist, and a Church of England layman, with Africans and missionaries seated around a big room, was the nearest we probably will ever get to those earliest days of Christianity, after the love feast was instituted by our Lord."

Opposition and unity

Official opposition to the revival continued in Tanganyika and Uganda through 1942. Some churches went so far as to discipline revival clergy. In some districts of Uganda they refused to allow any preaching by people who were associated with the "Ruanda Mission." The critical stance some church authorities took to the revival did not weaken the determination of the revived brothers and sisters to remain within their churches. On the contrary, it strengthened their resolve to stay in their own churches and work in them.

Meanwhile, the Ruanda Mission proposed an agape communion service similar to the one recently adopted by the newly formed Church of South India. "Symbolizing the great sense of unity among the Protestant churches at this time was the free exchange of evangelists and the large interdenominational gatherings characterized by oneness of spirit and great spiritual zeal."[39]

The nine churches that made up the Protestant Alliance in Ruanda were already working closely together, largely due to the strong influence of the revival. For several reasons the dream of a single Protestant Church of Ruanda never came to fruition, although the climate for it was created by the unity that many of the leaders experienced as brothers and sisters in the early 1940s.

The public ministry of Simeon Nsibambi came to a close in May 1941. That month he had preached at the Kabarole Convention in Toro, western

Uganda, but then fell ill. Poor health confined him to his house on Namirembe Hill thereafter, but his ministry was far from over.[40] Nsibambi served as a wise brother and counselor year after year. His most notable contribution to the brothers and sisters was his determination to allow nothing to blur the vision of Jesus Christ crucified, risen, and now interceding for those who love him. Nsibambi had a special gift of discernment that could detect anything detracting from the centrality of Jesus Christ. He no doubt had a prayer life that carried his friends in ministry. His house became a special place where people who were confused could once again see the Lord.

In summary, even though each nation, tribe, race, and economic or social group had its own view on world and local issues, those who humbly received God's grace testified to the life-changing power of the atoning work of Jesus. First, waves of conviction for sin swept across the communities. Then those who received the message repented and put things right. After that, testimonies of the saving and liberating power of Christ rang out. Invariably those who experienced the life-changing ministry of the Holy Spirit met regularly in fellowships of light. They studied the Scriptures, encouraged one another, and planned their ministry of love and evangelism in their communities and beyond. They assumed that everyone who had received the blessings of salvation should give witness to that fact. In these local fellowships the saved ones held one another accountable to the Lord, who was saving them.

In the early days of this movement of God's gentle wind, the stage was set for the next wave of missionaries, and particularly Mennonite missionaries, who would be blessed in this work and would in turn bless their friends at home.

—4—

Fresh Winds Blow Across
Tanganyika
1942

This book is an attempt to describe how a revival movement that began in Ruanda and southern Uganda influenced the lives of many people in North America. An important part of that story is how this movement of God's Holy Spirit blessed the American missionaries and how they shared their newfound freedom in Christ with their friends "at home."

The Mennonite portion of the story begins in Pennsylvania, where the Lancaster Conference of the Mennonite Church was located. It was one of twenty or so Mennonite conferences in North America and had the distinction of being the largest, with about 16,000 members at that time. This was also a rather culturally conservative conference that had evidenced little interest in missions since the original immigrants from German-speaking Europe arrived as early as 1690. But things began to change at the end of the nineteenth century when, as a result of many influences, Lancaster Mennonites became much more evangelistic. They established a nascent mission board and sent their first missionaries to neighboring cities. They soon sought a "foreign field." When Africa emerged as a possibility, they sent their first deputation in 1934 to scout a place to minister.

After a good deal of exploration, they felt that a door was open for them in Tanganyika, and the government and other mission societies there welcomed them. The Mennonites were directed to consider working in an area of many tribes and at least twelve different languages, just north of where the Africa Inland Mission had been working in the Lake region of Tanganyika. The AIM was an American-based interdenominational mission and had enough to do in evangelizing the huge Sukuma tribe south and east of Lake Victoria. So they suggested that the Mennonites begin ministries to the north, all the way to the Kenyan border.

Orie O. Miller, secretary of the Eastern Mennonite Board of Missions and Charities (EMBMC), and Elam Stauffer, the first prospective missionary, were warmly received by the AIM field director of Tanganyika, Emil Sywulka, who was himself a member of the Evangelical Mennonite Church. He took Stauffer to Shirati, just south of the Kenya border and on Lake Victoria, which the two men agreed was a good location for the first Mennonite station. Stauffer quickly obtained permission to begin a mission on that spot.

After establishing a station at Shirati, the mission then placed missionaries at Bukiroba, near Musoma; at Mugango, further south; then at Bumangi, to the east of Musoma and near the Serengeti Plains; and at Nyabasi, to the east of Shirati. By 1940 there were approximately twenty Mennonite missionaries.

That was the picture in the early 1940s, when the winds of revival began to stir in Tanganyika. The Mennonites were busily starting bush schools, establishing little fellowships of believers, and doing some medical work. The baptized adult membership numbered about one hundred. There were about ten fledgling churches.

Would the Mennonite missionaries be open to the fresh wind of God that was blowing across East Africa? The missionaries were rooted in the Anabaptist movement of 1525. They were pacifists, insisted on strict separation between the church and the world, and grew up in strong North American Mennonite communities that placed a premium on strict biblical interpretation and unassailable ethics.

Mennonite missionaries establish a mission in Tanganyika

Elam and Grace Stauffer wed near Lake Victoria, with attendants John and Catharine Leatherman.

Elam and Elizabeth Stauffer sold their farm near Manheim in Lancaster County, Pennsylvania, when the Eastern Mennonite Board of Missions and Charities asked them to go to Africa. Stauffer had experience as a farmer, schoolteacher, and home mission superintendent. Later in 1934 John and Ruth Mosemann from Lancaster city, along with Elizabeth Stauffer, sailed to East Africa to join Elam Stauffer. Mosemann's father was a Mennonite bishop and pastor of the East Chestnut Street Mennonite Church in Lancaster. The Mosemann family had a wholesale grocery business and manufactured peanut butter and other products.[1]

Other missionaries soon joined them, and the mission expanded its work from Shirati to Bukiroba and Mugango within the first year. EMBMC, the mission board, recruited John and Catharine Garber Leatherman as teachers for the leadership training school at Bukiroba, and in 1936 they arrived in Tanganyika. John Leatherman was the pastor of the Doylestown Mennonite Church when he accepted the mission assignment. He was born-again and had been baptized while a high-school student at Goshen Academy in Indiana. After high school, he held an office job in Philadelphia. God's call to service was so strong within him that he sold his car and went to Harrisonburg, Virginia, for advanced Bible study at Eastern Mennonite College to prepare for whatever God had for him to do. After his appointment to the mission, he did further study at Eastern Baptist Seminary.

At the newly formed Mennonite Bible School at Bukiroba, John taught all the Bible and church history courses while Catharine taught secular subjects. In 1940 John began publication of a bimonthly magazine in Swahili, *Mjumbe wa Kristo* (*The Messenger of Christ*).[2] This periodical

John and Catharine Leatherman at Bukiroba.

would be an effective vehicle for spreading the message of revival.

In 1937 Mennonites Clyde and Alta Barge Shenk and others "began the difficult task of entering Zanaki land with the gospel," in the highlands east of Musoma. They made Bumangi their headquarters. Alta Barge was a schoolteacher in Lancaster when she and Clyde Shenk, a young farmer

Clyde and Alta Shenk
with children David
and Joseph.

from near Millersville in
Lancaster County, were married in 1935. She had trained at
Eastern Mennonite College to
be a teacher.[3]

In 1940 EMBMC assigned
Simeon and Edna Hurst of
Ontario to Nyabasi, a
Mennonite mission station
located among the Wakuria
people, near the Kenyan border.
Simeon was born on a farm

Edna and Simeon Hurst with son Elwood.

near St. Jacobs, Ontario, in 1913. His parents belonged to the Old Order
Mennonite Church, but his father had bought a truck to help with the farm
work, and as a result the church excommunicated him. (Old Order
Mennonites, like Amish, used only horses and mules at that time.) Simeon
completed only elementary school before going to work full-time. When he
was twenty, he met Edna Schmiedendorf, a Mennonite girl from near
Preston (now Cambridge), Ontario, who hoped to go overseas as a missionary nurse. In 1935 Simeon began high school, while working a milk
route early in the morning. After completing high school, he entered
Eastern Mennonite College. Edna was already there. She had taken her

nurse's training in Ontario and was completing her studies to be a missionary. The couple were married in 1939 and went to East Africa the following year. "I grew up in a Christian family and joined the Mennonite Church," Simeon reflected. "But I felt I had only a surface piety."[4]

Phebe Yoder was a rather short, extremely active woman who knew the rigors of growing up on a farm in Kansas. She excelled in her profession of nursing and loved to deliver babies. Phebe was a leader in her own right; she combined a sincere love for the Lord with an open heart that welcomed everyone, no matter what their status or class. Above all, Phebe had a burning desire to be a friend of Jesus and work with him in ministering to the needs of those around her. Even though she did not perceive herself as an influential woman, she most definitely was.[5]

Phebe Yoder, early revival enthusiast and highly effective missionary.

When she was twelve, Phebe read a book about Alexander Mackay of the Church Missionary Society and the martyrs of Uganda. From that day she had a conviction that God was calling her to Africa. Mennonites did not volunteer for mission work: that was considered to be prideful. She reckoned that no member of the Eastern Mennonite Board of Missions would ever invite a Mennonite from Kansas to consider joining their mission in Tanzania.

To her utter surprise, Phebe was completing her training at University Hospital in Denver, Colorado, when she received a letter from Orie Miller, secretary of the mission board, telling of their fruitless search for a nurse, "mature in years and Christian experience," and inviting her to consider a call to Africa. She was thirty-four years old and had been waiting all her life for this invitation.[6] Phebe arrived at the Mennonite mission in 1937, a new missionary nurse who was also a qualified teacher.

"Phebe was basically a teacher. She said, 'I'd rather teach than eat,'" recalled colleague Catharine Leatherman.[7] But Phebe had undertaken nurse's training in order to go overseas, since at that time the Mennonites would not permit a woman to teach the Bible in the mission field or at home. Phebe received a broad education at Hesston (Kan.) and Goshen

(Ind.) Colleges, both Mennonite institutions. She began her missionary career as a nurse, but after a few years another calling began to dominate her life. Her vision to advance education among the Mennonites in Tanzania plunged her into an effort to establish schools and to enable those who were qualified to pursue further education. Her fellow missionaries were not convinced that the mission should become involved in running accredited schools. "Just before her arrival, the government had announced that only graduates of accredited schools could proceed to higher levels of education."[8] This underlined Phebe's conviction that education must accompany spiritual growth.

Mennonite missionaries join AIM in prayer for revival

Mennonites maintained a close relationship with their neighbors in AIM and knew of the changed lives among AIM workers. Hungry for such blessings, Elam and Elizabeth Stauffer attended the AIM prayer conference at Nasa in 1941. Lillian Elliott recalled: "Bill Stier read portions of Scripture and eighteen or twenty missionaries were on our knees all day, praying for revival." When the group prepared to leave the chapel for a meal, Elam Stauffer remained on his knees, in a corner, facing the wall. He later shared with them that God had dealt with everything in his life, especially his bondage to custom and tradition. "I [had] bound myself and I [had] bound my wife." Elizabeth Stauffer testified to the Lord meeting her. This was the first time that the rather timid Elizabeth spoke in public and prayed in public.[9]

The first stirring of renewal within the Mennonite mission came in March 1942, when another of the missionaries publicly confessed a serious moral failing. Elam Stauffer came to the new station at Nyabasi to inform Simeon and Edna Hurst, the missionaries there. The Hursts were shocked, but that night, Simeon felt led to confess to his wife failures in his own life, and she to him. They accepted Christ's forgiveness and felt closer than ever before to each other and to the Lord.[10]

Wind blows from an unexpected source

In May 1942, Rebeka Makura visited the Mennonite mission station at Mugango, in the Musoma district of northwest Tanganyika. She figured prominently in the early days of revival among the Mennonites. Rebeka lived in Mwanza, the lake port on Lake Victoria's southern shore. She was not a Mennonite but was a member of the AIM. She and her friends felt a burden to pray for the Mennonite churches on the Eastern shores of the lake. They detected a spiritual dearth among both missionaries and church members.

Rebeka had suffered difficulty in life. When she became a believer in Jesus Christ, her Muslim husband turned her out of their house and left her penniless. She carried water from the lake and sold it in the town of Mwanza for a living. The AIM Christians were suspicious of this poor Muslim woman who claimed to be one of them. But her life testified to the reality of salvation in Christ, and the church in Mwanza accepted her. She became a Bible woman, a kind of lay mission worker, with an effective witness. God then used her for revival in Mwanza.[11]

Like most Africans, Rebeka was accustomed to walking many miles on foot. Mennonite missionary Phebe Yoder heard her speak in a prayer meeting at Mwanza and knew at once that God would use Rebeka to answer the prayers for revival among the Mennonites. Phebe arranged for her to come to Mugango, the southernmost station in the Mennonite mission, and share from the Word and her own testimony. "She was invited to our Mugango station for a ministry, and God used her there. This was the beginning of revival on our field."[12]

Rebeka seemed an improbable messenger of renewal. "She was a weak speaker. Her ministry was one of prayer." She was illiterate, too, although she had memorized large sections of the Bible. Mahlon Hess, another Mennonite missionary, admitted:

> To the church elders she was a stumbling block. "What can she teach us; she doesn't even know how to read!" They continued: "What is more, it is contrary to the Bible for a woman to preach! She may lead us astray." Rebeka was not fazed by their opposition. She warned the young energetic Ezekiel Muganda regarding sin in his life and urged him to repent.[13]

Ezekiel Muganda was a respected church leader and had been an evangelist for AIM, and later for the Mennonites. He was aghast that a number of church members confessed their sins. He remained aloof, then he railed against Rebeka. He was so offended by this unlettered woman preacher that he decided to follow Rebeka around and tell people to ignore whatever she said.[14]

Rebeka and Phebe traveled twenty-five dusty miles on foot, from Mugango to Butata on Lake Victoria, where there was to be a mission-wide meeting. Since that was his home area, Ezekiel felt obliged to attend. He did so, and the Lord met him in a new way there. From this time onward, his life was completely changed. Often he would praise Jesus for saving him and naming his sins, and his testimony touched other hearts. He became a leader in the fellowships that then sprang up around the lake.

From Butata, Rebeka and Phebe went with a team to each of the Mennonite churches in the area, holding meetings with women and testifying to what the Lord had done in their lives. The two women came from quite different backgrounds, but they shared a love of the Lord.[15]

The response of Africa Inland Mission

Phebe owed her new spiritual vitality to the ministry of AIM's Rebeka Makura. Phebe soon became active in sharing her witness with AIM missionaries. Though the mission leaders were lukewarm if not outright hostile to the revival, Phebe reached out to the AIM missionaries who were finding the same liberty in the Spirit as she was. This served to build strong bridges between some of the AIM and Mennonite missionaries, as we shall see.

The revival was a breath of fresh air to some of the AIM missionaries, including Minnie Magnin, a British worker who taught in an AIM school for girls. She lived a life of prayer and encouraged many to go deeper with the Lord. Minnie built a little prayer hut, and her zeal touched others, such as Lillian Elliott, Florence Tilley, Sallye Higgins, and Virginia Stier. Virginia's husband, Rev. William A. Stier Jr., was at first hostile to the movement and his wife's deepening spirituality. A year later he came to the Lord in a fresh way. A soft-spoken and sometimes halting speaker, Bill Stier found a new confidence as well as a new message. Some of his colleagues were amazed at the transformation.

Simeon Hurst and Clyde Shenk went with Elam Stauffer to the AIM station at Nasa in July 1942 to attend a prayer conference with AIM workers. They heard a sermon on Romans 6:6: "We know that our old self was crucified with him so that the body of sin might be destroyed, and we might no longer be enslaved to sin" (NRSV). They were broken by the realization that "all had been done; Jesus did it for me." Elam declared: "The truth of our union with Christ in his death and resurrection bringing new life (Rom 6:1-10) came to us with new force. We saw the cross as God's provision for deliverance from the self-life."[16]

The annual mission conference at Nyabasi in July brought further blessings. Emil Sywulka and Metusela Chagu, an AIM evangelist, taught from the Bible. Elam Stauffer reported to his bishop colleagues in Lancaster in October:

As we gathered at Nyabasi this year there seemed to be a common burden that our ministries have been too barren of real spiritual fruit and great heart-searching and crying unto the Lord was made for a deeper working in our own hearts. The first prayer meeting prior to the conference was marked by the missionaries humbling themselves before the Lord in confessing their failures, barrenness, spiritual pride, carelessness, and sins.[17]

The conference conducted its business in a spirit of harmony so that "important questions were discussed and acted upon without difficulty," and "all returned home burdened and praying for the reviving of the church." More was to come. Stauffer continues:

> The Lord had begun at Mugango prior to conference. Since conference, there has been a mighty working at Shirati. Bukiroba and Bumangi have also seen his working. These workings have the form of deep conviction and confession of sin and of yielding to God's will, followed by a zeal for the glory of the Lord in the church. Souls need not be coaxed nor taught how to confess their sins but often with trembling and weeping they cry for forgiveness.[18]

John Leatherman also wrote of "an unprecedented confession of sin, and that particularly on the part of church members, elders, and teachers who were supposed to be in good standing." There had always been confessions, "but usually of such a nature that the one confessing would take no pains to seriously incriminate himself and would withhold matters that would involve costly restitution," but these confessions were different. "Another characteristic has been the rolling away of the burden of sin as the truth dawned that 'He was wounded for our transgressions and bruised for our iniquities'" (cf. Isa 53:5). Leatherman wrote that a third characteristic was "their burden and zeal for the salvation of others."[19]

The whirlwind at Shirati, August 1942

Shirati was the last of the Mennonite stations to experience a mighty working of the Holy Spirit. Elam Stauffer reported:

> On August 8, 1942 we had planned for our quarterly Communion time for the district. Christians from the out-schools gathered for the occasion. In the forenoon we had regular worship services.

Communion was scheduled for 2:00 p.m. Over the noon hour several of us, missionary and African, got together for counsel. We felt we should not serve Communion but rather call the church to prayer for revival. We felt to just go on as we were was adding darkness to darkness, sin to sin.

When we gathered in the church in the afternoon, I opened the meeting and explained the change of program and exhorted everyone to pray earnestly for God to revive us. Then I turned the meeting over to Hezekiah Odero, a church elder. I retired to the rear of the church to pray and wait.

Hezekiah exhorted the members to repentance. He asked them since they called Jesus Savior, why cannot He save them from their sins? Must He come back and die again? Must God send another Savior? After such exhortation, he called on everyone to pray. We all knelt in prayer.

After some time I heard a sound as a breeze come over the group. Soon I recognized [that] it was weeping. After some time I went to the front of the church. I began singing to get their attention. All sat up on the benches and awaited instruction. I told them, since God had convicted them of their sins, they were to confess them and find forgiveness. To facilitate this, I divided them into smaller groups—men, women, youth, boys, and girls in separate groups. I appointed a church elder to each group just to be in charge and hear.

I moved round from group to group. Such pouring out of sins. Sins of long ago and up to date. Sins we had not known to preach against. So burdened were they that they could hardly wait to confess. Some impatiently walked back and forth awaiting their turn. Eventually some began to sing spontaneously. The burden was gone. They were praising God for forgiveness and a new life. We gathered in the church again as one group to praise. Great was the joy. The meeting continued well into the night.[20]

Zedekia Kisare, a young man at the time, recalled his own experience. He was amazed and overjoyed to see that the Lord Jesus Christ was creating a new community based on heartfelt confession of need:

That August evening in 1942 the Holy Spirit gave us the insight that both the missionaries and the Africans were all lost from that one true village, the new village of God our Father. It was sin that kept us only concerned with our own earthly families, our ethnic villages. The Holy Spirit showed us that Jesus' sacrifice made it possible for all of us to be brothers and sisters in the same village.

At first I could not accept that God wanted me to be the brother of the missionary, that God wanted me to account the missionary to be of the same village with me. How could I accept that, when I felt the missionary's own ethnic pride so keenly? . . . But that evening we all saw Jesus. By that I mean that we saw the crucified Lamb of God whose blood removes the walls that separate people from each other and from God their Father. A great light from heaven shone on us, and each saw his own sin, and each saw the new village of God. We all saw this revelation together, so it was easy to confess to one another and to forgive one another. . . . It was only because of Jesus' blood that Elam Stauffer and I were able to recognize each other. Without that sacrifice he was nothing to me.[21]

Confession of sin can be an inward-looking, individualistic experience, or it can be profoundly revolutionary. Community can be no more than a sentimental way of looking at friends and neighbors in a church setting, or it can be a reorientation of society. Breaking down barriers between Africans and Westerners in the new community, as described by Kisare and a host of others, signaled a new beginning. People who abandoned all pretense and were transparent about their most secret sins and weaknesses could not settle for a superficial fellowship. But where would it lead? Were the churches prepared to accept this new way of living?

The East Africa Revival had reached the Mennonites. The message of renewal that Rebeka Makura and Phebe Yoder brought on their long walk together took deep root at the Mennonite mission stations on the eastern shore of Lake Victoria. Fellowship meetings united Africans and Americans in prayer and shaped the way both sought to follow Christ in their daily lives. Elam Stauffer's leadership was crucial in Mennonite acceptance of the revival, but nearly all of his colleagues shared his conviction and witnessed to a change in their lives, too.

The Mennonites who came to Africa to preach the gospel to "the natives" were conditioned to submit humbly to the church in matters of daily life. Though they would have denied it, that submission fostered a certain level of legalism. It was in their contact with *balokole* that they discovered afresh the centrality of Jesus and recognized a wider community of believers.

The revival struck a deep and familiar chord in the experience of many Mennonite missionaries. As with the CMS and AIM, not all Mennonite missionaries responded to the revival in the same way. Some believed it would undermine the doctrine and practice they came to Africa to teach; others feared public confession of sin and fellowship meetings would lead to a faith based on emotion. As a body, the Mennonite mission neverthe-less accepted the revival and played an important part in carrying its mes-sage to North America. The seed planted by the water seller from Mwanza and the missionary nurse took deep root. As Joe Church observed, Phebe Yoder's "testimony with that of others was used to revolutionize the think-ing of her mission and to challenge her church leaders in Pennsylvania."[22]

While the Mennonite missionaries were largely participants themselves in the revival fellowships, only a few in AIM continued in their relationship with the "saved ones." The Mennonite missionaries who became firm advocates for revival did so because they were substantially changed by it. AIM discouraged their missionaries from being involved. Because AIM was a nondenominational mission, the few missionaries who were involved in the revival had no denomination "back-home" because they were selected as individual missionaries, not commissioned by a single denomination. The Mennonites, on the other hand, were accountable to denominational leaders in their conferences, which meant that those touched by revival had a means to impact their denomination. For the East Africa Revival to bless North America, the role of missionaries became crucial. Local believers could not do it, so the involvement of the Mennonite missionaries was the bridge along which the revival message traveled.

The Fellowship Deepens and Widens 1942–1944

Zedekia Kisare

Zedekiah Marwa Kisare, destined to play a major role in the Mennonite Church in Tanzania.

Revival did not always manifest itself in great sins confessed. Signs of new life could be as simple as a man carrying water. Zedekia Kisare came from the Luo people on the borders of Kenya and Tanganyika, and he and five of his brothers worked for the Mennonites at Shirati. He was among the first students enrolled in the fledgling Mennonite Bible School. Reading his Bible, Kisare "began to see that in Christ my wife, Susana, and I were equal before God." He had always insisted on having the last word and making her an obedient wife. Once he saw from his study of the New Testament that a husband and wife are to work together, all quarreling ceased. He found a way of demonstrating this new way:

> I began to go to the lake to bring Susana water. In my father's village no man carried anything on his head. Heading was for women. A man carried things on his shoulder, not his head. But you cannot carry a *debe* (metal container) of water on your shoulder. People laughed at me when they saw me carrying water for Susana. They said I was ruining my wife. "She will become like a white woman, telling you what to do." But I continued to relate

to my wife in this new way I had seen in the New Testament. . . . It was several more years before my faith began to make a difference in how I related to the missionaries and to Africans who weren't from my father's village.[1]

For Kisare that expanding world began with confession and repentance at Shirati in August 1942 and grew as he experienced more of the revival fellowship. Kisare continued: "After the Holy Spirit's blessing came to us at Shirati, other brethren from Kenya and Uganda, African members of the Anglican Church, men who had earlier received God's blessing, came to visit us." They recognized the Mennonites as brothers in a community that looked beyond tribe, nation, and denomination. This was no superficial relationship. It meant that one could go among strangers and "be welcomed as dear, honored relatives." It extended to economic need. Kisare learned that "if a brother wished to marry but was so poor he didn't have the bride dowry, other brethren across ethnic and church boundaries would get the dowry together for him, just as they would were he their own blood brother."[2]

Exciting new relationships

William Nagenda was among the brothers who came from Uganda to visit the Mennonites. John Leatherman wrote in a letter to family and friends in America:

> I had the great privilege of laboring a bit with an African evangelist who has not been officially ordained, but whom God has filled with the Spirit and wonderfully blessed with a fruitful ministry. During one of his messages he said he was often asked how one can know if he is filled with the Spirit. He answered in words that burned into our souls: "You are filled with the Spirit when Christ is sweet and precious to you above all things. Didn't Christ say that the Spirit would testify of Him?"[3]

John and Catharine Leatherman recognized the revival as the work of the Holy Spirit, but they were not among the Mennonites who found the Lord in a new way in 1942. Catharine Leatherman recalled a conversation with Phebe Yoder after she returned from Capetown, South Africa, in July 1943. It helped Catharine in her own pilgrimage:

When revival came to the Mennonite missionaries, Phebe was one of the first to experience the new dimension of life. I saw and felt this new outflowing of love and grace and reality in her as she returned from a rest leave in South Africa. I yearned for the same thing, but I could not see any reason for my lack. I said to her, "Tell me how to get this new aliveness in Christ. I don't care what it costs; I must have it." Her response was, "I can only give you my own testimony. I felt just like you. I prayed, 'Lord, show me how I am in your sight.' What he showed me was dreadful, but now I know I'm joined to Jesus. I am reckoning myself to be dead with him, and alive with him."[4]

In later years an African brother told John and Catharine Leatherman, "When we sit around the fire in the evening, we don't part before someone begins telling what God has done for Pastor Leatherman." The Leathermans did not have their own new beginning until several months later, when they were staying at the AIM station at Mwanza. It came without any fanfare.

"Since no angel spoke to reassure me," Catharine Leatherman wrote later, "finally in 'cold faith,' without any warmth of emotion, I covenanted with God that from now on it would not be I any longer who directed my life, but that Jesus would be in control." For her husband too, revival came as a conviction rather than an emotion. John Leatherman described his experience: "Now I see that in this portion of death with Jesus, it is no longer our striving and groaning to be holy and trying to appear to others what we know in our hearts we are not, but it is His glorious self within, the new man, no longer I, but Christ, now raised up together with Him and made to sit together with Him in heavenly places." This did not mean that sin was no longer possible, but "since he no longer lives to defend himself," the Christian "is free to judge and confess sin whenever it becomes apparent." Leatherman had also learned that "ordination does not make me a privileged character before God, nor does it guarantee to me the filling of His Spirit."[5]

At this time John and Catharine Leatherman mailed another letter, this one requesting the mission board to stop sending their regular monthly stipend. It left them with "no way of proving to the heathen or to ourselves that we have left all to follow Jesus [when] we always knew where the next month's allowance would come from apart from any exercise of faith." They believed that "the riches of the missionaries are a constant hindrance to the gospel of him who had no place to lay his head."[6]

The mission board received similar letters from Phebe Yoder and Elam and Elizabeth Stauffer. Phebe had talked with her African housemaid after they had been praying together and asked her how she felt about Phebe being a salaried mission worker while she was paid a small sum to cook and clean. We do not know the outcome of Phebe's transparency on that matter, but the Holy Spirit made her to be keenly aware of irritations that destroy relationships. It must have come as a surprise to the maid to have her employer open that issue, which was taboo. It was just another step in Phebe's obedience to Jesus Christ. The board decided to continue paying their missionaries, but the issue of fair compensation for African workers was not abandoned.[7]

New possibilities—fellowship that shatters barriers

The revival influence had a tendency to blur denominational lines, too, because the winds of revival often blew through other missions and churches first, eventually blessing the Mennonite missionaries. Simeon Hurst recalled:

> The East Africa Revival hit me in the early 1940s when my first wife and I were touched by the fresh wave of the Holy Spirit as He moved to us through the Africa Inland Mission and the Church Missionary Society in Uganda and Tanganyika.[8]

Hurst and Clyde Shenk met the revival at the AIM mission at Mwanza. In 1943, Metusela Chagu, an AIM evangelist, came by invitation to the Mennonite stations. Shenk wrote at the time:

> Last week a visiting native evangelist spent a few days here at Bumangi. He had been at our native conference also. One evening while he was at Bumangi, I went to the native prayer meeting, which was held at the house of Jonah, who is the native church elder on the station. I was a little late and found that this visiting evangelist was seated in a corner wrapped in a blanket and speaking on John 3:30: "He must increase, but I must decrease." The burden of the message was that all men who have been and will be overcomers found their overcoming strength in the fact that they gave themselves to God, to be completely and unreservedly controlled by Him. He stressed death to the "old man" and "newness of life" in Christ Jesus. To see him was to understand that he lived as he spoke."[9]

Metusela Chagu was then invited to preach at the annual Mennonite conference that year. Mahlon Hess recalled:

> Many more experienced revival in the annual conferences which met at Mugango in 1943. In the missionary conference William and Virginia Stier [AIM missionaries] led the Bible studies, while Metusela Chagu preached in the spiritual life conference which followed. He appealed to God's people to leave the wilderness and to enter the promised land, to give up the controls to their lives so that the Spirit could work through them. Many were helped to take the next step in spiritual growth, and many met the Lord for the first time. In September 1944, Brother Metusela returned for a preaching circuit to every station, meetings which many remember with gratitude.[10]

Later in 1943, Simeon and Edna Hurst spent some weeks in Uganda with the CMS workers at Kampala and at Leslie Lea-Wilson's tea plantation at Namutamba, some sixty miles from Kampala, where William and Sala Nagenda made their home. They joined in fellowship meetings

Mahlon Hess, an early missionary

where African and Briton, farmworker and manager met for earnest prayer. Every day all the workers and staff came together for a fellowship meeting and shared deeply, confessing faults and "walking in the light."[11]

First witness abroad—South Africa

Although the Mennonite Church was a small denomination, workers from the Mennonite mission in Tanganyika had a role in bringing the East Africa Revival to Christians in other countries. During her 1943 stay in Capetown, Phebe Yoder encouraged some of the churches there to invite Joe Church and William Nagenda to speak. When the invitation came, it was the first request for them to speak outside East Africa. Everyone agreed that what South Africa needed was "a team in action, especially a team of black and white working in absolute oneness." But the authorities refused to issue permits for either William Nagenda or Yosiya Kinuka.[12]

Ken and Agnes Buxton of the Ruanda Mission also went on furlough to South Africa. "As a result of their testimony there to what God was doing in revival in Ruanda, Urundi, and Kigezi (Southern Uganda), supported by that of a few Mennonite missionaries working in Tanganyika who had been equally blessed, a call came to Joe Church to take a team to visit churches and ministers' gatherings in South Africa."[13]

When an all-white team from the Ruanda Mission finally came to South Africa in response to that invitation, they found some Mennonite missionaries en route to their American homes for a year's furlough: Phebe Yoder, and John and Catharine Leatherman and their children. They left Tanganyika in August 1944 as the first Mennonite missionaries to return home with firsthand experience of the East Africa Revival. But due to wartime priorities, their ship had to wait several months for needed repairs, and they were stranded in Capetown until it finally sailed early in February 1945.

Catharine Leatherman wrote, "Some dear Christian people gave us the two vestry rooms of a gospel hall to live in, and loaned us a small one-burner kerosene stove and dishes, and pans, all that we needed." Their unexpected stay in South Africa coincided, in part, with the conferences held in Capetown by Joe Church, Lawrence Barham, and Godfrey Hindley in October and November 1944. Phebe Yoder went every night. The Leathermans alternated, one parent staying with the children. The three Ruanda Mission evangelists visited them in their humble digs more than once and Catharine recalled "their fellowship built us up so much."

First witness in the United States

The next stage of their journey saw them in Buenos Aires for four weeks before they could catch a flight to Miami. Phebe went directly to her home in Kansas, while the Leathermans reached Pennsylvania at last. They found the home church as much in need of revival as the mission churches.[14] We will pick up this story in the next chapter.

With few exceptions, the Ugandan clergy in 1943 comprised "a formidable group opposed to the young enthusiasts for revival." Bishop Cyril E. Stuart tried to bring about reconciliation between the revival brothers and sisters and their critics in the Church of Uganda. He believed they had achieved this in a meeting at Ibuye in Urundi in February 1943. It seemed to some *balokole* that he was asking them to soft-pedal revival lest they give offense to anyone.[15]

Simeon Nsibambi found this a great strain, and ill health confined him to his house on Namirembe Hill through most of the year. He received visits from all the leaders of Christian work who came to Kampala.[16] Joe Church, Godfrey Hindley, and Lawrence Barham called on him to hear his opinion of the bishop's effort at reconciliation. Church recalled:

> He listened patiently to the story of the meetings at Ibuye, then he walked over to his bookshelf and pulled out a well-worn copy of Finney's *Revivals of Religion*. He pointed to a passage and asked me to read it. "If those who are laboring to promote them [revivals] allow themselves to get impatient and get into a bad spirit, the revival will cease." He pointed to the words "bad spirit" and asked me to read them twice. Then he said, "Isn't there another word in English—sweetness? Be careful not to lose sweetness."

Nsibambi stayed in his compound on Namirembe Hill because of bad health and as a way of avoiding conflict. Bishop Stuart regretted that Nsibambi no longer took part in the life of the parish. Nsibambi continued to be a leader of the revival, but he no longer preached, and he met with revival brothers only in his home.

Despite Nsibambi's counsel of charity, some *balokole* leaders resented Bishop Stuart's "efforts at controlling the revival" and began to see revival as "a battle against entrenched prejudiced authoritarianism in the Church." But the Lord was about to use the East Africa Revival in ways that no one had imagined in 1943.[17] The wind of the Holy Spirit blows where it will, and opposition cannot thwart it. That wind was destined to touch thousands of lives beyond Uganda. Those who maintained a critical attitude isolated themselves from blessings that open-hearted, hungry people enjoyed. Others whose first response was criticism found themselves kneeling with others at the foot of the cross, finding reconciliation with God and with one another.

—6—

American Churches in Need of Revival 1944–1946

Our story now switches to the United States and eastern Pennsylvania. It was a most unlikely place to receive the gentle wind of the Holy Spirit of God that first stirred in far-off Ruanda, a land that few in Pennsylvania had heard about. But in the providence of God they were visited by the same life-giving wind that brought renewal and freedom to thousands in East Africa. It happened through the missionaries they had sent to Tanganyika.

The problems that faced the Mennonites in Pennsylvania differed radically from the problems Africans faced as they shared their faith among their fellow Africans. Could the message of revival, lived out in the boiling caldron of tribal hatred in Ruanda and in conflict between Africans and whites, speak to the needs of Christians in entirely different circumstances? American Mennonites did not hold to a worldview that remotely resembled the worldview of African cultures. This was the acid test for the authenticity of revival. Does it leap cultural walls and produce reconciled brothers and sisters?

Even though the missionaries represented a culture quite different from African cultures, they discovered that what was good news to Africans was also good news to them. The revival message had just as much impact on the missionaries as on the local believers in far-off Africa. So the revival made its leap across cultures, binding missionaries and Africans together in the love of Christ. To their delight, both parties discovered the very thing the New Testament church discovered—the gospel of Jesus Christ is for all people and has the same affect on one culture as on the other. That old truth became a new reality for the missionaries.

The Mennonite missionaries returned home as World War II was winding down and found the church in eastern Pennsylvania dealing with difficulties quite unlike those in East Africa.

Mennonites struggle to maintain their faith

At that time mighty forces were eroding the traditional faith of the Mennonites. Many counted it as a time of theological disarray, as though the church had lost its sense of direction. So the denomination set about to establish new guidelines to bring Mennonite communities back together again. In 1943 a proposal came before the Mennonite Church's general conference to make nonconformity (separation from "the world") and nonresistance (noninvolvement in the military) tests of church membership. The nonresistance issue was fairly clear-cut and a reaffirmation of traditional Mennonite Christian pacifism. But nonconformity to the world involved myriad rules and regulations about dress, possessions, and conduct.[1]

Since the birth of the Anabaptist movement in the sixteenth century, simplicity and discipline have marked the Mennonites. Each local Mennonite conference established rules of conduct and strenuously enforced them. Lancaster Conference Mennonites were subject to the *Rules and Discipline of Lancaster Mennonite Conference*, which contained prohibitions designed to provide boundaries beyond which faithful Mennonites should not stray. The idea of living a simple, disciplined, holy life was not a strange thing for Mennonites. The difference was that now Lancaster Conference was determined to enforce a revised code of behavior to serve as a test of membership. Those considered lawless forfeited their membership.

The Mennonites' determination to uphold evangelical theology by codifying it was not unusual at that time. In many denominations liberal theology was taking a toll on evangelical beliefs. North American churches were emerging from a long struggle over modernism and liberalism. In many cases evangelical churches erected barricades of doctrine and practice to protect the faith handed down from the apostles. They wanted to return to the "fundamentals." Rules about personal adornment and behavior loomed large in the life of church members of many denominations. This was the situation in Lancaster Conference when John and Catharine Leatherman arrived in the United States in 1945.

Revival speaks to a new situation

The Lancaster Mennonites welcomed the Leatherman family home. They were barely settled when churches began inviting them to report on their experiences as missionaries, as expected of returned missionaries. John had many invitations to preach in Mennonite churches and describe how God was working in Africa. One of the first opportunities came from

East Chestnut Street, a large urban congregation in the city of Lancaster. John spoke there on the third chapter of Paul's letter to the Philippians. One person who attended the sermon reported, "The air seemed to be electrified."[2]

Not since the stirrings that occurred at the end of the nineteenth century had an evangelical message made such an impact on the Mennonites of Lancaster Conference. Their own missionaries had found something new that changed them. These missionaries had been nurtured by the same spirituality as their listeners. Therefore, the people could relate to what these missionaries were testifying to. There was a latent longing or yearning in their hearts to break out of their dry spirituality in order to enjoy the freedom that comes from walking moment by moment with Jesus Christ. These missionaries witnessed to the fact that it was not only possible but was, for themselves, an actuality. The missionaries were not only interpreters of the revival; they were also shaped by the liberating message of the gospel and were the results of its power.

There was nothing new about Mennonite missionaries reporting on other movements of the Holy Spirit that they encountered around the world. It was commonplace, but these missionaries were not simply reporting on a revival they had observed: they were speaking from within it, as people who had been blessed by the Lord. That infused the message with a life-giving immediacy.

Why did this message appear as something new, powerful, and life-changing? Why did it stir hope in some, agitation in others, and an invitation to a new life of freedom in Christ to others?

For many Lancaster Mennonites, the moment was one of amazing grace because it offered another way to live the holy life—by following Jesus in repentant faith. The key to spirituality was not obedience to a set discipline but abandonment to Jesus Christ. The missionaries never doubted the worth and the necessity of discipline, law, and order. Their concern was that by overemphasizing obedience, one's attention might be drawn from the source of salvation, the atoning work of Jesus Christ. With their whole hearts they believed that people are saved by grace and not by human striving or achievement. In Africa they had seen that when people experienced the new birth by grace, their behavior changed radically. They also experienced this transforming power themselves. They wanted to obey the Savior who walked with them in their salvation experience. They knew that grace properly received and lived produced law-abiding saints who produce good fruit. The people of East Africa who committed to shaping their lives according to the teachings of Jesus knew instinctively that a life of grace is a life of holiness. Parenthetically, at times others accused them of trying to be "too holy," which meant that their behavior was exemplary.

First witness from renewed missionaries

The Leathermans and Phebe Yoder returned to the United States as Lancaster Conference issued its requirements for holy living, demands that were producing intolerable tensions among the members. It was a time of great need, which the Leathermans heard more about from friends who had been with them in Tanganyika, John and Ruth Mosemann. The Mosemann's had spent a term in the Mennonite mission there just before the revival broke out. The Leathermans visited the Mosemanns in Lancaster, and John Leatherman reported:

> For dinner we went to John Mosemann's place and all afternoon John and I talked on the situation here at home. Many people are dissatisfied and the bishops seem unable to deal with the problem. Consequently they are fighting their last ditch, strongly asserting their authority. They have been in the wrong in a number of instances, but have not humbled themselves and confessed it.[3]

Second work of grace?

American Mennonite churches had begun to hear about the East Africa Revival, and not always positively. Elam Stauffer observed in 1944:

> It appears, judging from letters from America, that there are suspicions, fears and rumors at home in regards to the revival. . . . Some seem to have concluded that there is "second work of grace" teaching here, others suggest "eradication of the sinful nature" doctrine, still others that we are destroying the faith.[4]

The Lancaster Conference faced a crisis related in part to the East Africa Revival. They were aware of the worldly influences eroding the religious life of their members. The conference was determined to purify the church by requiring obedience to the discipline. When the time came to reappoint these "renewed" missionaries for return to their African assignment, what the conference leaders heard from the missionaries clashed with their vision of fostering spiritual growth through church discipline. The bishops were combating worldliness by enforcing rules of behavior, and it must have been unsettling when they heard the missionaries testify to release from what they discerned as legalisms of all sorts. The missionaries spoke not about success in their work but of new freedom in Christ as Jesus dealt with sin in their hearts. That was not what the church leaders expected. The concerned church leaders questioned the East Africa renewal movement because it treated denominational boundaries and church rules and regulations as of secondary importance.[5]

Leatherman met with Mosemann and other ministers, then reflected in his diary:

> We all have a common burden for the condition of unrest throughout the conference. Our question for discussion centered around how far it was possible for there to be a revival within the walls of the conference, and the misemphasis upon ordinances.[6]

Varied responses to the revival message

Phebe Yoder returned to Lancaster after a short visit with her family in Kansas. She spoke in a number of churches with John and Catharine Leatherman, including the Mount Joy Mennonite Church, which planned an African program for a Wednesday evening service. John Leatherman wrote, "The house was crowded and the Lord was there in blessing. Phebe especially had a good message." The three missionaries also spoke at Lititz Mennonite Church on a Sunday evening. Women could share their experience of the mission field, but only men could bring the Sunday morning message or speak from the pulpit.[7]

News of the great things the Lord was doing in East Africa began to spread. John Leatherman returned to the East Chestnut Street Church early in May 1945 for a week of meetings. On the first night, "the church was packed. [Pastor] Stoner Krady said there may have been 1,200 people there." John Leatherman's nightly sermons provided firsthand testimony of the East Africa Revival and its theological message. After the service, John and Catharine talked with individuals "and gave our experiences." What most people remembered was the testimony of their own renewed life. They wanted the same thing for themselves. Leatherman recorded in his diary: "The meetings continued throughout the week. There were a total of 24 or 25 people who responded, a number of whom found real victory in the Lord." One who came forward for prayer was Erma Longenecker Maust, a young mother who was a friend of Catharine Leatherman. Erma's husband, Herbert K. Maust, was the deacon in the Marietta mission church. For Erma Maust the meetings at East Chestnut Street marked a new beginning.[8]

Ruth N. Graybill heard John Leatherman preach at East Chestnut Street Mennonite Church. She later recalled:

> The church was packed to the doors. The air seemed to be electrified. He spoke about knowing Jesus as the One who brings revival to our hearts as we constantly keep repenting and receiving forgiveness for our sins. One of the hymns that night has become so meaningful to me ever since: "Out of my bondage, sorrow, and night, / Jesus, I come, Jesus, I come. / Into thy freedom, gladness, and light, / Jesus, I come to Thee"[9] [William T. Sleeper, 1887].

Abner and Betty Miller also went to the East Chestnut Street services. They were busily engaged at the Mennonite mission in Steelton, but Betty Miller was depressed and unhappy. "I was aware of my need, but too proud to acknowledge it." She knew Erma Maust and others who asked for prayer, "but I could not respond as she did."[10]

Mervin and Mary Keener Miller were at John Leatherman's meetings in Lancaster. Mary later recalled his messages as a turning point in her life. She testified: "I had yielded to the Holy Spirit's conviction some weeks before I heard John preach, but his message was just what I needed to help me all the way down and be filled with the Holy Spirit."[11]

In addition to speaking engagements in the Lancaster and Franconia conference[12] churches, John Leatherman accepted invitations to deliver the commencement address at Eastern Mennonite College, Harrisonburg, Virginia, and at Lancaster Mennonite School, and he taught a short course at Goshen College. In each case he brought the essential message of the East Africa Revival.

Leatherman noted that his commencement address at Eastern Mennonite College in May 1945 "was really a sermon." He thought it went well. But some of his remarks did not sit well with college president John L. Stauffer, well-known as a winsome, wise, and conscientious defender of the Mennonite faith. His opinions carried extraordinary weight among the Mennonites. Leatherman wrote that Stauffer "opened his 'inquiries' by asking me what I meant by referring to our 'denominational pride.'" Their conversation did not continue long, "but it was pointed enough to mark me down as 'questionable' in Bro. Stauffer's mind."

Leatherman did not temporize and "told him that I thought our church's emphasis upon ordinances was misplaced."[13]

First serious caution

In a letter written a few days later, Stauffer commented on Leatherman's message. He reported that he had received "a number of expressions of appreciation for your message" and the positive response from those "who heard your testimony from either yourself or Sister Leatherman." Stauffer was an exceptionally kind man and made his point graciously. "Relative to the distinction that you make between major and minor truth as I gathered it, I have sympathy for you." Stauffer appeared half-apologetic when he pointed to the time when, as a young pastor in the Mennonite mission at Altoona, Pennsylvania, he too found fellowship with "interdenominationalists." He then concluded, "I could not continue as a minister in the Mennonite Church according to my ordination vow if I could no longer hold the distinctive truth for which the Mennonite Church justifies her existence as a separate group." Stauffer, because of his ordination vow, broke off those relationships. Perhaps he wished that Leatherman would take heed and do the same.

In reply to this letter, Leatherman wrote:

> I only want to reiterate my testimony as to what the Lord has done for my soul. At a time of deep inner need, brought to a climax largely by the consciousness of a generally unsatisfactory ministry and manifested by such things as cynical attitudes towards others who did not view the truth as I did, the Lord showed to me that "I" needed to die and revealed the truth to my heart that "our old man was crucified with him" [cf. Gal 2:20]. The meaning of the love of Christ has come to me in a way I had never seen before, and I know that no matter how doctrinally correct I may be, if I have not love, I am nothing. Christ in a new way has become my all and I want to exalt Him as the head. By emphasizing the supreme need of love and the holding of the head, I do not wish to disparage in the least the importance of correct doctrine, or make excuse for any doctrinal misapprehension I may be found to entertain at any time. The cross at least means to me that I must be open for instruction and correction. However, should it become apparent that the leading of the Lord in my life has brought me into conflict with the promises I made at the time of my ordination, I realize my obligation to honestly face the implications.[14]

Mosemann seeks softening of regulations

John H. Mosemann and his wife had returned to Lancaster on furlough from the Mennonite mission in Tanganyika in 1940, before revival had reached the Mennonites. He was asked to stay in the United States and work with the Civilian Public Service program set up under the Selective Service Act of 1940. Mosemann maintained a close relationship with the leaders of Lancaster Conference. He admitted that he had misgivings about the revised Lancaster discipline and urged the bishop board to take a more compassionate view of members who could not live up to all the particulars of the document.[15]

In June 1944 the bishop board began considering a petition written by Mosemann and signed by fourteen other ministers and deacons, calling for "a conference-wide appeal for confession, contrition, and repentance—especially on the part of our ordained brethren—as the only possible path to revival, which in turn is the only hope in our present crisis."[16]

On the eve of his meeting with the bishop board, John Mosemann reflected:

> Our people, here and there, speak of a revival in Africa, but little discern the utter and desperate need here at home. Of course the terms in which our missionaries speak are an "unknown tongue" as far as many of our folks are concerned. At the very least the doings of the Lord on the field are causing no little stir. We earnestly pray that this may be the portent of a mighty upheaval, an earthquake in spiritual things.[17]

Many touched by the message of revival

The message that returned missionaries brought to Lancaster Conference Mennonites was good news for many who felt bound by legalism. J. Kenneth Fisher, a young husband and father who served as superintendent of the mission Sunday school at Parkesburg, Pennsylvania, was one who found release from this burden when he heard John Leatherman preach. Fisher recalled:

> At first I was happy in my Christian walk, but as time went on I became rather legalistic in my outlook. Surely my good works had a lot to do with my salvation. God began to deal with me so strongly by His Holy Spirit that for several years I was completely miserable. It became very apparent to me that though I obeyed

all the rules and regulations of the church, and appeared so holy on the outside, inside I could not control lustful and evil thoughts.

One Sunday evening in 1945, when we didn't have services, I visited the church in Coatesville to hear John Leatherman preach. When John stood up to preach I knew, by his countenance, that he had what I so sorely needed. Of course his message was about the power of the cross in bringing victory to broken, failing Christians like myself. It seemed to me that all of the missionaries who came home on furlough from East Africa, during this time, men and women alike, glowed with the light and love of God's Spirit. Not long after hearing John Leatherman's powerful message, God gave me a taste of His grace and power like I had never experienced before.

After the morning chores and breakfast, I hitched up a team of horses to a grain drill to sow winter wheat. As I plodded back and forth behind that grain drill, God did a work of grace in my life that I shall never forget. He showed me many things, perhaps the most important being that salvation is by grace, not works, that all my good works could not bring me to a place of peace and victory.[18]

Others found a different release. Esther Mae Longenecker was sixteen when the first Lancaster Conference missionaries went to Africa. Simon Garber, her pastor at Bossler Mennonite Church, kept every family in the congregation informed about the Tanganyika mission by giving each one a copy of the most recent *Africa Circle Letter*. She noticed "a definite shift to a spiritual emphasis" after the revival began. Esther reported:

I'll never forget meeting in Abram Gish's meadow with those who came home on furlough from Africa. They sang the song "Glory, glory, Jesus saves me." And two lines in the song caught my attention: "But when I gave over trying, simply trusting, I was blest." I did a lot of trying—and crying—to manage my impatient spirit, but with no success. I am the oldest of six siblings and practically raised the youngest three. But I was so impatient with them. Finally, I got to the end of my rope and said, "God, I quit trying to manage me; you take over." He did.[19]

The meeting in Abram Gish's meadow was apparently in July 1945. Abram and Laura Miller Gish, members of the Bossler Mennonite Church, were active in the mission congregation at Marietta. John Leatherman addressed a similar outdoor service near Elizabethtown on a Sunday evening in July: "I spoke at the lawn gathering at Frank Hertzler's above Elizabethtown. We had a most blessed meeting. There were seats for 200 but there were others standing. I spoke on Ephesians 3:8 and the Lord gave great liberty."[20]

John Leatherman returned to study at Eastern Baptist Seminary in 1945 and 1946. He continued to carry a full schedule of appointments for Sunday morning and evening services in Mennonite churches across Pennsylvania and as far away as Ontario.[21] His message made many suspicious, particularly among the leaders of Lancaster Conference.

John Mosemann complained to the board of bishops of Lancaster Conference about their "cool and critical attitude toward the ministry of John Leatherman." They had not yet asked for a time to speak with Leatherman. The grapevine had it that the church leaders had decided "to send no missionaries to the field until more knowledge of the situation could be gained from returning workers." Mosemann reported one bishop saying publicly that Leatherman would not be sent back to East Africa "if he does not change his position."[22]

The Issue? Communion!

The Leathermans assumed that the opposition to them was so intense that they would not be reappointed to return to Tanganyika. But the stance of some on the bishop board had begun to soften. To the amazement of John and Catharine Leatherman, the bishops informed them that they had "passed" the doctrinal exam, which was a standard questionnaire all missionaries were required to complete. John had expressed "questions on the validity of several of the ordinances, as the holy kiss, the devotional covering, and foot washing." His examiners did not object. He rejoiced that the board reappointed them "without having to make any compromise." John Leatherman and one of the prominent conference bishops, Henry Lutz, both preached at an Easter communion service at Kraybill Mennonite Church, and the next day the Leatherman family left for Africa.[23]

In the last days of their home furlough, John Leatherman finally had had a chance to talk with the mission board about African problems, including the relations with the home church, forming a truly indigenous church, and "the communion question." The latter was a crucial issue. Did sharing the bread and cup symbolize participation in the new village of Jesus or a willingness to be at peace and in order with the Lancaster Mennonite Conference?[24]

Elam Stauffer, as bishop of the Mennonite Church in Tanganyika, defended the missionaries and the mission board in his personal letters to the leaders. He explained that it was a long-standing practice whenever Africans from other missions "who are known to be worthy Christians" were staying at the Mennonite mission: "they are extended the privilege of communion with us." This was necessary because people often moved from one mission area to another for temporary employment, and it would be inappropriate to ask them to change their church membership. But "during the first years we kept strictly close [open only to communicant Mennonites] communion." When Mennonites attended conferences of other missions, they withdrew and did not share in communion services. "During that time some of us felt that having been together with other Christians and having had a spiritual feast together in the Spirit, it grieved the Holy Spirit to withdraw when communion time came at the end of the conference."

Bishop Stauffer recalled that as early as 1941, he and his wife, Elizabeth, had accepted the hospitality of a Plymouth Brethren family in Dar es Salaam and communed with them in their home. In sharing this with his colleagues in 1946, Stauffer wrote, "I then learned more fully that others of our group had been having the same problem." Some of the missionaries had shared communion with non-Mennonites but did not speak of it. The breakthrough came with the revival, as Stauffer reported:

> In 1942 the Lord brought the revival among us. He had been getting liberty in other parts of Tanganyika. I feel I should add that He used an African sister of another mission to begin the revival among us that uncovered much sin. Through her testimony and prayer life, she was used of the Lord to do the work that He, for some reason, could not do through us. Following that revival, others came to us to share with us in the things of the Lord. Several times we had guest speakers at our conferences who gave us rich spiritual food. We extended communion privileges to them and they rejoiced in the privilege.

Stauffer wanted it clearly understood that he and his colleagues did not favor entirely open communion, but simply "a variation from strictly close communion such as would enable them to fellowship in communion with faithful missionaries from other groups who are one in the Spirit with us."[25] The communion issue did not go away. Lancaster Conference leaders did not quickly resolve this problem. At the 1946 annual field conference of Mennonite missionaries in Tanganyika, there was no communion. The reason: "We had three visitors from Kenya this year again who were richly blessed among us, but because of their presence we could have no communion service." One Mennonite missionary, a critic of the revival, refused to participate if the Mennonites invited the visitors to join the communion service, and the others declined if some were barred from communion.[26] It was all very confusing.

Reaffirmation of restricted communion

After long consideration the bishop board reaffirmed the practice of offering communion only to those who were in compliance with the discipline of Lancaster Conference. The conference eventually made this requirement an integral part of a statement on foreign mission polity, which meant missionaries had to abide by it. The polity was initially drafted by Amos Horst in 1946 but not issued until 1949. Letters from overseas missionaries commenting on the proposed document were read at a meeting of the Bishop Board in October 1949. Simeon Hurst wrote:

> The matter of close [open only to those adhering to the discipline] communion with making no provision for communing with those outside the Mennonite church whom the Lord may have used to lead us into closer fellowship with Himself and whose lives give evidence of being filled with the Spirit is I feel contrary to the teaching of our Lord on the oneness of the body of Christ. This likewise applies to non-Mennonite speakers whom the Lord has used in the past to bring to us messages that our hearts needed and to show to us our own needs before Him.[27]

The East Africa Revival demonstrated how Christian men and women could unite in fellowship at the foot of the cross without ceasing to be Free Methodists or Anglicans, Mennonites or Lutherans. Could the missionaries carry this lesson to the churches of North America and Europe?

Many Mennonites in North America suspected that if the door to communion was opened wide, they might soon lose denominational distinctives like nonresistance and nonconformity to the world. If that happened, it would be the first step toward denying the reason for the existence of the Mennonite church as distinct from all others. Nevertheless, many church members shared the views of Leatherman and Mosemann.

The Mennonite missionaries whose furloughs were delayed because of World War II had by now completed their leaves and prepared to return to Tanganyika. As the missionaries saw it, they were now returning "home" to the place where they had found true liberty in Jesus Christ. While they were in North America, interacting with friends there, new developments occurred in East Africa. The missionaries were eager to return to the saved ones they had come to love and appreciate.

—7—

Growing Influence of Revival Following World War II

After their furloughs, the Mennonite missionary team returned to Tanganyika and immediately bonded again with local believers seeking to follow Jesus as the Spirit directed them. The missionaries were eager to enjoy the full blessing of life in Christ as a new community, a new fellowship of light and love. They envisioned new possibilities of hope that could take them through the demanding days of integrating the mission and the local church, preparing leaders, providing schools, maintaining outreach programs, and effectively evangelizing. The revival message and experience gave missionaries and local church leaders a basis for fellowship that enabled them to walk hopefully into the future.

A breakthrough among the Mennonites

In 1946 four African Anglican schoolteachers came to the Mennonite mission at Bukiroba, near Musoma, to hold three days of renewal meetings. Mahlon Hess recalled that the meetings began with each team member confessing his own sins and failures. One had stolen from his employer and returned the goods, with well-grounded fear of punishment, only to be forgiven. Another had difficulties with his wife until "he was willing to humble himself and help her with what were regarded as women's chores." In one afternoon testimony meeting, "after songs and prayer, the Mennonite station carpenter walked forward, placed a box on the pulpit, and showed the tools he had stolen while he worked in a government shop." As soon as he said that he would return them to the district commissioner, the congregation burst into praise, singing, "Glory, glory, halleluyah/Glory, glory to the lamb." Others followed. "Each time someone made a clear commitment, the congregation responded with another verse of the glory song,"

"*Tukutendereza, Yesu* [We praise you, Jesus]," which had become the signature hymn of the revival. (This hymn by Louise M. Rouse became popularized in Uganda in the language of Luganda. It was translated by popular usage into Kiswahili, the common language of Tanzania and Kenya. In the process the words of the chorus became simply, "Glory, halleluyah/Praise to the lamb/The blood has cleansed me, Glory to Jesus." This is the literal translation for the song as it appeared in the *Tenzi Za Rohoni*, a Swahili hymn book published by the Musoma Press of Tanzania in 1968.)

The visitors then told about the twice-weekly fellowship meetings in their home congregations that began with "walking in the light," sharing victories and defeats, reading and discussing Scripture, and praying for one another. They recommended this pattern at each of the Mennonite stations, and the Mennonite missionaries took their advice.[1]

Within a short time the revival had become part of the life of many Christian churches. In Kenya, where the first *balokole* visited in 1937 and the Rev. Obadiah Kariuki and his parishioners had to meet under the trees because the church at Kabete was closed to them, the influence of revival blew like a gentle wind in one church after another. "Anglican services all over the country were followed by revival meetings outside church [buildings], spontaneous and yet keeping to a certain orderly pattern. The saved ones greeted one another warmly with singing, handshakes, and embraces." A structure emerged. "Local fellowships formed, usually meeting on a weekly basis, if not more often, and meetings of fellowships on a district level every month or so. At each level they planned for on-going meetings and for witness in their communities and beyond."[2]

Revival was now a unifying force, bringing together Christians of many denominations. Until about 1945, especially in Kenya and Uganda, the revival movement reached mainly Anglicans, but the East Africa Revival became a source of renewal in other churches after that. As opposition to revival faded, Anglican, Methodist, and Presbyterian churches in Kenya welcomed its influence. The AIM stations alone remained aloof.[3]

Fellowships, a new basis for living

The Mennonite mission continued to be blessed and helped by Christian men and women from other missions. The missionaries thus testified to their own experience of the oneness of the body of Christ. The unity of Christ's body in its reality as a living, breathing community was becoming visible all over East Africa. Fellowship meetings and conventions testified to the corporate nature of revival. The teams that gave leadership to these powerful meetings were quite ordinary people, linked together by the atoning work of Jesus Christ. Norman Grubb, director of the World Evangelism Crusade, saw this team approach as a counter to Western individualism and an important lesson taught by the revival in East Africa:

> Further, we are beginning to learn, as a company of Christ's witnesses, that the rivers of life to the world do not flow out through one man, but through the body, the team. Our brokenness and openness must be two-way, horizontal as well as vertical, with one another as with God.[4]

A breakthrough at Kabale, Uganda

In 1945 the revival brothers chose Kabale in western Uganda, near the border with Ruanda, as the site for a major convention. They had previously met at Namirembe, near Kampala, under Bishop Stuart's patronage. The last of these meetings was in August 1944 and on the theme "Christ and Him Crucified." The *balokole* tried their best to please the bishop and other clergy of the Church of Uganda, who wanted to blend all forms of renewal in these meetings. It was not easy and proved to be a strain on both sides. Nevertheless, the convention was a marked success: many lives were transformed. Those who attended witnessed the movement of the Holy Spirit in profound ways. But the time had come to move out of the limelight of the cathedral city, Kampala. Moving away from Namirembe was a strategy of withdrawal to avoid conflict.

In December 1945 some fifteen thousand *balokole* gathered in Kabale, this time including many brothers and sisters from the district of Kigezi where the conference was held and from Ruanda, Urundi, Tanganyika, and Kenya. These large conventions soon became characteristic of the revival and continue to the present day.[5]

Some converts wept over their sins, and others shook or leaped with joy at their liberation. Such outward signs of conversion were not uncommon, but they were not especially encouraged. As often happens, however, there were some who wanted to prescribe what the outward signs of conversion should be and wanted to find a formula to repeat in every case of true repentance. Nsibambi and others resisted this trend.

The temptation to codify revival

Elam Stauffer reflected on the revival after he left East Africa:

> Not all that posed as revival was real. . . . Some learned the right
> words to say and the songs to sing but evidenced no changed lives.
> There were those who tried to add laws to the new life. Others
> began adding certain externals to the new life. Others denied that
> God had revived because it did not fit their concept of what that
> should be. All this was combated by holding that when one is in
> fellowship with Jesus, He is adequate. Nothing can be added to
> the risen Lord Jesus Christ.[6]

Legalism always threatened to creep into the revival as in every renewal movement. Festo Kivengere's struggle was typical. After he met the Lord
and was transformed by the power of God's mighty grace in 1941, the
question arose as to how to sustain that walk with God. He devoured spiritual books as a desperate soul and later reported:

> I nearly killed myself to be perfect. I became completely bogged
> down with all the Christian books which told me, if you want to
> crucify your old man, do one, two, three, four [things]. These
> writers were true men of God who had written their books to help
> other Christians. They had learned valuable lessons, but when
> they set them down in such a systematic manner, I, hungry and
> seeking, came along and said, "If only I do this and that, and the
> other, then all will be well, and my sinful nature will be dealt with
> forever."

Festo wrestled a long time before he found the answer in prayer. He
needed to go to the cross. "I wanted to find the key to perfection in order
to please him; but he was the key. . . . In order to present myself perfect
before Jesus, I had been looking for a solution other than Jesus."[7]

Thus, the message of renewal was simple, but even the most respected
leaders sometimes got it wrong. After listening to a preacher in Uganda
deal with the familiar text of Romans 6:6, even stalwarts like William
Nagenda and Yosiya Kinuka felt the need to spend time in prayer and solitude and "crucify the old man once and for all." When they returned home
to their families, they were irritable and hard with their children. William
continued to be troubled. One day Nagenda went to see Nsibambi, who
greeted him and said, "What is the matter, William?" The reply came, "Oh,
I am really seeking to crucify the old man in these days." Nsibambi then
looked at him sadly and said, "Don't you know, William, that your old

man was crucified for you, long ago, at Calvary! Go home and rest, Brother, rest in the finished work of Calvary!"[8]

After that Nagenda and the other brothers rejected any need for some additional experience leading to a higher plane of Christian life, "beyond the decisive and primary conversion experience of being saved by the blood of the crucified Christ, and in the light of that experience living a life of continual 'brokenness' and daily repentance."[9]

Many missionaries were learning these truths step-by-step, alongside African brothers and sisters, in small weekly fellowship meetings and in massive conventions like that at Kabale. American Mennonites were among them.

George and Dorothy Smoker find freedom in Christ

George and Dorothy Waterhouse Smoker arrived in Tanganyika in March 1943 after a harrowing journey around South Africa amid naval conflict. Both Smokers had worked in the Mennonite Publishing House in Scottdale, Pennsylvania, before accepting an invitation to East Africa. Both graduated magna cum laude from Wheaton College, where Dorothy out-stripped George by a fraction of a point. He often said later that if he could not be number one, he would marry number one. Both George and Dorothy were blessed with an extraordinary sense of humor that made them fun to be around. God did not bless them with children. Dorothy was from a long line of missionaries: her grandfather had been one of the first missionaries to Hawaii, and her father had a special ministry among Japanese. George's father died when he was quite young, so he and his mother started a little peanut butter manufacturing and distribution busi-ness in the town of Scottdale, Pennsylvania. George took that skill along to Tanganyika, where he continued to produce quality peanut butter from local peanuts. As young American missionaries George and Dorothy believed that they had something to share with Africans.

They settled into the work at the Bukiroba station under demanding wartime conditions and did their best to fill the gap left by the missionar-ies on furlough. The couple endured trying times at their mission station. After being there only a short time, they were exhausted and badly needed a rest. So the mission leaders decided that when the Leatherman family returned from furlough in June 1946, the Smokers would have a vacation in Uganda.

The Lake Victoria steamboat that brought the Leatherman family on the last leg of their journey from America to Africa tied up at the pier at

Musoma, Tanganyika, on the morning of June 9, 1946. Elam and Elizabeth
Stauffer, Mahlon and Mabel Hess, and George and Dorothy Smoker were
waiting on the dock to greet them. John Leatherman wrote in his diary that
"the Smokers came in to see us and also to leave on the same boat for their
leave [a local leave to Uganda]. After lingering for a while, we said goodbye to the Smokers and left for Bukiroba."[10] John Leatherman could not
have known what an important trip that would be for the Smokers.

At Simeon and Edna Hurst's suggestion, the Smokers took their annual leave at the CMS station at Kabale, in western Uganda, where the revival
convention had met a few months earlier. The Hurts knew that the
Smokers were discouraged and had doubts about whether this was the
place for them. They were even considering returning to America before
their allotted term of five years was over. The Hurts wanted them to see
the East Africa Revival at work.[11] Dorothy Smoker reported:

> We began to "see" the revival on the lake steamer. There we met
> a team of young Africans from the Tanganyika side of the border
> of Ruanda. We heard their remarkable testimonies and knew that
> here were truly Spirit-filled men who had learned to suffer for
> their Lord. On the same boat we met a missionary doctor and his
> wife returning to Kampala, who told us not simply of blessings in
> their African brethren but [also] in their own personal lives and
> home through their daily appropriation of the blood of Jesus and
> through a willingness to be broken before the great searcher of
> hearts.[12]

Years later Dorothy recalled that "their faces shone. We were glum."
George and Dorothy had to take "a rickety old bus going to Kabale" from
the nearest lake port. The bus stopped overnight at Mbarara and, since it
was still light, the Smokers went for a walk. "From the road we saw a
group of thirty to forty Africans sitting together, singing joyously, talking,
and then singing again." They asked an English missionary, who showed
them the Anglican church, whether the Africans were members of his congregation. They were members, and the missionary said they met every
afternoon to sing and pray.

The next day the Smokers continued on to Kabale and went to the district commissioner's office for a permit to buy the supplies they would
need.

When we went to the government offices to get a ration coupon for flour we found a young official quite upset over the quantity of stolen army equipment which was being returned by ex-army men, Africans, who all came with the same story that now they are saved and they want to return everything they had stolen.

At Kabale we found groups spontaneously stopping to sing and praise God even along the roads and in the town. Singing began before sunrise and could be heard from every direction around. It was in the atmosphere. Such joy could not be permanent and grow and spread as this has without some very real obedience to God's spiritual laws for revival. The African team on the boat had first told us, and others told us again, that the basis of it was a radical dealing with sin, and of being cleansed by the blood of Jesus. Faith in Jesus' blood, with confession of sin and honest restitution, is what is preached. . . . The standard for the Christian is brokenness before God and transparency in love with his brothers.

The Smokers knew they needed a closer walk with the Lord but weren't sure what to do next. On their final afternoon in Kabale, an African schoolteacher visited with them. He told how God had saved him and how that very day he had to repent of selfishness in taking the best for himself at dinner. That night George and Dorothy confessed and walked in the light with each other:

George and Dorothy Smoker in California, renewed by revival.

> We went aside to observe the miracle of the burning bush that burned with fire but was not consumed, and we ended by being burned ourselves with the flame of God that sears and reveals the dross. We began to learn in a new way together, with the hand

of God heavily upon us, what it means to be broken and to call sin sin. Also we know in a new way the joy of release and pardon and could sing the praise song in their language with our brethren, "the saved ones," as they are called. They insist the breaking process must be repeated over and over and that the joy flows from broken vessels. We agree.

They had learned the lesson of the revival. "God is no respecter of persons or races or missions or churches. Can we not have what they have if we will pay the price? And can you not have it too?"[13]

When George and Dorothy Smoker returned to Bukiroba, John Leatherman met them. Leatherman reported in his diary:

But the big event to record is that a new George Smoker came back. He was wonderfully revived and blessed. In prayer meeting this evening he humbled himself and confessed to much [and] that he has been refreshed. This I believe will be the beginning of new blessing in the mission.[14]

As the result of the Smokers' testimony, Mahlon and Mabel Hess also experienced renewal a few days later. At the mission conference in August, "George gave his testimony, which was heart-searching. A number of confessions followed and the way of fellowship was wonderfully prepared—this advantage to be realized during the discussion of the hard problems before the mission."[15]

In November 1946 a team of African brothers came to the Mennonite mission from the Anglican CMS and Ruanda Mission churches. They were Erisa Rwabahungu, a former school teacher who had been part of a team with Joe Church and Simeon Nsibambi in 1937; Frederick K. Bategeaza, a teacher at Katoke College; and Gabriel Rwandindi and Yohana Baishumike of CMS Tanzania. When the brothers arrived, John Leatherman met them on the pier in Musoma and took them to the church where Ezekiel Muganda was preaching. "They each gave their testimonies, which were very penetrating, yet simple." Later in the week John Leatherman recorded:

The meetings continue in the power of the Spirit. I do not recall having heard such a ministry of the Word from any European minister. The theme of these brethren was sin and the blood of Christ. I got a new vision of the meaning of Christ's death for my soul. He despised the shame—should we not do the same in acknowledging our sins and sinful heart? On their last night at Bukiroba, the brethren gave us instruction on how to proceed in fellowship meetings. After supper we had a very informal meeting in which they gave still more testimony as to what the Lord has done for them. And such joy in singing "Are you washed?"[16]

The next day the team went on to Mugango and spent time at each of the Mennonite stations in turn. They returned to Bukiroba early in December, where local Seventh-Day Adventists came to attend their meetings alongside the Mennonites. On the final evening "Frederick gave a message on how they walk together in the light. We too want to walk in the light."[17]

Leatherman summed up his impressions of their visit for *Africa Letters:*

During November and on into this month we were deeply blessed in our souls by the visit of four African evangelists, one from Ruanda, and the other three from western Tanganyika. These brethren were filled with the Spirit of God. . . . Again we saw the power of the blood of his cross to cleanse from all sin when we consent to be truly broken and bring our sins out into the light.

These messengers of our Lord were representatives of the great revival movement that has been in progress for some years in Ruanda, Uganda, and in western Tanganyika. It is gaining in power and influence as increasingly missionaries of various societies are confessing it to be of God and are conforming their lives and ministries to its demands. Again God is demonstrating before our eyes that no one missionary society or church is regarded by him as having more of the truth than any other, but wherever there are hearts that are prepared to follow the Lamb whithersoever he goeth, consenting to be thoroughly broken with respect to all religious or worldly pride, he again demonstrates his ancient power to redeem and sanctify.[18]

The exciting possibilities of a new community

As in every generation since the Holy Spirit descended in power at the first Pentecost, the Lord was forming his people into a new community that superseded the old ties of nation, race, and church membership. This was obviously John Leatherman's experience:

As a result of former contacts with this revival working, as well as of hearing the testimonies and messages of these native brethren, I have been deeply impressed with the fact that when God works in revival blessing, He causes His servants to lay the ax to the root of the tree, irrespective of race or status, whether ecclesiastical or social. A common feature of this revival is that all are addressed with the common needs of the human heart in view, and not one's status in life. That is, if there is a needy missionary sitting beside a so-called "heathen African," the missionary is expected to humble himself and confess his sins just like anyone else, and in doing so he brings great glory to God for he proves that he too has no other fellowship with God than the fellowship of the Blood. Fellowship meetings, new to the Mennonites, were really family gatherings. Like any family, the new community of believers needed to be together and to share honestly and openly.

As is the practice wherever this revival has continued, we have fellowship meetings at various intervals on our stations. Here at Bukiroba we find it well to have them twice a week. At these meetings we pray for one another, and in the Spirit seek to admonish one another and give help where the Spirit so leads. These meetings are unique in that all meet together on one common level, solely on the ground of the shed Blood. Here there is no such distinction as "missionary" and "native," for before the Cross we all see the unspeakable need of our wicked hearts irrespective of how good or how bad our backgrounds have been, and no one man holds the floor. A catechumen, baptized Christian, or missionary may confess a need and request the help of his brethren. Whatever teaching one may give another in the fellowship, he gives not from a superior standpoint of teacher to pupil, but in the form of a testimony as to how the Lord gave him the victory over lust, anger, pride, mentioning the circumstances in which the victory was experienced. This kind of fellowship meeting seems to resemble the "class meetings" of the Wesleyan revivals. It is here that things get "ironed out" before they have time to take root and thus stop whatever revival may have begun."[19]

Mahlon Hess had his own testimony, too, as he wrote in a letter home:

I thank God for the new dependence on him which I know. In the words of an African brother, I praise Him that I know the place where I can get rid of my sins. . . . By walking together in the light, not only do we enjoy a most precious fellowship, but we [also] become means of grace to each other. An African brother was telling me of the fellowship that has grown up between another brother and himself. They are members of different tribes between which strong feelings of antagonism still exist. Both these brothers have committed themselves to go absolutely all the way with the Lord. Said he, in brief: "We share all our trials and victories with each other. No one can accuse one of us to the other, for we already know all about each other, and can show the accuser his untruth." That testimony made my heart hungry. And that same day God began to satisfy it. Among ourselves as workers and with a number of African brethren we are beginning to enjoy just such fellowship. But I have come to learn more of the pride and perverseness of my own heart—I am just not quite willing to lay myself completely open before other brethren who are also committed to go the whole way with God.[20]

Learning the way of wholeness through brokenness in fellowship

Such openness did not come easy to reserved Mennonites, but they learned how to walk in the light with transparent honesty. John Leatherman reflected: "I feel I am more and more learning how to appropriate Christ's sufficiency for my introverted and self-conscious personality as I come into contact with others." Fellowship meetings were sometimes stiff, "and we seem to be afraid of each other." But hidden faults came to the surface in healing confession. "Right at the opening of the meeting," an African elder "confessed to his murmuring attitude against those who came from a far country to bring the light." Another elder acknowledged adultery with his sister-in-law. A missionary asked the forgiveness of a servant for speaking harshly to him. A church leader asked forgiveness for lying.[21]

The practice of confession brought self-knowledge and humility. "I know I have no message for the African people apart from that which divine grace bestows upon a sinner," John Leatherman admitted. And "walking in the light" gave a fresh basis to community. Phebe Yoder testified:

Because of his [God's] working which is constantly going on in our hearts, we have a unity and fellowship among us which I had not thought possible between black and white, between native and foreigner. Such oneness had never been our experience in the first years in Africa. Praise God for . . . the unity possible through walking together in the light.[22]

Frequent fellowship meetings on the local level had their parallel in the large conventions that drew people from many districts. In July 1947 John and Catharine Leatherman traveled with an Australian, the Rev. Lionel Bakewell, the energetic and winsome Katoke School Headmaster, to a convention at Murgwanza in western Tanzania. "We went in the consciousness that we are one with all those who confess themselves as sinners saved by grace." On the way they took a long detour to stop at Katoke Training School to visit with Frederick Bategeaza, who was ill with fever.

Arriving at last at Murgwanza, John Leatherman reported: "It was a great joy to meet Gabriel Rwandindi again. All the convention arrangements have been his responsibility." People kept coming to the CMS station at Murgwanza. "What struck me as various groups arrived on the grounds from widely separated places was the spontaneous songs of praise that burst out of happy hearts and the mutual recognition of those who are in Christ."

The Leathermans had a strong sense of the oneness of the body of Christ. "The unity that Christ has given Catharine and me with all of God's people made us one with this happy throng. . . . Here we were, a handful of missionaries from different countries with different customs, and from missions with opposing traditions, along with a large number of Africans from many tribes."

At the first session Erisifati Matovu, "a live man of God," preached. Converted in 1937, Matovu sold his shop to work as an evangelist. In 1940 he and his wife settled at Rubungo, near Katoke Training School, where he was the church teacher. (When Matovu retired in 1966, the bishop made him an honorary canon of the Anglican diocese.) It was customary for the team to meet in prayer and thus determine who each day's speakers would be. They asked John Leatherman to preach. "The Lord helped me to speak simply of what he has done for my soul. A number of times they broke in with 'Tukutendereza [We praise you, Jesus].' I was filled with joy at the spiritual union the Lord has brought with our Africans." The team asked Ezekiel Muganda of the Mennonite mission to give the closing message of the day.

During the convention the leaders endorsed John Leatherman's plan for a publication dedicated to revival news. "After the meeting the team gathered on the lawn, at which time I presented the matter of the *Mjumbe wa Kristo.*" John edited this Swahili magazine, *The Messenger of Christ*, for the Mennonite mission; it had become a vehicle for news of the revival, and he offered to open its columns to all. "The native brethren were all very enthusiastic over it. The leaders at various places proposed to take responsibility for distributing the papers at their respective places and also to accept testimonies of revived individuals to be sent to me for printing."[23]

The convention closed on the same note of joy in the Lord. "This morning the Ibuye and Buhiga people left. What a farewell it was!" That afternoon the Leathermans and Bakewells "attended a fellowship meeting which was a blessed one. Matovu is a mighty man of God because he is so humble and broken." Early the next morning they drove with Erisifati and Edita Matovu to their home at Rubungo, where they stayed overnight, and the next day went on to Katoke, where they were guests of Charles Maling, the new head of the Katoke Training School and one of the revival brothers.[24]

Dorothy Smoker returned from a brief stay in South Africa the same day that the Mennonite contingent came home from the Murgwanza convention. "God had greatly blessed them, and the singing that surprised the town people came from full and rejoicing hearts as we all shared God's goodness to us."[25]

The deep unity among Africans, Europeans, and North Americans demonstrated at the revival convention was a matter not of emotionalism but from recognizing that the mission churches had much to teach the sending churches. Leatherman declared:

These revived Africans are spiritual giants and many of them far exceed in spiritual power and discernment the missionaries who came to save them. This includes those of our mission, too. Too long have we missionaries lived in the pride of our national, racial, and religious traditions and regarded the black man with somewhat of a patronizing air. God is turning the tables and is beginning to provoke to jealousy the proud orthodoxy from the West by pouring out his Spirit upon a people lightly esteemed.[26]

American Mennonite officials visit, approve education and church development

Mennonites in Tanganyika with mission board officials, 1956.

As we've seen, the revival impacted the missionaries as well as church leaders in Lancaster Mennonite Conference, which paved the way through some potentially difficult times. The Lancaster bishops and mission board were preparing a foreign-missions policy guide, intended to help missionaries and the Lancaster leaders move forward in unity. Two of the bishops, Paul Graybill and Amos Horst, met with missionaries and church leaders in Tanganyika in 1947 to present their concerns. Leatherman recorded in his diary:

> We spent the morning on church matters and it was decided to organize the African church. I praised the Lord for his own way of working. Prior to the coming of these brethren from the states I had envisioned how I was going to make a dramatic and epoch-making speech on Christian principles as they should apply in Africa. However, the Lord yesterday pretty well closed my mouth and even this morning it did not seem right. Mahlon [Hess], however, rose to make some remarks which embodied very succinctly all that I wanted to say. It was much better for him to say it than for me.[27]

A day later the Mennonite missionaries met to settle issues facing them. They decided to reverse earlier policy and accept government aid for mission schools. The same day they made a momentous decision. "Late this afternoon we worked on church organization and we have decided to proceed in the direction of ordaining African pastors and organizing the church." Under the influence of the East Africa Revival, the Mennonite mission had come to maturity.[28]

With permission from Lancaster Conference, the missionaries with the local church ordained Ezekiel Muganda and Andrea Mabeba in October 1950, and Zedekia Kisare and Nashon Nyambok in December. "The coming of revival in the spiritual life of the church did much to break down the barriers between the two races. . . . But as the Lord led in establishing fellowship in all areas, the conviction grew that there must be fellowship in financial policies, at least with the leading African brethren." From 1953 onward, African pastors and elders had copies of all the budget figures, and from 1954 onward, they participated fully in the budget-making process. John Leatherman called this decision to share complete financial information "one of the incidental fruits springing out of that fellowship in which we are already sharing our lives with a number of our African brethren."[29]

Erica Sabiti and Lawrence Barham, a dynamic team.

Experience of revival brought appreciation for believers of other traditions. In place of their usual spiritual life conference, the Mennonites felt free to invite the Anglican schoolteacher Frederick Bategeaza to return with a team to each station in 1947, "bringing public messages and counseling with the fellowship groups."[30] They invited William Nagenda and Erica Sabiti, both Anglicans, to lead the annual missionary conference in 1948. Elam Stauffer reported: "Their messages were simple from the Word and related to life. God used them to challenge me to see deep need in my own heart and to set me free."[31]

In 1949 another team came, including the Anglican Erisifati Matovu and the AIM evangelist Methusela Chagu. John Leatherman reflected:

> Today was the last day of the conference and there were some real victories won. A number of our brethren were delivered from their bondage to shillings [money]. The theme of the conference was "We would see Jesus," and we certainly saw him as he led us to the [self-] renunciation of the cross. It is here that we rest from all our striving and self-will. Elam had a powerful message yesterday afternoon and Matovu was at his best this morning. If we really have Jesus, we are able for anything.[32]

Recognition of spiritual oneness with Christians from other churches affected every aspect of the Mennonite mission. For help in upgrading the mission schools, Phebe Yoder and her education committee turned to three CMS teachers who visited the Mennonite stations in 1946. "After discussing the matter with the Anglican educationalists, Lionel Bakewell and Charles Maling, the Mennonites invited two CMS teachers to assist the church as they took their first steps toward providing formal education. "Within six weeks, in January 1947, two teachers arrived." They also arranged to send two African Mennonite teachers for further training at Katoke.[33]

The revival message carried abroad by Africans

By 1947 the African churches had reached another level of maturity. John Leatherman recorded:

> It was commonplace to suggest that the time will come when the Africans will be sending missionaries to England and America to warn a dead orthodoxy and dying civilization. Well, at this present hour this suggestion is in the first stages of reality. For several months now, two Spirit-filled Africans are making widespread contacts in England and are witnessing with power to the perfect salvation of the Lord Jesus. Their names are William Nagenda and Yosiah Kinuka. I recently had the privilege of reading a letter from William in which he wrote that the people of England would like to have revival but they are looking for something new and spectacular. They need to realize that revival is "just Jesus." To men of this holy caliber Jesus is the living mighty Savior just as the

Scriptures set him forth, and they are free because they are not bound by the fetters of a cold orthodoxy and an intellectual theology. They have only the testimony of Jesus.[34]

—8—

Changing Lives in Europe and Abroad 1946–1955

While missionaries from both Great Britain and North America found a spiritual home in the East Africa Revival, they naturally wanted to share their testimonies with their friends in their home countries. As we examine what happened in Britain and North America just after World War II, we will see some parallels and some striking differences.

From East Africa to the UK

Missionaries in the Ruanda Mission of the Church Missionary Society had access to thousands of prayer partners in Britain. The missionaries shared freely about what God was doing in revival. After World War II travel restrictions were lifted, an African revival team traveled to Great Britain in 1947 for the sole purpose of giving witness to the grace of God in Jesus, which they found to be life-transforming. This marked the beginning of many visits, thus further simplifying and strengthening the message of the East Africa Revival. Will the revival message have effects in Britain like those witnessed in America?

British evangelicals learned more of what the Lord was doing in East Africa when the Worldwide Evangelization Crusade sponsored a visit of William Nagenda and Yosiya Kinuka to the British Isles.[1] The Ruanda Mission Council approved a plan for "Revival Teams of Witness" to visit churches in England, and Nagenda and Kinuka flew to London to be part of this effort. They joined Joe Church and Lawrence Barham, both British, for a series of meetings that summer.[2]

The two Africans stayed at the headquarters of the WEC in London when they were not meeting speaking engagements. Norman P. Grubb, WEC executive secretary, later reflected:

From them I learned and saw that revival is first personal and immediate. It is the constant experience of any simplest Christian who "walks in the light," but I saw that walking in the light means an altogether new sensitiveness to sin, a calling things by their proper name of sin, such as pride, hardness, doubt, fear, self-pity, which are often passed over as merely human reaction. It means a readiness to "break" and confess at the feet of him who was broken for us, for the blood does not cleanse excuses, but always cleanses sin, confessed as sin; then revival is just the daily experience of a soul full of Jesus and running over.[3]

As a result of his own encounter with revival, Norman Grubb wrote a book published in 1952 as *Continuous Revival*, which carried the message around the world.[4]

Nagenda and Kinuka brought no new message to England. They did not teach a new understanding of a Scriptural doctrine or bring a new emphasis in theology. There was no new way to a holy life, no spiritual discipline for all to learn. "Every Bible-believing Christian already acknowledged what they came so far to preach." Roy Hession, the British evangelist, put it succinctly: "It was not a case of systematic theology but rather of *life*, which was flowing everywhere among tens of thousands of Africans and missionaries."[5]

This was true of all the revival brethren. Some of their expressions like "being broken" and "walking in the light" might be unfamiliar, Neville Langford-Smith explained, but there was nothing new about it. "What has really happened is that accepted doctrine has become alive."[6]

Roy Hession, a zealous British evangelist, asked Ruanda Mission Council in Britain to provide three speakers for a conference for young Christians during Easter week 1947 at Matlock in Derbyshire, near the geographical center of England. They agreed and designated Lawrence Barham, Bill Butler, and Peter Guillebaud, all revived clergymen who had served in Ruanda and Uganda.[7] This brings us to the story of Roy Hession, who was to have a dominant role in spreading the revival message of new life in Jesus Christ.

Roy Hession touched by the Calvary way of revival

Roy Hession left his job as a banker in 1935 to devote himself to full-time evangelistic work with the National Young Life Campaign. Roy had a Churchillian face that could in a moment brighten up like the sun. He was a consummate communicator and as zealous as they come. Youth responded to his appeals, and he had every hope for a bright future as an evangelist. His wife, Revel, was highly gifted in her own right, and her pleasant, sincere personality endeared her to many people.

Over the years Hession conducted many successful campaigns in England, Wales, and Scotland, but in March 1947 he and Revel had just come from one at Margate, an English seaside resort, where they both experienced failure. He acknowledged that it was more than an isolated incident. "I had somehow lost the power of the

Revel and Roy Hession on early visit to North America.

Holy Spirit, which I once had known in the work of the Lord, and yet I had to continue to conduct evangelistic campaigns without his power—a terrible experience!"[8]

The British evangelist had much to learn from the men he invited:

> The team's message was simple, and they made no attempt to preach in the strong way to which we had become accustomed. . . . But this much they did do—they laced everything they taught with their personal testimonies, sharing their experiences of failure and weakness on the mission field and how grace had restored them—and this in the event proved inescapable to everybody.[9]

The biggest lesson for Hession was his own need to repent, not mechanically or superficially, but with a searching honesty and willingness to bring everything into the light and begin to make amends to those he had injured:

> When at the end of the conference others testified as to how Jesus had broken them at his cross and filled their hearts to overflowing with his Spirit, I had no such testimony. It was only afterwards

that I was enabled to give up trying to fit things into my doctrinal scheme and come humbly to the cross for cleansing from my own personal sins.[10]

God began by convicting Roy of his attitudes toward his wife. Over time, Roy found more and more that needed to be confessed. The Matlock conference changed Roy and Revel Hession and prepared them for a new ministry. "It was as a direct result of Jesus' showing himself to us again at that time that Revel and I wrote jointly the articles that became *The Calvary Road*."[11] Roy and Revel Hession published a little monthly paper called *Challenge*, "intended to lead young Christians into a deeper experience of the Lord." In the next four issues after the Matlock conference, "we simply put down the themes the team had brought to us and the telling illustrations they had used." Requests for these issues came in startling numbers from readers in Britain and overseas, so many that the press run was soon exhausted. Eventually the Hessions incorporated these messages into a small book, *The Calvary Road*, which was published in London in 1950.[12]

In 1947 and 1948, William Nagenda and Yosiya Kinuka teamed with missionaries on home leave and British evangelists like Roy Hession to bring the message of revival to conventions and meetings throughout the British Isles. They developed a team to share the truths that had become so powerful in Africa. "The testimony of these together, black and white, missionary and African, reached many churches, university and college Christian Unions [Fellowships]."[13]

The revival message proved to be for all

How did the message of revival find fertile soil in Western cultures? How did people so readily understand it? The answer must certainly be that life brought life. People everywhere recognized the quality of life in the revived ones. It was the messengers as well as the message that rang true. According to the official report of the large evangelical convention at Keswick in northern England in 1947, "It was heart-stirring to see the shining face of William Nagenda, an African Christian from Uganda, and to hear him tell of the Revival there."[14] The testimony was always the same, whether *balokole* preached in a village marketplace in Uganda, a missionary conference in Tanganyika, among university students in England or a crowded church in the United States: "We saw their shining faces. We knew they had something that we wanted."[15]

Many Africans came to Christ as first-generation Christians, like the converts in first-century Ephesus or Corinth who heard and heeded Paul's sermons. It was different for Westerners accustomed to the practice of Christianity for centuries. Christianity had somehow immunized them against the simple message that characterized the revival. At first, the British asked the usual theological questions about the East Africa Revival. Was it rooted in the Holiness movement? Did it imply a second work of grace? Was it compatible with (Scofield's) premillennial dispensationalism? Did it fit with the (Anglican) Book of Common Prayer or the (Reformed) Westminster Standards?

Revived missionaries did not even try to respond to these probing questions, which were often a foil for criticism. They simply spoke of their experience. This connected with their audiences, just like it did in Africa. In telling their stories to Westerners, they used the language and thought patterns of their listeners. They tried to make relevant what they had learned and experienced. They avoided theological controversies because they wanted to focus on the centrality of walking with Jesus.

Some listeners concluded that heresy lurked in the theology undergirding the revival and simply turned away. Nevertheless, if theological tradition kept some people from accepting revival, it enabled others to understand clearly that it was nothing new, but rather an integral part of Christian experience through the ages. The convincing argument, however, was in the changed lives of the missionaries and others who shared in their experience of renewal.

Communicating the revival message to Westerners presented a challenge to the message itself. People from the West were looking for formulas and wanted to know, "How do you do this?" The temptation was to reduce revival to a formula. Lawrence Barham and Joe Church both commonly used a five-point scheme "in the form of five steps up to Calvary," but Nagenda and Kinuka "refused to be limited by what appeared to them as a kind of jargon." Others wanted formulas for everything that surrounded revival in East Africa, including public confession of sins.[16]

Through books like *Continuous Revival* and *The Calvary Road*, news of the East Africa Revival reached a worldwide audience, and invitations came from many places for a team to visit. As a result Joe Church and William Nagenda traveled to Switzerland, France, Germany, Malawi, Angola, and even to India in 1952. Some felt that Ruanda Mission personnel belonged at their own mission stations and hospitals, but the council decided, "As long as God was using them, we could not withhold their tes-

timony from the worldwide church, hungry for revival."[17] Mission personnel from the Ruanda Mission and the CMS in Kenya, Uganda, and
Tanganyika opened doors in British churches and university fellowships for
the message of revival. Likewise, missionaries from two small American
missions in Tanganyika were responsible for bringing the message to the
United States and Canada, AIM and the Mennonite mission.

It was left for the North American Mennonite churches to open doors
for William Nagenda and Joe Church. Already the revival brethren had
invitations to preach in America. As Church recalled:

> Beginnings are always interesting, especially when we can trace a
> tributary to its source. One of these springs was a sister in the
> strict American Mennonite mission, Phebe Yoder, who was work-
> ing at Musoma on the east side of Lake Victoria in Tanganyika.
> . . . Her testimony with that of others was used to revolutionize
> the thinking of her mission and to challenge her church leaders in
> Pennsylvania. Letters began to come asking for a team to visit
> America, but we hesitated before going to that great country.[18]

Missionaries told of their experience of new life in Christ, but no team
went to the United States or Canada until 1953. Furloughed AIM missionaries, like their Mennonite counterparts, wanted to share with friends and
relatives in America what the Lord was doing in East Africa. In some
places, though, their message was not welcome. It seemed to conflict with
expectations of how God works. Many church leaders saw the revival
teachings as a source of confusion both on the mission field and in
American churches.

AIM struggles to understand revival

Lillian Elliott recalled that before she left Tanganyika in 1945, a delegation from AIM headquarters in New York visited her station. Some of
the mission leaders feared that the revival was "all emotion," and others
expressed concern about Africans and Americans holding lengthy prayer
meetings and sharing deeply together. They called a meeting and questioned some of the sisters who stood with the revival—Sallye Higgins,
Minnie Magnin, Florence Tilley, and Lillian herself—"on our beliefs." In
the end, each of these women testified to "the wonder of the Lord and how
he changed our outlook." When the meeting ended, everyone shook hands
and one of the visitors said, "I would give all to have what you've got."[19]

But AIM leaders remained uneasy about revival, as were many of the Mennonite mission leaders. So Henry F. Garber and Amos S. Horst of Eastern Mennonite Board of Missions, and John L. Stauffer, president of Eastern Mennonite College, met with AIM leaders to discuss their common problem. Horst informed the Lancaster Mennonite Conference Bishop Board, "The Africa Inland Mission representatives reported that some of the missionaries in the Uganda-Tanganyika area have created confusion in several of their missions on the field and in their home communities through their extreme emphasis on spiritual experience, which they think other Christians should accept, too."[20]

Florence Tilley and Lillian Elliott of the AIM station at Mwanza in Tanganyika returned to America together late in 1945 on their first furlough after six years in the mission field. Lillian Elliott had met the Lord before she went to Africa, but in Tanganyika she saw the Holy Spirit working and learned the meaning of the cross and of crucifixion with Christ. Both women came from the Philadelphia area and shared their African experiences with friends and neighbors and occasionally in churches. A North Philadelphia fellowship developed at this time. Florence Tilley had a cottage at the American Keswick in New Jersey and had a strong prayer ministry with many individuals there during missionary furloughs and after her retirement from the mission field.[21]

Why did revival have such limited impact upon the AIM constituency in North America? One reason is that AIM had serious misgivings about the theology of the revival, which they considered to be focused too much on sin and repentance and not enough on the resurrected life. Their theology of what it meant to crucify the old man and to live in victory did not square with the revival message of walking day-by-day with Jesus in repentant faith.

A second reason, as mentioned earlier, was the interdenominational nature of AIM, whose missionaries were not members of a single North American denomination. As missionaries such as Tilley and Elliot returned home, they no doubt gave testimony to their friends, but the message did not impact large denominational groups. This stands in contrast to the experience of the Mennonites, who dispatched their missionaries and held them accountable to the denomination.

So even though the AIM missionaries had a muted message among their constituency, they encouraged the Mennonites who embraced the revival message. In February 1946 Erma Maust, "a sister who this summer came into a realization of our relationship with Christ in personal union," traveled with her little girl to visit the Leathermans. They took her to meet Florence Tilley and Lillian Elliott in Philadelphia.[22]

The Mausts, faithful teachers and encouragers

Erma and Herbert Maust, influential proponents in North American revival.

When John Leatherman opened his heart at East Chestnut Street Mennonite Church in 1944, Erma Maust fell before the Lord and found a new freedom and joy that changed her forever. She was to play a vital role in spreading the revival message in North America. Yet she was a quite unlikely choice for this demanding calling. The Mausts lived in Maytown, a village in northwestern Lancaster County. The Church of God parsonage was across the street, where the Rev. Gerald Marzolf and his wife, Lela, lived in 1945–46. Lela recalled her first meetings with Erma Maust, "when she came and helped me get ready for open house at the new parsonage. She also came and cared for me after my hospitalization when my husband had to go to conference."[23] It was characteristic of Erma Maust to pitch in to help a neighbor with housecleaning and baking.

Erma was a bundle of energy. She was of average height, with a generous head of wavy hair tucked neatly into the devotional covering required of Mennonite women in Lancaster Conference at that time. Her eyes took in everything and beamed with goodwill. She was adept at everything from cooking to wallpaper hanging and interior decorating. Her speech was rather rapid, like her step.

Erma's husband, Herbert, was about the same height as Erma. He was methodical and deliberate in his actions. Even on his best days, he felt uneasy about taking leadership in a public way, but he was always figuring out ways to increase the couple's effectiveness. He seemed perfectly content to see Erma take initiatives. She wrote the letters; he typed them on the latest typewriter with the most attractive type.

Erma did not hesitate to help where she saw a need. On one occasion, when John Leatherman spoke at the Steelton Mennonite Mission at Sunday evening service, Erma saw tasks that needed to be done and did them with-out asking. When she did this, she offended Betty Miller, whose husband was assigned to the mission. "I was irritated to see Erma parading around, being of help." That Sunday night Betty fired off "not a nice letter" to Erma, tak-ing her to task for her faults. "She answered my letter, thanking me and say-ing, 'I am everything you said and more.' 'Also,' she added, 'I know you've been ill quite a lot and not been able to keep after your work. I'll be glad to come and help with your work.' And she came, when I'd been so nasty."[24]

Years later Betty had this to say about the relationship:

> I was overwhelmed by this response of humility and generosity. Erma began coming to help me with housework, but more impor-tantly, we began to fellowship in the things of the Spirit. I feel indebted to Erma for showing me the way of the Cross.[25]

Abner and Betty Miller lived on a farm near Elizabethtown. John and Catharine Leatherman were aware of Betty's poor health and called at the Millers several times. John wrote, "She is physically low and is expressing great conflict. We tried to strengthen her in the Lord and had prayer."[26] Unlike the Leathermans, Erma was not a close friend of Betty, but she knew that a mother with two small children always needed help. Betty recalls, "She came and did my ironing" and other housekeeping chores. She was touched by Erma's humility, "her coming and showing love, instead of defending herself." They talked about the Lord. Late in the afternoon when she was leaving, Erma paused on the other side of the screen door and said: "All the Lord has given me for you is Psalm 37, verse 5 'Commit thy way unto the Lord; trust also in him; and he shall bring it to pass.'" "How do I do that?" "We'll talk about that next Tuesday."

Erma returned on many Tuesdays to do housework, and to pray and study Scripture with Betty. They became friends. Betty Miller recalled: "She had a message and I needed to listen. It was a long journey to freedom for me."[27]

It was also the beginning of a long journey in ministry for Erma. A busy wife and mother whose education stopped after the eighth grade, she had no formal training in Bible or theology. She read her Bible in an exis-tential way, as the coming alive of God's Word at this time and this place, without any attempt at exegesis or fitting the text into a larger scheme of historical criticism or dispensationalism. It was not uncommon to find open Bibles in every room in the Maust house in Maytown. Already steeped in Scripture, she let the Word shape her life.[28]

Erma was born in 1910, the oldest of Samuel and Annie Lehman Longenecker's six children. Her father was converted at a revival service held in the newly built Elizabethtown Mennonite Church in 1906, and the family grew up in that congregation. Erma was deeply influenced by the integrity of her own parents. An unpretentious man, Erma's father, simply known to many as Uncle Sam, was well-known both in religious circles and in the communities in which they lived. After suffering bankruptcy during the Great Depression, he eventually made restitution to all his creditors. He was known for his interest in Jewish evangelism and prison ministry. Like many Mennonite families in that generation, the Longeneckers also helped with mission Sunday schools.[29]

There were also Bible classes and singing groups, where Mennonite young adults met. Erma Longenecker sang in a young people's chorus in Elizabethtown, organized and directed by Ezra O. Brubaker, cashier of the First National Bank in Elizabethtown. The Elizabethtown Gospel Chorus nurtured more than one Mennonite couple in deepening friendship. When Herbert Maust first came to Elizabethtown in 1932, he joined the Elizabethtown chorus. Herbert and Erma were married in April 1933.[30]

Herbert Maust, born in 1905, graduated from Eastern Mennonite High School in Harrisonburg, Virginia, in 1925. In preparation to be a teacher, he also studied at Eastern Mennonite College and Millersville State College in Millersville, Pennsylvania. He then taught school in Somerset and Dauphin Counties in Pennsylvania, and in Dover, Delaware. Eventually the young couple settled in Maytown, Pennsylvania, Erma's home area, and assisted with the newly developing Mennonite mission in Marietta.[31] Herbert Maust was ordained as deacon of the Marietta Mennonite Church in 1942, and the same year he began working for the Pennsylvania Railroad as a clerk in Elizabethtown.[32]

First weekly meetings in Maytown

Following Erma's experience at East Chestnut Street Mennonite Church under the ministry of John Leatherman, she began to seek fellowship with other like-minded women. This soon developed into a weekly meeting for prayer in the Maust home in Maytown. God was reordering Erma's understanding of biblical faith and practice. This is apparent in comments of Lela Marzolf in 1996. She recalled being in a discussion group with Erma when the subject was faith. Erma said, "Faith that only trusts when it can see, isn't faith at all; it is wicked unbelief."[33]

Both AIM and Mennonite missionaries frequently nurtured Erma's Bible study groups while on furlough. Dorothy Smoker, for instance, returned to the United States from Tanganyika in October 1947 because of her mother's ill health and stopped in Lancaster County on her way back to Africa.[34]

She joined Erma and other women for prayer and fellowship in June 1948. Erma reflected:

> O how I praise God for bringing Dorothy Smoker into our midst, if it was only one meeting with the prayer group. Our prayer fellowship had gotten to the place where the enemy had succeeded in bringing in jealousy and thereby breaking up the unity. Mary [Miller] and Betty [Miller] and I were standing for a breaking and convicting of sin. . . . But the Lord gave us a most challenging message on walking in the light, and the Spirit has been working the past week. Some victories have been won, for which we praise our faithful God, but there is still more that needs to be uncovered and brought into the light. Dorothy and I had a most precious time of fellowship in him Tuesday A.M. [June 29]. Now we are looking forward to Elam [Stauffer]'s coming.[35]

Frequent letters and periodic reports from East Africa also nurtured the fellowship. Erma wrote, "Truly the articles in the *Revival News* have been a real blessing to me, and I long to know more of being truly broken and walking in the light for his glory."[36]

Erma was learning more of being broken and walking in the light day by day. In July 1948 she wrote to a friend:

> One thing that the Spirit has taught me which has been such a blessing to me in the past weeks is this—when the Lord shows me something which is not of the Spirit, some manifestation of the flesh, He may do it by some brother or sister challenging me. . . . It is the so-called little sins that rob us of the power of the Spirit. Some weeks ago I was challenged on my not waiting for someone speaking to finish, but if they halt, perhaps not knowing just how to say it, and knowing about what they wanted to say, I would butt in and perhaps carry off the subject for a minute or so. I asked the Lord to show me why I did this. . . . He showed me it was a desire to be on top.[37]

In June 1948 the Mausts moved "into the country, which was truly God's provision for our growing boys." A neighboring farmer of the Millers bought a small farm "about four miles west of Elizabethtown" to add to his own farm but had no use for the house on the property, so he was more than willing to rent it to Herbert and Erma Maust. The prayer fellowship moved with them.

The idea of moving came from Mary K. Miller. John, Herbert and Erma's teenage son, had been helping Mervin Miller with his farm work, but transportation to and from Maytown had become difficult. John needed to be within walking distance so he could help with early morning farm chores. The new house, according to Erma, "needed much in the line of repairing and fixing up," but everyone was pleased with it at first. However, after they had been there for two years, the well failed. The Mausts had to come to Millers' well for water each day.[38]

Mervin and Mary K. Miller

Mervin and Mary Keener Miller also met as members of the Elizabethtown Gospel Chorus. Mary recalled:

A highlight of my teenage years was attending a mixed chorus directed by Ezra O. Brubaker. My older brother Sam and I usually went unless the busy time on the farm took priority. This was our main social outlet with other young people. We sang at the Marietta Mission cottage prayer meetings quite often. We also went with the men's chorus sometimes and sang between their standings when they gave public programs. We counted that a real privilege! One of their programs in 1937 was at Philadelphia. That

Mary and Mervin Miller with daughter, Janice.
Fellowships met regularly in their home.

occasion marked the first date I had with Mervin Miller, who three years later became my husband.[39]

They began working the dairy farm owned by his father, Levi Z. Miller, near Bainbridge, and attended Goods Mennonite Church, where his father was a minister. They hoped soon to have a farm of their own. In October 1945 Paul M. Miller put his farm up for sale. Mary Miller recalled, "Very unexpectedly, we found ourselves the highest bidder on the Miller homestead, owned by Uncle Martin Z. Miller and farmed by his son Paul. Paul was leaving the farm to heed the call of God to prepare for ministry in the wider church."[40]

Mary Miller had a spiritual awakening of her own early in 1945. She was dissatisfied with her life and "more and more aware that I was not right with God." Attending church bored her. "I admit that I would have quit going had I not cared what people would think of me." Mary told her husband that she feared she was not saved. They asked Paul and Bertha Miller to come that night. "The Lord used Paul to minister the Word to me, to show me that my basic sin was unbelief. That's where I began, without any feeling, just sheer faith; I thanked him for forgiving me and cleansing me." There were still things she had to make right with other people, but she hesitated. When John and Catharine Leatherman came home, John's "message was just what I needed to help me all the way down and be filled with the Spirit."[41] "All the way down" refers to complete surrender of one's will to the will of God.

Bertha Mumaw and Paul Miller, while courting.

After that, she was involved in the women's group that met once a week in Maytown. Mary had known Erma a long time, but they were not close friends. "Erma was nine years older than I, which is a big difference when you are young." Sharing in the women's fellowship brought them closer. "She began to stop at our house, after taking Herbert to work." When Mausts moved nearby, the two women got together for sharing and prayer more frequently. With no water at Mausts' house, Mary thought of converting the second floor of the Miller farmhouse into an apartment. The Maust family moved there in 1950.⁴² The men were not all that enthused about the idea but, taking the way of brokenness, they agreed and made the plan work.

In September 1950 Mary Miller arranged for a meeting of women who taught Sunday school at Goods Mennonite Church and invited the members of the prayer and sharing group as well. She thought of asking Erma to speak but decided against it. "A lot of people didn't like her. She was outspoken and turned some people off." Instead, the committee invited Elva Lehman, who was known as an effective speaker in Mennonite women's groups. She accepted but had to change the date because of prior commitments. After several attempts at finding a mutually agreeable date failed, Elva withdrew. Mary then invited Erma to speak. There was a good turnout and the room was full. Erma shared on 1 John 2:28. . . . She asked, "What does it mean to abide in him [Christ]?" She made her points with examples from everyday life, as was always characteristic of her Bible teaching. ⁴³

Later in life Mary told of her own struggles at this time:

I had a Sunday school class of teenage girls one year and the Lord was helping me with them. Then the next year I didn't get that job, but rather was elected substitute of a women's class. I felt "put on the shelf" and it was hurtful. I shared these feelings with Erma Maust [my prayer partner], and we talked to the Lord about this. The answer that came was to thank the Lord for this disappointment and keep in right relationship to God. We agreed that having a ministry was not to be of greatest concern, but rather, being usable, and ready when the Lord needed them.

Erma and I prayed together regularly. Erma was beginning to be controversial because she had made a clear-cut surrender to the Lord to have him work deeper in her heart. This is what had attracted me to have fellowship with her. But a lot of ladies were repulsed at what they would have considered too great a concern about things that didn't matter so much. They were in a church where regulations were very clear-cut—you were instructed for baptism at a certain age and you joined the church and agreed to follow all its rules and regulations, the most obvious being dress regulations. So what more could you possibly need than to live an outwardly ordered life.

Erma and I wanted to go beyond just having a form of godliness; we wanted to know Jesus. I brought my women's Sunday school class [to] our Monday night prayer time at our home. There were about a dozen ladies including Florence Stauffer, Evelyn Miller, and Florence Zeager, all of whom were touched with Erma's disarming and deeply challenging message [on] 1 John 2:28: "And now little children, abide in him; that, when he shall appear, we may have confidence, and not be ashamed before him at his coming." She gave a testimony of how God had shown her she was not abiding in him and how she could abide in him. The Holy Spirit brought such conviction as Erma asked if anyone had anything to say, and then she waited quietly. Several women began to cry and some prayed.[44]

When she finished, one of the women said what she thought about Erma. Erma only said, "I didn't know you felt that way." Everything grew so quiet that one might even hear a pin drop. Mary Miller remembers that she was tempted to do or say something to get over that tension. But Erma waited. After a long silence, someone confessed a fault and asked for prayer, then another and another came into the light. "Each one shared something and each one heard what she needed."[45]

The last one of all to say something was Florence Stauffer. She had responded as a girl in an evangelistic meeting and never doubted that she was a Christian, but she recognized her sinfulness and she openly acknowledged her failings. This marked a new beginning for her.

Years later Florence Stauffer reflected:

Jesus became real to me in that meeting. I realized later that this was my "new birth" experience. I had never really known the Lord in this personal way before. God removed the feelings I had against Erma, and Erma was able to help me then and many times afterward. Through the years and to the present time, God is working in my life, enabling me to be truly Christian in situations that would otherwise be impossible.[46]

Another Florence, Florence Good Zeager, knew God began a work in her heart that night that made it possible for her to move to New York City with her husband for mission work. Each one felt the presence of the Holy Spirit at that meeting. The spontaneous confessions that marked this meeting, as in Africa, made a new beginning. Their burdens were faults that one might easily overlook, but in laying them at the cross and openly acknowledging unkind thoughts, gossip, jealousy, or whatever interfered with their following Jesus Christ, the women from Goods Mennonite Church found themselves in a new community. As in East Africa, these American *balokole* knew they needed to meet regularly in fellowship.

Florence recalled:

I always wanted to live in the country and never wanted to be a pastor's wife. But God did a work in my heart that night and following, that it was possible for me to move to New York City later, with my husband, and he was then ordained to the ministry. My husband saw such a change in me after this meeting that he was interested in attending these class meetings. God did a deep work in his heart and life as a result of these fellowship meetings. We lived in New York City 21 years.[47]

Emma Ebersole was one of those whom God's grace set free. She recalled, "I and my husband, Clarence, were farmers living near Goods Mennonite Church when the Lord poured out his Spirit at the Mervin Miller home, and many persons were saved and began to walk in openness. I was part of all that and appreciated the love and concern that Erma Maust and Mary Miller had shown toward me."[48]

Following that meeting these women spread the news that they had seen Jesus in a new way and invited others to open their hearts to him. One of these was a young man who lived in the Miller home, Tom Hess. He was later to become a pastor and remembered:

Those women who were touched by Jesus in that meeting ministered to me and God invaded my life. They then showed me how to walk in the light, repent of my sins, and rejoice in my Savior. Like them, I was restless because I was not in "ministry." The Holy Spirit spoke to me through them that I must rest in the Lord and turn my concerns over to Him about not feeling like I had a ministry. They encouraged me to just "abide in Him" and leave the ministry part to his leading.[49]

Two weeks later the women who had been at the first meeting asked to have fellowship gatherings every week. They met at Millers' home, all women at first, but then men began coming with their wives. These first groups were small, but gradually they filled the house. Eventually they had to meet in a building that had been a poultry house. "The Lord gave Erma little messages. She didn't change when the men came." She continued to teach the Word and apply it to everyday life.[50]

Like the earlier meetings in Maytown and at the Millers' home, prayer was at the heart of the fellowship. John and Florence Miller, who lived nearby, took part in "daily early morning prayer meetings at Mervin and Mary Miller's home, with prayer for revival in our churches." They also participated in weekly fellowship meetings, with both men and women attending. Mary Miller remembered that this was in 1951. "A bit later we had a Wednesday morning women's fellowship where we were accountable to each other in our daily walk with Jesus."[51]

The Miller home was a center for fellowship. Mary plays the piano as Mervin and Janice sing along.

A woman in leadership?

The idea of a woman teaching and delivering messages offended some Mennonites and other Christians, too. Ira Z. Miller, pastor at Goods Mennonite Church, saw the Lord's hand in what was happening. But most church leaders were critical. Mary K. Miller realized that this could cause trouble. "The meetings in our home were not under their authority. Opposition came from everywhere." In 1951 a well-known Mennonite evangelist attended the fellowship meeting. After Erma spoke, he proceeded to preach a sermon explaining why women should not be teaching the Bible.

Now what? As a faithful church member, Erma Maust was troubled and stopped speaking, although the fellowship meetings continued. This was a time of confusion for her.[52] She wanted to be a submissive sister in the Lord and yield to authorities over her, and yet the message burned unquenchably in her soul. So she deferred to authority. But her witness could not be muzzled.

Ongoing uneasiness among some church leaders

This was a time of confusion for the Lancaster Mennonite Conference. The testimony of returned missionaries brought new life to the church, but its leaders were still uneasy with the revival. The bishop board endorsed George and Dorothy Smoker's return to Tanganyika for another term on the mission field in 1948. "It was also suggested that the concern of the bishops be registered with them before they return." The bishops decided that "more care be exercised in examination of prospective missionaries."[53]

Elam Stauffer, the obvious leader of the Mennonite mission in Tanganyika, returned to Lancaster in July 1948 for a year's furlough. During that time he brought the good news of the East Africa Revival to many Mennonite churches and institutions. Stauffer also nurtured growing fellowships, like the women who met with Erma Maust.

Paul M. Miller recalled that he became aware of the revival through Elam Stauffer. As bishop of the Tanganyika Mennonite mission, Stauffer was able to explain the revival and its transforming influence on some of the missionaries. Revival critics acknowledged that God was working through the revival to draw people to himself, but there was a gnawing concern that they found hard to express. It was difficult for them to see how the revival in East Africa—with its emphasis on continually repenting and accepting God's forgiveness and cleansing—fitted their understanding of salvation by grace. It seemed to them like a new kind of legalism or works righteousness.[54]

Stauffer's testimony in words and life eventually silenced the criticism. After many conversations on doctrine and discipline, the bishops reappointed him as a missionary to Tanganyika. They also authorized him to "proceed with plans to ordain several native brethren as pastors [ministers]." He returned to Africa, following a farewell service at his home congregation, Erisman Mennonite Church, on May 1, 1949.[55]

Popular Scofield Bible courses, visions of new freedom

To further complicate matters for Lancaster Mennonite Conference, a significant number of their members in the Elizabethtown area were becoming absorbed in the "Scofield Bible Course" offered by Moody Bible Institute. The eagerness with which so many enrolled in this program indicated a hunger for deeper insight into Scriptures. Several prominent Mennonite pastors and lay teachers became so enamored by the course's schooling in premillennial dispensationalism that they began to criticize the teachings of Lancaster Conference. The conference issued a long-standing caution, reiterated in 1946, warning "against the use of the notes and comments of the Scofield [Study] Bible."[56]

Some who found new freedom in the revival also continued their interest in the Scofield course. Harold Longenecker, Erma's youngest brother, recalled, "While we were profiting from the ministries of the Stauffers and Leathermans, Esther and I were also involved in the Scofield course taught by Abe Gish [a gifted Mennonite teacher] and enjoyed the pastoral impact of John Hiestand. God used all these instruments to stimulate our Christian life and prepare us for Christian service."[57]

Mervin and Mary K. Miller attended Bible classes taught by Abram Gish, working out the lessons each week. Mary declared, "This was a great help to us and gave us a fair working knowledge of God's Word." Abner and Betty Miller also enrolled in Gish's course. Abner took Bible courses from Moody for seven years. He testified that "Abe Gish taught me how to study the Scriptures."[58] Many others shared their enthusiasm for the Scofield course. The Scofield program opened the Bible for the hungry hearts in the Elizabethtown area, but those studies were not meant to bring people into a personal relationship with Jesus. The message of personal revival did that.

Abram L. and Laura Gish were active in the Marietta mission, where the Mausts attended and helped where they could. In November 1945 Abram Gish began teaching a Scofield Bible class there, and then he taught the course at Paul Garber's in Elizabethtown all summer and into the fall. More than seventy persons enrolled. In these classes Gish directly challenged some Mennonite beliefs. His pamphlet on *Washing the Saints' Feet* was issued at Elizabethtown by a publisher identified as "The Scofield Bible Class." It asserted that literal foot washing was not an ordinance and was to be practiced only when reclaiming a brother who is out of fellowship and being led back to the Lord.[59] The Mennonites considered foot washing, taught in John 13, as an ordinance. The gauntlet was dropped.

In the autumn of 1949 the Lancaster Conference Bishop Board decided to suspend Gish "from council, communion, and church activities," ostensibly because he continued to teach the Scofield course.[60] The bishops considered the foot washing issue as minor. Their real contention was not foot washing but communion. The Gish group believed in offering communion to all who acknowledge Jesus Christ as Lord. The conference, however, taught that communion was open only to those who were in compliance with the conference discipline.[61] The Lancaster bishops agreed to meet with Gish, but he declined, and the bishops dropped the matter from their agenda.[62] Consequently, Gish was out.

In 1951 many of the group led by Gish organized as Word of Life Fellowship. They adopted a statement of "commonly held doctrines," including verbal inspiration of Scripture, salvation by grace, evidences of salvation, unity of the body of Christ, and the rapture. They then called Gish as their pastor.[63]

Of all the members of the Marietta Mennonite Church, where the split occurred, only Herbert and Erma Maust, Warren and Minnie Hertzler, and Barbara Witmer remained loyal to Lancaster Conference and the Mennonite Church. The schism cut the Mausts off from some of their dear friends. They must have often remembered this situation as they later found themselves under suspicion for their part in the revival fellowships. Weekly fellowship meetings and daily prayer sustained them through those difficult days.

Members of the revival fellowships called to missions

Several participants in that little revival fellowship found courage to respond to calls to mission work. Abner Miller, for instance, had long felt a call to pastoral ministry. A Mennonite church in Cumberland, Maryland, knew of his work in the Steelton mission and asked him to consider coming there as their pastor. Betty was reluctant to think about being a pastor's wife or leaving her Lancaster County home, and she struggled with it for more than a year. One afternoon she prayed, "Lord, I'm not willing to do this, but I choose to do it and I trust you to work in me." She felt no different as she cooked supper, took care of the children, and got them off to bed. The next day, after preparing lunch, Betty went out to the chicken house where Abner was collecting eggs and surprised him by saying, "We should look at those churches this weekend." Abner had several invitations, and now he was impressed with the change in her attitude. They visited Cumberland Mennonite Church, and the congregation called Abner Miller to serve as their pastor (1954–56).[64]

Betty's broken spirit and Abner's patience not to move forward without her full cooperation were hallmarks of the revival. In a similar fashion Alvin and Ethel Miller answered

Abner and Betty Miller, early witnesses to new life in Christ.

a call to mission work in northern Pennsylvania. Ethel described how it happened:

> It started during the early morning prayer meetings and the Monday evening fellowship meetings at Mervin and Mary Miller's. I went with a hungry heart and was given the opportunity to share my need. It was a time of spiritual awakening for me. I was very glad to attend those meetings. It was at one of those meetings that the Lord gave me a new heart and mind. Several weeks later we were asked to go to Potter County in mission work. Several months before, we were asked to go and I said no. Now I was willing and ready. The Lord had really changed my attitude.[65]

Glenn and Florence Zeager sold their farm near Bainbridge and moved to New York City, where Glenn began his alternative service (I-W) at Bellevue Hospital. They also assisted with a new Mennonite mission work in Harlem, where they lived.[66]

Glenn and Florence Zeager, active in the New York City fellowship.

The good news from East Africa was also spreading to Christians in Europe. On their journey home from Tanganyika in July 1951, John and Catharine Leatherman traveled through the continent. Max Showalter met them at the airport at Mulhouse in Alsace, France. Leatherman wrote that "Max had met Joe Church and William Nagenda when they were in Switzerland. He is revived and earnest for the Lord."[67]

The Hessions and Nagenda visit North America in 1953

Americans read about the revival in Roy (and Revel) Hession's *The Calvary Road* and soon invited Roy and Revel to visit the United States.[68] Norman Grubb offered to set up a six-month tour of churches and other preaching appointments. The Hessions shared the invitation with their British team. They were learning the benefits of walking in light, even on matters such as this. The team decided that Joe Church and William Nagenda, then ministering as a team in Wales, would go along. But they had been in Britain for some time and first needed to go home to Africa. It was agreed that the Hessions would go to America first, then Church and Nagenda would join them four months later.[69]

Joe Church finally arrived in Montreal in May 1953. William Nagenda and Roy and Revel Hession joined him in New York. Their first engagement was a residential conference at the Christian Literature Crusade/World Evangelism Crusade headquarters in Fort Washington, Pennsylvania. On the day of the event, every corner of the building was filled with eager, expectant listeners. Some Lancaster Conference Mennonites were among them.[70]

Jean Griswold embraced the message of revival early and continued to be an effective witness.

One of the people who came that night was a young wife and mother from a Philadelphia suburb. Jean Griswold had suffered the loss of her little son, and she and her husband were drifting apart. Roy Hession and William Nagenda spoke to her need.[71] Nagenda always spoke simply and directly. One of the images he used was the simple picture of the learner-driver in Uganda displaying the *L* sign on the vehicle to alert others that the driver was a beginner. "In God's kingdom," he pointed out, "we never stop wearing that *L*, for Jesus said, 'Come to me; . . . learn of me.' That sign speaks not only of a heart that is willing to be humble and accept from God what he wants to teach, but it also indicates that here is someone who is learning. Furthermore, it is a warning to fellow-travelers that the one wearing the *L* is not perfect and needs love, light, fellowship, and encouragement."[72]

William Nagenda set the theme of the entire tour: Jesus must be lifted up that "in all things he might have the preeminence" (Col 1:18). In England, Nagenda was concerned about an emphasis or teaching that might take the place of Jesus in the center; he was far more concerned about that in America. He found a strong and lively evangelical church in North America, which employed every conceivable emphasis and technique purported to be the answer to the church's need. But Nagenda saw all of it as competing with a focus on Jesus as the central place, and he felt that revival would come from none of these things. Out came the little white circle in the center of Nagenda's Bible, to which he pointed again and again. "It is not this or that in the center, but Jesus," he preached.[73] He was wary of "revival" becoming an idol, and he refused to allow their visit to become a promotional tour for Christian books, even *Continuous Revival* or *The Calvary Road*. The team had come to talk about Jesus!

This was what the North American churches needed. In the weeks that followed, the team spoke before large crowds throughout North America. They visited Park Street Congregational Church in Boston, where Harold Ockenga was senior pastor; Oswald Smith's People's Church in Toronto; Moody Bible Institute; and A. W. Tozer's Southside Alliance Church in Chicago. "So God led us to the heart of America, as we ended in Lancaster, and in the Mennonite homes of Pennsylvania."[74]

Nagenda returned to the United States the following year, 1954, to speak at the missions conference Urbana 54, organized by InterVarsity Christian Fellowship. The conference brought thousands of young Christians and a score of well-known evangelical speakers to the campus of the University of Illinois at Urbana. In his talk, Nagenda went straight to the point:

> When we come to such a conference as this and the Lord begins to speak to us about things which concern us, things which we value, and we face a crisis, the thought comes that God may be calling us to renounce and surrender certain things to Jesus. . . . There are many, many conditions of discipleship, but God has been telling me that the most important condition in our lives for us to be disciples [those who are taught by the Lord Jesus Christ], is to seek first the kingdom of God and his righteousness.

William used his own false starts and wrong turns as examples, telling how he went to Ruanda to be "a successful missionary" and how he tried to "crucify the old man" by his own efforts. "For a long time I was looking for experiences, something which was going to come, a second blessing, fullness of the Holy Spirit, this and that." But what he needed, he said, was to learn to acknowledge his sins and repent. Discipleship was not a matter of heroic self-denial, but of abiding in Jesus. And abiding meant to keep his commandments. "We don't look for experiences. We don't even wait for a crisis. Jesus Christ is waiting for us. . . . You don't have to wait. Deal with that thing that has brought separation between you and the Lord." He urged his hearers not to let anything else take the place of Jesus or separate them from him.[75]

William Nagenda and Roy Hession again spoke at the American head-quarters of the World Evangelism Crusade at Fort Washington, Pennsylvania. It was there that Roy Hession brought together Jean Griswold and Erma Maust.[76] It was a friendship that was to endure.

The central message of the East Africa Revival had reached an ever widening audience in America through the preaching of William Nagenda and Roy Hession, and lives were being changed, one at a time. Nagenda told his listeners at Urbana 54 about the way the Lord was working in East Africa:

We don't see hundreds and thousands. No. We see one man brought to the Lord at a time, but when he comes to the Lord, you know for certain that that man has found Jesus Christ as his per-sonal Savior, for he makes him Lord at once. And this revival has been spreading slowly but surely, and the way has been, "Abide in Me." Call sin sin. Don't try to excuse it. If you fail, don't try to be what you are not; be what you are.[77]

—9—

Revival Takes Deeper Root in North America 1955–1959

The seeds of revival were planted in North America by missionaries such as the Leathermans, the Stauffers, the Shenks, and the Smokers, along with the visits to the continent by evangelists such as William Nagenda, Joe Church, Roy and Revel Hession. The message of revival also spread through the writings of Roy and Revel Hession and Norman P. Grubb. With no fanfare at all, Erma Maust emerged as a most effective spokesperson for revival, both by word and work. She and Herbert carried major responsibilities as revival fellowships formed in North America.

The Mausts travel with William Nagenda in 1955

Erma and Herbert Maust, the plainly dressed, conservative Mennonite couple, were a touchstone for visiting evangelists and church leaders from East Africa and Europe. On their way to mission conferences like that at Urbana, Illinois, or to speaking engagements at a seminary or major-city church, they invariably scheduled a week in Lancaster County with Erma and the small group who met with her in fellowship. These well-known churchmen sought her counsel and relied on her to arrange all or part of their American itinerary and often traveled with the Mausts.

In February 1955 George and Dorothy Smoker arranged for William Nagenda to speak at Scottdale, Pennsylvania, where the Mennonite Publishing House was located. The Smokers had lived in Scottdale before they went to Africa so it was fitting for them to arrange for Nagenda to speak in the Mennonite church there.[1] Many there found his message liberating, but others had difficulty assimilating his testimony with their own theology.

Marvin and Mildred Plank were among those who responded to the Lord through William's preaching. They were already familiar with what

God was doing in East Africa, and they knew the Smokers and the Leathermans. "We followed every bit of news about them, after they went to Africa." The Smokers visited the Planks on their first furlough home in 1947 and again in 1954. Mildred recalled, "I'm sure they gave us our first copy of *The Calvary Road*."[2]

Marvin Plank offered to drive Nagenda to Harrisonburg, Virginia, where he was to speak at Eastern Mennonite College. On the way they stopped at Abner and Betty Miller's home in Cumberland, Maryland, for a meal. Erma Maust was there at the time. "There Marvin first met Erma, and in that short meeting he perceived that he had just met one of God's anointed."[3]

Marvin and Mildred Plank, of Scottdale, Pa.

Herbert and Erma Maust were already committed to "a ministry of helps," humble service to those in need. Herbert gave up his job with the Pennsylvania Railroad and his pension benefits in 1954, "because of convictions about the labor union tactics and closed-shop policies."[4] The Mennonite Church discouraged membership in unions because of the coercive tactics often used by organized labor. His fidelity to church discipline created financial problems, but opened the door to a new kind of servant ministry. Erma explained:

> We believed that we were a part of the gift mentioned in 1 Corinthians 12:28 ["helps"]. At that time the way seemed clear that part of that job was giving assistance in a physical way whenever there was an opening.[5]

A growing number came to fellowship meetings and sought Erma's counsel, but her circle also expanded geographically as the church called many to mission work far from Lancaster County. Abner and Betty Miller were then pastoring the Mennonite church at Cumberland, Maryland. Glenn and Florence Zeager were in New York, working with John and Thelma Kraybill in a new Mennonite mission in Harlem. The Alvin Millers were planting a church in Potter County, Pennsylvania. Herbert and Erma's ministry of helps began with visits to these mission churches and letters of encouragement and spiritual guidance.

Through their visits to the Zeagers in Harlem, the Mausts came to know all of the Mennonite mission workers in New York City. This was a particularly difficult time for Mennonite home missionaries just as it was for those overseas because Lancaster Conference required them to enforce the newly adopted Conference Discipline. Located in poverty-stricken neighborhoods in Harlem and the South Bronx, their storefront churches attracted children for Sunday school and other programs, but most adult city dwellers were not much interested in becoming Mennonites. Since the mission board provided no financial support for home missionaries, they all worked at other jobs to support their families and had to juggle church planting and work schedules. It is not difficult to see how the most dedicated mission workers could be discouraged at times.

A letter Erma wrote to Paul and Miriam Burkholder at the Glad Tidings mission in the Bronx is typical of this aspect of her ministry:

Just had a letter from Glenns, in it they shared something of your problem. The easiest thing to do when we are going through trials, misunderstandings and so on, is to think we ought to get out of the situation, to remove ourselves from the circumstances, but that is not God's way. His way is for us

Paul and Miriam Burkholder at the mission church in New York City, with children Judy, Glenn, Renee, Marilyn and Jim.

to submit to him in the trial, get the lesson, and be conformed by the circumstances. Now I realize this is not easy, but thank him for all this, because he says: "All things are of God" [2 Cor 5:18]. "All things are for your sakes" [2 Cor 4:15]. "All things are for your good" [Rom 8:28]. "And in all things give thanks" [1 Thess 5:18].[6]

In addition to writing personal letters, Erma began sending a more general mimeographed letter to a wider circle:

The Lord has wonderfully led step by step, until I began to realize he did want me to enlarge my mailing list to include all those with whom I have correspondence and are interested in revival, and to send the messages he speaks to my heart to all such, in this way working with God for revival. For we do need this linking up with all God's people who are longing for his return and for a mighty Holy Ghost revival.[7]

The Mausts began a pattern of extended visits that they continued for several years. In June 1955 the couple spent two weeks at Cumberland, Maryland, helping with the vacation Bible school at Abner Miller's church, "but most of all working with God for revival." For July they stayed with the Zeagers in Harlem, working in their summer program.[8] Erma wrote from Cumberland: "These are busy days. Bible school each morning, visiting homes in the afternoon, studying and preparing for Bible school, ministering to souls in need. He has put us in a new school, but praise, He is leading on in His way."[9]

After their month in New York, the Mausts went to Springs, Pennsylvania, where Herbert's parents lived. The Allegheny Mennonite Conference was holding its annual meeting at the Springs Mennonite Church, and they naturally attended.[10] Marvin and Mildred Plank also attended the sessions. There Marvin introduced his wife to Erma Maust. Mildred long remembered their meeting:

At my first meeting Erma at the Allegheny Conference in Springs, Erma invited us, with others, to Herbert's [parents'] home for refreshments between the afternoon and evening sessions. On the front porch, while eating, we had a little "fellowship" time. I was an extremely bashful person but I did screw up my courage and said a few words, prefacing my remarks by saying I was a bashful person. Immediately Erma challenged me by saying, "Would you like to ask the Lord why you are bashful?" I did ask the Lord and when I saw Erma later I reported that he had shown me it was pride. That was the first of many challenges God brought to me through Erma.[11]

The Mausts and the Planks became close friends, encouraging one another. Both couples recognized a common commitment to Jesus Christ and a common concern for revival.[12] Mildred Plank later recalled the Mausts' initial visit to the Planks' home and lessons learned over a long time of working together:

I remember that first visit in our home. It was a hot summer day and since we had no air-conditioning we took our chairs out in the yard and listened spellbound as Erma told about how the Lord began to work in her life. She was free to use the expression "the Lord showed me," or "the Lord spoke to me." She made us so hungry to know God in an intimate way. I think one of her main emphases was to make people hungry and then immediately challenge them to be honest with themselves and with God. That meant being open to the Holy Spirit and then being quick to admit what He showed you by being willing to share with other people what you had seen and responded to.

She taught the importance of calling sin sin and not faults, then repenting and giving thanks for the freedom of forgiveness. One big lesson Marvin and I learned from Erma was the importance and necessity of giving thanks in all things.[13]

While Herbert Maust worked as counselor at a Christian camp for the rest of the summer, Erma Maust visited Ruth Truesdale, an AIM missionary to Kenya who was not allowed to return there because of her association with the East Africa Revival. Erma also spent time helping in the New York City Mennonite churches.[14] Wherever they went the Mausts did painting, carpentering, upholstering, housework, and farm chores for people who were sick, depressed, or simply overwhelmed by daily life.

The Hessions minister again in United States

The Hessions paid their second visit to North America in September 1955. Their book, *The Calvary Road*, was published by the Christian Literature Crusade and was very popular that year when the first American edition was released, five years after its publication in England. They began their speaking tour, as they had done with William Nagenda in 1953, at the headquarters of the Christian Literature Crusade. Erma Maust reported: "The simplicity of the way, the way of repentance, was so clearly brought out in the messages at the Fort Washington conference which we were privileged to attend."[15] Before they left England, the Hessions made arrangements to spend several days with the Mausts in Lancaster County. Erma invited everyone on her mailing list to come for fellowship during that time. "The afternoons will be open for informal fellowship, with fellowship meetings each evening." Mildred Plank recalled her excitement about traveling from Scottdale for this meeting.[16]

Reflecting on the ten days she and Herbert spent with Roy and Revel Hession, Erma told Paul and Miriam Burkholder:

> We also saw the need of not only confessing our sin as sin and forsaking it, but also the need of being in the light about it. This was made very clear to me through our time together. . . . When we were in fellowship alone with Roy and Revel, I was free, but not in fellowship meetings. I couldn't understand and was seeking the Lord about it. I began to get light [on] Sunday and had liberty in our fellowship Sunday afternoon, but only as we opened our hearts wide to one another on our way to the Sunday evening meeting. We all began to get light and see where we had failed.[17]

Roy and Revel continued their preaching tour through the winter months. Their final engagement was at Keswick, New Jersey, in March 1956. Herbert and Erma Maust were there. "We had a most blessed fellowship with the Hessions and sixty other brethren in the Lord, whom he had gathered together for a retreat at Keswick before the Hessions sailed for England."[18]

Learning to follow Jesus in fellowship with others

Erma went back to New York City for two weeks in April, while Herbert was helping to paint at the Steelton Mennonite mission.[19] Erma was usually assigned to teach children in Sunday school and vacation Bible school. "I have never felt called to children's work, but rather to adults, and this time the Lord did the seeming impossible and gave me adults."[20] When Erma returned to New York the following summer for vacation Bible school, she was happy that "my little tots are not so restless and hard to manage." She acknowledged that "I find it quite difficult with children's classes. I always feel such a failure."[21]

Erma realized, as the revived brother and sisters had learned, that revival is best maintained by regular, committed, Christ-centered fellowship with fellow pilgrims. In East Africa, they called it "walking in the light."[22]

With so much traveling, the regular Bainbridge fellowship meetings suffered. In June 1956 Erma sought to maintain a firm commitment to more frequent fellowship meetings:

> [The Lord] has been working afresh in our hearts here in our community and Saturday evening, June 2, in a time of fellowship gave

us a deep oneness in desire for again meeting regularly for fellowship. So if he continues to so lead, there will be a fellowship here at Mervin's every second and fourth Monday evening at eight o'clock. He has also made us deeply one in seeing how each needs to wait upon the Lord for what He would have, rather than looking to one or two to lead the meeting.[23]

Erma and Herbert Maust established regular times for fellowship. "Our fellowship meetings each second and fourth Monday of the month continue to be times of rich fellowship, and the Lord continues to work among us, bringing new ones into the fellowship, and working deeper in those He had set free."[24]

Fruitful ministries of Norman Grubb and the Hessions

There were stirrings of renewal among Lancaster County Mennonites that summer in a series of spiritual life meetings at Steelton, Pennsylvania, as well as in fellowship meetings like those at Mervin Miller's home. Erma wrote, "The Lord surely began to pour out his Spirit during the meetings at Sharon Church in Steelton. . . . He has been deeply uniting the groups who are praying for revival." Among them were the fellowship groups that met at the Millers' place, at Mellinger Mennonite Church in Lancaster, and at Steelton.

The idea of larger fellowship meetings, akin to the conventions held by *balokole* in East Africa, came from a Baptist pastor. Erma reported: "Jack Ludlam, pastor of a Baptist church in Chester, Pa., took care of the business end of the conference at Keswick, N.J., when the Hessions were with us. Several weeks ago he, with several others, met here at our house to seek the Lord and plan for another time of fellowship such as we had then."[25]

Ludlum sent an announcement of the first such gathering to everyone on Erma's mailing list in May 1957:

Fellowship meeting for those interested in a deeper walk with our precious Lord is planned for June 6th at Messiah College, Grantham, Pennsylvania. The speaker will be Mr. Norman Grubb, director of the World-Wide Evangelization Crusade, and author of *Continuous Revival* and other books.[26]

The Messiah College meeting brought another large group together. In his talks Grubb emphasized the corporate aspect of renewal, which had

Revival conference at Messiah College, Grantham, Pa.

struck him when he first heard William Nagenda and Yosiya Kinuka. Revival was not simply something that happened in the hearts of individual believers; it created a new community of brothers and sisters for whom Jesus Christ is all in all. Erma testified:

> As the Spirit opened the Word to us through Bro. Grubb Thursday on fellowship, what it is, why we need it, we were made to see again, [how] it is of the most vital importance and how the church today is suffering because we have gotten so far from the pattern of the early church in this very thing. We were also reminded [that] "real fellowship with God implies real fellowship with one another."[27]

Messiah College is an institution of the Brethren in Christ Church, and the East Africa Revival had an impact on the church through the school. Lucille Wolgemuth, the wife of a Messiah College professor, was part of the fellowship group that met at Mervin Miller's place. She suggested to the college president, C. N. Hostetter Jr., that he invite Roy and Revel Hession to be the resource persons for a week of services in the fall of 1957. At the same time, Erma Maust was holding weekly fellowship meetings on the campus with student and faculty wives.[28]

Roy and Revel Hession again stayed with the Mausts, for ten days in

October 1957. Erma announced, "Our home will be open for fellowship afternoons and evenings."[29] During his week at Messiah College, Roy encouraged those who counseled with him to

Herbert and Erma Maust, with children James, David, John, and Miriam in front.

keep in touch with Erma. Ronald and Marjorie Lofthouse, a student couple from Ontario, were among them. Marjorie remembers:

> We met Erma when she was leading a fellowship for faculty wives and married student wives on Messiah College campus in the fall of 1957. We were living on campus and Ron was a student. She often came to our house for noon lunches after the meetings. Roy Hession told Erma to stay close to us as Ron met Jesus in a new way while Roy had meetings at Messiah College.[30]

Marjorie and Ron Lofthouse, touched by revival at Messiah College and active for many years.

Erma's care was not always welcome. Ron Lofthouse was studying for the ministry in the Brethren in Christ Church and later commented:

> When Erma would come for lunch at Messiah College and she'd get talking about what Jesus was doing in their ministry, I wished she'd shut up or go home. After some time I shared with her how I felt and asked whether I could be jealous of her, to which she said, "Why don't you call it that and take it to Jesus to cleanse you?"[31]

A meaningful retreat at Keswick

Reflecting on her time with Roy and Revel, Erma confessed: "We praise the Lord for the quiet working of the spirit at Keswick" and "for what the Lord did for me the week [the Hessions] were with us. The Lord cleansed me of a covetous spirit which manifested itself in wanting Roy and Revel to think I was broken and a feeling of inferiority around them and some others."[32]

Among those at the Keswick fellowship retreat was a young pastor from Maryland named Bill Scott. He had been five years in the ministry but was burned out and ready to quit. A friend suggested going to hear Roy Hession. His wife, Marian, encouraged him and "prayed that the Lord would do something for us." Hession's sermon on God's rejection of Saul as king hit home. Scott recognized that he had failed in his "little kingdom" and that the Lord would send a better man to take his place. Then Hession made clear that Jesus is the one chosen as king, and that we have to yield our rule to him. Bill Scott acknowledged this when Roy invited responses. Erma Maust heard him and asked, "Will anyone pray for Bill?" She then prayed for him. They had already talked and she knew the depths of his discouragement. When everyone was leaving on the final day of the retreat, Erma told him, "The Lord has met you. I'd like to come and share with Marian."[33]

Marian Scott was burdened with housework and soon to give birth to a child. "Erma was able to work with her hands and talk at the same time," she recalled. "And she worked, doing dishes, cooking, mending, talking all along on that first visit." Thereafter, the Mausts drove down to Cecil County, Maryland, two or three times a year. "She became our mentor." The Scotts began attending some fellowship meetings at the Mausts' home, despite the distance, especially when Roy Hession or William Nagenda came.[34]

Bill and Marian Scott of Northeast, Maryland, continued to serve on revival teams.

A vision for fellowship grows

At this time Erma came to a new conviction about the fellowship meetings at Mervin Miller's farm:

> Years ago when the Lord first began to work in the fellowship here, He gave the word: "Behold, I have set before thee an open door, and no man can shut it" [Rev 3:8]. This word has come back to us with new meaning the past months as the Lord has been opening more doors for fellowship with individuals and groups than we have been able to enter. . . . For the past year or so, we

have been having fellowship each second and fourth Monday evening, until about two months ago when we felt the Lord would have us meet each Monday evening. So now we meet each Monday evening at 7:30. In those who have been coming we have seen a fresh work of God and a new diligence.[35]

Other fellowship meetings sprang up around the country. Glenn and Florence Zeager and several other Mennonite mission workers in New York City began a regular fellowship in 1956. Initially, it was just the Zeagers and Burkholders who met together for prayer. Erma counseled Paul and Miriam Burkholder about it in one of her letters to them:

> Had a letter from Glenns—and praise, you have been getting together for fellowship. Florence said you have faced quite a problem with the situation there. Here is a thought—why not be in the light with Harold Thomas [mission superintendent]; don't try to hide anything or be secretive about it. Tell him you and Glenns have been getting together for fellowship, simply sharing what God speaks to you and praying for revival, and that anyone is welcome to join you. Then you can trust the Lord to work out the details.[36]

Erma Maust understood that revival was both personal and corporate. She also knew the importance of love as the bond of unity. Using 1 Peter 4:7-11 as her text, she wrote to her friends in the New York mission:

> The chief thing is not doing mission work or witnessing but to carefully see that he is allowed to cleanse us of those things which hinder our having "servant love" for one another as brethren; then he will see to our missions and our witnessing. What good does all our service do when we have bitterness in our hearts toward one another? How it must grieve him.[37]

Although they invited other mission workers, the New York group remained small. Erma wrote a year later: "Don't strive about their getting there. God will gather together those he purposes to get together."[38] The New York fellowship continued nonetheless for many years. Glenn and Florence Zeager eventually purchased a large house on University Avenue in the Bronx "in order that they may give themselves more effectually to the ministry of the saints who pass through the city." Missionaries and visiting Africans stayed there on their journey to or from America.[39]

Returned missionaries carried the message of the East Africa Revival to Mennonites at home and shared their testimonies of God's working in the lives of thousands there. After Clyde and Alta Shenk, George and Dorothy Smoker, and Elam and Grace Stauffer went back to Tanganyika in 1954, more than three years passed without any missionary furloughs.

◦

The revivalists in America

At the close of 1957 John and Catharine Leatherman had their turn at a North American assignment. Back in Pennsylvania, the Leathermans renewed contact with the fellowship meeting at Mervin Miller's farm. They were living in Doylestown, Pennsylvania, so the long trip ruled out weekly attendance. John wrote: "There were quite a few there and I find that the need is great. A number have made a start but have been perplexed because of 'holiness' agitation. I left the meeting feeling great love for these folks. O Jesus, teach me thy brokenness."[40]

A few weeks later John and Catharine returned to "the fellowship at Mausts'." Just as in East Africa, men and women from different backgrounds shared openly. An attending professor from Messiah College "was quite hungry and open with his problems." Another brother "who was sour the last time I was there began to open up and found release."[41] They went as often as they could. On a Sunday afternoon in August, for instance, "Catharine and I went over to Erma's, where we had a fellowship meeting. A Rev Bill Scott and wife were there. He is seeking."[42]

Glenn Zeager invited John and Catharine Leatherman to New York for the fellowship meeting there. The Lancaster bishops were pressuring the group to enforce the conference rules, thus creating new strains for the fellowship. Leatherman reported:

> Glenn took us to Paul Burkholder's home at the Glad Tidings mission, where we had supper. Others came in and we spoke of the Lord's dealings with us and how we go on in fellowship. They are eager to go on but have felt themselves hemmed in by ultra-conservative requirements in their work.[43]

The Hessions were again in North America in 1958. Erma Maust planned a weekend with Roy and Revel at Harmony Heart Camp in the

Pocono Mountains of northeastern Pennsylvania.[44] John and Catharine Leatherman attended the conference:

> A meeting was held in the evening and the general theme was grace, using Elijah on Mt. Carmel. We want the fire—truth and conviction, but God sends the refreshing rain. We were surprised to find a number of Mennonite folks from EMC [Eastern Mennonite College, Harrisonburg, Va.] and others from Scottdale [Pa.]. Also the Mausts were there. Roy and Revel were eager that we work together as a team.[45]

Leatherman found the preaching filled "with warmth and the blessing of the Spirit." He recorded: "The afternoon messages by Roy and Revel were excellent on the vine and branches. Yes, we surely saw Jesus afresh as the vine containing all the fullness of God. Roy wondered if I would have any message but I felt only to give my testimony, which I did." In one of the team meetings, Leatherman learned that he was to preach the next day and spoke on Naaman.[46]

Roy and Revel Hession, visiting the Lawtons in Washington, DC. Revel died shortly after this trip.

The Hessions planned to return to England after one final meeting in New York. They arranged for the Leathermans to join them. "We teamed up and Roy and myself gave messages and Catharine followed with a testimony." They parted "with love and oneness" and "gave them our warm greetings to William Nagenda, Joe Church, and Yosiya Kinuka."[47]

Before they left, Roy and Revel gave the car they used on their American tour to Herbert and Erma Maust. Erma could hardly believe it:

> The Lord has opened the way for us to get a car after being without one for over four years. It is one of those "exceeding, abundantly above" things he sometimes does. He would have been gracious to give us any car, but he has led we should get the car Roy and Revel Hession had while touring the States, a 1958 Plymouth. We can only praise the Lord who has made this possible.[48]

In October, Erma arranged a one-day fellowship meeting at Kenbrook Bible Camp, north of Lebanon, Pennsylvania. Some forty people attended, among them some from Messiah College. John Leatherman noted: "We had team meetings to arrange for the programs. I met Ronald Lofthouse of the Brethren in Christ Church. He is really a brother."[49]

In November 1958 the New York City Mennonite churches united for a series of renewal meetings and invited John Leatherman to preach for them. The Lord enabled John to deliver clear messages on union with Christ and quickness to acknowledge sin and wrong. Attendance grew larger at each service as New Yorkers heard and appreciated these East Africa Revival themes.[50]

In 1958 a young Eastern Mennonite College student from Uganda named Thompson Sabiti visited the Mausts and the Leathermans over the Christmas holidays. This paved the way for a visit by his father, Erica Sabiti, in 1960. Erica was the new Anglican bishop in western Uganda. The message he gave in the college chapel led at least one person to open his heart to the Lord. Rev. Robert Crewdson completed his studies at Virginia Theological Seminary that year and was assigned to a little Episcopal mission church in eastern Rockingham County, Virginia, as deacon-in-charge. A friend invited him to hear Erica, who in his sermon compared the river of life and the Nile. It was the beginning of a full conversion for the young minister, who recognized that until then his relationship with the Lord was "in my head, not in my heart."[51]

Joe Church and Roy Hession teamed up for a mission to Brazil in 1959. They planned to meet with American friends between flights. Erma informed her contacts:

> Roy Hession of England and Dr. Joe Church, missionary from Ruanda, who had been at Fort Washington with William Nagenda some years ago, plan to be with us for a weekend fellowship meeting that together we may see Jesus afresh.[52]

To reach the greatest number in the short time available, Erma planned "an all-day fellowship meeting to be held Saturday" at the Mennonite House of Friendship in the Bronx, and another all-day fellowship on Sunday "at the Marcus Hook Baptist Church, where Dr. Church and Roy Hession will be speaking" in the morning service. The Marcus Hook Baptist Church, near Chester, Pennsylvania, was Jack Ludlam's congregation.[53]

The Mennonite House of Friendship, opposite the entrance to the Bronx Zoo, was the most accessible of the Mennonite missions in New York. John I. Smucker, the pastor there, was also touched by the revival through the ministry of Erma Maust, whom he recalls as "a Mennonite saint." After Joe Church and Roy Hession preached there, regular fellowship meetings were held at this church, too.[54]

Not long afterward Joe Church wrote of this visit to New York and Pennsylvania:

> We gave our own testimonies. Mine was that of a missionary belonging to a keen evangelical mission, going out to Africa to teach the Africans about the love of Jesus, and how he died for them, and about the victorious life: but how very soon under the testings that God allowed to come upon us in those early days at Gahini, it was not more about Jesus, but less and less about Jesus, that the Africans began to see, and then God in his goodness led me to the first saved African I had met, away in Kampala, in Uganda, and there he gave me a new vision of revival. That was in October 1929; to me it was "in the year that King Uzziah died" [Isa 6:1]. I began to see slowly that much more of me had to die; first I think it was my anger that I called "righteous anger!"
>
> Secondly was the sin of departmentalism—independence in running my hospital and not wanting others, especially my fellow missionary, a clergyman, to "interfere," that horrible word, in it. Thirdly, there was a deep-seated but subtle despising of the Africans, as somehow inferior to me, who was the superior paternal missionary.
>
> These things and many others had to die, and many times we have had to cry "Woe is me." But we have learnt this place of breaking to be the gateway to revival, but we have to keep on and on coming back there, in fact we have to live there, before the Mercy Seat, where we hear the cry "Holy, holy, holy" continually [Isa 6].
>
> Roy gave his testimony of how, as a successful evangelist, he had become mechanical and found his evangelism, although still bringing results, becoming a strain. He could go on no longer. Then he began to see that he, Roy, must die. In time God led him out to Africa and so we have come to travel together, taking this message to the Americas.[55]

More input from missionaries on furlough

Mennonite missionaries on North American assignment were again bringing the message of renewal to the sending churches. Elam and Grace Stauffer and Clyde and Alta Shenk returned early in 1959. Phebe Yoder came back to the States in April of that year.[56] John Leatherman was taking courses at Goshen Biblical Seminary in Indiana, an opportunity to become reacquainted with developments in his own denomination. On one occasion he met with members of the Reba Place Mennonite Church in Chicago, "a group of folks who have agreed to live on a communal basis, pooling their resources and sharing the vicissitudes of life together." They had him tell of the African fellowship, "and I felt great liberty in doing this."[57] Their life together resonated with John Leatherman.

Back in Pennsylvania after his courses ended, John had other invitations to share his testimony. The Leathermans left for Leverett, Massachusetts, to visit Ruth Truesdale of AIM, who had scheduled meetings for them in churches and at a missionary conference at Northfield. "We found Ruth a real sister in the Lord. She has not been able to return to Kenya because of the AIM's strong position against the [revival] fellowship in the field."[58]

The Hessions returned to New York City in June 1959 for a series of meetings at the Alliance Gospel Tabernacle. Glenn Zeager and John Leatherman, in New York at the time, attended the meetings and had meaningful fellowship with Roy. Leatherman found Roy's message on King Saul to be especially searching. He recalled that this word from the Lord touched Bill Scott at Keswick. Leatherman affirmed:

> We, too, must accept that God has rejected our kingship in favor of another who is better than we. Our willingness to have it this way will be demonstrated in our attitude toward our brother. If we become jealous in his choice of our brother it means we don't want to be overshadowed by him, which means the same for Christ. . . . We should not mourn the rejection of Saul but rejoice that Jesus [our David] is now king. Samuel made all the sons of Jesse pass before him. Yet God rejected all. We try out many "sons" before we accept the lowliest, the "ruddy" one. When he comes, "then we sit down and rest."[59]

After the New York meetings, Roy Hession's last engagement before returning to England was a fellowship retreat at Harmony Heart Camp that Erma Maust planned. Here he was one of a team, rather than a visiting evangelist as in other settings. "The theme as it developed was God's rightness against our wrongness as we seek to establish our righteousness." Roy Hession gave the message on the first evening. The next day Hession, John Leatherman, and Jack Ludlam spoke. On the final day, Hession preached in the morning, "and this afternoon he, Erma, and myself again gave messages." Leatherman noted in his diary that "the meetings were deep" and that there were "a number of heartbroken responses and victories."[60]

Erma was asked to speak, along with a Baptist minister, a Mennonite minister, and an Anglican evangelist. She never thought of herself as a preacher or of sharing as a sermon or message whatever the Lord had shown her in Scripture. Neither she nor her church believed in calling women to preach. As in East Africa, the revival freed men and women from cultural bondage to share deeply what God had done for them. There was no doubt that Erma was a free woman in Christ.

Erma never had any difficulty in working with other Christians on a one-to-one basis or in setting up meetings for non-Mennonite speakers like William Nagenda, Norman Grubb, or the Hessions. Her fresh insight was that denominational distinctives were secondary and should not impede unity in Jesus Christ. One could share that common core with anyone.[61] She did not apologize for being a Mennonite nor did she expect others to apologize for their affiliations. On the contrary, she delighted in the grace of God, which simply disregarded denominational distinctives as sinners, like herself, met at the cross. To Erma, that was powerful testimony to God's reconciling grace:[62]

> We have been seeing anew this is what God is wanting to do, "gather his saints together unto him," from every denomination, where we in fellowship with one another see Jesus afresh and experience his cleansing us of those things which hinder that oneness Jesus prayed we as believers should have. What blessed oneness when we gather unto him, not unto a church, nor a doctrine, or a cause, but simply unto him and to glorify him.[63]

The evangelists and the Mennonite denomination

Since Herbert Maust had returned to teaching at Kraybill Mennonite School a year or two earlier, Erma traveled with Emma Good, a friend from her Lancaster County church. Her travels were more extensive now than earlier. She wrote: "We are praising the Lord for all he is doing these days as we are going from place to place. The Spirit is giving liberty in the messages and takes it home to the hearts who hear."[64]

Erma was engaged in a speaking ministry but remained a faithful member of Lancaster Conference and observed all the regulations of the conference discipline. On one occasion Ronald and Marjorie Lofthouse, Emma Good, and Erma Maust drove to New York for the weekly fellowship meeting there.[65] Mennonite churches in the city still observed traditional standards of plain clothes, but the Brethren in Christ Church had relaxed its rules in the interest of making the church more accessible to the people they were evangelizing. This raised questions that Erma Maust answered to her own satisfaction:

> I believe it is right for Ronald's, as their church does not require it, but it would not be right, or of the Lord, for Emma and . . . [me], for how can we teach brokenness and submission if in this one area we would not be so? By Ronald's not wearing the plain clothes, even though Emma and I do wear our bonnets, it will be a real testimony to the people that those who are so different could be so deeply one and work as a team.[66]

Ongoing suspicion, and its resolution

John and Catharine Leatherman and Elam and Grace Stauffer were going through a difficult time in the summer of 1959. Mennonite Church leaders were still not convinced that the East Africa Revival was a good thing. The Leathermans and Stauffers had many interviews with the mission board and bishop board before they were permitted to return to Tanganyika. The mission board gave final approval to the Leathermans in September 1959. "It was a big and glorious day. We were at last reappointed for Africa by the board, and without any objection from anyone."[67]

During this time the support of revival brethren (*ndugu*) in Africa and America was important. John Leatherman recorded that he and Catharine

> went on out to the fellowship meeting with Erma, Ronald Lofthouse, and Dan and Nancy Wegmueller. The latter are from Urundi and are real *ndugu*. We had a heart-searching time in which I expressed my own present need—being under a cloud and not praising. How blessed to have brethren who love and care![68]

As the Leathermans and Stauffers prepared to return to the mission field, Erma organized another large fellowship conference at the Harmony

Dan and Nancy Wegmueller, Free Methodist
missionaries to Urundi, with children Priscilla,
Patricia, Susan, Marybeth.

Heart Camp in October 1959. She announced:

This will be the last fellowship John and Catharine Leatherman will be able to share with us for sometime as they plan D.V. [*Deus volens*, the Lord willing] to sail for Africa a few days after the conference. We do praise the Lord for the way he has opened the door for them to go back, and that he has allowed them to be with us for this retreat before they leave.[69]

The tail end of a big hurricane reached eastern Pennsylvania the day the conference opened, and travelers had rain all the way to the camp. Many others waited for the weather to improve. "A few of the folks came early for a team meeting and we had a gathering in the afternoon." John Leatherman spoke in the evening "on the simplicity of Christ." The next day brought a large number to the meeting. Ludlam and Erma "gave messages in the morning." In the afternoon Lofthouse addressed the group, and in the evening Leatherman spoke "on Christ making himself of no reputation" (Phil 2:7). "We had a closely knit fellowship and one marvels at the light and liberty." On the final day Ludlam and Leatherman both preached on the woman with the issue of blood (Mark 5), and Don Jacobs brought the closing message from Revelation 5. "The whole group gave Catharine and me a gift in view of our leaving for Africa," Leatherman wrote. "We were much touched by the love of our brothers and sisters."[70]

These were busy days for the Leathermans. There was a farewell meeting at Doylestown Mennonite Church, where John had first served in the ministry. A day later they drove to New York for a fellowship meeting at Glenn and Florence Zeager's new home in the Bronx. "Paul Burkholders, John Freeds, and Erma [Maust] were all present." The following day they went to Leacock Presbyterian Church at Paradise, Lancaster County, Pennsylvania, where Norman Grubb was preaching. There they again said goodbye to Elam and Grace Stauffer and Clyde and Alta Shenk. They flew from Idlewild International Airport the next day, on their way to Nairobi. "Don Jacobs and the New York brethren were also there" to see them off.[71]

—10—

Revival Enables Relationships for the Life of the Church 1954–1960

The argument could be made that the key to the spread of revival across cultures is for God to call out a few who translate or tell the story of revival convincingly to people in other cultures. It was a blessing that East Africa produced many effective interpreters of revival for all the world to hear. Notable among them were articulate Africans like William Nagenda and Festo Kivengere, who traveled and wrote. But God used many non-Africans as well. For this translation to really work, the "carriers" of revival, whether African or not, had to be invested in the revival fellowships. Proponents of revival do not simply report; they testify to the new life in Christ that they have experienced.

Translation across cultures is not a one-person exercise. People may well question the authenticity of an individual. But when several persons from each culture receive and embody the same message, that is powerful and persuasive.

The story this book tells alternates between Africa and the Western world. We digress now from the American narrative to reflect on events in East Africa during the postwar period. What was occurring there ultimately impacted the spread of revival to the world.

The fifteen years after World War II marked a time when many nations in Africa struggled for independence from their former European colonial masters. It was a struggle that also occurred in the churches. The history of missions in this period demonstrates stresses and strains between African church leaders, who desired freedom to run their own affairs, and Western missionaries and mission boards, who were often reluctant to grant autonomy to the local churches. During this stressful era the revival fellowships were frequently able to foster relationships that could be maintained in love.

Revival and the Mennonite ethos

We begin this chapter by walking with an American Mennonite missionary as he struggled to make sense of all that was happening in those days of change and challenge. He was a typical product of the Mennonite Church, which traces its roots to the Anabaptist movement that began in Zurich in 1525. The Anabaptists called for a radical following of Jesus Christ in every area of life, in fidelity to the clear teaching of Scripture. This religious awakening spread rapidly across Dutch and German-speaking lands during the years of the Protestant Reformation, pioneered by Martin Luther. The Anabaptists were mercilessly persecuted by Catholics and Protestants alike; they found security in their close-knit communities. "Instead of primarily confronting the evils of society, which did not go away, they concentrated on their own purity and life as a people of God."[1] In time Mennonites and other Anabaptist-related groups created communities that tended to isolate themselves from the national societies where they lived.

> This is hardly surprising. It is, in fact, inevitable. From the very beginning, the missionary message of the Christian church incarnated itself in the life and world of those who embraced it. It is, however, only fairly recently that this essentially contextual nature of the faith has been recognized.[2]

Our missionary prototype is Donald Jacobs, who was blessed by the refreshing wind of God in East Africa. He was critical of the revival at first but eventually found himself as a joyful repentant sinner.

Reflecting on revival and culture, Jacobs observed, "Renewal movements often become concretized in cultural forms peculiar to the setting in which they occurred." The history of his own denomination clearly illustrated this. The once-dynamic and evangelistic Anabaptist movement took on characteristics of the folkways and worldview of the modern times. For several centuries Mennonites lived out the gospel as best as they could in Germanic cultural forms, even after locating in North America. Things began to change, however, in the twentieth century, when the larger groups of Mennonites abandoned the German language and adopted a more contemporary American lifestyle while maintaining strict discipline and high ethics. The denomination experienced great internal debates in the early decades of the twentieth century as it struggled with the essence of Mennonite identity.

"I have met the Anabaptists and they are Africans!" Donald Jacobs wrote to Mennonite theologian John Howard Yoder not long after Jacobs and his wife arrived in Tanganyika in 1954. He and Anna Ruth, his wife, heard stories of martyrs who refused to take up arms during a Mau Mau uprising that was just coming to an end. Don mused over a revival that produced martyrs: wasn't this like the Anabaptists who went through similar fires in sixteenth-century Europe?

Don came to teach at Katoke Training College in northwestern Tanganyika. In graduate school he

Don and Anna Ruth Jacobs, fledgling missionaries in Tanganyika, beside a typical granary.

had specialized in the history of the Protestant Reformation, and as a student of the Anabaptist awakening, he had read accounts of the Anabaptists' vision for following Jesus Christ in all of life. Now he met people who acted like the early Anabaptists did, walking with Christ in the same way.[3]

The comparison was an apt one. Like the East African brothers and sisters, Anabaptists had a Jesus-centered approach to faith that impacted every aspect of daily life. To Anabaptists, following Jesus emphasized the life and teachings of Jesus as normative for the Christian life, not just for salvation. Anabaptists "were not interested in either doctrinal correctness or spiritual experiences that did not result in changed lives, faithful discipleship, authentic church, and courageous mission."[4] The same insistence on Jesus as the center made the revival a source of renewal for many Christian churches in East Africa.

"Our arrival in Tanganyika more or less coincided with the great tidal wave of Christian renewal known as the East Africa Revival," Jacobs recalled many years later.

In East Africa, for the first time in my life, I found a community of faith that had the markings of my Anabaptist dream. I was fascinated to discover that these Christians represented many different denominations, from Lutherans to Seventh-Day Adventists. That was my first reaction to the revival. The second was the realization that something must change within me if I was to know the living presence of Jesus Christ like these people did. But my spiritual pride and independent spirit, mixed with unwitting prejudice, conspired to build up a resistance.[5]

His desire to learn more about "the spirituality that fueled the faith of my own spiritual ancestors" in the Anabaptist movement reflected the interest he shared with others in renewing the Mennonite Church through recovery of the Anabaptist vision. As he was aware, "Mennonites had managed to turn a spiritual movement into a sociological community that preserved the virtues of the faith but lacked the immediacy of the living presence of Christ."[6]

He had also read widely in the writings of Paul Tillich and other modern theologians, finding liberal Protestant thought supportive of much of his own Mennonite tradition with its emphasis on the ethical aspects of Christian living. "I could still make a complete theology out of Christ's ethical teaching that exposed evils in society as well as in the human heart."[7]

"When we arrived at Katoke," Jacobs recalled, "I walked into the new freedom of the revival." It did not take long before Jacobs learned a new way of following Christ from African colleagues. "I changed my orientation completely during my first year there, as I discovered the freedom of walking in the light with students and staff." He said he found a strong revival group among the teachers at Katoke. "A teacher from Uganda was the leader. Eliezer Mugimba had been one of the students expelled from Mukono Divinity School with William Nagenda, Yona Mondo, and six others in 1941. Mugimba studied at Oxford University, one of the first Ugandans to go there, and took up a teaching career. He was keen in revival. Mugimba had a great influence on my life," Jacobs admitted. Eliezer Mugimba took the new teacher from America as his own mission field and helped him to a fresh relationship with Jesus.[8]

Jacobs found a warm welcome from the revival brethren when he repented and made a new beginning:

As I shared what was happening to me, the community reached out and embraced me as a "brother sinner" saved by grace. Immediately I felt at home. The East Africa Revival movement blended well with my Anabaptist theology, producing a vision much like that of the New Testament church. From that moment I found great delight and meaning in walking "in the light" with that vigorous community of faith.[9]

It was not at all strange that Katoke Teachers College became a center for the practice and spread of revival. Residential colleges like it dotted the nation, and when a revival movement occurred in one of them, teams of revived ones fanned out across the countryside on the weekends, inviting people to come to Jesus. In the providence of God several Ugandans who carried the fire of revival to the schools, where they contributed greatly to the spread of revival. As early as 1939 Simeon Nsibambi and Joe Church ministered at the Katoke College. "One way that revival spread was that Church of Uganda young people would opt for mission service, often as teachers," Jacobs recalled. "Festo Kivengere, for instance, was sent to Dodoma to teach." Kivengere was teaching in that dusty town in arid central Tanganyika in 1954 when he joined William Nagenda and other *balokole* on a visit to other places in the country, including the Mennonite and AIM mission stations.[10]

"Teams of revived Ugandans and Kenyans came regularly to Katoke College," Jacobs said. Jack Bennett, a captain in the Church Army, was headmaster when Don and Anna Ruth Jacobs arrived at Katoke. Bennett too was greatly impacted by revival and became an important person in their lives. "He was elected to Tanganyika Legislative Council and was gone more than half the time. I was his assistant and became acting headmaster when he went to Britain a year later."[11]

Revival and cultural insights blend

Don, Anna Ruth and young Jane Jacobs, 1958

Jacobs represented a new generation of missionaries. Earlier missionaries of every denomination arrived in Africa with profound knowledge of Bible truths and deep commitment to teaching Africans about salvation in Jesus Christ, but they had to come to grips with African ways on their own. The mission board appointed Don and Anna Ruth to Africa in 1953 but sent them first to the School of Oriental and African Studies at the University of London, where Don learned about the cultural dynamics surrounding the mission enterprise. The main purpose of the year in London was for Don to become qualified to teach in British territories.[12] Anna Ruth was already a qualified teacher in the American system.

Don had earned bachelor's and master's degrees in American and European history from Franklin & Marshall College in Lancaster, and from the University of Maryland. He had planned on a teaching career in America before a conversation with the Mennonite mission board, which resulted in a teaching assignment in East Africa. "We were eager to give ourselves to one term as educational missionaries and then return home to pursue careers as teachers. We ended up spending twenty years there."[13]

Katoke Teachers Training College, an interdenominational enterprise

The Mennonite mission became involved in formal education somewhat reluctantly, but joined with other missions in upgrading the Katoke Teachers Training College on the western shore of Lake Victoria. This was far from the Mennonite stations in the Musoma district, east of the lake. The school was the result of a cooperative effort by the Church Missionary Society, the Church of Sweden, the Swedish Free Mission, the Mennonite mission, and the Africa Inland Mission,[14] which formed themselves into the Lake Missions Educational Council in 1950. The Katoke board met for the first time in 1953, with Archdeacon Lionel J. Bakewell as chair and John E. Leatherman as secretary.[15] Not all the missions shared the same view of revival, but they worked together amazingly well, preparing an entire generation of teachers for the schools that soon dotted the landscape around Lake Victoria in Tanganyika.

As part of the intermission agreement, Mennonites started a boys boarding school at Bumangi, near Musoma, while the Mennonites and AIM together prepared study guides for Bible classes in all the cooperating missions. Dorothy Smoker, and Catharine Leatherman worked with AIM missionary Florence Tilley, Methusela "Matt" Nyagwaswa in writing the Bible Study manuals that were used by several denominations.[16] Like the three missionary women, Nyagwaswa found a new beginning in the revival. He was active in the AIM church at Mwanza when William Nagenda and Festo Kivengere preached there as part of a revival team in 1950. His conversion caused him some difficulty with AIM leaders, but for him it was the start of a life in union with Jesus Christ. Nyagwaswa was to figure prominently in the spread of the revival message not only in Tanzania but also in North America.

Leadership training

The small but significant Bible school at Bukiroba, on the eastern shore of Lake Victoria, proved to be an instrument of God for the spread of the gospel. John Leatherman and his colleagues George and Dorothy Smoker taught at Bukiroba Bible school. This paragraph from Leatherman's diary reflected the enthusiasm for God's work there. He ascribed it to the spirit instilled by revival:

> Again we must feel that this happy year of Bible school was large-ly the fruit of the closer bond of fellowship in Christ that existed among the students themselves and between students and faculty. Each day was begun with a worship and fellowship period in which the Word was permitted to speak to each one in accordance with his or her need. Pupil and teacher were on one level here. Murmurings, criticisms, doubts would be confessed and cleansed in the blood, with the result that minds and hearts were free from darkness to approach the work of the day. We can only thank God for his help in this ministry when we remember our own very lim-ited abilities and shortcomings, and our frequent need of cleansing from sin. We were constantly reminded that his strength is made perfect in our weakness.[17]

Elam Stauffer, by this time a bishop, recognized that the East Africa Revival had given the entire Mennonite mission fresh purpose and power:

We believe that the foundation of strength for carry-ing on the work, and of wisdom for solving problems, is invariably found as we walk in the light, in fellow-ship with him, and with one another. The revival bless-ings of the past have been price-

Teaming in the gospel. Front row, Dorothy and George Smoker; back row, Eunice Byler, Anna Ruth and Don Jacobs.

less in value, and it would be painful to contemplate what would be the state of the church apart from these blessings of cleansing from sin. And yet we seek for ourselves and our African brethren a fresh vision of the cross that will cause many to say, "Here I am, send me." In addition to this seeking the face of the Lord for the calling forth of laborers, we have replanned our Bible school curriculum.[18]

As African and American pastors and teachers shared deeply in fellowship meetings about their daily walk with Christ, missionaries recognized that "closer spiritual fellowship seems to require a sharing of financial knowledge with our African leaders." The executive committee of the missionaries on the field took the decision to make this information available.[19]

Greater educational opportunities and greater responsibility for Africans pointed to the inevitable day when Tanganyikans first and Tanzanians later would have full control of their churches and schools, but the most important ingredient was to be found in spiritual growth. "Largely through the channel of closer fellowship between missionaries, African pastors, and elders, the Lord has given these leaders a new concept of the part they will increasingly need to play in the indigenous onward-going church." The revival fellowship meetings brought unity and resolved differences. Leatherman wrote to the mission board, "When one observes how barriers created by suspicions and misunderstandings are broken

Ordained Mennonite clergy in Tanganyika, almost all touched by revival.

down through the medium of these fellowship gatherings, their value can hardly be overestimated."[20]

The revival message spreads and deepens

Twelve years after Rebeka Makura shared her testimony of God's grace at the Mennonite mission stations, the effect of the East Africa Revival was still visible in the lives of many. The sweeping nature of the early revival and the large-scale confessions and restitutions, however, were things of the past, and Leatherman saw the need for renewal:

> The church as a whole continues to give various evidences of the need for a new breath of revival, but we are nevertheless encouraged to see the little nuclei of brethren and sisters in each congregation who love the Lord and one another, and who are going deeper to possess new land. It is among these where one can witness even a deeper work of the Spirit than what is normally seen in more spectacular movings of the Spirit. Spontaneous fellowship meetings continue in a number of the congregations which satisfy the needs of those who are going on in this way.[21]

The Swahili periodical that Leatherman edited spread news from the revival. Each issue of *Mjumbe wa Kristo* printed "testimonies from brothers and sisters in many parts of East Africa" and reported what God was doing in the Mennonite mission. This helped to open the door for Mennonites to spread the gospel far and wide. "From time to time Muganda, Leatherman, Kisare, and Stauffer were invited to preach in Mwanza, in Bukoba, in Maseno, and in Mombasa."[22] These places covered an area of hundreds of miles and included both Tanzania and Kenya.

The work of the Mennonite mission increasingly reflected the impact of revival. "What we have to report, then, we believe to be meaningful because God has been walking among us, showing us our weakness and sinfulness and pointing us anew to Jesus, the fountain of living water." In fact, Leatherman wrote, "Revival is really nothing more than Jesus coming in to satisfy hungry hearts, and this is the revival that is still going on in a number of us in the church here."[23]

Church meetings were invariably renewal meetings. Elam Stauffer wrote of a conference at Bukiroba: "I am sure there are few who have not seen themselves needy. Many have opened their hearts for the Savior to come in and cleanse [them] anew."[24]

Recognizing the need for strong indigenous leadership

Spiritual growth was important as Stauffer sought to find and train African leaders. "The Lord keeps reminding us graciously from time to time that the days of our being conspicuous leaders is past," he told a member of the mission board. "We must permit our Africans to lead, and in fellowship with them, and in training them, make what spiritual contribution we can to the work here."[25]

Stauffer recorded "a thought brought out" at a fellowship meeting that "became very precious to all of us," especially in the light of the need to nurture African leaders for the African church. He wrote to his mission board:

> Every member baptized into the body of Christ by the Holy Spirit has some gifts and calling given to them for the body. All callings and gifts fit together for the welfare and edifying of the body and the body always has within itself whatever is needed for its edifying. When any new need arises, we must believe that the Spirit has right within the body the material that is needed to meet that need. Thus does Christ build his church in any land. May we labor together with him, as he builds, not as we think nor desire. It is his church and he must always be the head in every respect. To him be the glory.[26]

Walking in the light was crucial to building the church as the body of Christ described in the letter to the Ephesians. It took on quite practical aspects, as Elam Stauffer reported to the board back in Lancaster:

> We are assured we moved in the right direction when we took our African brethren into counsel in making our budget and in the use of our finances. It is not always easy nor without its problems, but it has dispelled ignorance and suspicion, and has enabled us to work together with more confidence, unity, and faith. Darkness can only be ousted, and kept out, by full light. Where this is, there will be humility, brokenness, and fellowship in the blood of the Lamb. This is never easy to the natural or carnal man. It is always working death, but from this death comes new life, resurrection life.[27]

Missionaries had much to learn, too, from their African converts, as Dorothy Smoker explained at the time:

From the old tribal life, with its absolute loyalty to the chief and to the members of the clan, the African brings to the new tribe of God a loyalty to the chief [Christ] which counts neither possessions nor life itself as important in comparison. He also can teach us something of fellowship and tender concern for the brotherhood that we do well to learn.[28]

The revival brothers and sisters took very seriously the need to bear one another's burdens. Walking in the light meant for them a willingness to give and receive counsel and correction. As a result, as Kevin Ward observed, "the *balokole* see themselves as a new clan, operating along the same lines as traditional clans, but also cutting across traditional clan obligations."[29]

The armed Mau Mau struggle tests the revival in Kenya

Christians in Kenya endured a fiery ordeal when many of them refused to take a ritual oath of support to the Mau Mau rebellion and were targeted for death as "collaborators with the enemy." They generally sympathized with Mau Mau aims of restoring Kikuyu land and gaining national independence, but "they could not accept the goat's blood, the curse, the promise to kill, and the banning of Jesus" that the oath implied. In 1953 and 1954 attacks on Christian villages were commonplace. Many Kikuyu chose to die rather than renounce the Lord Jesus Christ. It was a time of testing whether loyalty to Jesus could continue to bind the revival brothers and sisters of different nations and tribes.[30]

"During those dangerous days, one after another of our community was killed by the Mau Mau," one Kenyan recalled. "But we went on praising Jesus as we lovingly buried our dead with singing and testimony." When a certain teacher disappeared, Heshbon Mwangi and Neville Langford-Smith went together to look for him and found his body. Heshbon Mwangi was savagely beaten and his teeth knocked out with a tree limb. But the revival leaders stayed at their posts with their people. "Two brothers who faced death day after day by refusing to take the oath and helping and encouraging people hiding in the villages were Obadiah Kariuki and Heshbon Mwangi." Obadiah Kariuki, later bishop of Mount Kenya, was the brother-in-law of Jomo Kenyatta, leader of the Kenyan move for independence.[31]

The situation in Kenya continued to worsen, and the colonial authorities responded in kind. There were 72,000 detainees and prisoners behind barbed wire. The Christian Council of Kenya saw an opportunity for ministry and appealed to Orie Miller, executive secretary of Mennonite Central Committee, the relief arm of the Mennonite church. Miller brought this concern to the mission board, and they directed Elam Stauffer and John Leatherman to investigate the possibilities for Mau Mau prisoner ministry in Kenya. The missionaries concluded that they did not have the personnel to undertake a major expansion of this sort.[32] The mission board subsequently appointed Victor and Viola Dorsch to Kenya, but in the summer of 1956 decided to send them to Somalia instead.[33]

A pivotal conference for Mennonites, 1956

For the Mennonite spiritual life conference of 1956, William and Sala Nagenda and Festo Kivengere were invited as speakers. Mahlon Hess recalled that "attendance overflowed the shelter built in the center of Bukiroba station. As customary, the Mennonite hunters brought a number of game animals to provide meat to garnish the *ugali* [cornmeal mush], rice, and vegetables served to conference guests."[34]

Amos Horst, an American Mennonite bishop, and Paul Kraybill, mission board secretary, were also present. Horst was not pleased that the program committee, composed of Africans and missionaries, invited "several of the East African revival brethren to come and speak in the African Inspirational Conference held annually for the native Mennonite Church members." He reported to the board that "William Nagenda, Festo, and others of the revival leaders were there. . . . A few of our missionaries are still promoting the revival ideals, which give me no little concern."[35]

Elam Stauffer received their report in due course and wrote a personal letter to mission board secretary Paul Kraybill:

Mission secretaries Paul Kraybill and Orie Miller, with Bishop Amos Horst in Tanganyika.

Gamaliel's advice is quite good for revival movements, too. What is of man will come to naught, and we need to be careful lest we criticize what is of God. I feel certain God is working among us. We have much to learn yet, more than we thought at first. We want to go on with him who is walking among us. Your letter has put no distance between you and me.[36]

This Mennonite conference was one of the last engagements on Festo Kivengere's calendar before he left his teaching at the Alliance Secondary School in Dodoma and went to England that summer. The Anglican bishop in central Tanganyika, Alfred Stanway, secured a scholarship for him to study at London University for a diploma in education, beginning in September 1956. During his year abroad Roy Hession invited him to speak in the United Kingdom. William Nagenda also visited England. Festo and William spoke together to the Cambridge Intercollegiate Christian Union. A student remembered Festo's "irrepressible, infectious high spirits and joy in his faith." This was Festo's first opportunity to preach outside East Africa.[37]

The first wave of revival testimony included persons like Joe Church and William Nagenda, an Englishman and a Ugandan, both exceptionally gifted in communicating what God was doing in revival so that diverse audiences could understand. The next generation produced people like Festo Kivengere, who were zealous, thoughtful, loving interpreters and proponents of this new freedom in Christ. That generation was determined to shape the religious, social, and political activities around the profound understanding of new life in Christ, which was the hallmark of revival.

We now consider the careers of Kivengere and a few others who demonstrated that walking in light with Jesus Christ as committed fellowships was not self-centered pietism, even though it was known for its profound piety, but represented a new way of thinking and acting at all levels of life. They knew that following Christ was not a way to avoid the demands of life but was the way God had designed to strengthen and embolden disciples with an entirely new way to meet the daunting challenges of life. God used Festo Kivengere to help an entire generation to put into practice in every area of life what they kept experiencing every day—new, fresh winds of the Holy Spirit. Festo and those like him brought the gentle wind of God to blow with grace and truth.

Revival and the desire for political independence

A fresh political wind was blowing in Africa and around the world. Africans insisted on taking charge of their own political and economic destinies. They were no longer content to supply the West with raw materials and accept the crumbs for payment. In 1957 the British government gave their Gold Coast colony in West Africa its independence as the new nation of Ghana. Everywhere else decolonizing plans moved to the top of the agenda.

The wind was also blowing in British East Africa. Elam Stauffer observed that "in East Africa there have been such large and rapid changes from a variety of causes, that we have been challenged to adapt and adjust ourselves and our work to the changes. One of the great changes we face daily is the demand for freedom. Africa wants freedom in full measure, political, religious, and industrial freedom."[38]

As part of the effort to prepare a new generation for the challenges ahead, the educational authorities asked the Mennonite mission to set up two new boarding schools. Morembe Girls School began in 1958 with Mennonite missionary Rhoda Wenger as headmistress. The boys school, Musoma Alliance Secondary School, opened in 1959 under headmaster John S. Shellard, a CMS missionary. The school was not ready for the students recruited in 1958 so they took their first year at the boarding school in Dodoma, where Festo Kivengere was headmaster.[39]

Kivengere resigned his post as headmaster at Dodoma, effective the last day of 1958. The Anglican bishop in central Tanganyika, Alfred Stanway, an Australian, then invited Bishop Yohana Omari, his assistant, and Festo Kivengere to minister in Australia. Stanway was an accountant turned missionary clergyman. People knew him as a man of the Word, an excellent Bible teacher. At the same time he was an astute and meticulous administrator. Bishop Omari, his assistant, emerged as a Tanganyikan with extraordinary vision. He planted churches wherever he could. His rotund body and deep voice disguised his tender, Christlike simplicity. He had both feet in revival.

The team of Omari and Kivengere was a good choice for ministry in Australia. Both Omari and Kivengere were brothers in the Lord. The plan was for Omari, the bishop, to preach in Swahili and for Kivengere, the school teacher, to translate into English and give his own testimony. They left in December 1958 for a stay of several months.[40] As it happened, Kivengere remained in Australia on a preaching tour until November 1959, and Omari returned to Africa several months earlier.[41] That visit to Australia gave Kivengere a new way to look out onto the world. He would become a worldwide witness for Jesus Christ.

Changes occurring in the worldview of a missionary

In Tanzania, Don Jacobs struggled to reconcile his Western cultural outlook with what he was learning in Africa. "The new life I was living in the East African context challenged many of my Enlightenment-rooted pre-suppositions," he recalled.[42] The mission board assigned him to the Bukiroba Bible School when John and Catharine Leatherman returned to the United States in 1957 for their regular furlough. The Leathermans expected to return to teach in December 1958, but were delayed another year because of misunderstandings that had arisen as a result of their identification with the revival. This state of affairs prompted the mission to move Don and Anna Ruth Jacobs and their family from the Katoke Teachers Training College to the Mennonite Bible school at Bukiroba. While teaching at the Bible school, Jacobs' first experience in teaching Bible and theology in Africa, he wrestled with issues dividing Western theology from African understanding and wrote of the challenge:

> To further complicate my life, after three years as a teacher/principal in the national educational system, the church appointed me as principal of its fledgling Bible school. The in-service church leaders of the Bible school had no stomach for my worldview at all. These people believed in the immediacy of Jesus Christ as a living presence, the power of the Holy Spirit to enthuse life, the authority of the Bible as written, and the integral relationship of the natural and supernatural. It became clear to me that my African friends held to a worldview much akin to that of the New Testament writers, and to that of Jesus Christ, in particular. I saw that much of what I was teaching missed the mark because I was teaching out of one worldview while the listeners lived in another. They confided that my course on biblical theology would be more helpful and relevant to their pastoral work if I dealt with life as they were experiencing it.[43]

Don Jacobs as a young missionary, fetish burning in Tanganyika.

Jacobs discovered that he stood between two worldviews: one shaped by the Enlightenment, which discounted the supernatural or spiritual world in favor of a more materialistic world; and the other decidedly spiritual outlook, informing the Bible and, incidentally, African cultures too. For a time it created a struggle in Jacobs's spiritual life.

> A battle raged in my soul for quite a long time until at last I made a great leap. I agreed that the sayings of Jesus in the New Testament were actually his sayings, if not verbatim, at least true to his original meaning. That led to the next step of agreeing that Jesus' worldview was the real worldview. I had genuine problems with some aspects of Jesus' description of things. But the moment I relaxed on that point and identified with Jesus Christ's view of the world, the Bible made sense. Prayer took on new meaning, and the whole of life lit up in a new way. Serendipitously, I stood innocently but squarely in the world of the people with whom I was sent to live and minister.[44]

Determined to teach a contextualized theology, Jacobs pursued a doctor of philosophy degree at New York University when he returned to the States in 1959, concentrating on religion and cultural anthropology. He was coming to new understandings:

> Just as middle-class Americans meet a Jesus "who affirms the individual, penetrates his loneliness, and puts people back in touch with their own feelings and with one another," because this is where they sense their need, people around the world meet Jesus in the context of their own culture. As missionaries in East Africa we were impressed by the way Jesus broke right through and met people where they were. For example, he set people free from fear of evil spirits. He also liberated men from male chauvinism, so that monogamy became not only possible, but [also] desirable. He also gave women a new understanding of their worth before God.[45]

There was a paradox here. The good news of Jesus Christ had to come to the hearers in terms relevant to the life they were experiencing if they were to make it their own. But the gospel would inevitably change the hearer's worldview. The gospel could not come to Africans (or to Americans, for that matter) wrapped in the guise of an alien culture without disastrous results. Preaching Jesus Christ in Europe's African colonies as part of a "civilizing mission" often brought superficial conversions. Elam Stauffer considered these conversions as losses. When Africans took a harder look they sometimes recognized the shallowness of their understanding of Christianity:

> In the past he saw the white man as a clever, rich, powerful some-body. He reasoned that his god or religion must therefore be much more powerful than his own African beliefs. We are coming to realize that much of our heavy loss comes from this delusion of the African. Having tried the white man's religion, he finds it inadequate and unsatisfactory to his way of life.[46]

As Don Jacobs' concern with contextual theology grew, so did his wonder at the ability of revival to cross cultural boundaries. "How did missionaries absorb an African movement and make it applicable to Western theology?" he asked. The East Africa Revival was authentic in its African context, but no less authentic in the lives of men and women whose thought was thoroughly Western. "Dr. Joe Church and others did the theologizing and reflecting that proved helpful for British evangelicals to understand it and keep on track." He believed that *Ruanda Notes*, the publication of the Ruanda Mission, interpreted the revival for Anglicans at home. "John Leatherman and Elam Stauffer did this in our group. The Africans who came through later reinforced it." In this way, "missionaries were part and parcel of the movement, and the mechanism for its transfer."[47]

—11—

Revival Message Clarified and Unity Promoted 1959–1961

African society experienced the euphoria of independence as former colonies quickly moved to self-rule. Those were heady days as new economic and educational opportunities opened, not just in government and commerce, but also in churches that were themselves centers for development and growth. Some African believers enthusiastically entered this new world, joining political parties and adopting new methods of evangelism. Others clung to the tried and true ways.[1] These were not uniquely African problems or solutions. Worldwide evangelical Protestantism found itself in much the same situation in countries yearning to live free of outside domination.

With a desire for political freedom in the air, it was not surprising that the churches established by missions also demanded independence. This desire for self-determination often led to incendiary disputes among the leaders of the African churches, the missionaries, and mission agencies that sent the missionaries. Would the revival way of walking in repentance and in the fullness of the Spirit make any difference?

The revival fellowships that dotted East Africa did not need independence from any mission board or denomination because they were not birthed by any formal organization. They were completely self-reliant and established their own system of relationships, which they never recorded or codified. When they planned for a mission or a conference, for example, they relied entirely on the generosity of the fellowships. They handled large sums of money on their own. They simply walked in the light about finances. Don Jacobs reported, "I do not recall any accusation of misuse of finance in the years I was intimately involved in the ministries of the fellowships."[2]

So even though they were entirely autonomous, the fellowships did understand and sympathize with the groundswell of opinion pressing for independence.

Disturbing signs of unrest in the 1960s

The year 1961 was a time for constitution making as former colonies inched closer to full independence. It was not a year without disappointments and false starts, even turmoil in some places. It was definitely an opportunity for new directions for both churches and for governments.

The quickened pace of change affected everyone. In Kenya, Jomo Kenyatta, who'd been incarcerated during the Mau Mau troubles, was still in jail. But the British were now preparing Kenya for self-government.

Tanganyika was also moving toward independence, guided by Julius Nyerere. Nyerere, a Roman Catholic, was born and raised near the Bumangi station established by Clyde and Alta Shenk. Nyerere became the carrier of the torch for independence in Tanzania. He was highly regarded by Mennonites and others. It was a special occasion, therefore, when Julius visited Musoma during the heat of the independence movement, at the very time that Mennonite Conference was meeting there. John Leatherman recorded:

> March 15—Everyone went to see Bwana Julius. A great crowd awaited the plane which came about 11 a.m. We then went into our conference. At 3:30 we went to hear Julius speak at the post office field. . . . March 29—Today was Tanganyika's big day. It was officially announced that May 1st is the beginning of full internal self-government and December 28 [actually 9] complete independence. . . . May 1—Today was a big day in town marking the installment of Julius Nyerere as prime minister of Tanganyika and full internal self-government.[3]

Independence thus came to Tanganyika in 1961 and to Zanzibar in 1963. In April 1964 the two countries would form the United Republic of Tanganyika and Zanzibar, renamed United Republic of Tanzania in October 1964. Not every transition was as peaceful as the one in Tanzania. Bloodshed marked the last years of Belgian rule in Ruanda. A writer in *Ruanda Notes*, a publication of the Ruanda Mission, summed up the situation at the end of 1959: "Civil war had descended on peaceful Ruanda like a cloud, almost overnight, and no one seemed to know where it had come from and why people were fighting." Refugees poured over the border into western Uganda. Joe Church became entangled in the ethnic web in 1961 since he had "become a centre of political controversy in the Gahini area" through his friendship with members of the royal family, who were Tutsis.[4] In both Ruanda and Urundi the Hutus comprised about 80 percent of the population and the Tutsis about 20 percent. Even though the Tutsis were the minority, they usually held the positions of political power in both Ruanda and Urundi. Now and again the Hutus asserted themselves, demanding a greater voice in government. That was the situation in Urundi in 1961 when the leader of the Hutu political party was assassinated. From that moment any semblance of unity between representatives of Hutus and Tutsis disappeared. Worse was to come in later years as politicians and tribal leaders stoked the fires of hatred.[5] This presented a daunting challenge to the little flocks of brothers and sisters who walked in light and love as revival fellowships, embracing those of the other tribe with Calvary love. They were hated by the tribal leaders, who insisted on absolute tribal loyalty.

As we have seen, the East Africa Revival united men and women of different tribal and ethnic backgrounds, different denominations, different cultures. The revival brothers and sisters deplored any political system that set tribe against tribe, denomination against denomination, class against class. In 1962 political independence would come to these two East Central African districts, with Ruanda renamed as Rwanda and Urundi as Burundi. Yet continuing tribalism in both Rwanda and Burundi presented a huge challenge to the revival. Many brothers and sisters remained true. But that was costly because every time there was another mass killing between Tutsis and Hutus, it appeared that the revived ones were among the first to be slain.

Don Jacobs told of an incident that occurred several years later involving a person he greatly admired, Israel Havigumana. He was a Hutu who worked in reconciliation among tribal leaders in the early 1990s. He was the team leader of the African Evangelistic Enterprise in Rwanda. Havigumana was formed in revival. He had married a Tutsi wife. This was unacceptable to the hard-core tribalists. Havigumana served as the Rwandan team leader for African Enterprise. He was committed to apply the reconciling power of the cross of Christ and so gave himself to peacemaking between tribal leaders. When he lost his beloved wife through cancer, Havigumana was responsible to care for his three daughters. As tribal animosity escalated prior to the great bloodletting of 1994, the Hutu extremists warned Havigumana to stop trying to make peace. They tossed a grenade into his house; it destroyed the living area. Havigumana survived the blast. He must have topped the list of tribal enemies, because on the day the genocide started in July 1994 Israel Havigumana and his daughters were gunned down in their home. Only one daughter survived. Martyrdoms such as these were not at all uncommon.[6] Havigumana's "crime" was that he was a peacemaker.

God had provided the answer to lasting peace in Rwanda. It was the open door of reconciliation at the foot of the cross. Tribalism was so intense, however, that tribal leaders ordered their people to deal harshly with any meaningful spiritual or social relationship between the tribes. According to Rwandan brothers and sisters, this is a factor that blunted the impact of revival on the churches in Rwanda.[7]

The revival brothers and sisters were not organized in a way to protest to the evils of tribalism. They simply died as martyrs. Those revival brethren who were ordained as clergy did confront the political and tribal powers, with mixed success.

A more complete story of the brave martyrs of Rwanda was told in the book *Faith Under Fire*, by Antoine Rutayisire.[8] He gives examples of people who took the classical stand of the brothers and sisters in revival. They loved Jesus, and they loved people of the other tribes. That was a crime! Who knows how many brothers and sisters died during that horrifying time? Certainly thousands. They stand in the same line as the Kikuyu martyrs and the Ugandan martyrs.

There were no doubt some, maybe many, who abandoned the claims of the Cross of Christ and took up arms to defend their people, but they did so, not as "saved ones" but as backsliders.

The Rwandan experience stands in contrast to what happened in Kenya during the Mau Mau uprising, which was more of a racial war between the colonial settlers and the Kikuyu tribe. Nevertheless, the Kenyan brothers refused to take up arms either in defense of the Kikuyu or the settlers' interests. The brothers knew that the tribal oath declaring loyalty to the tribal ancestors was contrary to the gospel. In Kenya, martyrdoms of the brothers and sisters aroused the nation and ultimately assisted peacemakers to come to terms with the potentially destructive hostile feelings.[9]

The Mennonite missionaries were amazed at the response of the revived ones in Kenya to the escalating violence in the Mau Mau movement. As soon as John Leatherman returned from furlough in 1961, he and Don Jacobs set out for the revival convention at Butere in western Kenya, where they found another expression of unity:

There was an enormous crowd at the convention and the Spirit of God was present. Don brought a good message on Potiphar taking Joseph into his house. We again saw most of the brethren. After the afternoon meeting Festo [Kivengere] met with the Tanganyika group and made us hungry with an account of how God is reviving in Uganda again.[10]

Among the nine thousand people at the Butere convention was a student from St. Andrew's University in Scotland. She wrote in her diary that "Festo gave a masterly exposition of the story of Jesus at Bethany with Lazarus. . . . He is very lively and makes the Bible stories come alive."[11]

The meeting ended with messages by Joe Church and William Nagenda and several testimonies.[12] After the suffering of the Mau Mau uprising and the painful struggle for independence, the churches in Kenya moved forward, many of them united in revival.

Ongoing issues between Mennonite missionaries and their home churches

Mennonite missionaries who returned to the United States often met a chilly reception from Lancaster Conference leaders despite sincere efforts by the missionaries to understand the problems the conference leaders faced. Some in the conference leadership remained cool to the revival; they felt that they could not depend upon missionaries like Stauffer and Leatherman to enforce the conference's rules of behavior in Tanganyika/Tanzania.

Notable among Lancaster Conference's stringent rules during those years were an insistence on certain types of apparel, and for women, uncut hair and the prayer head covering. In order to enforce the rules, the bishops insisted on "exclusive communion," excluding from communion anyone not in harmony with the written conference discipline.

It was not easy for the bishops of Lancaster Conference to enforce these rules in their own districts. Some of the bishops felt that if the conference permitted missionaries to ignore the rules and regulations in their church-planting efforts overseas, their own positions would be weakened. They held that rules governing Mennonite behavior were universal and should be applied everywhere. So the conference pressed the missionaries to promise to enforce the rules in their work overseas.

Some missionaries felt that the conference was putting so much emphasis on rules of behavior that it contradicted a core belief held by the Mennonite Church since 1525: people are saved by grace and not by works of the law. Missionaries and many others in the denomination feared that pressing for obedience to a set of behavioral rules fostered a false notion of salvation by works. All could point to examples of Mennonites who obeyed the rules to the letter but lived untransformed lives.[13]

The theological underpinnings of the East Africa Revival were a strong insistence on conversion and the indwelling of the Holy Spirit, a daily walk with Jesus in the community, and an unquestioning belief in the authority of the Scriptures. These were doctrines that the Mennonite Church had embraced for centuries. The differences came in describing what the holy life should look like and how the brothers and sisters should be disciplined. Lancaster Conference pressed the missionaries to be more specific in how they were going to enforce discipline in the churches that they were planting. The missionaries were reluctant to make these kinds of pronouncements and preferred to see the African believers working it out in the African context. The missionaries' deference did not sit well with some bishops.

The Leathermans and the Stauffers had many interviews with the mission board and bishop board before they were permitted to return to Tanganyika in 1959. The bishops were responsible for faith and practice in the Lancaster Conference and were the supreme body when it came to decisions about the fitness of missionaries to represent them. The mission board, which presided under the authority of the conference, had some influence on the bishops, but the bishops had to make the ultimate decisions. So the conversation emerged as triangular, with the bishops in one corner, the mission board in another, and the missionaries in a third.

The internal debate had less to do with what was good for the newly planted African churches and more to do with the welfare of the Mennonites in North America. The discourse was often intense and led to many times of prayer. Ultimately, the bishops were satisfied with the stand that Stauffers and the Leathermans were taking and finally came to an amiable agreement with the missionaries. The mission board gave final approval to the Leathermans in September of 1959. "It was a big and glorious day," Leatherman wrote. "We were at last reappointed for Africa by the board, and without any objection from anyone."[14]

A month later, the bishops also approved Elam and Grace Stauffer for an additional term. Being the bishop of the Tanganyika Mennonite Church, Stauffer was seen as being a more pivotal person than Leatherman in matters relating to church discipline. Elam expressed his desire to work in harmony with the Lancaster bishops as much as possible. At the same meeting, however, the bishops requested changes in the proposed constitution of

Transition from mission to new Tanganyika Conference smoothed by message of revival.

the Mennonite Church in Tanganyika to include exclusive communion, feet washing at communion, and the devotional covering for women.[15]

Rather than debating the decisions of the bishops, Stauffer and the other missionaries quietly received the request. While appreciating the concerns of the American bishops, the missionaries realized that ultimately the Tanganyika Mennonite Church would determine the wording of its constitution with their own understanding of faith and practice. At this stage in the maturation of the Tanganyika church, some of the issues dividing the missionaries and the bishops seemed rather inconsequential. There was no significant difference between the beliefs of the Tanganyikan Mennonites and the American Mennonites. The fuss had to do with cultural issues and church discipline.

The missionaries felt at home in an ever-expanding array of churches because they had experienced fellowship with many in those churches. The era was one of ecumenicity, and the larger denominations welcomed the Mennonite missionaries to become engaged in the discussions and help where possible. The missionaries remained aware of the fact that their own denomination would frown upon joining any ecumenical movement. But as the winds of ecumenicity blew, the "saved ones" were looked upon for any help they could give.

An international fellowship emerges

On the way back to Africa in the fall of 1959, John and Catharine Leatherman were met in London by Roy Hession, who took them to his home for supper. Lawrence and Julia Barham were the other dinner guests. Lawrence Barham was a part of the East Africa Revival from the beginning; after thirty years at Kabale in western Uganda, he retired in 1958 to become general secretary of the Ruanda Mission. Later the church called him out of retirement to become bishop of Rwanda and Burundi. The Leathermans stayed with the Rev. John Collinson. "He is vicar of Penge and a dear brother." On Sunday friends took them to a Baptist church where "the pastor is Ken Furlong, another brother." Both John and Catharine spoke in the service and took communion. In the evening they "attended another communion service at John's church [Anglican]. After this a fair-sized group moved to a schoolhouse where a fellowship meeting was held. Here we met various folks who love the Lord, among them Robin Church, Joe's son."

Collinson took them to the airport on Monday night, and they arrived in Nairobi early Tuesday morning, to be met by another crowd of witnesses to the Lord's work in East Africa. It was surely a worldwide fellowship reaching across national, tribal, and denominational boundaries.[16] The Leathermans welcomed the idea of Christians living in harmony with one another, something that they were appreciating more and more as they experienced life together in revival.

They started a day later for Tanganyika and stopped at Tarime, "where a large group of our *ndugu* [brothers and sisters] had met for fellowship." Tarime, near the Kenyan border, was the first Mennonite station on the main road from Nairobi. John Leatherman wrote in his diary: "It was a tremendous time and our joy at reunion was unbounded. Someone finally called [a] stop [in the celebrating] or we might have become hysterical. How good of the Lord to bring us back again." They had "another huge welcome" when they reached Bukiroba a day later.[17] Elam and Grace Stauffer returned in the last days of December and met a similar tumultuous welcome.[18]

Reestablished in Tanganyika but moving broadly to promote unity

Home again in Tanganyika, John and Catharine Leatherman returned to the Bible school and fellowship meetings with revival sisters and brothers, who now included Jack Shellard, Anglican headmaster of the Alliance Secondary School. Leatherman and Shellard led teams on preaching missions to Musoma, the nearest large town.[19]

Don and Anna Ruth Jacobs returned from the United States in July 1961. Don took up his assignment as principal of the Bukiroba Bible school, recently upgraded to a theological college. John and Catharine Leatherman went to Nairobi to meet the Jacobs family, and the next day all went to a fellowship meeting at St. Stephen's Church with a number of *ndugu*.[20]

Back at Bukiroba, Jacobs was focused on the message of the revival in his preaching and teaching. John Leatherman testified: "This morning Don had a message which stirred my heart. There was sin in choosing my own way. We have turned everyone to his own way." And again, "Don had closing message again with subject—The Forward Look. This was looking to Jesus and was again stirring."[21]

Scarcely settled in, Jacobs was off to Kampala, Uganda, to arrange a peace conference to be held at Limuru, Kenya. Leatherman, on the other hand, left for Dodoma as a delegate to a church union conference. On his arrival the brethren had a fellowship meeting. The conference began the next morning at Mackay House, named for the pioneer CMS missionary Alexander M. Mackay (1849–90). Leatherman notes in his diary:

> There were about 30 delegates of Moravian, Lutheran, Anglican, and Mennonites. The discussion was rather general. Bishop [B. G. M.] Sundkler was the chairman. This afternoon they appointed a thesis committee which consisted of a Mr. Johnson [Lutheran from Dar es Salaam], myself, Theofilo, Musa, and another African. Our job was to outline the main points to be covered in the work tomorrow.[22]

They met at the home of Bishop Alfred Stanway, Anglican bishop of Central Tanganyika, and found no obstacle to closer union. "A working agreement was worked out for proceeding with union, and we finished up early this afternoon." After that expression of unity in spite of differences, "Tea was served for all at Stanway's house."[23]

The determination on the part of some to bring all denominations in East Africa together into a Christian church of East Africa never materialized. But that does not discount the unity that was already present, fostered in large part by the unifying effects of revival. This is certainly true of John Leatherman, who became an enthusiastic proponent of church unity because he experienced it in the revival fellowships.

Billy Graham campaigns

An effort at evangelism on a larger scale was taking shape early in 1960. Billy Graham planned campaigns at Moshi in Tanganyika, and at Kisumu and Nairobi in Kenya. This was the first time Graham held an evangelistic campaign in East Africa. "Festo Kivengere was somewhat dubious of the American evangelist's methods such as 'going forward' and 'follow-up,' but agreed to serve on a local team making arrangements for the crusade." Kivengere was already known as a gifted linguist, and Graham asked him to translate or paraphrase his sermons for meetings to be held in Moshi, at the foot of Mt. Kilimanjaro. Through this invitation, the American evangelist and his team came to know and respect the school superintendent (Kivengere) from Kigezi in western Uganda as a brother.[24]

John and Catharine Leatherman went to Kisumu on Lake Victoria to hear Billy Graham and meet with Kenyan *ndugu*. Revival brethren lent their full backing to the Graham meetings. John recorded in his diary:

> We got to Kisumu late morning and went to where Yosiah Kinuka, Jona Mondo, and Heshbon Mwangi were staying. Then to the Graham meeting. A huge crowd, perhaps 15,000, and the preaching was powerful.[25]

A bump on the revival road—"reawakening"

For the revived ones, a Jesus-centered faith meant an emphasis on discipleship. They had entered into an ongoing relationship with the Lord, and they determined to follow Jesus in everyday life. The cross was central. The life and teachings of Jesus as revealed in the Gospels provided a pattern of life in the shadow of the cross. This was essentially a matter of the heart.

But discipleship also has a social, cultural dimension. How should believers live out the new life that they were experiencing within? Throughout the history of the Christian church, followers of Jesus have faced the temptation to freeze their own experience and make it normative for everyone. It is common for people to believe that since they met the Lord in a certain way, others will surely encounter him in the same way. In addition, Christians who set out on the road of discipleship have always been tempted to codify rules for living faithfully. Both tendencies surfaced within the revival movement in the 1960s, and many of the faithful responded with a call to a reawakening.

As the Leathermans returned to East Africa, they encountered this call to be "reawakened." While in Nairobi en route to Tanganyika, they went with CMS friends to a large fellowship meeting at St. John's, an Anglican church in Pumwami, in Nairobi's industrial section. Leatherman learned of problems in the Kenyan revival movement. "Numbers of brethren were getting off the track with an over-emphasis on *kuamka* [Kiswahili word for 'arise,' as from sleep] but they now feel this is healed."[26] This was Leatherman's impression after limited exposure. He little realized that the reawakening was to have a profound impact on the revival in both Uganda and Kenya.

This call for a reawakening originated in Uganda and had strong appeal for those who felt that the revival brothers and sisters had relaxed in their zeal to follow Jesus.

The Reawakening gathers strength

During 1960 storms of more than ordinary force tested the revival, particularly in Uganda. That summer Yona Mondo and others in Kampala called the Church of Uganda to a reawakening. Why the need for a reawakening? Was not the original awakening of the early 1930s sufficient? As revival became more integrated into the life of the churches, some brothers and sisters felt that the movement had fallen away from the enthusiasm and zeal of the first generation. Mondo's message was, "The things we did ten, twenty years ago were marks of true spirituality. If we are to be truly spiritual, we must recapture them." He invited Christians to "awake from sleep" and repent of worldliness, which extended to such things as elaborate plaiting of the hair, immodesty in apparel, the questionable use of guitars, and buying insurance policies.[27] The revival folks needed to awake. The very word echoed Blasio Kigozi's call to "awake" (*zukuka* in the Luganda language).

Yona Mondo was a respected leader of the revival. He was one of the young men expelled from the seminary at Mukono with William Nagenda. Mondo had no desire to split the fellowships, and the leaders of revival did not want to break fellowship with him. The brothers and sisters continued to welcome him in team meetings and conventions long after he began preaching reawakening. William and Sala Nagenda and others at Namutamba welcomed his invitation for a fresh start and only later recognized the legalistic side.[28]

Simeon Nsibambi, still a highly respected voice in the East Africa Revival, did recognize the need for a fresh commitment, but he discerned that the "reawakening" road took a wrong turn. One person observed, "This search for a reawakening came to be expressed in conflicts over dress and fashion, about whether brethren should take out loans and become burdened with debt in order to improve their material standard of living."[29]

Nsibambi was reluctant to criticize Yona Mondo, an old and trusted friend, until he saw the direction Mondo's preaching led, which was that reawakening was the final stage of one's salvation. In short, it insisted that a person is saved, but that salvation is of no avail if one is not reawakened. Nsibambi observed: "This 'awakening' has been exalted, taking away the preeminence of our Lord Jesus and the salvation he offers, because that salvation is no longer important without 'awakening.'" Nsibambi perceived the error of "striving to gain righteousness and holiness by the laying down of rules and regulations of conduct and raising any Christian experience above that of walking with Jesus." Festo Kivengere, William Nagenda, and a host of others did what they could to keep the revival fellowship together through this difficult time. But in time the reawakening did cause division as "reawakened" brothers and sisters sought to exclude others and broke fellowship with those who did not obey their rules.[30]

As the controversy swirled, the usual fellowship meetings continued unabated in the churches or under the trees. Teams continued to preach in village schools and churches and in the marketplaces, and to meet in larger gatherings for teaching and renewal. And many thousands were "saved" by their witness.

Revival brothers become church leaders

The East Africa Revival was by now an integral part of the life of a number of churches. Young men beginning to study for ministry in Kenya, Uganda, and Tanganyika, regardless of denomination, were almost all shaped by revival fellowships. Church leaders, too, like Zedekia Kisare and Ezekiel Muganda in the Tanganyika Mennonite Church, were impacted by the revival. The African bishops who were starting to take charge of the Anglican Church in East Africa were nearly all *balokole*. In many parts of Uganda, particularly in the southern regions, the revival fellowships were the norm for Christian initiation and nurture.[31]

An early example of a revival brother taking on church responsibilities was Festo Olang, later Anglican archbishop of Kenya. Olang, along with his wife, visited the Mennonites on several occasions on the shores of Lake Victoria. Olang participated in the ministering team at memorable meetings in churches and schools in the region. That he was an Anglican clergyman seemed to make little difference as people came to Christ through his witness. Leatherman wrote: "The meetings were a blessing from heaven. I confessed my lack of love to the students this morning. One of them came to bring a number of things into the light."[32]

The question arose as to whether the brothers chosen to be church leaders would continue in open, candid fellowship with "ordinary brothers and sisters." Don Jacobs recalled hearing testimonies to the effect that the clerical collar can play tricks on the person that wears it if he is not careful. The collar has a tendency to grow: first it stiffens the neck; then as it grows, it covers the mouth, and finally it suffocates by covering the nose itself.[33]

The revival did not stand against denominations. Rather, it simply disregarded them since the leaders knew one another as repentant, joyful, Spirit-filled repentant sinners. In November 1960 the Leathermans and other Mennonites attended an ecumenical meeting in Nairobi, staying at the CMS guesthouse, "where we found Matovu and Erica Sabiti, Capt. [John] Ball, and Neville Langford-Smith." All of these were steeped in revival. They learned that their meeting would not start for another day, so "we then went up to the Mwika Bible School [operated by the Church of God] where Matovu and Omari are having meetings." Yohana Omari was then assistant bishop of Central Tanganyika. "Omari gave the messages this afternoon, and Catharine and I followed with testimonies."[34] This array of different denominations was impressive. Leatherman writes:

> The purpose of the Nairobi meeting was closer unity among Christians, a unity already experienced in the revival fellowships. The conference began this morning with delegates from a number of missions. Bishop [Lesslie] Newbigin was present. He is the secretary general of the Inter Missionary Council, also a bishop in the South India Church. Father [Trevor] Huddleston was also present. He is a notable personage who has recently been expelled from South Africa because of his defense of African interests.[35]

Each morning Newbigin gave expositions on Ephesians. During the day "interesting and profitable" discussions continued. In the evenings, John Leatherman, Erica Sabiti and many others went to the meetings at Mwika.[36]

As reported, these efforts to produce a unified church of East Africa never materialized. The revival brothers and sisters were not dismayed, however, because they had learned how to be truly one in the Spirit, whatever the names of the denominations.

A few weeks later there was a revival convention at Tabora in central Tanganyika. As usual, Africans and Westerners from many denominational backgrounds found closer unity as followers of Jesus. John Leatherman, along with his co-workers Nyerere Itinde and Zedekia Kisare, traveled from Bukiroba to Mwanza by bus. They found brothers there, Pastor Shem of CMS and Bill Stier of AIM, and they all took the train to Tabora:

> Quite a large group continued to come. Had morning and afternoon and evening meetings. The team meetings and early morning

fellowship meetings were heart-searching. The brethren all over recognize their much backsliding.[37]

Catharine Leatherman, Phebe Yoder, Elam Stauffer, Jack Shellard, and some African Mennonites came later. The morning and afternoon meetings were at the Moravian Church. Yona Mondo of Uganda and Bishop Omari of Tanganyika spoke in the morning; Pastor Matovu, a Ugandan serving as a pastor in Tanganyika at that time, preached in the afternoon. According to Leatherman, they brought "blessed messages of love and power."[38]

Dorothy Smoker expressed the attitude of missionaries of all denominations who had shared in revival blessings:

> We who are here in Africa have been learning afresh from our African brothers a great deal of the joyousness and carefreeness of walking together in company with Jesus in unbroken fellowship, swift to repent and be washed of whatever mars that fellowship on any side. So, it is no more that we feel ourselves to be always on the giving side, as parents to children. On the contrary, we need humbly to recognize the great contributions Africa has to make to us, and then to see what God expects us to share with her.[39]

Mission/Church relations resolved

Would this same spirit of unity ease the integration of mission and church? Mission boards of many denominations recognized the need to give Africans control of their own churches. In 1960 the Lancaster Conference mission board and bishop board decided to grant autonomy to the Tanganyika Mennonite Church and sent a deputation of three to meet with the general church council at Shirati in August. John Leatherman expressed his amazement at "the liberty the deputation is offering to the Tanganyika church. . . . I see how these men are making no attempt whatsoever to tell the African church what to do." The meeting went smoothly. "There was the official turnover of responsibility, and we were constituted a separate conference." Mahlon Hess recalled: "The draft constitution was adopted. Everyone joined in the revival song. That was on August 25, 1960."[40]

Early in 1961 Tanganyika Mennonite Church met to adopt their constitution and to choose delegates to visit Mennonite churches in the United States and Canada the following summer. They sent Ezekiel Muganda and Zedekia Kisare, two revival brothers, on this mission.[41]

—12—

Africans Strengthen Fellowship with Americans by Visits and Residence 1960–1964

Mennonite missionaries on furlough first introduced the revival message. They did their best to interpret the message and testimony of revival for their friends and audiences in America. From the witness of many, the message came through with powerful conviction and living hope, profoundly blessing hungry hearts. At the same time the writing and speaking of people like Roy and Revel Hession and Norman Grubb bolstered the witness of the missionaries, though neither of them worked as a missionary in Africa. They were extremely helpful in spreading the good news of freedom in Christ. But the circle would be complete only when Africans appeared with the message.

The time had come when African brothers and sisters would interact more intimately with the Western culture. To some, the impact of their message was oversimplification or even naive, while for others the message struck as a sword into their hard hearts, convicting of sin and leading to repentance, renewal, and new power in the Holy Spirit.

Africans traveling to North America with the message of new life in Christ represented the return of the tide, a "blessed reflex," as Wilbert Shenk noted in the foreword of this book. The church had sent out missionaries with the message of salvation in Jesus Christ—a message that produced abundant fruit. The visit of African brothers and sisters to America was a gentle wind of God, a breeze of blessing and an arresting phenomenon. They were calling Americans to cast off accretions they had allowed to bind and strangle them, and thus find true freedom and salvation in Jesus Christ. Their message was as simple and as demanding as that.

This chapter details how the ministry of African brothers and sisters stirred the hearts of hundreds, and how North Americans bonded with those who became true members of one family of faith—refreshed by the same wind of God that was bringing life to so many in East Africa.

Nagenda among the Mennonites in 1960

The first to travel to North America was William Nagenda, from Uganda. After ministering in Brazil with Roy Hession, Nagenda arrived in New York in March 1960. Hession had to cancel his American appointments to go back to England, but Nagenda was available.[1] Erma Maust arranged a busy schedule for the days following his arrival. Emma Good and Erma Maust drove to New York to meet him.[2] Clyde and Alta Shenk, missionaries home on furlough, also traveled with Nagenda on this long tour. Erma found it a learning experience. In this way the bonding between the revived ones in North America and Nagenda grew stronger. Traveling together and sharing in ministry together, as a team, gave them ample opportunity to follow the simple way of walking in fellowship with Jesus Christ and with one another.

The whirlwind of Nagenda's engagements included a fellowship meeting in the Bronx; a fellowship meeting at Mervin Miller's home in Lancaster County; a night service at Moore's Brethren in Christ Church in Lewisberry, Pennsylvania; the chapel at Messiah College, Grantham, Pennsylvania; an evening fellowship meeting in Westover, Maryland; a fellowship meeting at Rev. Wayne Lawton's Free Methodist mission in Washington, DC; chapel service at Eastern Mennonite College, Harrisonburg, Virginia; a fellowship meeting at Marvin Plank's home in Scottdale, Pennsylvania; a fellowship meeting in East Liverpool, Ohio; then onward to Niagara Peninsula in Beamsville, Ontario, and a fellowship meeting at Wainfleet, Ontario.[3]

Erma reported:

> As you know, our brother William Nagenda from Africa was with us in April, and I with Clyde and Alta Shenk had the privilege of traveling with him for about ten days as we went to the different places. We were coming home from New York City the day after William arrived when as we drove along William said, "The Lord has been helping me to be very weak." I was challenged and came to the Lord to know in my own experience what William was talking about.[4]

Nagenda's messages struck a deep resonance with his listeners everywhere. Paul and Miriam Burkholder wrote that they were praying for the travelers and testified to what they heard in the New York meeting:

> We want you to know that we have been standing with you these days as you and William have been linking up with the brethren in this end of the country. We are believing that God has been doing great things as Jesus is lifted up. The word that night at Glenn's [Zeager] was certainly what I needed. In all this upheaval with our churches here in N.Y.C., it is so easy to begin to carry our burdens instead of giving them to Jesus.[5]

Driving from place to place with Nagenda, Erma Maust also learned more of what he meant by being weak. It was not always an easy lesson:

> As we traveled many hours together the next week and had many deep talks, I seemed to know less and less, nothing seemed to work, and the devil would put me under a cloud again and again. . . . For it seemed to me William never understood me and I dare not explain or I'd be vindicating myself, but at once I knew that was pride and the Lord helped me to quickly repent and continue to open my heart as we drove along. . . . I had to come to the Lord and confess that deep down I don't really want to be weak. Then I saw that it is one thing to know one is weak, even confess it freely, but quite another to be willing to be weak. Since then the Lord has put a very deep longing in my heart to be weak that Jesus may be all and in all.[6]

As soon as Nagenda concluded his meetings in Ontario, he flew to the West Coast, where an equally grueling schedule awaited him. Don Widmark met his plane and drove him from one appointment to the next. His experience was much the same as that of Erma Maust and Clyde and Alta Shenk: "You cannot live with a man who is as transparent before the Lord as William Nagenda is for sixteen days without coming to know him intimately." Widmark had not shared in the revival fellowships in East Africa, so some things seemed strange to him:

> The first day William began to repent as he looked at the schedule as there were so many meetings and he was so long away from his home. Tired in body, he just couldn't see how the Lord could see

him through it. He was repenting so much, and on such little matters, that I thought he was carrying this matter of confession of sin and repenting too far.[7]

Weary he might be and, as he confessed in his first meeting, cold and dry, but William kept on sharing at meeting after meeting what he had learned of walking with Jesus in discipleship. At a women's prayer fellowship in Fresno he preached on Jesus meeting the woman at the well. "It was in such power, so fresh, as ear had never heard it before." He used his illustration about the mirror, "how when we looked into it we not only see the mirror [Jesus] but we also see ourselves." An early morning breakfast meeting in Hollywood presented a special challenge. They were reading the ninth chapter of Revelation that morning. William had never spoken on that chapter before and wondered why they had not read from the Gospels. This chapter is about the first two woes, a grim text to preach on, and William had no time to prepare a message.

> There were two thoughts that he asked us to consider: the greatness of the love of our God toward all his creation—how concerned he was for the grass of the earth, all green things, and the trees, then how much more [concerned for] man, whom God seeing in his need and fallen state came down in his Son to redeem such as us back to himself. Second, he asked us to see the holiness and righteousness of God, and yet he considered men who would not repent. Then from this he drew some practical everyday applications to the men present that would give one to think that he had personal insight into the problems of almost everyone there. Truly we all went away seeing Jesus as Lord in a new way.

William was the speaker at an Abundant Life Conference held over a weekend. He saw this as the high point of his West Coast visit "for it gave the Spirit time to give a more complete picture of Jesus Christ to be all we need." Widmark reported:

> At the Friday night meeting he spoke on the Holy Spirit from Acts, chapters one and two, seeing all the preparation preceding the coming of the Holy Spirit, the mighty wind, tongues of fire, and other tongues—[these] were all set in the background when Peter stood and preached Jesus Christ. The message was not the gifts

but the giver. It was a precious night for again we saw more clearly the work of the Holy Spirit was to exalt Jesus. He came and did just that for us on that evening.

Reflecting on the impact that William Nagenda made on his life, Don Widmark recalled an event that he could not forget:

> We were driving north from Los Angeles to Fresno. The sun was just coming up and casting long shadows from the hills over Bakersfield and the valley below. William had just awakened from a snooze and was looking around, when he said, "Don, do you have any weak brethren who know that they are weak?" I asked what he meant. William went on to say, "You Americans are wonderful people. You are so strong. You just know how to do things, get things done, organized, so efficiently." I was beginning to be really confused. "You know how to do things so well you really don't need Jesus too much. Don, do you really have one person who is weak, who knows it, and so in all things he can trust him who alone is strength to do for him all and in all?"

Weakness and complete reliance on Jesus was one of Nagenda's favorite themes, an understanding that shaped his own spiritual life as well as his preaching. But in this conversation he recognized a problem in sharing that insight with American audiences. From his first speaking tour in England, Nagenda had resisted any attempt to translate revival into a formula or a series of stages in the Christian life. He was equally emphatic in his visits to the United States and Canada that Jesus must be at the center and believers must let nothing take his place. Christian churches were busily promoting great evangelistic crusades, to which many thousands responded. Many Protestant denominations were engaged in mergers and ecumenical dialogue. Programs for adults, children and youth, small groups, and renewal movements were everywhere part of congregational life. No one could disagree with Nagenda's message, but without a book to buy, a course to enroll in, a committee to form, there was no need to organize around it. Is this one reason why the revival changed individual lives in North America but never took deep root in the churches as it did in Africa? Or did Nagenda's insistence on avoiding formulas liberate the message? It was hard to tell.

There was no question that Americans found new life in the preaching of Nagenda and other African visitors. Paul Burkholder wrote from New York: "Erma, there does seem to be something about the messages of our African brethren that brings such freedom as they say 'of soaring birds.'"[8]

Nagenda, like others touched by the East Africa Revival, was not hostile to the gifts of the Spirit, so long as everything exalted Jesus Christ. Similarly, he preached a powerful sermon in a church that was established in what some called the Holiness tradition, seeing holiness as a permanent state rather than an ongoing experience of being continuously made holy by the blood of Jesus. His message of the need to repent of sin every day did not fit well with their theology, according to Widmark:

> As William spoke it seemed what he was saying was in direct conflict with the teachings of the church, yet no one could doubt that Jesus had spoken deeply to those in the service that night, for as the altar was opened for those who saw themselves to be unclean before a holy God, young and old alike came forward and plunged beneath the cleansing stream.

After speaking in churches all over California, in as many as three different pulpits on Sundays, Nagenda and Jacobs flew from Los Angeles to Tucson, Arizona, where Clair Richardson had arranged for William to meet with friends. "We met in the Christian and Missionary Alliance Church with Lutherans and Methodists and many other denominations in attendance." He had other meetings in Tucson before he left for a final appointment in Phoenix. Then he flew off to Uganda. Widmark recorded, "William stopped on each step ascending the plane and waved a white handkerchief with a glow of heaven on his face."[9]

The Mausts increasingly active in sharing testimony and teaching, in 1960

God was calling Erma and Herbert Maust to a most significant but equally demanding ministry. It required long absences from their home and family and was quite tiring. They visited people who were touched by Nagenda and others. The Mausts knew the value of an ongoing relationship with Jesus and of fellowship with one another. They knew that this was the key to spiritual growth. And they stretched themselves to fulfill that ministry of love and encouragement.

The Mausts had a busy summer with their ministry of helps. When the school year ended in June, they traveled to New York to help with vacation

Bible school at Seventh Avenue Mennonite Church, as they had in other years. At the end of July they went to Homer, New York, where Erma was scheduled to speak each day at the weeklong Central New York Bible Conference.[10]

In September Erma attended a large fellowship meeting at Laurelville Mennonite Church Center in western Pennsylvania. Instead of one visiting speaker as customary, there were several, as Erma observed: "George Smoker, Don Jacobs and his wife, Anna Ruth, and Rhoda Wenger from Africa were with us as well as K. V. Cherian from India. . . . The word of the Lord for us Thursday evening was 1 Samuel 22:2: "Everyone . . . in distress and . . . in debt and . . . discontented . . . [came unto David], and he became a captain over them." We saw we are all poor, weak, and needy, but if we will but come into the cave of Adullam [to Calvary] to our David, Jesus, he will be our captain and fight our battles."[11]

Erma Maust shared one important lesson from the Laurelville meeting with those on her mailing list: "Just because I was broken yesterday does not mean that I am broken today. Just because I was broken this morning does not mean that I am broken now. The important thing is, Am I broken now?"[12]

In her diary she recorded another thought that seemed to speak to her own situation:

Revival conference at the Laurelville Camp near Mt. Pleasant, Pa., 1960.

If the prayer of Jesus is to be fulfilled, that we all may be one as the Father and Son are one, it must begin in our homes. We must be willing to break before the Lord and then put all into the light with one another. It is not giving in to one another that brings us into this oneness, for this oneness produced by the Spirit is only maintained as we are both willing to break before the Lord and put all into the light with one another.[13]

Herbert and Erma Maust left Laurelville Church Center and headed toward Chicago. Their plan was to drive across the country for fellowship meetings in California. Changes in class allocations eliminated Herbert Maust's teaching position at the Kraybill School, so he was free to travel with his wife. They had arranged speaking engagements at different places on their route. Erma had a meeting in Baraboo, Wisconsin, one night and in Blue Earth, Minnesota, the next. "We sat in a circle in the rear of the church. . . . Herbert opened the meeting and then turned it over to me for the message from Luke 19." At other stops Erma found her listeners disappointed that she did not speak on gifts of the Spirit. Her emphasis, as always, was on Jesus Christ, God's invaluable gift to all who would believe.

At Glendale, California, Don Widmark greeted the Mausts, and they prepared for a weekend fellowship meeting with old friends on the team.[14] "Our brother K. V. Cherian had arrived early that morning. Dorothy Smoker called and, as soon as she could, came over, and we had a precious time of fellowship." Don Phillips from Brazil and Clair Richardson from Tucson were also on the team that week at the Falling Springs Lodge fellowship. They all recognized "how important it is that the team meets for a time of prayer and walking in the light with one another and that we are deeply one."[15]

More opportunities to speak were coming to Erma Maust. During their California trip she addressed a revival prayer fellowship at Pacific Palisades and chose Matthew 15:21-28 as her text. There were other fellowship meetings in Costa Mesa and Fresno. "Each Monday and Tuesday evening we have been attending the two fellowships going regularly here in the L.A. area. . . . There are a number of young people attending, and it is precious to see the openness in them. It reminds me of those early days back home when the Spirit was stirring up people and one told another what the Lord was doing and the fellowship grew." Erma had other speaking appointments in San Diego and at the Brethren in Christ Church in Upland and in Pasadena. Dorothy Smoker was asked to join Erma in one meeting. Erma was excited: "It will be wonderful to work with her as a team; the Lord has made us so deeply one."[16] Erma had more meetings in Phoenix and Tucson and then returned to California for the Los Angeles Fellowship Retreat in November.[17]

Erma was also learning more about the meaning of discipleship herself, noting on this trip:

> One thing came home to me very forcibly: it is so easy to be satisfied in praying for revival, get lifted up on a wonderful plane, rather than seeing revival is simply going the way Jesus walked, the way of coming down, of being weak, that Jesus may be all in all. I saw as never before the one thing hindering revival more than anything else is—God would not get the glory. Either we would take it ourselves or we would give it to another.[18]

Yustasi Ruhindi of Uganda joins the New York fellowship

As God was setting people free on the West Coast, precious things were happening in the East as well, in the absence of the Mausts.

The New York fellowship that met at Glenn and Florence Zeager's home was regularly fed by visiting Africans and missionaries. Yustasi Ruhindi, an Anglican minister and one of the revival brothers, came to the United States to study at Berkeley Divinity School in New Haven, Connecticut. He made contact with the revival fellowship in the Bronx.[19] "He has been getting down to New York and has been a mighty blessing to the brethren there." Over the holidays he visited Herbert and Erma Maust in Pennsylvania, and Erma responded: "The Lord sent him over to us with Glenn Zeager during his Christmas vacation. He was such an encouragement to me."[20]

The fellowship welcomed young men who came to the city for alternative service in hospitals and social-welfare agencies. The Selective Service Act had a provision for drafted conscientious objectors to perform alternative service. David W. Shenk, born in Tanganyika in 1937 to Mennonite missionary parents Clyde and Alta Shenk, was literally raised in revival. He gave his life to the Lord as a child and grew up completely surrounded by revival brothers and sisters. When he returned to the United States in 1952 for schooling, David became aware of the gulf between "the mainstream of Mennonites in Lancaster Conference" and his father's "Jesus-centered and grace-filled message." The objections raised by the bishop board to his parents as representatives of the Mennonite Church shocked young David.

Bill Scott with David Shenk, son of Clyde and Alta Shenk.

The censure of his parents and other missionaries for their role in the East Africa Revival clarified his own beliefs, and he identified completely with the revival brothers and sisters. David went to New York to do his alternative service and was soon made unit leader for the Mennonite conscientious objectors in the 14th Street unit. David and his wife, Grace, were part of the revival fellowship and introduced fellowship meetings at the unit residence, Menno House. Church authorities thought this divisive and did not permit the younger Shenks to return to Tanganyika/Tanzania until David had proved his loyalty to Lancaster Conference by teaching two years in Lancaster and attending a conference church.[21]

Fellowship, teams, and conventions in the United States

The Mausts seemed to have little rest as they returned to their Pennsylvania home. They were soon busy in organizing fellowships again. As in East Africa, people came from local fellowships to meet as a team and arrange for larger conventions. Erma wrote of one such gathering:

> Today we had one of the best team meetings we have ever had. It was so good seeing them coming in from the east and the west, the north and the south. Paul Burkholder and Glenn Zeager from New York City; Marvin and Mildred Plank from Scottdale; Ronald and Marjorie Lofthouse, Charles and Pearl Bonner, and Lucille Wolgemuth from Grantham; Ellis Rowe from Dalmatia; Jean Griswold and a friend from West Chester, Pa.; Wayne and Mary Lou Lawton from Washington, DC; Abe Minnich from Westover and Bill Scott from North East, Maryland; and Don Jacobs from Africa [home on furlough].[22]

They planned a Fellowship Convention at Keswick, New Jersey, although there were no special speakers:

> The evening meeting opened with great anticipation as about sixty of us met for the first session. Before the meeting as a few of us

met to wait upon the Lord for his word to us, someone read 1 Peter 1:18-19. As this portion was read, the Holy Spirit began to put within our hearts a great longing for the Lamb of God. With this also came the realization, it is the Holy Spirit who reveals the Lamb, that we need to depend wholly upon him to do it and not upon wonderful speakers or messages.[23]

Revival conference at Keswick Grove, N.J

As soon as the convention was over, Herbert and Erma Maust left for Ontario, where they spent time with Simeon and Edna Hurst on furlough home from East Africa. "Tuesday evening they had three other ministers in to spend a time in fellowship. They are hungry and Simeon sees the need of carrying on as the Lord opens the way." They spent a day in Kitchener, where "Simeon had the chapel period at the Rockway Mennonite High School and then had a class on missions over at the Ontario Bible School."[24] The Mausts completed their circuit of the east in New York City and left there March 16 by plane for Tucson.[25]

They held meetings in Arizona, California, Washington, and Oregon over the next two months. Roy Hession had written to ask them "to get into fellowship with Canon Dick Wooton, an Episcopalian missionary from West Pakistan, whom God had met in a new way through Dr. [Joe] Church, William [Nagenda], and Roy [Hession]." Wooton arrived in Los Angeles when the Mausts did, and they traveled together much of the time they were on the West Coast.[26]

One Sunday evening the Mausts, Don Widmark, George and Dorothy Smoker, and Dick Wooton attended a fellowship meeting of charismatic Episcopalians and Lutherans. "God has been working among these people; some of their priests as well as their laity have been saved, filled with the Spirit, and are exercising the gifts of the Spirit." But Erma Maust was still uncertain about the charismatic movement:

At first I was a bit fearful as to what we might get into. But the Lord helped me to repent of all my fears and by faith he helped me take the oneness Jesus prayed we as believers might know. He did the rest. We had a most blessed

Zedekiah Kisare and Ezekiel Muganda visit Paul Jacobs, Don's father, in Johnstown, Pa., with Edna and Simeon Hurst, on left and son Elwood on right.

time. They received us warmly. Dick Wooton first told how God had worked in his heart and how Jesus had cleansed. Dorothy followed with how God brought her to a consciousness of her need through the testimony of saved Anglicans in Africa; how Jesus had come in with his cleansing blood and changed her relationship with her husband, fellow missionaries, and the Africans. Then I followed by sharing how God had first stirred up hunger in me through the testimonies of the missionaries, bringing it up-to-date how Jesus is saving me now.

The message of the East Africa Revival was unfamiliar to these good people, who did not fully understand their own experience. This cleansing day by day is new to them, for it seems these people were saved, filled with the Spirit, speaking in tongues, and exercising the other gifts of the Spirit all at once. They hardly know themselves what is happening. When we speak of daily cleansing in the blood of Jesus and light concerning the daily walk, this is all new to them. The door is wide open to go back, and how I long to meet with them each week, not to counter them on exercising the gifts or speaking in tongues, but to lovingly help them to see how to "walk with Jesus" also.[27]

In Seattle the traveling group took part in a large Spiritual Fellowship Conference at King's Gardens. "On the team were George and Dorothy Smoker, Don Jacobs, Charles Higgins [Nazarene pastor from Pasadena],

Harriet Smith, Don Phillips [Seventh Day Baptist minister], Herbert and I." They drove there with Harriet Smith, "a missionary on furlough from Uganda and in fellowship with the brethren there."[28]

While Herbert and Erma Maust were still on the West Coast, the East Coast brothers and sisters held a fellowship at Camp Pinebrook near Stroudsburg, Pennsylvania.[29] Marvin Plank reported that they felt lost without Simeon Hurst, Don Jacobs, Yustasi Ruhindi, or the Mausts present; and that someone remarked: "Yes, we have always been saying, we are come together to see no man save Jesus only. So now it looks like Jesus is saying, 'We will see whether these folks really mean what they say.'"[30] They saw Jesus!

At a June fellowship in Scottdale, Herbert and Erma Maust met Zedekia Kisare and Ezekiel Muganda from the Mennonite church in Tanganyika. Erma testified:

> The Lord arranged that the brethren from Africa who are visiting the churches these months should be at the Planks for a fellowship that evening. It was a precious time. One of these revival brethren said in closing, if revival stops it is always one of these three points—an unwillingness to really repent, or an unwillingness to be utterly broken, or an unwillingness to walk in the light fully about that which God has done for us.

Erma Maust felt personally convicted at the Scottdale fellowship meeting. These men, Kisare and Muganda, were not returned missionaries, sharing their testimonies; they were Tanganyikans touched by the same message of new life in Christ as the missionaries. Their testimonies amplified what the renewed missionaries were talking about. "I praise the Lord for the new work he has been doing in my heart just since Monday evening. How blind we can be to our own sin." The Mausts invited the two visitors to their Lancaster County home for another fellowship meeting.[31] Erma also found new freedom in this second meeting with East African Mennonites:

> I feel we have just barely begun to experience revival when we sit in fellowship with these brethren. Not that they are wonderful people, they are not. Not that they have a wonderful message, it is not, for it is so simple one might be tempted to think, "Why make so much of that?" But the most amazing thing is that the Spirit has liberty to go deep in one's heart and search you out; you cannot go on as you did after meeting these revival brethren.[32]

In another letter Erma remarked on the impact Ezekiel and Zedekia made in their rather quiet ministry:

> I praise very much for fellowship with our two African Mennonite brethren who are here in the States visiting the home church. The Lord so challenged me about this matter of brokenness through fellowship with these brethren.[33]

At the time of their visit Erma wrote to another friend:

> I know what you were speaking about in your letter when you said you feel so weak and inadequate for the task the Lord has called you into. I so often feel the same way when counseling people. But the Lord helped me in this manner—he showed me this was just what he wanted, this was just where he would have me, this was where he could do all if I came confessing my utter helplessness to him but then not stop there, but as I come to him in my weakness then to begin to thank him for this need I do have Jesus. The phrase "Thank you, Lord, [that] for this need, I have Jesus" has become more than a phrase, it has become life with a capital "L."[34]

In July 1961 there was a farewell fellowship meeting at Messiah College "for the Don Jacobs and George Smoker families, who will then almost immediately be returning to the African mission field."[35]

Herbert and Erma Maust were on the road again after the Messiah College fellowship meeting, traveling to northern Pennsylvania, western New York, and Ontario for more meetings and speaking engagements. Marcus Lind invited the Mausts to spend a month visiting Mennonite churches in Oregon, but Erma hesitated to leave fellowships closer to home. She felt a call from God to strengthen the local fellowships near their home:

> There are calls coming from new ones in whom God is working right here in our own Lancaster County and in our own church where up to this time we have had little or no opening. God has begun to work in a group about 30 miles south of us in a Mennonite church, and they are almost begging for us to come and fellowship with them as they meet every two weeks. We plan to meet with them this coming Sunday afternoon. Now I know personality is not the answer to the needs of these people, but if

this is the Lord's call and all these things are an indication that we are to stay here at this time, we need to know and heed. We do need light on all this.[36]

In October Erma reported that she and Herbert had been meeting with these new fellowships on a regular basis. "We have been having some precious fellowship with new groups in whom God is working and who are meeting for fellowship in our own Mennonite church. Praise the Lord also that this revival does not take us out of our churches, but rather Jesus frees us to allow him to live his life in us right where we are."[37]

Fifty-six people came to the fellowship retreat at Pinebrook in the Pocono Mountains of northeastern Pennsylvania in October, although it was "the first time we have ever met when we did not have someone we could look to through whom the Lord would minister to us at some time during the conference. But Jesus was there."[38] They relearned the lesson of dependence on Jesus to raise up message bearers.

With the Smokers and the Jacobs family back in Tanganyika, the revival fellowship had no obvious speakers for their conventions. But this was soon to change. After the regular fellowship meeting in Scottdale, the Mausts and the Planks finalized plans for the next convention when William Nagenda, Festo Kivengere, and Roy Hession would all be part of the

Don Widmark introduces Roy Hession to U.S. inner-city ministries.

speaking team. They also talked with Don Widmark about West Coast meetings for the three men.[39]

Festo Kivengere had an invitation to speak at the InterVarsity Christian Fellowship Missions Conference at Urbana, Illinois, in 1961. William Nagenda was also coming. He and Festo planned to stay for about two months. Roy and Revel Hession were to be in the United States at the same time, and William agreed that they might all be together for one conference. Roy asked Erma Maust, "Might it not be right for you and those on the West to look to God for a conference center or a school in a central place for such a conference, when folks from the East, West, and South [Ernie Gilmore and friends from the Southern Presbyterians], and from Canada would come together, along with hungry ones they might bring, for a glorious time together?"[40]

Roy Hession.

Roy Hession was developing a quite close relationship with Ernie Gilmore, the pastor of the First Presbyterian Church in Moultrie, Georgia, during the late 1960s and early 1970s. Ernie longed to see persons in his own congregation enter into the freedom of Jesus Christ as he had under the ministry of Roy Hession. Ernie Gilmore's personal secretary through those years, Betty Sanders Hendrick, commented about him:

> He was a man of great stature, very open and honest in every way, and when he was right he was very, very right and when he was wrong, he was very much so, but that was seldom. He brought life to our congregation and was responsible for bringing a tremendous revival in 1973. Some in the church, like me, think that it was the greatest thing that ever happened, but alas, there are others who would differ.
>
> He introduced us to Roy Hession through his books, quotes from him in the sermons, and a weekend of teaching by him in person. It was a very moving time. Ernie wanted an honest relationship with the Lord for his congregation, and in my case, he succeeded.[41]

The University of Illinois in Urbana is where William Nagenda and Festo Kivengere began their American visit together. Urbana 61 took place December 27-31. Erma attended the meetings:

> The first meeting opened with a message by Billy Graham, with other nationally known speakers . . . as well as William and Festo taking part in subsequent meetings. The message that gripped most hearts was the one by Festo on "Jacob," which we

can share with you when we see you. There were over 5,000 at the convention. Through the convention many more doors were opened for William and Festo during the week in Chicago.[42]

The sermon on Jacob spoke to many at the conference. Kivengere's biographer noted that he introduced the East Africa Revival to educated and affluent America through the story of Jacob and Esau. "I am not Jacob. I am not defeated. I am a victorious Christian. I have had a wonderful upbringing and belong to a very evangelical church. I am Esau. And then we wonder why the blessing has not come."[43]

Herbert and Erma Maust met Nagenda and Kivengere at Urbana

Rowena Freelend, Miriam Maust, Mary Lou and Wayne Lawton, Betty and Ted Grable, Nathan Wanyanga, Erma and Herbert Maust at Free Methodist Mission, Washington, DC, 1962.

A memorable conference at Pinebrook Camp near Stroudsburg, Pa., 1961.

according to plan and provided transportation for them to their appointments in the eastern United States in January. Don Widmark had responsibility for their stay on the West Coast. The planned itinerary took them to the Moody Church and Wheaton College in Chicago, Goshen College in Indiana, Malone College in Ohio, then to Scottdale, Messiah College, World Evangelism Crusade headquarters in Pennsylvania, and Washington, DC. John Mosemann, who had moved from Lancaster to Indiana, arranged their Goshen College visit, and Wayne Lawton planned meetings in the Nation's Capital.[44]

Driving across the wintry Midwestern landscape and speaking more than once a day took a toll on Kivengere and Nagenda. This was the origin of Kivengere's jealousy of and coldness toward Nagenda, a story Kivengere told many times in later years.[45]

> William Nagenda and I were sharing an exhausting preaching itinerary overseas. Along the way I became jealous of the success of my brother. I became critical of everything he said. Each sentence was wrong or ungrammatical or unscriptural. His gestures were hypocritical. Everything about my brother was wrong, wrong, wrong. The more I criticized the colder I became. I was icy and lonely and homesick. I was under conviction by the Holy Spirit, but I went on seeking to justify myself and put the blame on William. At last I repented and then had to face the difficult task of admitting my bad attitude to William. We were about to start off for a meeting where we were to preach together, and I said, "William, I am sorry. I'm very sorry. You sensed the coldness." "Yes, I felt the coldness, but I didn't know what had happened. What is it?" "I became jealous of you. Please forgive me." That dear brother got up and hugged me, and we both shed tears of reconciliation. My heart was warm, and when he preached, the message spoke to me deeply.[46]

Traveling with Nagenda and Kivengere was a privilege for Herbert and Erma Maust. On the way the Mausts stayed with old friends like Paul M. Miller, then teaching at Goshen Biblical Seminary, and his wife, Bertha.[47]

Paul and Bertha Miller with children, John, Rebecca and James. They moved to Goshen, Indiana, to teach.

It was a real joy to travel together for six weeks while they were here in the East. To sit in meeting after meeting with them and see the Lord Jesus lifted up brought new hunger to my heart—to see Jesus and have him do in me what I saw him do in these brethren and to know the genuine humility I saw in these brethren.[48]

Always humble, Nagenda was ready to accommodate to his listeners. After speaking to Mennonite students at Goshen College, he was interested in bringing the message at the Mausts' church in Pennsylvania. And he was willing to follow Mennonite custom in his attire when he appeared there. Erma wrote Mary K. Miller to make arrangements:

William would like to get into a Mennonite church. Would it be of the Lord to have him at Goods Saturday evening the 27th and Sunday morning the 28th? If there is no church at Goods the 28th, have him at Goods Saturday evening and Elizabethtown Sunday morning. . . . He said he will take off his tie.[49]

After preaching in Lancaster County on Sunday morning, Nagenda joined Kivengere for afternoon and evening meetings at World Evangelism Crusade in Fort Washington, Pennsylvania. They then went on to Washington, DC, where they hoped to meet with African-American pastors and share their vision. Festo was given ten minutes to share at a large meeting of Baptist pastors. The Holy Spirit flowed through him in that short talk and pastors extended invitations for him to speak to their congregations, which he did speak at more than one church on the weekend. That week Festo also spoke to a Bible club of about 60 African-American students at McKinley Technical High School. He also met with Abraham Vereidi, founder of International Christian Leaders and his successor, Doug Coe. Then Carl F. H. Henry, editor of *Christianity Today*, interviewed him.[50]

Later William and

William Nagenda and Festo Kivengere, a powerful team, resting in the Lawton home in Washington, DC.

Festo flew to Los Angeles for a full schedule of preaching appointments in the West in February. They returned to the East Coast in time for the Fellowship Conference at Pinebrook Camp. "We believe the Lord has taught these brethren something of the secret of walking with Jesus, which we who are longing to know Jesus in a deeper way need also to learn. . . . We expect, the Lord willing, to have Roy, and perhaps Revel also, with us for this time."[51]

Despite this grueling schedule, Nagenda and Kivengere maintained a sense of joy. Charles and Pearl Bonner recalled an example. After William Nagenda and Festo Kivengere preached that morning at Moore's Brethren in Christ Church they invited them to their home for dinner. Then in driving them back to Grantham William spotted a herd of cattle and exclaimed "Our Father's cows!" He and Festo laughed heartily.[52]

Nagenda and Kivengere's final preaching engagements were in New England. The Mausts again provided transportation for the last stage of their American visit.[53] "We had a very profitable time with the brethren as we traveled to New Haven, Connecticut, and Boston, Massachusetts, then back to New York." The Mausts saw them off on their morning flight to London.[54]

Even before they left home for their American visit, Nagenda and Kivengere were anxious to be in contact with African-American churches. During their time in the United States, they met Arthur Cash, a Mennonite minister with a church in Fort Wayne, Indiana, and Ernie Wilson, a Baptist pastor in Philadelphia. They arranged for the two pastors to come to Kampala in May 1962 and witness the East Africa Revival at first hand. Cash and Wilson also visited the Mennonite churches in Tanganyika in June as well as other Christian communities influenced by revival.[55] Soon after Cash and Wilson returned to the United States, they visited with the New York fellowship and with Herbert and Erma Maust at their home. Erma recalls:

> We were so happy to have Ernie Wilson, Philadelphia, Pa., and Arthur Cash, Fort Wayne, Ind., with us the other weekend. They are two Negro brethren whom William and Festo had invited to come to Africa to sit with the brethren there and then prepare the itinerary for a team to come and work with the American Negro. Our hearts were so challenged as they told what God had done for them through their fellowship with the brethren in Africa.[56]

Ernie Wilson and Arthur Cash met other revival brethren at the Fellowship Conference at Messiah College in August, as Erma Maust reported:

Ernie Wilson of Philadelphia, powerful lifelong preacher of the revival message, and wife, Lucille.

Since our two Negro brothers, Ernie Wilson, Philadelphia, Pa., and Arthur Cash, Fort Wayne, Ind., have come back from fellowship with the brethren in Africa, you too would want to have a time of fellowship with them. A number of us were privileged to meet them in New York and also at Bainbridge, where we had precious fellowship. There is a possibility of Dan and Nancy Wegmueller, just returning from East Africa, being with us.[57]

Later in August, Ernie and Lucille Wilson traveled with the Mausts for meetings in Wainfleet and Nanticoke, Ontario.[58] Ernie returned to East Africa in 1965, meeting with revival brothers in Uganda and Tanganyika. He preached in schools and churches around Musoma and at the Mennonite Theological College in Bukiroba in several eventful days in June.[59] In following years Wilson would preach the message of revival from his own Philadelphia pulpit and in churches across the country and abroad. He was a gifted man, with a huge heart for God and people. Wilson had the rare ability to employ stories and illustrations to bring the message of the gospel to light. Through his messages people in the African-American communities were blessed. Others such as Kivengere and Methuselah Nyagwaswa had only limited access to the black communities of America.

The unique ministry of Sala Nagenda in the United States

Then the completely unexpected happened. Sala Nagenda, William's wife, came to the United States on her own that autumn. She and Erma Maust were close sisters in Jesus. Erma wanted everyone to meet Sala and arranged to meet her at Fort Wayne, Indiana, where she was staying with Arthur Cash and his family. Erma set up a full itinerary for her. "We expect Sala, William's wife, with us for the month of November. The Lord has graciously granted me the privilege of linking up with her for meeting and fellowship during that time."[60] It stretched Erma because she was used to a subdued role, as a woman, in her own denomination.

This was a unique team—a Ugandan woman and an American woman, one an Anglican, the other a Mennonite—yet one in the fellowship of Calvary love. Furthermore, they were ministering without their husbands but with the blessing of their husbands. They were traveling solely to encourage people, men and women, who were discovering new life in Christ Jesus together. After visiting fellowships in Pennsylvania and

Sala and William Nagenda, a strong ministering team.

Washington, DC, they flew to the West Coast, where they visited brothers and sisters and ministered in California, Oregon, and Washington and then proceeded to Saskatoon, Saskatchewan, where Ron and Marjorie Lofthouse were pastoring. On the way back to Pennsylvania, they visited Art Cash in Indiana. That was a most unique ministry tour and was powerful in witness to the uniting grace of the atoning work of Jesus.

This was a good time for Erma: "I praise the Lord for these days with my sister Sala and the way he has been making us a real team."[61] Erma Maust was beginning to be more open to a speaking and teaching ministry herself:

> Herbert and I were at a fellowship meeting near West Chester before Christmas. After the meeting a Pastor Cerato came to me and asked, "Do you ever speak in churches?" The Lord has been working in his heart and those of his people. It was arranged that I go down January 21-24 at least. I'm also to meet with the pastors of the area who have their regular monthly meeting, Monday morning, 21st, at his church near Kennett Square, Pa.[62]

Erma's ministry of helps continued to take precedence. Marian Scott was in the hospital in January 1963. Erma brought Marian's mother and

Virgie Keener to the Scotts' home in Zion, Maryland, and took two of Scotts' children to Mary K. Miller, and two to Florence Stauffer. "Monday Herbert and I are going down to help give the interior of the house a 'face-lift.' There is furniture upholstering to be done as well as floors to be sanded and varnished and curtains to be made."[63]

At about this time Erma enclosed a brief text she had written in a letter to Paul and Miriam Burkholder. It was later printed as a tract:

Accept the Situation and Praise God

"Those hard situations are put into your lives to change you.
Stop praying for them to change,
but pray that they may change you." —H. Markham.

What a blessing the above has been to me since the Lord has been cleansing me of a deep unwillingness to accept all he allows and to thank him for it, seeing he is allowing it all to consume my dross and refine my gold. If I find I cannot accept any situation and thank him for it, then I come to him confessing, "Lord, I am not really willing to accept this hard situation, and I am not willing to thank you for it." Then I begin to say, as these difficult situations arise, or depression or heaviness come upon me, or I lose my peace over my own wrongdoing or the wrongdoing of others, or frustration, accidents, or ill health, "My Father, this is another one of those things you are allowing to consume my dross and to refine my gold, and I thank you for it." As I continue to confess the unwillingness and thank him for all just as often as it raises its ugly head, I soon see [that] I am being changed, I am being delivered from the self-life. And now I would not have had the situation changed as I can see what he has been doing in me through it as I learn to accept all with thanksgiving. Praise the Lord! Praise for the blood to cleanse and for Jesus who "took the cup of our iniquity and gave thanks," so now as we repent deeply he is also our enabling to take our cup and give thanks.[64]

William and Sala Nagenda were a team again in 1963. Erma Maust set up a busy speaking schedule in the early months of that year. In April they went to Greensburg, Pennsylvania, for a revival fellowship conference. It was a hugely important meeting, and the Greensburg newspaper reported on it:

The revival fellowship meeting held Friday at the Greensburg Antioch Baptist Church brought 125 religious leaders from Florida, Chicago, New York, and Canada together to hear East African leaders speak on the development and effects of Christianity in Africa.

Zeb Kabaza, Pastor Lanier, Sala and William Nagenda in Greensburg, Pa.

Participating in the program were Zabuloni Kabaza of Uganda and a Chicago Wheaton College student; Mrs. Sala Nagenda of Uganda; Mrs. Rahabu Gatu and Rev. John Gatu, executive secretary of the Presbyterian Church in East Africa; Rev. Ernest Wilson of Philadelphia, an international evangelist; Richard Hightower of Philadelphia, representative of International Christian Leadership; Rev. William Scott of Zion, Md.; Marvin Plank of Scottdale; and William Nagenda of Uganda, East Africa.[65]

A new vision for revival challenges the Mausts

Herbert and Erma Maust were busy moving into a new home in the spring of 1963. "The Lord has been helping me these busy days of moving, gathering furnishings for the house the Lord has led us to. It was neither to buy nor build, but to rent."[66] They had been living in a trailer on Mervin Miller's farm. When that was no longer available, they bid on a house not far from the Miller place, but lost it to another buyer.[67] Their new home was only six miles south of Mervin Miller's farm, so the Monday night fellowships also moved with them to their new place.

Erma found a new direction in her own life and, after several years of traveling, she felt called to concentrate more of her energies on renewal in her own church and community. Weekly fellowships met at her home on Monday evenings and women's fellowship meetings on Wednesday mornings. She wrote in 1964:

It is now more than a year ago the Lord began to lay the burden for revival upon my heart for this area, as never before perhaps, challenging me with 2 Chronicles 7:14: "If my people, which are called by my name, shall humble themselves, and pray, and seek my face, and turn from their wicked ways, then will I hear . . . and forgive . . . and heal." It was around this time the Lord led Mary [wife of Mervin Miller] and me together again to team in prayer for revival. Through our being away so much through the past eight years and also partly because of the darkness we had been in for a number of years, we had somewhat lost the vision for revival here, or at least we were not pursuing it diligently.[68]

Erma Maust had occasional invitations to share her testimony with larger groups of women, as at a Bible conference at Homer, New York, in 1963.[69] Her ministry was largely with individuals and women's circles at churches. She wrote friends: "D.V. [the Lord willing], I will be going to Jean Griswold for a time of fellowship Thursday and then with the women of the Philadelphia churches Friday evening. I will appreciate your prayers that I may be hidden in Jesus, abiding at that low place that Jesus may be seen."[70]

Erma was an extraordinary person. Another old friend, Russell Krabill, gave his impression of her in his diary:

She is much occupied with the revival emphasis which she got from Africa about 20 years ago. Feels she was not a Christian before that. Seeks to live "honestly, openly, and in the light" before God and others. Confesses that she is a failure, that she is nothing; Christ is everything.[71]

All-day fellowship gatherings continued. There was one at the Mennonite Church in Scottdale, Pennsylvania, where Glenn and Florence Zeager shared their testimony.[72] Erma Maust organized another fellowship conference at Messiah College in June 1964.[73] A month later she wrote to everyone on her mailing list:

Now, we have good news for you. Festo Kivengere from Uganda is in the States and also Matt [Methuselah] Nyagwaswa. Matt is the brother whose wife passed away several years ago, and some of us were so challenged by his letter of praise which Catharine Leatherman shared. Matt has been going to school in Arizona this past year, and we are trusting the Lord to bring him to us for this conference, which is planned for Saturday, August 15, at Messiah Bible College, Grantham, Pa.[74]

African brethren study and witness in the United States

Festo Kivengere, like Nyagwaswa, came to the United States for further education. After wrestling in prayer for some time, Kivengere decided
in the summer of 1963 to seek ordination as a minister in the Anglican
Church. His friends, especially the revival brothers and sisters, generally
opposed this idea. He was already preaching the Word as a lay evangelist
and school administrator. Why take time out for years of study? Joe
Church doubted any need for his further training. Archbishop Leslie
Brown, head of the Anglican Church of Uganda, was unconvinced and had
to be talked into accepting Kivengere as a candidate for orders. He came to
America to speak at United Presbyterian Missionary Conference at New
Wilmington, Pennsylvania, in 1964 and was offered a scholarship to
Pittsburgh Theological Seminary.[75] Kivengere accepted the offer. "As this
was decided without the approval of the brethren in Kampala, it was considered a betrayal of group solidarity."[76] In their custom, a question of such
importance should be taken to the fellowship for counsel. Many East
African brothers were disappointed that Festo made the decision on his
own. The breech did not diminish Festo's ministry when he eventually
returned to Uganda.

Kivengere moved to Pittsburgh in the summer of 1964 to begin his seminary studies. Rev. John Baiz, his pastor at Calvary Episcopal Church,
recalled Kivengere as "the most mature and convinced Christian man, let
alone seminarian, whom I had ever met. He served with grace and influence
in the life of the parish." Many calls to preach around the country began
coming as soon as American Christians
learned that Festo Kivengere would be
in the States for the next three years.[77]

He made himself available to the
revival brothers and sisters in North
America. Erma Maust arranged a
schedule of monthly fellowships where
Kivengere was the speaker, and Marvin
Plank drove him from Pittsburgh.
Mildred Plank wrote:

Festo Kivengere with Marvin Plank.

> We were blessed so much in our contacts with Festo during his
> years at the seminary in Pittsburgh [1964–67]. Marvin was avail-
> able to drive him once a month to the fellowship meetings held at
> various places in the East.[78]

The first of this new series of extended meetings was held at Messiah College from December 31, 1964, to January 2, 1965. It brought together Festo Kivengere, Roy and Revel Hession, and Stanley Voke, an English Baptist minister and "author of the Abundant Life leaflets many of us have been finding very helpful." Erma Maust announced, "It is planned to have an all-day fellowship the last Saturday of each month with Festo Kivengere meeting with us. If you can come, get in touch with the Mausts for details."[79]

The coming of Festo Kivengere and Methuselah Nyagwaswa breathed new life into the North American churches and the revival fellowships.

The message of revival was becoming ever more clear. The way of revival was to avail oneself to continuous, daily, moment-by-moment cleansing of all that hinders and destroys fellowship with God and with those with whom one is in contact. This was not a culture-specific message; it penetrated all cultures with the same impact.

As the brothers and sisters in North America took the revival message to heart, they discovered that the basis of true freedom in Christ is the same for all peoples. It must have been gratifying for all concerned to realize and to experience the fact that the cross of Jesus Christ is "home" for all who believe. They discovered, anew perhaps, that the atoning work of Jesus, which included his sacrificial death and glorious resurrection and ascension, is the key to the salvation of every human being. Not only is it the essential message for all people; it is also the essential message for all denominations. This realization gave the revived ones a liberty to witness in every circumstance, among all churches and movements.

Erma and Herbert Maust figured largely in this story because they were activists. But many others were equally blessed by the fresh understanding of victorious living in walking moment-by-moment with Jesus. The Mausts were noteworthy inasmuch as they shouldered the responsibility for making sure that those who found new freedom in Christ would continue to walk in the light and spread the good news to others that Jesus satisfies, totally. The history of revivals teaches that God chooses key persons, often most unlikely ones, not only to embody the message but also to broadcast it as widely as possible. The Mausts exemplify that calling.

Transitions
1964–1970

The Stauffer family and the Hurst family left Tanganyika in June 1964. Elam Stauffer was the senior bishop of the Tanganyika Mennonite Church, and Simeon Hurst was his colleague. Both were walking in unity with the revival fellowships. They realized that it was their time to retire, because of age, and did so. Their leaving, however, left a huge hole in the Mennonite Church and among the brothers and sisters.

It would have been a most appropriate moment for the selection of a Tanganyikan to become bishop. Even by 1962 Stauffer and Hurst sensed that it was time to retire and turn over leadership to a national bishop. The original plan was to select a Tanganyikan bishop for the newly autonomous church, but tribal loyalties proved too strong at this time. Two names were suggested, but neither man had overwhelming support. After nearly two years of prayer and con-sultation, in 1964 the church agreed on Donald R. Jacobs to lead it as bishop.[1]

Leatherman wrote in February 1964, "The big event of the day was Don being chosen as bishop to take Elam's and Simeon's place."[2]

The brothers and sis-ters held a farewell fel-lowship for Stauffer and Hurst and their families when they were ready to

Elam Stauffer and Festo Kivengere, longtime fellow laborers.

leave in June. "The Musoma Church was full, and it was a good meeting. Some Muslim and R.C. [Roman Catholic] friends were there."[3] The church bade farewell in a special worship service at Shirati, another station further north, with more than 1,600 present. Elam, Simeon, and Zedekia Kisare each brought messages, and there was much special singing by different choirs. The service ended with 450 people taking communion.[4]

On June 24, 1964, Leatherman wrote of church members and friends traveling long distances to say a last goodbye: "This afternoon a number from the station [Bukiroba] went to see Stauffers off [in Musoma] as they leave Africa permanently." There was again much singing and praising.[5] A month later the Hurst family left on the first lap of their journey home to Ontario.[6]

Jack Shellard served as headmaster of Musoma Alliance Secondary School, an institution that served all of the Protestant communities on the east side of Lake Victoria. Jack and Florence, friends of Festo and Mera Kivengere when they taught together in Dodoma, were also known as supporters of revival. They had tried their best to assure that their replacement at the school would be a revival brother. They had in mind Methuselah Nyagwaswa, who had returned from United States with advanced degrees. But it was not to be because of matters beyond Shellard's control. In 1964 the Shellards left Tanzania, also with the blessing of the revival fellowships.

Joe Church and his family left Rwanda in 1964 also. He moved back to England with his wife, but within two years they were back in Africa and took up residence in the house that William and Sala Nagenda owned on the fabled Namirembe Hill in Kampala.[7]

John and Catharine Leatherman left Tanganyika in 1965, fully planning to return there. About their farewell session with the brethren, John wrote: "The word was 'Tell the people that they go forward.' It was a great time, such great love is a rebuke to my selfishness."[8]

It is hard to overrate the contribution the Leathermans made to the spread of the revival, both in East Africa and beyond. Their departure from Tanganyika was keenly felt. They fully intended to return to Tanzania (as renamed) the following year, but in July 1965 they realized that God had other plans for them. They remained in America.

Leadership training becomes a priority

A changing of the guard was under way. It was prompted by the exodus of seasoned and trusted missionaries, but also by the transforming of the local congregations into autonomous bodies no longer under the control of foreign missions. It all meant that leadership training had to become a priority in the churches.

The departure of these missionaries, while difficult for the revival fellowships, did not impact them greatly because by that time local people were leading all of the fellowships. It was the churches that were impacted.

So the training program at the Mennonite Theological College at Bukiroba took on added significance as it became clear the church would soon be calling a new group of leaders to carry the work forward. The college opened at Bukiroba in 1962 to train pastors and church leaders, following the syllabus of the East African Association of Theological Colleges. Donald Jacobs and Dorothy Smoker were in charge, and also teaching were John Leatherman, George Smoker, Phebe Yoder, Robert Keener, and Paul Waterhouse, Dorothy Smoker's father.[9]

Jacobs was not only the new bishop but also the founder and principal of the Mennonite Theological College. At that time the student body included most of the active leaders and, blessedly, almost all were walking in fellowship. The entire class stayed together for three years, pursuing a three-year curriculum. That gave ample opportunity for true community to develop among staff and student body. Out of that initial group of sixteen men came those who led the church for the next years.

Fortuitously, Festo Kivengere arrived at the Mennonite mission station at Bukiroba in March 1964. He conducted meetings for students at Morembe Secondary School and met in fellowship with *wandugu* (revival brothers and sisters).[10] He also spoke with students in the theological college. His ministry was timely.

Leatherman wrote in his diary, "Everyone at Bukiroba station went to the fellowship meeting at Musoma Church, where Festo gave a powerful message on Hagar: 'Return and submit yourself.'" On the next day was a fellowship meeting "at Jacobs' where Festo gave a message on Genesis 8—Noah leaving the ark to a world of desolation and standing at the altar." A day later Kivengere spoke in the Theological College chapel "on 1 Samuel 9, about Saul wearing himself out looking for donkeys while a kingdom was awaiting him." John wrote, It was "a tremendous message." One of the students, Shemaya Magati, experienced it as a turning point in his life. As a result of those meetings, Leatherman wrote that as he closed the class he was teaching at the college, probably the following day, Shemaya stood "and began to open his heart." He and other students from the college came to the regular fellowship meeting for the first time that afternoon.[11] Almost the entire student body became an authentic fellowship, in the revival sense of the word.

Preparing for Zedekiah Kisare's ordination as bishop. From left, Elam Stauffer, Eliamu Mauma, Bishop David Thomas, Bishop Donald Lauver, Elisha Meso, Zedekiah Kisare, and Don Jacobs.

Jacobs' role was to prepare Tanzanian Mennonites to take leadership roles and help them in the transition. In February 1966 he again called on the pastors to choose a new bishop from among themselves. They were nearly unanimous in selecting Zedekia Kisare, a devout brother who was set free by Christ in revival.[12] When Kisare was called, he was teaching at the college, where his clear testimony shaped the lives of many who would lead the church in the future.

The transfer of leadership from missionary to local leadership was not just occurring among the Mennonites. It was happening all across East Africa in the maturing churches. It was not uncommon for the denominations to choose men formed by the East Africa Revival. As this happened, the revival took on enhanced importance. This was especially true among the Mennonite mission neighbors in Tanzania—the Anglicans, the Lutherans, and the Moravians.

The same thing occurred in the Anglican church in Uganda. Kosiya Shalita, who was on one of the first teams at Gahini, became bishop of Ankole in Uganda in 1957, and Erica Sabiti was ordained a bishop in 1960. In 1965 Archbishop Leslie Brown of the Anglican Church of Uganda, Rwanda, and Burundi announced his decision to retire and left the choice of his successor to the bishops of the province. A year later they chose Erica Sabiti, a revival stalwart, to be the first African archbishop.

In Kenya, Obadiah Kariuki, the first Kenyan clergyman to become part of the revival, was appointed bishop of the new diocese of Mount Kenya in 1962. His brother-in-law, Jomo Kenyatta, became Kenya's first president in 1964. Two other revival brothers headed dioceses of the church in Kenya: Festo Olang was bishop of Maseno, and Neville Langford-Smith was bishop of Nakuru. In 1970 Olang was elected archbishop of the Anglican Province of East Africa.[13]

In contrast to the slowness of Westerners to "catch" revival, East Africa *balokole* had transformed the life of their churches. Paul M. Miller, sent to East Africa as a consultant on preparation for ministry, observed while in Tanzania: "In some areas the movement is remarkably well-integrated into the life of the organized church and is functioning as the mid-week prayer meeting of the church." He believed that, at least in those areas, 80 percent of the pastors were part of the revival fellowship.[14] In Kenya, by 1973, at least 90 percent of all Anglican, Presbyterian, and Methodist clergy and prominent laypeople identified with the East Africa Revival.[15]

The revival an example of economic self-reliance

One of the problems that faced the Africans who were, in a sense, replacing missionaries was the issue of finance. At this time emerging churches, which had received considerable assistance from mission boards, faced the challenge of becoming financially self-sustaining. The revival movement was one shining example of how it could be done. It never did depend on outside finances, or on outside direction, either. It was all the more remarkable because the movement had no officials, no executives, no salaried workers, no headquarters, and little structure of any kind. In Kenya, for example, there were district team meetings of some twenty brothers every two or three weeks, a provincial team meeting of twenty or so brothers representing the districts, and a Kenya team meeting representing the provincial teams. When funds were needed, spontaneous gifts went into the Lord's bag (*mfuko wa Bwana*), but no one felt obliged to make a contribution. Team meetings had responsibility for distributing funds for organizing conventions, for travel, and for helping needy people.[16] Funding for revival did not normally threaten the flow of funds into the churches.

The revival brothers and sisters deliberately avoided setting up administrative bodies. This was not well understood by many Western church leaders, who were accustomed to large organizations with professional staff and large budgets to be raised. Some have speculated that the simplicity of the East Africa Revival proved to be a stumbling block, which no doubt it was to many who, like modern Naamans (despising the small Jordan River in which he was told to bathe), expected something more spectacular than repenting and confessing sin and coming to the cross.

African Anglican Bishops challenge the Lambeth Conference

The tenth Lambeth Conference of the worldwide Anglican Communion opened July 25, 1968, in Canterbury Cathedral. Archbishop Michael Ramsey's opening sermon developed the theme of Lambeth X: the Renewal of the Church in Faith, Ministry, and Unity.[17] The conference demonstrated the remarkable shift in the African churches from Western to African leadership and the distance between them. Ten of eleven bishops from the Province of Uganda, Rwanda, and Burundi and eleven of eighteen bishops representing the Province of East Africa were themselves Africans.

The first subject on the agenda was renewal of the church in faith. It was at once clear from the draft document that many Western church leaders understood the meaning of faith in different ways. An American participant commented: "Anyone who read the report to find some hope or encouragement in personal faith was predestined to disappointment, if not disheartenment and confusion."[18]

Bishop Silvanus Wani, of Northern Uganda, was the first to criticize the tone of the document. He was followed by his primate, Erica Sabiti, the archbishop of Uganda, who was to be one of the men most frequently heard at Lambeth X. Time and again with old-fashioned evangelical zeal, he stood to draw back the conference to "sin" and "forgiveness" and other basic terms. "Renewal means going back to where things are at their best—or at least it does in my country," he said in a slow, direct voice that always seemed tinged with sadness. "In all of our technological progress, the sinful mind is still the same. There is no mention of 'sin,' yet the Lord's Prayer still mentions it. And there is no reference to the cross, although we know there can be no renewal unless we are driven to the cross."[19]

Sabiti brought the bishops to serious thinking in a later discussion on intercommunion. "To me, renewal means the

Erica and Geraldine Sabiti provided leadership for African Evangelistic Enterprise in Uganda.

facing up to the fact that we have been sinners and need repentance," he said. "In Africa, I have communion with others, and we are one at the cross—those who love the Lord."[20] This was the essential message of the East Africa Revival.

First major rift in revival

Apart from the minor schism led by Mary Ensor in the 1940s, the revival maintained an internal unity, but that unity was threatened in August 1964, when revival brothers from East Africa journeyed to Mombasa, a port city on the coast of Kenya, for a convention. The theme was "Jesus the Way" and more than twenty thousand people came together to praise the Lord.[21] Speakers on the first full day included Lawrence Barham, Elijah Kariuki, Yona Mondo, and William Nagenda. Mondo's message caused a stir. He called for a "reawakening." John Leatherman did not pick up the discordant note but recognized "the presence of the Spirit in today's meetings. . . . Neville Langford-Smith gave a very good message on Luke 7:19—'Art thou he that should come?'—and Festo Olang also gave a clear word. Don [Jacobs] spoke well on the leprosy of Naaman." On the train home, Leatherman sat with Lawrence Barham, "who is now bishop in Rwanda."[22] After returning to Bukiroba, he transcribed Langford-Smith's message and others given at the Mombasa convention for publication in the Swahili language monthly magazine of revival news, *Mjumbe wa Kristo*. This Mennonite periodical was widely circulated and had correspondents in many places.[23]

The massive gathering at Mombasa marked a transition in the revival movement. The reawakening (*okozukuka*) preached by Yona Mondo and others now began to splinter the movement. Reawakened brethren in some places started holding their own fellowship meetings. Some observers saw this withdrawal as a protest against growing organization that resulted from the large sums of money being handled. The Mombasa convention itself must have cost thousands of shillings.[24] Others noticed a legalistic emphasis on rules among the reawakened. Still others saw them "go off on a tangent with slightly new phraseology: They are emphasizing the gift of the Holy Spirit and talking about *okozukuka* (reawakening)."[25]

At the heart of the gospel is reconciliation—between God and his creatures and between human beings. The blood of Christ establishes a new covenant, uniting believers in covenant fellowship with God and with man.[26] The fellowship was committed to live this reality. To think of splitting into two movements pained everyone, but there seemed to be no way to reconcile their differences. The very gospel that they were preaching and the testimony that they were sharing was brought into question in the minds of some because they could not solve this internal rift. The sides did not line up according to national, ethnic, or racial lines. It was a purely religious matter. While the revived brothers and sisters had warded off the divisive influence of ethnicity, they failed to bring the "classical brethren" and the "reawakened ones" together.

Let us consider how new movements emerge from older movements. Revivals are marked by newfound freedom and joy in Jesus Christ and his atoning work. This leads to an emphasis on discipleship and holy living. At a certain point it is customary for the movements to codify the marks of holiness expected from all followers. That was the case in the East Africa revival in the 1960s. The movement was then in its second generation, almost thirty years old. At that time the revival had spread, and in the eyes of some it had lost its earlier fervor. In their lives some discovered sin that quenched the work of the Spirit. For example, many had gone into debt of one kind or another, and those debts hindered an open and free walk with the Lord and with one another. Financial matters were swept under the rug. "That is wrong!" they discerned, "and we must repent of that." The outcome was that the reawakened ones pronounced indebtedness as unfaithfulness to God and to the fellowship.

So it went with other issues in which the reawakened ones discerned that there had been compromise. They prescribed new rules for themselves as a hedge against backsliding. The question arose as to whether this tendency would lead to legalism or to freedom.[27]

Simeon Nsibambi and William Nagenda exercised a degree of control over the movement by the spiritual force of their character, the quality of their own personal walk with the Lord. Neither man needed organization or structure of any kind. Far from being showy speakers or dominating in a gathering of brothers and sisters, both were self-effacing, even withdrawn, and best in one-on-one counseling. At the same time, they shared an amazing capacity to stay on message and, as Max Warren observed of Nagenda, "to be terribly insensitive to any approach to God other than his own." Furthermore, both Nagenda and Nsibambi were landowning aristocrats, part of a highly educated elite, and belonged to the ruling class that ran the former kingdom of Buganda under British indirect rule (now a major part of Uganda, independent in 1962).

They, and the Kampala brethren with them, faced two new forces at work among *balokole*. One was a conservative impulse, represented by *okozukuka* (reawakening), which pressed for more structure, even codes of behavior, so that they and future generations would follow the identical path. This involved a kind of withdrawal from Ugandan society. The other tendency, represented by the somewhat freewheeling brother Festo Kivengere, wanted to integrate the revival into modern life. A whole generation of educated *balokole* had grown up who wanted to bring revival Christianity into the new East Africa taking shape around them.[28]

In spite of these tendencies, revival brothers and sisters continued in fellowship with one another. In September 1964, for instance, Yona Mondo, Erisifati Matovu, and John Leatherman formed a team for a fellowship meeting at a church in Mwanza, Tanganyika (soon to be Tanzania).[29]

Simeon Nsibambi and other leaders made every effort to mediate differences rather than separate from one another. The new movement nevertheless spread to Kenya and Tanzania, and many were challenged by the call of the reawakened ones to repent and return to the Lord. This was the experience of John and Catharine Leatherman and Dorothy Smoker in a team meeting at Tarime, Tanzania, in 1965, where "the Kenya brethren spoke to us very frankly."[30] The reawakening message had a certain appeal for those who wished to recover the early revival fires: it was true that a coldness had developed among many who were at one time very keen in revived living.

When a team of the reawakened ones paid a special visit to Don Jacobs in 1965 to enlist his backing, he remarked that his own beloved denomination, the Mennonite Church, had tried to bring new life by codifying behavior, dress, and a host of other things, and he had no desire to repeat that tendency in the revival. If the reawakened brothers and sisters wanted to see a list of rules, he offered to produce one for them from his own denominational background.[31] Don was aware of the tendency to push Jesus to the side and concentrate on perfecting holiness by one's own effort.

Some among the brothers and sisters warned against any form of legalism within the fellowship. William Nagenda returned from an overseas mission early in 1964, convinced that the legalism of the awakening was a wrong turn.[32] But his own health began to weaken before the close of that year, and he was increasingly unable to travel to meetings.[33] He was still preaching in his familiar way that autumn. In the last days of 1964, John and Catharine Leatherman visited Thika, Kenya, where William Nagenda was having meetings. Nagenda characteristically invited John to come forward and share his testimony.[34]

Nagenda continued in failing health, suffering from the onset of Parkinson's disease and other neurological problems. In 1966 William and

Sala Nagenda left Namutamba, the Lea-Wilson tea plantation, where they had lived since 1941, and moved to Oxford, England, to work with the Overseas Hostel Association. William Nagenda's ministry had always been most powerful one-on-one, talking and listening, and he and Sala enjoyed personal contact with international students at Oxford University.[35]

Returning missionaries of every denomination found Christians in the West interested in what was happening in East Africa, but less ready to hear and accept the message of the East Africa Revival. With characteristic humility Elam Stauffer admitted the difficulties he faced:

> When I retired to America in 1964, I was asked to tell of the East Africa Revival at many places and to teach on the deeper life. Interest was keen. I often longed to see more genuine revival here. Looking back now, I fear I was more of a reporter of the revival than a simple demonstration of Jesus' presence in me and his risen power. I think I felt that the same truths, teachings, and methods here would produce the same results. The African brethren had often cautioned against putting the Holy Spirit on a schedule. I have felt since [that] I may have done just that. He is sovereign. He is here to meet the deepest need of anyone in his own way. I praise God for what he has done and is still doing. He will continue to draw hungry hearts to Jesus for new life and thus glorify him. I am counting on him to work his gracious reviving in the many seeking souls here. It may be the case that many are seeking in the wrong way and place, but if they are truly seeking, he will be found of them.[36]

—14—

International Teams Sharpen the Message of Revival 1965–1969

Festo Kivengere preached the simple truths emphasized in the East Africa Revival in a way that American Christians could understand. His association with Billy Graham and his articles in *Decision* magazine opened doors in many denominations, and he received more invitations than he could fill during his years at Pittsburgh Seminary. Methuselah Nyagwaswa had a similar experience on the West Coast in his time at Fuller Seminary. Both men found a new beginning through the revival and remained close to the brothers and sisters in Africa and America. Elam Stauffer first knew Festo and his wife, Mera, when Festo was a secondary school teacher in Tanzania. Stauffer affirmed Festo's development:

> His transformation was so genuine that one of the critics of the East Africa Revival had to admit to me that there was a great change in him. In East Africa and while he was studying at the Presbyterian Seminary in Pittsburgh, we had many times of precious fellowship with him. He was God's servant to me many times when I needed counsel.[1]

Growing acceptance of the revival message as Kivengere ministers in North America

It is one thing to hear a new and penetrating message from someone of your own culture, and another to hear it from an articulate and committed person of another culture. People tend to sit up and listen when the messenger is from afar, particularly if that person is internationally acclaimed. As Festo Kivengere moved among the American churches, he was recognized as authentic and deserved attention. Added to this was the fact that

Kivengere was a phenomenally gifted communicator in his own right.

As Kivengere ministered in the United States, he not only preached but also met with the local fellowships. This gave the North American fellowships a much needed boost, not only because Kivengere ministered the Word of God to them in a most unique and refreshing way, but also because he tied them into the network of the international revival fellowships. Kivengere delighted in sharing stories and learnings from his own African experience.

It was novel for North American audiences to hear the identical message of grace through the testimony of both Africans and white people. Kivengere teamed with white people as often as possible in the ministry of the Word. The message itself took on visible meaning as people of different cultures ministered together in love. America related to this message because racial issues dominated the history of the United States and were still a sore spot in the 1960s, a hundred years after the Civil War. Kivengere and other Africans preached a message of hope and reconciliation in America. Jesus broke down the walls that society had erected to separate peoples. This was good news indeed. So eyebrows were raised when American audiences saw brothers and sisters of entirely different cultures witnessing to the same life-changing power that has come from the atoning work of Jesus Christ. Their testimonies invariably alluded to the fact that Jesus makes one of all races and cultures. They could testify to that reality, and it was powerful.

Kivengere's message did not only point the way to reconciliation between cultures and races, but also between people, especially husbands and wives. Often Festo referred to his walk with his wife, Mera. In fact, they traveled together as much as possible. Festo recalled the time when he had a harsh word with Mera before dashing out of the house to preach somewhere. The Holy Spirit stopped him in his tracks, asking, "What are you going to say to others? You left Jesus in the kitchen, with Mera. Now go back and repent, then go out with Jesus."

Festo Kivengere was convinced that the only way to true unity is through the cross of Christ. He knew that the key to everything was to be found in the cross, the atoning work of Jesus. As he matured in his walk with Jesus, he often said: "I am just beginning to see the meaning of the cross of Jesus Christ, just beginning. There is so much to discover in that mighty work of atonement."

As often as he could, Kivengere used his weekends and times off to join the American teams, which were becoming quite active. Erma Maust delighted in teaming with Kivengere and a great variety of people who could and did witness to the same transforming power of Jesus Christ. Audiences could not fail to see that the revival paid little attention to denominational affiliation or to race and culture. The team was itself multidenominational. Kivengere was an ordained Episcopal priest, Erma Maust was a lay Mennonite, and Methuselah Nyagwaswa was a layman from the Africa Inland Church. Furthermore, they represented three different nations. The fellowships that appeared in America were invariably made up of disparate groups. In this way the gospel was not bound by any particular culture but was open to all who truly repent and walk in light with God and one another.

This year was full of groundbreaking experiences. The message Kivengere carried in his heart, which he conveyed with penetrating candor and insight, touched the hearts of hundreds. They applied what they discerned to be good news in their fellowships. In this way the core message of revival spread in ever-widening circles.

Erma Maust ministers with Kivengere

Erma Maust was happy to find Mennonite Church leaders supportive of the monthly fellowships with Festo Kivengere. The first one held in 1965 was at Perkasie Mennonite Church in eastern Pennsylvania. "The pastor and the bishop have been invited to this meeting; they are open and eager for this meeting."[2]

Erma gave her impressions of a fellowship held at Waynesburg in western Pennsylvania in March 1965:

> Festo spoke on Colossians 3:13: "Forbearing one another and, if one has a complaint against another, forgiving each other; as the Lord has forgiven you, so you also must forgive" [RSV]. We saw further that all unforgiveness and differences end at the cross. When two people meet there, there can be no quarreling, no unlove. We will be most patient with one another. The afternoon session opened with songs of praise, and then Festo gave a short word from Romans 15:7 "Welcome one another, therefore, as Christ has welcomed you, for the glory of God" [RSV]. As he often did, he used a homely image in a way that made his point memorable.
>
> We saw how Jesus so freely opened his heart to us and that as we are willing to take a sinner's place we too, because of our common loyalty to Jesus Christ will also freely open our hearts to one another. Festo illustrated it this way: If you take two balloons that are full of gas and try to bring them together, you cannot.[3]

Kivengere's messages spoke to a need in Erma. She was prone to give pat answers to perplexing questions. The Lord was dealing with her on this issue. About this time Irene Smucker, wife of a New York City Mennonite pastor, asked Erma to come and stay with a troubled woman for a week. While she was there, she met as usual with the New York fellowship.[4] Paul Burkholder, pastor at Glad Tidings Mennonite Church in the South Bronx, came into the light about his own problems and revival in his congregation. He was disappointed that Erma seemed to offer simplistic solutions to troubling situations and wrote to her about it:

> The Lord has been helping me to take cleansing for my attitude toward you, and I do want to again ask your forgiveness. I think for a long time I have looked at you as one who is perfect. Then, when I think I see some things, I find myself rebelling and not wanting to accept you as you are. This is one of the very things I have been accusing you of. . . . I keep getting this feeling that I am not a brother with you, but rather that you have very simple pat answers to my problems as well as those of others. The Lord Jesus has been speaking to me lately about my need to live a disciplined life. It is so easy for me to waste my time, especially since the congregation has called me to be full-time pastor. It is so easy to get involved in trifling things. God seems to be doing a new thing in our congregation as we are learning to share together much more deeply. This evening Elam Stauffer will be sharing with us at Glenn [Zeager]'s and speaking tomorrow night at our joint midweek service.[5]

Erma Maust responded characteristically to Paul Burkholder's letter, accepting his evaluation of her own weakness:

> There is no doubt that the things you saw were in me in some degree even though I may not have been aware of them. Forgive me, Brother, where I have been pat and not filled with his love and compassion as you shared your problems. Pray for me that I may know his tenderness, meekness, and utter dependence upon the Father. I do so need this for I can be so hard and matter of fact.[6]

At this time Erma's speaking ministry was increasing. She missed the April fellowship in 1965 because she was in Saskatoon, Saskatchewan, where Ronald and Marjorie Lofthouse arranged for her to speak at a one-day "ashram [religious retreat]" and in several area churches.⁷ She was also invited to speak at an Inter-Varsity Christian Fellowship meeting at Sault Sainte Marie, Ontario, and planned to meet Simeon and Edna Hurst at the Toronto airport for fellowship meetings at Wainfleet, Ontario.⁸

Calvary Presbyterian Church in St. Clairsville, Ohio, was the venue for the April fellowship meeting, with Kivengere participating. Erma Maust's announcement stressed the broad ecumenical tradition of the East Africa Revival and the North American revival fellowships:

> For those who have never attended such a meeting, we come together from different denominations basing our fellowship on our relationship with Jesus Christ rather than on points of doctrine. We believe all believers are one in Jesus Christ regardless of rank, station, denomination, race, nationality or social status. Our fellowship is around the living Christ with his cleansing blood as the central theme.⁹

Mary K. Miller wrote a report of the St. Clairsville meeting for those who could not be there:

> Festo opened his heart in the opening session and shared how he had come to the meeting very dry. He told Mervin on his way to the conference, "I dread to speak for I am very dry. Surely another brother must do the speaking this time for I have nothing." But he said something happened during the night: he met Jesus afresh and Jesus filled him to overflowing. They were meeting on the Saturday after Easter, and Festo took the gospel account of the first Easter as his theme. He shared with us how Mary came to the empty tomb early Easter morning so disappointed [that] Jesus was not there.
>
> We saw how often we too are looking for Jesus where we are not to find him, in past experiences. Mary saw the angels. So often we would be quite satisfied to see angels, but not Mary. She wanted to see Jesus more than anything else. When she saw what she supposed was the gardener, she said, "Tell me where you have laid him, and I will take him away" [John 20:15 RSV]. How could Mary have taken the body away? She wanted Jesus so desperately that she would have dragged him away. When Jesus saw Mary's determination to find him, his love could hold out no longer and

he said, "Mary." She turned about, not halfway, but completely, and wanted to hold him; but he said, "Do not hold me, . . . but go to my brethren" [20:17 RSV]. When we make a complete turnaround, we too see him; yet we must not hold him either, but go tell others. Festo used the story of Jesus overtaking the two disciples on the road to Emmaus for his second message [Luke 24:13-35].

In the afternoon we saw Jesus as he joined the two on the way to Emmaus. He was a stranger to them for their problems, endless talk, confusion, gloom, and despair blinded their eyes to their risen Lord. He knew they needed his understanding and sympathy so he drew near, instead of sending an angel to them. When Jesus is a stranger, we get into confusion, hardness of spirit in fellow-ship, and we become "sweetly hard." Outwardly we appear sweet, but hard toward others within.[10]

The fellowship meeting in May 1965 was at the United Presbyterian Church of the Atonement in Silver Spring, Maryland, just outside Washington, DC, with Rev. Stewart Rankin as pastor and Rev. Wayne Lawton handling arrangements. Kivengere preached on 2 Corinthians 5:17-18: "If anyone is in Christ, he is a new creation; the old has passed away, behold the new has come!" [RSV]. Erma Maust wrote of his mes-sage: "We saw [that] when Jesus comes to us, he sets us free—free to repent, free to turn to him, free to share what he has done for us, free to allow the transforming grace to go on." Kivengere also used a favorite image comparing believers to mirrors: "Our mirrors reflect that upon which they are focused. If we focus them upon the faults of others, that is what we see. If we focus our mirrors upon ourselves, that is what we see. But if we focus our mirrors upon Jesus, we see Jesus, and our lives are transformed into his wonderful image."[11]

The next fellowship meeting was at Mill Run Mennonite Church, near Altoona, Pennsylvania, where Kivengere took his theme from instructions in Leviticus about lepers. Erma Maust wrote that she found it "very diffi-cult to convey something of the spirit of the fellowship held at Altoona." Kivengere had given new meaning to religious language: "We have been indoctrinated with such words as 'cleansing' and 'forgiveness' until they become so familiar [that] they become mere head knowledge." His message brought those terms to life.[12] Early in August 1965 Kivengere teamed with Ernie Gilmore, a Presbyterian pastor from Moultrie, Georgia, for a three-day fellowship meeting at Niagara Christian College, Fort Erie, Ontario.[13]

The Leatherman family returns to US

John and Catharine Leatherman returned from Tanzania later in that August. John wrote in his diary, "This morning we went to Mount Joy [Mennonite Church]. Catharine gave her greetings and a review of our work in Tanzania while I followed with a sermon. I used the word of our last fellowship meeting at Bukiroba: 'Tell the children of Israel that they go forward.'"[14] The Leathermans began participating again in the Monday night fellowship meetings at the Mausts' place.[15]

Herbert and Erma Maust had already made plans for an extended trip across Canada to the West Coast, with stops in Tucson, Phoenix, Colorado Springs, Dallas, and Hesston (Kan.) on their way home. Mervin and Mary Miller were going with them. On the first part of their trip, Erma had speaking engagements at several places in southern Ontario, Saskatoon, and at the Prairie Bible Institute in Three Hills,

Mervin and Mary Miller in 1988, ever active in the fellowship.

Alberta. They would be gone from September to December.[16] What would happen to the two weekly meetings while they were away? Erma had made no advance plans for them:

> It didn't seem right for Mary and me to be away from the Monday evening fellowship and the Wednesday morning one for such a long time. Not that someone else couldn't take charge, but who? As we shared with the brethren Monday evening and the ladies Wednesday morning, the Lord gave assurance [that] he would provide and take care of this need. Before we left on the trip, the Lord had provided: John and Catharine Leatherman are home from Africa, so John plans to meet with the Monday evening fellowship and Catharine with the ladies on Wednesday morning.[17]

John Leatherman also took responsibility for the monthly fellowship meetings. The September meeting took place at Memorial Baptist Church in Huntingdon Valley, Pennsylvania, a Philadelphia suburb. The night before there was a team meeting at Elam Stauffer's. Early the next morning Elam and Grace Stauffer, John and Catharine Leathermans, and Clyde and Alta Shenk drove to the church. Leatherman recorded: "There were many there, including Marvin Plank, [Glenn and Florence] Zeager, Ernie Wilson, Festo Kivengere. I spoke in the morning with great love and liberty on Phil. 3. Bill Scott followed on Ezek. 37. Festo and Ernie spoke in the afternoon."[18]

There was another speaker at the Huntingdon Valley fellowship: John Wilson, a businessman from Kampala, Uganda, and one of the *balokole*. Later he would be called out as an evangelist in his own country and abroad.

Betty Shaeffer and Kathryn Hertzler, long-term members of Erma Maust's weekly fellowship, reported on the conference. The messages brought out ideas emphasized in the East Africa Revival:

John Wilson of Uganda, businessman turned evangelist, noted for his peace-making ministries.

Brother John Leatherman gave a searching message out of Philippians 3:7-10. One thing he made so clear to us [was] to always keep Christ as the center of our lives, and he will meet our every need. In giving his own testimony, we saw that "the Big I" who wants to be at the center must come down; and all at once we see Jesus, the one who came down, down, down for us (Phil 2:5-7), and we see that the things of God are revealed unto babes. Then Bro. Bill Scott told us of the cleansing stream, the precious blood of Jesus.

Speaking first in the afternoon, Bro. Ernie Wilson took as his text Ezekiel 37:11. When we withdraw and are afraid to speak for our Lord, we are like the bones spoken of in Ezekiel, dry, and our hope is lost. Everything we hold on to that will hinder our fellowship with our Lord is another piece of grave clothing.

Festo began his message with prayer, and [he] made us realize anew how great is our need for Jesus. The third and last speaker for the afternoon, Bro. John Wilson from Africa, said, "Even if you go through fire or water, Jesus will go with you. He cares for you." When we witness for Christ, we are to speak of him and not of ourselves. A challenging testimony indeed! The meeting was brought to a close with testimonies and prayer, and a sense of the nearness of our precious Lord.[19]

The next fellowship meeting met at Nairn Mennonite Church, Ailsa Craig, Ontario. This was too far away for most of the regulars. Kivengere came with Herbert and Erma Maust. She wrote:

> We were only a small group seated in a semicircle at the front of the church, perhaps about twenty-four for the morning session. Besides those from the local church and neighboring churches, Simeon and Edna Hurst from Hawkesville, Ontario, Robert and Sadie McPherson from Font Hill, Ontario, and several from Elmira, Ontario were there.[20]

The final conference of the year was again at Messiah College over the New Year's holiday. John Leatherman wrote in his diary:

> Elam, Festo, Wayne Lawton, and myself were the speakers. The theme was concerning Mary: "When her time was come, she brought forth. Our time is the end of our strength and righteousness."[21] [On New Year's Eve:] The meetings increased in power throughout the day. The attendance was also greater today. [On New Year's Day:] Festo and Elam were inspired, large number of responses. This afternoon was the last meeting.[22]

Another banner year, 1966

In January 1966 the monthly fellowship was again in St. Clairsville, Ohio. John Leatherman and Marvin Plank picked up Festo Kivengere in Pittsburgh. John wrote, "It was good to see him again." As soon as they got to St. Clairsville: "We had a team meeting and it was agreed to center about John 1 'the light' and Luke 15. Festo spoke first. The Lord led out in him wonderfully. I spoke in the afternoon with liberty."[23]

Steelton Mennonite Church, near Harrisburg, Pennsylvania, was the site for the monthly fellowship in February. "It was a large meeting and very good. Festo was with us and Marvin Planks from Scottdale. Phebe Yoder was also there."[24]

Erma Maust provided a long, glowing report of the fellowship at Steelton for those on her mailing list:

We were gathered together from western Pennsylvania, New York, Virginia, and from all around the surrounding area. This was perhaps the largest attended monthly conference we have ever had. Perhaps the deepest truth the Lord spoke to us was how we can get "principles, doctrine, and structure" and many other good things so in the center that Jesus Christ is no longer our focal point.

Perhaps the most amazing thing about the conference was the way the Spirit went right on working in the service at the Steelton church the next morning. By the reports we have had, it must have been a most refreshing time as the pastor [Russell Baer] opened the service before the message for testimony, confession, and so on, and the congregation responded spontaneously, one after the other, until it was time to dismiss, when the pastor who hadn't any time to give his message simply said, "My text this morning was 'We Would See Jesus,' and closed the meeting." They had seen him![25]

Erma shared a few challenging quotes from the Steelton fellowship meeting, probably drawn from Kivengere's message:

When principle, doctrine, or structure becomes the center instead of Jesus, before we know it we are left with our dos and don'ts and have lost the Lord Jesus. Are you willing to have the Spirit smash the structure or your principle, so that Jesus may have the preeminent place? When we see Jesus we see men from a different angle. Values change when we see the cross of Christ. The cross is the point of contact between God and man.[26]

The March Fellowship Conference of 1966 met at Manoa United Presbyterian Church in Havertown, Pennsylvania, another Philadelphia suburb, and again Kivengere was the main speaker. Betty Shaeffer reported what Kivengere and Florence Tilley, veteran AIM missionary, said there:

All the meditations for the day were drawn from the experience of Moses at the burning bush as found in Exodus 3. Festo explained: "There are times when we like Moses are not where we should be and these are places where we do not expect God to act. When we don't expect anything, this is when God steps in. . . . To come near to God's presence, we will have to come to the bush and look in."

Miss Florence Tilley saw Jesus from the other side of the bush. When God came to Moses and Moses turned aside to see, this is all he did. Nothing else he could do but come out of hiding. We only need to turn aside and look, and we will see Jesus. Every day he waits for us to look. When Moses turned aside, God called to him. He did not rebuke him; he looked down deep and Moses hid his face like a child. Moses was convicted and penitent, but God did not punish him but said, "Let me show you what is in my heart, only love." When we see into the heart of God, we see his people. When Moses saw into God's heart and saw God's people, that ended Moses. The loving tender heart of God will melt our hearts. When we get a glimpse of the heart of God, it will defrost our hearts. Festo Kivengere took us to the bush and Miss Tilley told us to look into the bush, where we saw the heart of God. At the bush the Lord met us and opened our hearts.[27]

Erma Maust and Jean Griswold were in Pasadena, California, when the conference met in March in Havertown (Pa.). Erma had been speaking in Phoenix and had more speaking appointments in California and Oregon.[28] At the monthly revival fellowship meeting in Los Angeles, Erma met Methuselah Nyagwaswa from Tanzania. "Ernie and Lucille Wilson from Philadelphia were there to link up with our brethren on the West Coast. Matt and George and Dorothy [Smoker] were also there and this linked us with the brethren in Africa."[29] While Festo Kivengere was a student at Pittsburgh Seminary, Nyagwaswa was earning a degree at Westmont College in California. He also spoke at fellowship meetings and in churches on the West Coast.

In April 1966 the fellowship conference met at Eastern Mennonite College in Harrisonburg, Virginia. Mary K. Miller reported Kivengere's sermons there:

Wayne Lawton opened the meeting with this question: "Shall I come just as I am?" The Lord spoke to us through Bro. Festo Kivengere from John 12:23-26. It is time for Jesus to be glorified. We sometimes spend hours on spiritual suicide, but we cannot crucify ourselves. To be where Jesus is, we must follow in his humiliation—this is the safe place. . . . This place of weakness is the safe place because this is where God meets us.

There are certain signs to show us that we aren't in the safe

244   *A Gentle Wind of God*

place. Do you ever feel unsafe or ashamed to open your heart to someone else? Do you ever weigh your testimony and eliminate those things which humiliate you? Are you afraid to come again and again with the same sin?

After lunch Festo shared with us the experience of an African brother who followed Jesus even though his church had excommunicated him. Instead of going to another church, he worshipped regularly just outside the church door. They even passed the offering plate to him. All the while he had such a sweet, forgiving spirit [that] the love of Jesus flowed out to those inside the church. Some months passed. The pastor was convicted and was unable to preach until he went outside and was reconciled to his brother.[30]

The next month-end fellowship convened at the Memorial Baptist Church, in the Philadelphia suburb of Huntingdon Valley, Pennsylvania, with Kivengere present. Franklin Vail was the local pastor, and John Leatherman recorded: "Festo was with us and spoke on our union with Christ at the cross. In the afternoon I spoke on cleansing from John 13, and he followed with a further most precious exposition. Erma also gave a short message and testimony."[31]

Kivengere's ordination in Pittsburgh

Festo Kivengere was to be ordained to deacon's orders in the ministry of the Anglican Church in June 1966, and many of his friends drove to Pittsburgh to attend the ceremony at Calvary Episcopal Church. The Mausts, the Millers and the Leathermans stopped overnight in Scottdale. Early the next morning:

> We left for Pittsburgh to go to Festo's ordination. It was at the Episcopal Church there and he was ordained in behalf of the Uganda bishop. It was an impressive service. We were invited to a luncheon immediately afterward and there we had a very nice fellowship time with Festo.[32]

Kivengere had another year of study at Pittsburgh Seminary before he returned to Uganda. It was not too soon to sort out what form his ministry would take after he returned home. Although he felt called to ordination, he did not want to give up the work of an evangelist for parish ministry. In

Revival friends attend Festo Kivengere's seminary graduation in Pittsburgh. From left, Mary Miller, Marvin Plank, Mildred Plank, John Leatherman, Mera Kivengere, Festo, Erma Maust, Herbert Maust, and Catharine Leatherman.

October Kivengere shared a written statement with the members of the revival fellowships in North America a vision that he believed to be of the Lord:

> While at Pittsburgh Theological Seminary, my wife and I have been laying before the Lord, who called us into his blessed service more than twenty years ago, the fact of where in his great vineyard back in Africa he wants us to serve and in which way. It is through these times of heart-searchings, desiring to know his will for us, that the idea of "WORKING ON AN INTERDENOMINATION-AL BASIS FOR THE MOBILIZATION OF AFRICAN EVANGELISTS INTO A UNITED FORCE FOR GOD, WHER-EVER THEY ARE" began taking shape in our hearts.

In his proposal Kivengere identified the need for "running conferences for evangelists and pastors in different parts of the Continent." The initial needs he foresaw included a home, a car, a fixed salary, "simplified litera-ture to equip the evangelists," an office and secretary, expenses for confer-ence facilities, and traveling expenses for those who need the help.[33]

After sharing with Festo and Mera Kivengere in the joy of Festo's ordi-nation, the Mausts returned home to host another revival brother from East Africa. "Next week we expect our Brother Methuselah Nyagwaswa to be with us. He expects to be at our house for fellowship on Monday evening, then on to New York for a few days and back to Los Angeles by the 19th."[34] John and Catharine Leatherman and other returned missionaries had a reunion with their friend from Tanzania. "This evening we had fellowship at Mausts' and it was a very large and special one. Nyagwaswa was present, having arrived from the

Mera and Festo Kivengere in Tanganyika, tireless advocates for revival.

West. Also Don [Jacobs] and Elam [Stauffer]."[35]

After ordination one of Festo Kivengere's first appointments was the fellowship conference at Messiah College. "We met Thursday evening as weak ones from as far west as Saskatoon, Saskatchewan, and also from Kenya, Tanzania, and Uganda."[36] On the first evening, John Leatherman noted, "There was no organization when we arrived, but the Lord took over and the meeting became free."[37] It was a hot weekend, but this did not quench the Spirit.[38] "The meeting continued through the day with Festo bringing the messages. There were morning, afternoon, and evening sessions. The Spirit spoke clearly in revealing the cross still deeper for me."[39] John Leatherman, Ernie Wilson, and Kivengere preached on Saturday.[40]

The July fellowship meeting at Clinton Hill Baptist Church in Union, New Jersey, was very different. Quite a few of the team were unable to come. "Jesus was there to meet us, and this was a fellowship, not a preaching service," Erma Maust reported. "We had no messages as usual, but rather the word came to us mostly through testimonies."[41] Kivengere was again available for the August fellowship conference in 1966. Erma wrote:

Close friends Ernie Wilson and Festo Kivengere.

Last Saturday we had a blessed time as we met in the Beverly Heights Presbyterian Church in Pittsburgh for an all-day fellowship. The night before about a hundred (mostly youth) met for a time of fellow-ship. The Lord spoke to us throughout the entire day on the story of the prodigal sons in Luke 15:11-32.[42]

An outreach to youth was again emphasized in September at a two-day fellowship at Steelton Mennonite Church, near Harrisburg. Erma reported:

> We had a precious time at the last conference at Steelton. The Friday evening meeting was a real blessing. Quite a few young people attended. The word of the Lord came to us in the portion from John 1:43, "Follow Me," not a teaching, not a doctrine, not a church, but Jesus Christ.[43]

A fellowship wedding—Methuselah and Josephine Nyagwaswa

The regular fellowship meeting on the last Saturday of October was at Goshenville Bible Church in West Chester, Pennsylvania. Erma was again on the West Coast that weekend. She flew to California for the wedding of Methuselah Nyagwaswa and Josephine Mwanbi at the Lake Avenue Congregational Church in Pasadena.[44] "Ever since I knew our dear brother and sister Matt and Josephine were to be married in Pasadena, California, I have had a desire to be at the wedding, for I knew Jesus would be there in a real way."[45] Kivengere also flew to California to preach the wedding sermon. Dan and Nancy Wegmueller, Free Methodist missionaries and *ndugu* (of the revived), acted as parents for the groom and Erma Maust as the mother of the bride. "The bride came down the aisle on the arm of Festo Kivengere, who acted as the bride's father." When it was time for the sermon, Kivengere began by reading the passage in Deuteronomy concerning the mercy seat in the tabernacle. "Matt and his bride exchanged glances of alarm; they couldn't see how such a passage could relate to a marriage ceremony. But Festo went on to draw an analogy between the young couple and the two cherubim that stood facing above the mercy seat, 'facing each other, but not looking at each other; but rather fixing their eyes and focusing on the mercy seat.'"[46]

Methuselah Nyagwaswa of Tanganyika, whose influence was felt particularly on U.S. West Coast, where he was a student.

Both Methuselah and Josephine had come to a deeper knowledge of the Lord in the East Africa Revival. Their wedding reflected their lives:

We watched with almost breathless silence as the ceremony went on. Then just after they had faced the audience and just before they went out, Matt said, "My wife and I are going to give our testimonies. My wife will give hers first, then I'll give mine." After they were finished, we burst out singing, "Glory, glory, hallelujah, / Glory, glory to the Lamb."[47]

Other significant meetings

Festo Kivengere was unable to join the fellowship meeting at Laurelville Mennonite Church Center in western Pennsylvania on the last three days of 1966. Eighty people came for the conference.[48] John Leatherman wrote in his diary: "Don [Jacobs] came last night and was with us today. He made up for Festo's absence. Our theme was [to] rest in the Lord, starting with the communication to the shepherds, 'Peace.'"[49] Ernie Wilson was also on the team.[50]

Kivengere's time at Pittsburgh Seminary was coming to an end, and he received more invitations in 1967 to preach than he could accept. To accommodate his schedule, the date of the February fellowship was changed. Erma explained: "Since he was not with us for the last two conferences, we arranged this one so he could be with us."[51] A large group met at the Baptist Church of Kennett Square, Pennsylvania, where Rev. John A. Cerrato Jr. was pastor. Festo brought the messages, and John Leatherman led the afternoon open session.[52]

Working within Kivengere's availability, Erma scheduled a fellowship conference at Glad Tidings Mennonite Church in the South Bronx.[53] Glad Tidings had a unique ministry in the form of a sandwich shop, a safe place in a rough neighborhood, where teenagers and younger children gathered after school, volunteers helped them with homework, and parole officers met young offenders. Paul Burkholder, the pastor, proposed that those attending the fellowship conference could buy their noon meal there.[54] "The meeting was very well attended and was very good. Bill Liner from Three Hills, Alberta, a very dear brother, was with us and also Festo. They both brought messages from the Lord."[55] Kivengere used the story of Jacob as the theme, a text he had often used before.[56]

Although Kivengere had many speaking engagements for his remaining time in the States, he accepted Leatherman's invitation to preach at Doylestown Mennonite Church, John's home church, on April 2, 1967. Since Kivengere would be in eastern Pennsylvania that weekend, Leatherman proposed to Paul G. Landis of the mission board a larger meeting in Lancaster County:

This morning I went to see Paul Landis about whether he would favor having Festo minister to a Saturday evening group in the Lancaster area when he comes for Doylestown on April 2. Paul is very much in favor and has started the ball rolling. I called up Festo this evening at Pittsburgh, and he will be able to do this.[57]

The regular monthly fellowship met at the Mennonite mission board building at Salunga, Pennsylvania, on Saturday, and in the evening a public meeting was scheduled at Hensel Hall on the campus of Franklin and Marshall College in Lancaster.[58] Leatherman recorded in his diary:

Festo was with us and was at his (the Lord's) best. Very penetrating message on the cross. A large number of responses in the afternoon. We brought Festo home for supper and then went to the evening meeting at Hensel Hall at F&M. This was sponsored by the Lancaster MYF. This meeting was also good. Festo stayed with us for the night.[59]

At Doylestown Mennonite Church next morning: "Again the Lord gave Festo full utterance in the word of the Cross."[60]

Kivengere also addressed the April fellowship conference at Eastern Mennonite College in Harrisonburg, Virginia. John Leatherman wrote:

We had a team meeting prior to the first meeting, which was held in the high school auditorium. Festo was at his best, and our dear Lord was surely glorified. There was a second meeting in the afternoon. Elam was also present and gave a good testimony. We were invited to Merle Eshleman's for supper in their home. [Dr. Merle W. and Sara Zook Eshleman had served with the first Mennonite missionaries in Tanganyika.] For the evening we went to Waynesboro, [Virginia] to attend a service in Wayne Lawton's church, where Festo also spoke.[61]

The next morning Kivengere spoke at the morning service in the chapel of Eastern Mennonite College. Leatherman wrote, "What a message for college people! It could hardly have been better."[62]

In May, Festo Kivengere and Ernie Wilson had a series of meetings at the Metropolitan Baptist Church in Manhattan. Glenn Zeager and John Leatherman went to one of the services. Leatherman reported: "To my astonishment they called me to the platform and invited me to give a testimony. There was great liberty—a warm meeting with Christ's liberating grace powerful."[63]

Festo and Mera Kivengere's time in the United States was rapidly drawing to a close. The two-day fellowship conference at Laurelville Church Center in June 1967 would be the last they could attend. "This will also be a farewell meeting for Festo and his family as well as the Don Jacobs family, who are all returning to Africa, leaving sometime in July."[64] Festo arrived in time for the evening meeting. The next day brought the revival team together. Leatherman reported: "The day saw three sessions, morning, afternoon, and evening. The Spirit spoke deeply—Don, Festo, and Elam brought searching messages."[65] After Festo returned to Africa, these monthly fellowship meetings came to an end.

More international revival visitors in Pennsylvania

Other revival visitors came to eastern Pennsylvania that summer. The Jack Shellards were on their way home to Australia from Tanzania, pausing to visit old friends like the Leathermans in America.[66] Zedekia Kisare and two other *ndugu* came from Tanzania to visit American Mennonite congregations.[67] Shemaya Magati, one of the visitors, had been converted when Kivengere preached at the Theological School in Bukiroba in 1964. John Leatherman interpreted from Swahili for them as they spoke in different churches. At Christian Street Mennonite Church in Lancaster and Line Lexington and Souderton churches, each gave a short sermon.[68]

Two conventions followed, one at Easton Mennonite Church in Easton, Pennsylvania, in August 1967; and another at Waynesburg, just south of Pittsburgh, in October.

Revel Hession's funeral

The revival fellowships in the United States learned at this time that Roy and Revel Hession, coauthors of *Calvary Road*, had been in an auto accident on September 3, 1967. Revel was instantly killed, and Roy suffered a broken arm, leg, and ribs. Festo Kivengere wrote to Erma Maust about Revel Hession's memorial service:

> The funeral on the 7th [of September 1967] at Bristol was a "heaven on earth." It was like a great convention—a feast of spiritual things. Death was indeed swallowed in victory! Stanley Voke, Ken Maynough, and John Collinson gave lovely messages, and the

whole service was permeated with the presence of the risen Savior. Roy was there in a wheelchair, full of joy and comfort in the Lord. It was indeed a shock to us all, but she is now with Jesus, whom she loved and served.

William was there with us at the funeral and rejoicing. Now as to the meetings Roy was planning in the States, Roy told us they are definitely off as he won't be able to come over this year and all the brethren are already committed. So all meetings will be canceled.[69]

Roy Hession sent a form letter to Erma Maust "giving much glory to God for his grace, yes, even the 'courtesy of God,' in taking Revel as he did, suddenly." He said he still hoped to come to the United States in 1968.[70]

The last fellowship conference of 1967 met at Laurelville Mennonite Church Center at the end of December. "Our brother Eddie Young from Dixon's Mills, Alabama, was with us for the holiday conference." He brought tapes of Revel Hession's funeral. "Matt and Josephine Nyagwaswa were with us also . . . before they leave us to go back to Africa."[71]

William and Sala Nagenda came from Oxford, England, in 1968 to visit their daughter and for fellowship with the brethren in America. William was in failing health, suffering from the onset of Parkinson's disease. In August they participated in an all-day fellowship at Camp Hebron near Halifax, Pennsylvania. William and Sala had always been a team, and in his weakened state William had to sit in a chair to preach. Sala held his hand and, after a few minutes, she would take over and deliver their message.[72]

John Leatherman also fell ill that summer, and there was little hope of recovery. "Our brother John Leatherman was confined to the hospital for several weeks, and during exploratory surgery there was discovered a tumor in the pancreas, which was considered inoperable." He died of cancer several months later.[73]

Roy Hession returned to the United States with his new wife Pamela (Pam) in October. Pam Greaves joined the Ruanda Mission in 1949 as a secretary and worked with Joe Church from that time on. Roy and Pam spoke in a number of places, beginning with meetings in New York City organized by Glenn Zeager. They held meetings at Penn Presbyterian Church in Verona, Pennsylvania; and in Scottdale, Pennsylvania, where Marvin Plank made the arrangements. Their itinerary included more meetings at the Christian Literature Crusade headquarters in Fort Washington, Pennsylvania, and with Ernie Wilson in Philadelphia. Roy and Pam spoke at Bob DuVal's church in West Chester, Pennsylvania, and Bill Scott's church in Zion, Maryland. They held another round of three-day meetings at Locust Lane Mennonite Chapel in Harrisburg, and then went on to the Faith at Work convention in Columbus, Georgia. They were the main speakers at the Revival Fellowship Convention

Pam and Roy Hession, effective ministering team from the United Kingdom.

organized by Erma at Laurelville Mennonite Church Center in November. Their North American visit ended with meetings at Park Avenue Methodist Church in Minneapolis and meetings arranged by Bill Liner at Three Hills, Alberta.[74] In all, it was a fruitful ministry tour for Roy and Pam. They encouraged the fellowships and spread the message of new life in Jesus in some new places.

Consolidation in 1969

After the fellowship conference at Laurelville in November 1968, there were other conferences at Chicago Avenue Mennonite Church in Harrisonburg, Virginia, in January 1969; at the Free Methodist Church in Trucksville, Pennsylvania, in April, where Wayne Lawton brought the message; and at Eastern Mennonite High School in Harrisonburg in May. Bill Liner was the featured speaker at the May meeting.[75] This was the last effort to bring people from a distance for fellowship. Erma wrote in January 1970:

> Some of you have mentioned missing the monthly report of the fellowship conferences. At present, we are not having such conferences each month. This does not mean God is not at work among us. . . . Since we have been confined here at home these past two years, the Lord has opened up many opportunities locally for "sharing the good news with needy people."[76]

The weekly fellowship was still meeting at Mausts', and Erma alluded to it in the same January 1970 letter. Other East Coast fellowships met at Glenn Zeager's place in New York City and at Ruth Graybill's in Philadelphia.

One of the West Coast fellowships met to share Jesus regularly in Canoga Park, California, at the Dave Bridgeford home. They were happy to announce that Festo Kivengere was coming back to Los Angeles in July 1969. Their revival fellowship covered his traveling expenses. There would be an all-day fellowship meeting at the First Baptist Church of Downey, California, two services at Glendale First Presbyterian Church, and another at the San Gabriel Union Church during this busy weekend.[77]

Festo Kivengere and Zeb Kabaza, headmaster of Kigezi High School and one of the Uganda *balokole*, came to the United States as a team in May 1969 to work with the Billy Graham Crusade in New York and meet with their American brothers and sisters. By early June Kivengere was preaching on Manhattan streets as part of the open-air ministry of the Graham crusade.[78]

Significant changes for Kivengere

Much had happened in the two years since Kivengere completed his studies at Pittsburgh Theological Seminary. Festo and Mera made their home in Kampala, Uganda's capital. In December 1967 Bishop Richard Lyth of the diocese of Kigezi ordained him as minister, leaving him free to accept the many invitations to preach outside the diocese. The bishop appointed him assistant chaplain at All Saints' Cathedral in Kampala. In May 1968 Festo Kivengere was one of the main speakers at an international congress on evangelism, held at the University of Ibadan in Nigeria. There he met a young South African Christian, Michael Cassidy, whose ideas about evangelism were congruent with his own. Cassidy, an Anglican layman who had studied at Fuller Seminary in the 1960s, shared his vision for teams of African evangelists and invited Kivengere to lead an East African team within the African Enterprise program.[79] Cassidy had already established an interracial team of evangelists in Pietermaritzburg, South Africa, and the program's work was expanding.

Although he worked closely with Billy Graham and already had an international reputation as an evangelist himself, Kivengere had serious doubts about Western success-oriented evangelism. He wanted to preach Jesus Christ, not manipulative techniques for tangible results.[80] The *balokole*, often schoolteachers on vacation, went out in teams to preach in nearby villages. Did the new urban masses of Africa need teams of trained evangelists with access to modern technology to bring them the same gospel message? Or could the best features of American mass evangelism be the vehicle African churches needed? These are the questions which Festo and Mera Kivengere considered as they reviewed their primary calling to evangelism and the training of evangelists.

Early in 1969 Festo Kivengere and Michael Cassidy went to Nairobi for a preaching mission. "Crossroads Mission to Kenya had the backing of nearly all the churches in this sprawling, hustling city of nearly half a million people." The meetings began at five o'clock each evening, to allow working people to attend. "The two preached in turn. Festo spoke in Swahili, with the American Mennonite bishop Don Jacobs interpreting for him."[81]

Revival leaders form African Evangelistic Enterprise

The African Evangelistic Enterprise team began to take shape over the next year. The East Africans decided to call their program African Evangelistic Enterprise. The umbrella organization was African Enterprise. Archbishop Erica Sabiti agreed to chair a board for the East African team. Don Jacobs joined as well, and Zeb Kabaza resigned as headmaster of Kigezi High School in 1971 to work full-time with AEE. John Wilson, a wealthy businessman in Kampala, hesitated because of other commitments, but eventually joined the team. So did Methuselah Nyagwaswa of the Africa Inland Church of Tanzania.

All of them were formed spiritually by the East Africa Revival, and all were active in the life of the revival fellowships. They determined to preach the revival message as evangelists in the new AEE even though it was not organically connected to the revival fellowships. This brought a strain within some of the revival fellowships.[82] The Kenya brothers and sisters, in particular, were troubled by the idea of anyone being paid a salary by "outsiders" to preach the gospel. To some it appeared as though Kivengere, for his part, wanted to be free of the constraint of having the brothers and sisters decide where and when he would preach. But the revival fellowships had definitely shaped Kivengere and his colleagues: they preached the same truths as other revival brothers. In this sense, they carried the revival to new places in the same Spirit. However, AEE was a bone of contention in the throat of many of the revival brothers and sisters from its inception.

The East Africa Revival drew thousands to the big conventions, as well as smaller fellowship meetings. The Mbarara Convention in western

Uganda in December1969 was "crowded and merry with old friends meeting up once again." Roy Hession gave the Bible readings, which Festo Kivengere interpreted into the local language of Runyankole and Methuselah Nyagwaswa put into Swahili.[83]

—15—

Troubled Times in East Africa 1970–2000

It was not uncommon for revived missionaries and local church leaders to share openly on financial matters. Don Jacobs recalled the time when the Spirit of the Lord enabled open sharing among brothers and sisters in the area of finance. This was difficult for the missionaries, for their own cultures had taught them not to talk freely about money, particularly in the church. A larger challenge presented itself, however, when mission societies turned over the leadership of the churches to local leaders. They had to talk about money. That was a stressful exercise for both mission and church.

The question arose as to what light the message of revival had to shed on the dangers of financial dependency. Many of the local churches established by mission agencies had come to depend on continuing financial help from abroad to maintain the church and to expand. It was difficult to move to financial self-reliance, more so because East African churches were relatively poor. It would be a breach of fellowship if Western mission boards unilaterally cut off their financial assistance once most of the churches had become independent. The churches still needed help from the mission agencies that founded them, even though they were fully in charge of their own affairs. Hence, financial assistance continued to flow into East African churches from the American mission agencies and conferences. This was good brotherhood, no doubt, but the financial dependency proved detrimental to the churches.

The East Africa Revival had been financially self-reliant. When "the saved ones" felt that God was calling them to do something locally or on a broader scale, they simply announced the need and received the funds from the local fellowships. What they could not afford they did not undertake. When they commenced huge projects, like the stratified evangelization of an entire town or city, they did so with their own finances.

Chuck Higgins, John Gatu of Kenya, Victor Dorsch.

Rev. John Gatu and the self-reliance movement

One of the leading brothers in Kenya, John Gatu, served as the first African general secretary of the Presbyterian Church in East Africa (PCEA) in 1964–79. Gatu knew what the revival fellowships could do in bringing together large sums of money for ministry. When he took office, roughly 85 percent of the funds necessary to run PCEA originated abroad. After a few years in office, Gatu determined to lead the denomination toward financial self-reliance. He encountered much resistance, but within twenty years, PCEA managed to reverse the numbers. They raised 85 percent of their budget from their own members and received only 15 percent from abroad. To set the stage for self-reliance, Gatu called for what he termed a moratorium during which the PCEA could get its house in order and pre-pare for financial self-reliance. The proposal was described in an article by Gerald Anderson, president of the American Society of Missiology:

An African church leader recently laid before the World and U.S. National Councils of Churches a proposal that there be a morato-rium on sending and receiving money and missionary personnel. John Gatu, general secretary of the Presbyterian Church in East Africa, said that their continuing sense of dependence on and domination by foreign church groups inhibits many churches in Asia, Africa and Latin America from development in response to God's mission. "[Our] present problems," he explained, "can only be solved if all missionaries can be withdrawn in order to allow a period of not less than five years for each side to rethink and formulate what is going to be their future relationship. . . . The churches of the Third World must be allowed to find their own identity, and the continuation of the present missionary movement is a hindrance to this selfhood of the church."[1]

The proposal startled some mission agencies and gave others a good excuse to cut off funds for the African churches. Gatu defended the idea as consistent with the ethos of the revival fellowships, which knew the freedom that comes from raising and using their own money. In the end, the controversy abated as John and others moved entire denominations into a new self-understanding of what it means to build what you can afford and praise God for it.

The revival fellowships loved their friends overseas, but they never wanted to be beholden to them for financial support. They had to believe that God would supply the money to do the things he wanted them to do.

Rwanda experiences unrelenting tribal hostility

During the 1970s East Africa suffered stresses and strains that challenged the revival brothers and sisters. Rwanda remained a boiling caldron of ethnic hatred. Waves of ethnic killing continued. The peace witness of the revival fellowships was incompatible with the violence routinely used to maintain tribal superiority. As reported earlier, radical tribalists viewed the revival fellowships as disloyal and even considered them dangerous.

The revival fellowships placed loyalty to Jesus Christ as paramount. Rwanda's Tutsi and Hutu peoples could have been spared decades of bloodshed if they had embraced the reconciling power of Christ. That was the tragedy of Rwanda. God gave them the answer to their woes, but they repeatedly rejected the Prince of Peace. Some people ask why the revival failed in Rwanda: It did not fail. It was rejected.

Nationalism puts new strains on revival

When the revival first spread across East Africa, the British controlled the region, and people could move about freely. Those days came to an end in the 1970s, when each of the three major independent nations that had emerged in the region—Kenya, Uganda, and Tanzania—took a different course. Kenya was relatively stable and pursued the capitalist path. Uganda was plagued by war, dictatorial rule, and economic ruin. Tanzania embraced a style of state socialism called *ujamaa*. Strife later developed between Uganda and Tanzania. The result was that the free-flowing revival that once enjoyed ease of movement and encountered little nationalism entered a new context.

This climate affected the revival in several ways. Each nation looked after its own affairs, with little knowledge of what was happening with its neighbors. The "saved ones" faced new manifestations of nationalism and patriotism. Earlier they had met tribalism with the love of Jesus and had succeeded in breaking down some tribal barriers among their own. But nationalism presented a new set of problems. Even though the revival was vital and growing in these nations, teams were unable to travel abroad, and contacts across national boundaries were limited.

The political situation grew steadily worse in Uganda, the heartland of the revival. In 1971 Idi Amin ousted Prime Minister Milton Obote and took control of the country as its new president. A capricious tyrant, he was friendly to the church one day and its enemy the next.[2]

Tanzania became embroiled in the conflict because Idi Amin spoke of snatching a strip of its land that would give Uganda access to the Indian Ocean. The revival teams of the two countries had developed a close relationship, but political relations between Tanzania and Uganda were tense during the Amin era. Zeb Kabaza and a busload of eighty revival brothers and sisters from Uganda on their way to a fellowship meeting in Tanzania were briefly jailed as security threats in 1972. It was the last attempt to hold an international convention for seven years.[3]

Against this backdrop our story of God's hand at work unfolded. The journey was not problem free. The brothers and sisters in East Africa were put to the test again and again, sometimes by problems from within, other times by problems from without.

One of the issues they dealt with was the establishment of an African Evangelistic Enterprise program, begun mainly by Festo Kivengere and other revival leaders. Would it prove to be a new way to spread the message of revival? Or would it confuse and cloud the message of following Jesus Christ in a moment-by-moment walk of repentant faith?

African Evangelical Enterprise strengthened

Early in 1971 Festo Kivengere established African Evangelistic Enterprise. "Because of Archbishop Sabiti's support for the work, . . . Festo launched the Uganda AEE that spring, with the sole help of Zebulon Kabaza."[4] The purpose was to evangelize the cities, towns, and schools of

Africa. The archbishop became the chairman of the Uganda AEE board, and Kivengere was the team leader. All involved were keen revival brethren. In time national boards and teams were formed in Tanzania and Kenya, and eventually an East African board coordinated the work of all. The East African ministry was supported largely by support boards in United States and England. Other nations joined later.

The formation of AEE in East Africa brought some confusion to the revival teams. AEE was a nondenominational evangelistic ministry. Yet it was staffed largely by well-known revival leaders, such as Festo Kivengere, Zebulon Kabaza, James Katarikawe, Erica Sabiti, John Wilson, Methuselah Nyagwaswa, Emmanuel Kibira, and Titus Lwebandiza. The misunderstanding was apparent when the Kenya national revival team decided not to get involved in the establishment of a Kenyan branch of AEE. They did not want to hinder the work of AEE but had concerns because AEE was supported largely from abroad. They feared that evangelists who served in AEE would be under its direct control, with little or no connection to the revival brothers and sisters.

In Uganda and Tanzania, the revival teams blended with AEE. The three key figures in the establishment of AEE in Tanzania were also well-known leaders in the revival fellowships: Emmanuel Kibira, who became chairman of the board, together with Methuselah Nyagwaswa and Titus Lwebandiza, staff persons.

About this time Tanzanian authorities required the revival to organize into a legal body before it could have an official bank account. They did so under the name New Life For All. Organizing like this was unique for the revival anywhere in the world. The development brought additional tension among the national revival fellowship teams and proved to be quite harmful for the propagation of revival in Tanzania.

The Kenyan teams stood isolated, so to speak, because of their stance toward AEE. The Kenyan teams disliked what they considered as a move to incorporate the revival. The former good relationship between the national teams was suddenly under heavy strain. This estrangement ran parallel to the political situation in East Africa, which saw the nations isolating themselves from their neighbors.

The East African AEE program was naturally built around Festo Kivengere, so it came as a great surprise when in May 1972 Bishop Lyth of Kigezi announced that he was about to retire. "Kivengere" was the only name the Kigezi diocese sent to Archbishop Erica Sabiti and the House of Bishops to be Bishop Lyth's successor. "Complete dismay settled like a cloud on the heads of Michael Cassidy and Don Jacobs and the rest of the team, both in Africa and the States."[5] They feared that if Festo Kivengere became a bishop in the Church of Uganda, his involvement as a key player in AEE would be minimized.

Kivengere made bishop

Plans were soon under way for Kivengere's consecration as a bishop in Kampala in November 1972 and for his installation in Kabale Cathedral, in his home area of Kigezi in December.[6] Festo was soon preaching around the world and, at the same time, trying to administer his populous diocese in western Uganda. With only Festo Kivengere and Zeb Kabaza on the AEE team, more invitations came than could be accepted. Happily, the team grew with the work. John Wilson, a Kampala businessman and rooted firmly in revival, was the first to step in and help. He became Festo's deputy in AEE, relieving him of many speaking engagements when diocesan duties pressed.[7]

John E. H. Wilson resigned from his position as sales manager for a multinational corporation to enroll at Bishop Tucker Theological College in Mukono, Uganda. He was ordained deacon at Namirembe Cathedral in April 1974 and a week later was on his way to America for a series of meetings with Titus Lwebandiza, culminating in a weekend at the High Street Church of God in Philadelphia at the invitation of Ernie Wilson.[8] Titus had recently resigned his post in the Tanzanian government to become a full-time preacher. John Wilson, an Anglican from Uganda, and Titus, a Lutheran from Tanzania, returned to the United States for their extended preaching mission.[9] Wilson had visited the United States several times and in 1972 conducted meetings sponsored by AEE.[10] He now moved with his family to California for further study at Fuller Seminary. During his year in the United States, he received many invitations to preach and fellowship with revived brothers and sisters.[11]

John Wilson came to ministry by a long road. After leaving Makerere College in 1945, he worked as a big game hunter, a welfare officer in the East African Railways, a subcontractor in building the hydroelectric dam on the Nile at Jinja in Uganda, and an automobile dealer—all before joining Caltex Oil of Uganda in 1961. He came to Christ in 1955 through the East Africa Revival and about 1960 began preaching on teams with Kivengere and other revival brothers.[12] He was ordained a priest in the Episcopal Cathedral in Los Angeles in May 1975, together with James Katarikawe, a new member of the AEE team, who was beginning a year of study at Fuller.[13]

Kivengere sought help in administering his diocese. In 1974 he installed the William Rukirande as his administrative assistant. "Rukirande, from a village near Kabale, had just finished a diploma in theology from Mukono and was serving as chaplain at Kigezi High School."[14] He too was formed by the revival. Kivengere wanted him to be assistant bishop, and in 1975 the new archbishop of Uganda, Janani Luwum, ordained William Rukirande as assistant bishop of the Kigezi diocese. More and more of the running of the diocese devolved on him.[15]

Invitations to Kivengere and his team came from around the world. In 1974 he preached with Zeb Kabaza in Japan, then participated in the Lausanne Conference on Evangelism. He was immediately off again, "this time back to Europe, beginning with a CMS preaching tour of England with Eustace Ruhindi, a senior clergyman from Kigezi diocese, and Zebulon Kabaza."[16]

Methuselah Nyagwaswa returned to the United States in the spring of 1975 for two months of renewal meetings in churches. He was still a senior education officer in Tanzania but used his vacations to preach the Word as part of the AEE team.[17] Although these men were not sent out as a team by the revival brethren, they carried the message of revival to North America and linked significantly with the North American fellowships.

Brethren in East Africa made plans for the fourth Revival Convention at Kabale, the center of Kivengere's diocese of Kigezi in western Uganda. The first convention met there in 1945 with the theme "Jesus Satisfies," and William Nagenda and Festo Kivengere had been the main speakers then.[18] Kivengere had chosen the theme this time: "Christ's Love Reconciles Us." People came "from Kigezi, Ankole and all Uganda, from Kenya, Burundi, Rwanda, Zaire, USA, Canada, England, West Germany, Norway, Switzerland, and even Japan."[19] It was a joyful reunion of old friends in Christ. Simeon Nsibambi was too ill to leave his home at Namirembe. Joe Church came from England.[20] Kivengere estimated there were "around 8,000 present Thursday through Saturday and 25,000 on Sunday at the closing services." The bulk of those attending, it was reported, were young people, an indication "that the forty-year-old revival has taken root in a new generation." As in other conventions, "the daily program of speakers was decided on the spot by a team waiting on the Holy Spirit for guidance." The physical needs of so many people took careful advance planning. "The Christians cooperated in growing the food to feed the guests and volunteered to cook for them." Drought that year gave them some anxiety, but in the end everyone was fed and housed and returned home while praising the Lord.[21]

Alarming confrontation with Ugandan authorities

The Kabale convention was one of the last happy events for Christians in Uganda. Idi Amin had overthrown the government. At the beginning of his regime, his relationship with the church seemed positive. John Wilson wrote: "One of the greatest challenges ever posed to the ten million Ugandans was when the new president said that all people should turn to God."[22] Amin intervened in the affairs of the church when a squabble arose over the fact that Archbishop Erica Sabiti was from Ankole and not from Buganda, a tribal issue that threatened the unity of the Church of Uganda. Through Amin's efforts the bishops were reconciled.[23] But in 1977 the amiable relationship between Amin and the church soured as the Church of Uganda began planning to celebrate the centennial of the first missionaries' arrival in Uganda.

By the mid 1970s things had begun to go very wrong for Uganda's strong man, Idi Amin. He was convinced that the church was out to destroy him. Early in February 1977 government agents searched Archbishop Janani Luwum's house in Kampala for evidence of a plot against the dictator. They found nothing. Luwum, like all the brothers and sisters in the revival fellowship, deplored the use of violence and made it clear in a statement to his beloved church:

> While the opportunity is there, I preach the gospel with all my might, and my conscience is clear before God that I have not sided with the present government, which is utterly self-seeking. I have been threatened many times. Whenever I have the opportunity, I have told the president the things the churches disapprove of. God is my witness.[24]

The next day the Ugandan bishops sent a respectful protest to the president. Ten days later Amin summoned Archbishop Janani Luwum and Bishops Festo Kivengere and Silvanus Wani to the Nile Mansions Hotel for interrogation. He ordered the archbishop taken away under guard. The next morning the government-controlled newspapers announced that Luwum and two government officials were killed in an automobile accident. Believing his own arrest imminent, Festo and Mera Kivengere fled to Rwanda. Their home and many others on Namirembe hill in Kampala were systematically looted. James and Muriel Katarikawe found refuge with Zebulon and Priscilla Kabaza in another section of Kampala, after their home at Namirembe was raided.[25]

All of these Ugandans were shaped by and deeply involved in the East Africa Revival. As in the Mau Mau uprising in Kenya, the Ugandan brothers and sisters witnessed to the grace and mercy of the Prince of Peace in the midst of appalling hostility. Janani Luwum was a demonstration of the power of the love of Jesus over hatred. These brave souls lived according to these New Testament words: "They [the martyrs] overcame him [Satan] by the blood of the Lamb and by the word of their testimony; they did not love their lives so much as to shrink from death" (Rev 12:11 NIV).

Other church leaders feared for their lives. After the archbishop's funeral, Bishop William Rukirande, another revival leader, drove back to his home area near Kabale, far removed from Kampala. He went to an isolated mission school to hide and pray for guidance. After a week there, he put his collar on and showed himself in Kabale as the bishop. Nothing happened to him, and he continued to administer the diocese without any difficulty from the government.[26]

Kivengere escapes, pleads for help

After Festo Kivengere's escape from Uganda, the Lord touched him regarding his feelings about Idi Amin. Kivengere repented. Then he had his answer when someone in the press challenged him: "Knowing how evil Idi Amin is, if you and he were in a room alone, and you had a gun and he did not, what would you do?" Kivengere replied: "I would give him the gun for that is his weapon, not mine. Mine is the love of Jesus."[27]

Having escaped Amin, Festo Kivengere felt obligated to alert the world to what was occurring in once-prosperous Uganda. He and his wife, Mera, arrived in United States in March 1977 for this reason. Soon after, "Don Jacobs, an old friend and occasional AEE evangelist, executive director of the Mennonite Christian Leadership Foundation, set up a number of appointments with senators and congressmen so Festo could alert them about what was going on in Uganda."[28] Kivengere was gratified with the outcome of his discussions. Don recalls when he and Festo were leaving the office of one of the senators, the senator whispered to Don, "Is this the next President of Uganda?" Don shared this with Festo as they were walking down the hall.

Festo as an Anglican bishop, witnessing out of his many years of walking in revival.

Festo stopped, pointed to his Bible, and said, "This is my politics!" He and Don had a good laugh at that.[29]

Festo Kivengere had many opportunities to preach in America, including the Billy Graham Crusade in Asheville, North Carolina, in September; and the same autumn at Messiah College, in Grantham, Pennsylvania, where he had often spoken at revival fellowships.[30] Dorothy Smoker and Festo Kivengere worked on a book about his experience, *I Love Idi Amin*, published in 1977.[31]

Many refugees fled from Uganda, finding their way to neighboring countries. Ugandan students found themselves stranded overseas without funds. The AEE set up the Committee for the Relief, Education, and Training of Ugandan Refugees, with John Wilson in charge of operations from his office in Nairobi, Kenya. They were able to raise millions of dollars to provide scholarships for Ugandan students and later, after Idi Amin's fall, to reconstruct Uganda. Some of the revival brothers and sisters had been hoping that the revival movement would become involved more in large-scale social service ministries. With the help of the revival fellowships, AEE responded courageously to a huge tragedy and humanitarian crisis.

We have recognized how the formation of AEE national teams presented huge challenges to the unity of the revival fellowships in East Africa. On the positive side, AEE enabled revival brothers such as Kivengere, Wilson, Kabaza, Lwebandiza, Katarikawe, and others to maintain contact with fellowships abroad. They were free to travel and had finances to make it possible. As they conducted their AEE work, they also encouraged the revival fellowships and people who were walking the Calvary way. The African Enterprise board in United States was especially helpful. They provided blocks of time when East African evangelists could minister among the revival fellowships as they traveled in the interest of AEE. So when the East African brothers and sisters were not in a position to send teams to spread the message of ongoing revival, as in the early days, the AEE filled that need to some degree for a while.

Tensions arise between East and South Africa

In the 1960s and 1970s, East African nations viewed South Africa, with its rigid apartheid system, as abhorrent and refused to allow its nationals to travel there. It was always a struggle to keep the two African Enterprise regions together. In many ways, it would have been much easier to simply separate. But that would have been a denial of the gospel of reconciliation. The East Africans took heart from the determination of the

South African teams to build multiracial teams there, but the pressure that the East Africans felt was intense.

One of the central themes of the East Africa Revival message was that the atonement wrought by Jesus Christ enabled people to love one another across all human barriers. Festo Kivengere and others struggled with this because what they were doing was not politically safe. Yet they felt constrained to love even where their societies placed boundaries.

Against that background it should not come as a surprise that strains developed between the teams, especially along North/South lines. Kivengere's biographer told how they were resolved at a meeting late in 1971 in an Alpine village in Switzerland, much as Kivengere and Nagenda had done by coming into the light years earlier:

> [Kivengere] began with a testimony. A couple of hours before, he said, he had been praying and expressing his love for Christ. Suddenly he had heard an inner voice say: "I know you love me, but do you love Michael?" Festo went on to admit that he had had to confess to a lack of love, and that the Lord had then poured love in.
>
> Don Jacobs recalled, "Having given us his witness, Festo crossed the room and embraced Michael before all of us. This was a moment which had about it the aura of eternity. The fellowship between the teams was built upon that little walk of ten steps that Festo took toward Michael."[32]

The revival story told in China and the Middle East

African Evangelistic Enterprise became a useful vehicle for the propagation of the revival message. Don Jacobs was in Kenya when AEE was formed and retained an ongoing relationship to that body through the years. Jacobs recalled that the effectiveness of AEE was demonstrated by three prolonged visits to China at the invitation of the Three-Self Church, registered with the Chinese government. There was always a small team, including Festo Kivengere, John Wilson, and others who were asked to share what God is doing in Africa. Sig Aske of Norway, a member of the AE International Board and a former missionary in China and Ethiopia, arranged for these visits with Bishop Ding in China.

The Chinese believers were eager to hear how the church was faring as the colonial powers were fading. Invariably the team told story after story of the mighty power of the gospel to satisfy the needs of the human heart and weld believers into tight, loving communities of faith. Chinese congregations were at the edge of their seats as the Africans spoke of how the atoning power of Jesus Christ enabled them to overcome the works of Satan, producing communities of faith.

Seminary students were also amazed by the love they heard about and witnessed in the team, a love that came from Calvary to bind men and women together, in spite of their differences. Bishop Ding and Festo Kivengere were good friends, which aided in the spread of the gospel as lived out in Africa.[33]

Another highlight included the several visits of AEE teams to Israel, the West Bank, Jordan, and Greece in 1982. This was a ministry organized by John Wilson, called "To Israel with Love." Jacobs long remembers the large meetings in Samaria, where Jewish and Arab believers gathered together for a time of fellowship, sharing, and hearing what God was doing in Africa. The large group of several hundred who picnicked together on a sloping lawn at the Baptist Village is a scene he will long remember.

Jacobs also recalls intimate, secret meetings on a Greek island, where there were significant breakthroughs. Arabs and Jews can love one another—in Jesus. Those meetings proved to be rather difficult at times, but the ministry of people like Festo Kivengere and John Wilson carried the day. People could see the value of Jesus' removing divisions at the cross, where we are all one in him.[34]

The AEE came under intense criticism at this time for relating to colleagues in the South African AE, in which whites had prominent positions. Many meetings between the AEE and South African AE teams and boards moved forward only through repentance. It is a tribute to the East African teams that they resisted the blistering criticism that resulted from their dealings with the South Africans, especially because the governments in East Africa forbade all relationships with that apartheid nation. The South African AE teams, headed by Michael Cassidy, insisted on being multicultural from the beginning. And those teams bore the criticism of those who wanted to maintain white rule in South Africa.

None of the East Africans could visit South Africa during that period because of visa restrictions placed on them by their own nations. The AEE teams and boards met regularly with the their South African colleagues in neutral venues, where they could share openly about what God was doing. In East Africa, brothers and sisters were living together in peace, in spite of their differences. Literature produced in East Africa, particularly the writings of Festo Kivengere, circulated freely and openly in South Africa.

Don Jacobs served as chairman of the International Partnership Board of Africa Enterprise from 1988 to 1994. Serving on the board were church leaders with a heart for evangelism from seven African nations—Kenya, Tanzania, Uganda, Rwanda, Malawi, Zimbabwe and South Africa—and others from the nations that supported them: the United States, the United Kingdom, Germany, Australia, Norway, Switzerland, and Canada. The partnership board supported and directed the work of the AEE. This put Jacobs into a context where he could continue to relate to and team with brothers and sisters of the East Africa Revival and the South African teams as well. He served as a bridge between the fellowships in Africa and in other parts of the world. In this way the message of the reconciling power of the atoning work of Jesus went forward. Under his leadership Africa Enterprise embraced reconciliation as a major ministry, along with evangelism and social concerns. This reflected Don Jacobs' theological orientation, which grew out of his own Anabaptist theology and the life and witness of the revival in East Africa and beyond.[35]

Dorothy Smoker tells revival stories

Dorothy Smoker, writer.

Dorothy Smoker's literary ability was put to good use in preparing African Enterprise publications at their Pasadena office. In 1972 she began writing and editing a monthly newsletter *African Enterprise Outlook*.[36] She included a lead column by Festo Kivengere in almost every issue. The message of revival was getting out. In addition, by 1976 African Enterprise was selling tapes of twenty different messages preached by Kivengere. They also widely distributed his two small books, *When God Moves* and *Love Unlimited*.[37] In 1975 Dorothy Smoker had prepared a small book of Kivengere's messages, taken from those in the Swahili monthly mission periodical *Outlook*, and called it *Love Unlimited*.[38] She revised *When God Moves in Revival* from a collection of his messages. It was published in 1973 at Accra, Ghana.

Festo Kivengere invited George and Dorothy Smoker to put together a book of his special messages for Uganda, in its needy condition. Kivengere had given the messages in *Hope for Uganda* at Bishop Tucker Theological Seminary in Mukono, Uganda, at Easter 1980. "The Smokers, feeling also the need for a definitive book on the East Africa Revival from the partici- pants' point of view, collected together an autobiographical book of Bishop Festo's own experiences as told in his messages. Thoroughly revised by the bishop, *Revolutionary Love* was finally published in 1983." Distributed by Christian Literature Crusade, it went through many printings.[39]

In 1980 George and Dorothy Smoker left California for Kenya, to work in the African Enterprise office in Nairobi. They returned to East Africa in time for the revival convention at Mwanza, Tanzania. Some five thousand *ndugu* (revived brothers and sisters) from Tanzania, Uganda, Kenya, Rwanda, and Burundi met there to be reconciled in Jesus Christ after their countries had been torn by war.[40] Forty years after they met the East Africa Revival, the Smokers went on evangelistic teams with John Wilson and other brothers.[41] Later Dorothy Smoker compiled the stories of the faithful witness of revival brothers and sisters in the sufferings of the Mau Mau years in Kenya; it was published in 1994 as *Ambushed by Love*.

Troubles beset East Africa in the 1980s. In 1985 Uganda was suffering from civil war. Milton Obote fled, and early in 1986 Yoweri Museveni became president of Uganda. John Wilson was murdered by unlawful sol- diers in Kampala.[42] The country was nearing total economic collapse.

The passing of William Nagenda and Simeon Nsibambi

William Nagenda had suffered a stroke in December 1971 while he was receiving treatment in a German hospital for Parkinson's disease. William and his wife, Sala, returned to Uganda later that month. William died on January 8, 1973, at sixty years of age. Archbishop Erica Sabiti con- ducted his funeral, and Bishop Festo Kivengere preached at the graveside.[43]

George and Dorothy Smoker notified the North American revived brothers and sisters and added their own tribute:

> This is a special bulletin to let you know that William Nagenda has gone home to be with the Lord. He entered glory on January 8th about 8 p.m., and Zeb Kabaza phoned us with the message about 10 p.m. He had been very ill for some time and died in the Mengo Hospital in Kampala, Uganda. Sala, his wife, is peacefully trusting the Lord. Brethren from all over East Africa are preparing a most triumphant farewell to William for Thursday, January 11th.

If you knew William Nagenda, you knew that God blessed and used him. He was the first spokesman for the East Africa Revival movement who carried the testimony of what God was doing by grace throughout East Africa and gave it with clarity and authority in England, Europe, and America. He first brought Festo Kivengere with him as a teammate, and later his mantle fell on Festo as William weakened in body.

William was heard at the Urbana, Illinois, IVCF Missionary Convention of 1954. He and Festo were approached by the Billy Graham team with the possibility offered that they become a part of that team. They had to decline, as they felt their African brethren could not understand the sponsorship of so great an American organization.[44]

William's message was never a pointing to "revival" but always pointing to the Lord Jesus Christ. Putting him in the center was the key to joyous living. [William's] own life was transparent before his brethren and in his preaching. He knew himself to be weak and a failure in many ways, but an excited recipient of the forgiveness and grace of Jesus, washed in the blood daily. Thank God with us for Brother William and all he meant in the personal lives of many of us.[45]

More than four thousand people came to William Nagenda's funeral at Buloba, near Kampala. This humble follower of Jesus had touched many lives.[46]

The brothers and sisters celebrated the home-going of another one of their beloved leaders when Simeon Nsibambi died on February 14, 1978, at the age of eighty-one. "A thanksgiving and memorial service was held for him on June 16, 1978, at which the retired Archbishop Erica Sabiti described him as 'Our father in Christ.' Nsibambi was, the archbishop observed, 'a man who could have been the *katikkiro* [the leading government official] of Buganda, but who instead devoted his life to bringing people closer to God.'"[47]

Charismatic renewal in East Africa

The 1970s marked the decade when Pentecostal and charismatic churches grew by leaps and bounds. This siphoned off large numbers of young people who had been converted and nurtured in the revival. Two streams were running—the revival, which began in the early Thirties, and

272 A Gentle Wind of God

the more recent charismatic movement, which presented the revival with new challenges.

But the revival stayed on the message in spite of everything. People became saved daily, and the local fellowships continued to nurture and care for one another. Those were not the most exciting years, but the revival remained strong and vibrant, with its message of grace. It might be noted that the Pentecostal and charismatic movements in East Africa maintained a strong emphasis on the mighty work of salvation, a bedrock belief of the revival.

Before the 1970s there had been a good deal of traffic between the revival fellowships in East Africa and North America. This soon slowed to a trickle because of the situation in East Africa. The fellowships there were so heavily challenged by the upheavals that were occurring that they had little leisure to consider sending teams abroad as they once did. As already noted, the limited contact between them was maintained through the visits of revival brethren who worked in AEE. But their visits were sporadic and did not fill the role that the earlier teams from East Africa had. This was both a challenging and a maturing time for the fellowships outside of East Africa. It was challenging because they could not rely on much encourage-ment from East Africa, and maturing in that they had to embrace the mes-sage as their own, regardless of its place of origin.

Blessedly, fellowship among the various teams in North America, Europe, and the United Kingdom increased. The trials and tribulations of the revival fellowships in East Africa meant that the revival outside Africa had to find its own way. It did so. The message of revival was embraced and lived out in Western cultures, just as it was in East Africa. The East Africa Revival became revival for Western culture. Revival in the West was coming into its own, appreciative of its African origins, but not dependent upon them.

The deaths of Sabiti and Kivengere

In these difficult days, two leaders of the East Africa Revival were called to their reward. Erica Sabiti, retired archbishop of Uganda, died peacefully at home on May 17, 1988, at the age of 85.[48] The next day Bishop Festo Kivengere died. He was sixty-eight years old and had been active almost to the last. Like Blasio Kigozi fifty years earlier, one of his last actions was to raise a question for the 1988 Lambeth Conference: "How can the experiences of renewal be turned outward in service to the commu-nity rather than inward in sentimentality?"[49] After preliminary services at

Namirembe Cathedral, Festo Kivengere was buried from his own cathedral in Kabale, with twenty thousand people present. The president of Uganda spoke "a heartfelt impromptu speech." Don Jacobs delivered the first of two funeral sermons; the second was by the archbishop of Uganda.[50] Jacobs preached on the text from Isaiah 52:7, "How beautiful on the mountains are the feet of those who bring good news, who proclaim peace, who bring good tidings, who proclaim salvation" (NIV). Festo fit that description perfectly.

With the passing of Nsibambi, Nagenda, Sabiti, and Kivengere, an era ended. Will the revival that they preached and lived survive as a shaping influence on the generations that follow? Only time will provide an answer to that question. But it is gratifying to know that the revival fellowships prospered throughout East Africa in spite of daunting circumstances. The way of walking with Jesus in a moment-by-moment cleansed relationship is still known and lived by thousands. Even some associated with Pentecostal-oriented movements continue to value the centrality of being "saved."

In Uganda the regular weekly local fellowships continue to shape lives. Because most of the leaders of the Church of Uganda are in sympathy with the revival, if not actually walking in fellowship with it, larger gatherings of the brothers and sisters are often held in collaboration with the renewal meetings of the church.

In Kenya, active regional teams carry the vision of revival and assist in the regional meetings. Together they form a nationwide Kenyan team that gives guidance to the affairs of the fellowships on a broader basis. Every other year there is a national convention, and a youth-oriented convention in the off years. With funds contributed by the fellowships and with the aid of the evangelists within the revival fellowships, they also mount evangelistic campaigns, usually in one of the major cities.

The Tanzanian fellowships had passed through a hiatus in the 1990s, but here and there new life is springing up. Tanzania has an operating team that meets with the other East African teams to pray, to share lessons of walking with Jesus together, and to discern what God is asking them to do. The East African team is now strong, with each nation represented. The banner year of 2000 brought representatives not only from Kenya, Uganda, and Tanzania, but also from Rwanda, Burundi, and even from northeast Congo.

It is truly amazing that the wind of God that began to blow gently in the hills of Rwanda in 1928 still brings new life in Jesus Christ to thousands. The wind is still a wind, not an organization or a program. As long as it can sustain life without human scaffolding, it should continue to blow blessings to the entire world.

—16—

Challenges and New Opportunities in North America 1970–1980

The revival message that spelled new life for thousands in East Africa was also marvelous good news to hungry hearts in North America. The message was disarmingly simple: The atoning work of Jesus is wonderfully sufficient for salvation, holy living, and for victory over Satan. Believers discovered that they can maintain a moment-by-moment open relationship with Jesus Christ by dealing honestly with their sinful nature, by repentance, and by walking in transparency and love with fellow brothers and sisters regardless of their status in life. Central to this message is the cross and resurrection of Jesus Christ. The challenge, both in East Africa and North America, was to add nothing to Jesus and to take nothing from him. Jesus is front and center. All practical theology flows from the reality of walking with Jesus.

There was nothing in this message that was novel to North Americans. The delight came when they realized it could be lived out, that it was actually possible to walk so closely with Jesus and with brothers and sisters that nothing could dismay or overwhelm the believer, even death itself.

The revival held the atoning work of Jesus Christ as foundational. As the hymn puts it, "His blood avails for me" (Charles Wesley). Christianity in North America tended to dilute the power of Christ's atoning sacrifice for sinners. The revival had no place for human self-effort, no matter what form it might take. According to the revived, holy living and doing good flows naturally from those who walk so closely with Jesus that his mind is formed in them.

The challenge that faced the revival fellowships in North America was to be as diligent as their counterparts in East Africa in keeping the accretions off the simple message of God's good news. We saw how new challenges faced revival fellowships in East Africa, and how the community of faith there dealt with anything that tended to blur the absolute centrality of the crucified, risen Jesus Christ. This focused devotion on the living Jesus, known and obeyed by his grateful followers, may account for the fact that this revival endured as a vital movement for more than seventy-five years, and is still a powerful force in the lives of many thousands in East Africa and beyond.

But the question is posed: Did the North Americans affected by the East Africa Revival succeed in guarding the centrality of the crucified and risen Jesus Christ? This, among other issues, will emerge as the story of revival unfolds in North America.

Learning from and relating to the charismatic movement

When questioned about spiritual gifts, Zeb Kabaza, an early participant in revival, responded, "We experienced the gifts of the Holy Spirit from the very beginning."[1] He recalled that Pentecostal phenomena—such as speaking in tongues, prophesying, demonstrative healings and the like—occurred in quite a few places in the early days of the East Africa Revival. Notable was what happened at Katoke, near Bukoba, on the western shore of Lake Victoria. The revival fellowship experienced an outbreak of dramatic Pentecostal expressions in 1939 there, and revival leaders did not question the authenticity of these signs of the Holy Spirit's presence. But they cautioned the Katoke fellowship against making too much of the dramatic experiences. They encouraged believers to just lift up the crucified, risen Christ and not to allow anything to distract from Jesus. It was not long until the group blended their experience of the Holy Spirit with the central revival message of intimate, cleansed, open fellowship with Jesus Christ, and on walking in submission to Christ in the fellowship of believers. This happened many years before the wave of the modern charismatic movement swept over many churches in America and Africa.

By about 1970 American Christians of many traditions were talking about the charismatic movement. Lutherans, Presbyterians, Episcopalians, Catholics, and Mennonites had discovered the gifts of the Spirit in a fresh experience of grace, often with speaking in tongues and other manifestations of spiritual gifts.

Erma Maust, a key promoter of the revival, encountered charismatic experience as early as 1961, when she ministered among a group of recently blessed Episcopalians and Lutherans on the West Coast. It was rather strange to her, but she warmed to their genuine love of the Lord. As charismatic experience became more common, Erma welcomed it as a sign of revival; so did John and Catharine Leatherman, John I. Smucker, and other revival brothers and sisters.[2] However, the excitement tended to overshadow the simple Jesus-centered message from East Africa. During that era the charismatic movement did not produce new denominations. That tendency came later when the difference between those who were being filled with the Holy Spirit and those who weren't became so pronounced that the only solution seemed to be to establish new denominations.

Bill Liner and others identified with North American revival fellowships were far from convinced that charismatic movement was a good thing. They saw congregations divided over speaking in tongues and other signs. They feared that the movement was separating those baptized in the Spirit from other Christians, and they detected a tendency in charasmatics to set up new rules for the Christian life.

The revival fellowships in East Africa took no stand on what was then known as the Pentecostal movement, neither endorsing nor condemning it. In the United States and Canada, however, disagreement over speaking in tongues and the baptism of the Holy Spirit disturbed the revival fellowships. Erma Maust's acceptance of charismatic experience and her later association with Kathryn Kuhlman, an extraordinarily successful Pentecostal-style evangelist in Pittsburgh, and Women's Aglow, a fellowship for women in the charismatic tradition, cost her some old friends who consequently rejected her leadership.

Refocusing the message, Switzerland 1970

The European and North American revival fellowships tried to revisit the heart of the message of revival in light of the much more popular charismatic movement. Roy Hession and other revival leaders convened a special conference at Oberageri, Switzerland, in June 1970. A review of the messages given at this conference reveals no attempt to overtly examine the pros and cons of the movement. Rather, the speakers stayed on the central message of Jesus as revival and then clarified and updated the revival message.

Chuck Higgins, a Nazarene pastor from California, and Bill and Gladys Liner from Alberta, Canada, represented the North American fellowships at the conference. Bill Liner reported: "Seventy representatives convened from Africa, England, Scotland, Germany, France, Canada, the

International revival team meeting in Switzerland, 1970.

United States, and Switzerland." Stanley Voke, a Baptist pastor from England, delivered the keynote address "to form the basis of our thinking and praying in the days together."

Liner was particularly struck by Archbishop Erica Sabiti's message: "When God came in reviving power to Uganda, he made what was only religion and mere Christianity to become life. He made it very simple for us. A religion full of things to do became just a life to be received." Claire-Lise de Benoit, Scripture Union worker from Switzerland, told of the beginnings of revival there in 1947, when William Nagenda and a team from Rwanda visited her country. Other speakers included Ernst Krebs, evangelist from Switzerland; Rev Jim Graham, Baptist pastor from England; Rev. John Goring, minister from Scotland; Rev. Geoffrey Jones, Methodist minister from England; Dr. Ken Moynagh from London; Joe Church; Roy Hession; and Rev. John Collinson.[3]

Bill and Gladys Liner, effective advocates for revival in Western Canada.

Elam Stauffer did not attend the Switzerland conference, but his views of the charismatic movement reflected the views of most of those within the revival:

I have long felt that the Spirit must and will raise up servants of his, filled full with the Spirit, who will praise and magnify him without tongues, . . . just to keep his saints balanced. Neither history nor Scripture says that all his Spirit-filled ones will speak in tongues. Some will and some will not. This is the message we must give and demonstrate. . . . The Spirit may be reviving the charisma these days to give new evidence of the reality of his presence. Praise him for this. But the emotional side of Christians must not carry them away to emphases and experiences that will not stand the test of time and of reality, and of proper exegesis of the Word.[4]

To organize or not to organize?

Chuck and Marge Higgins and Bill and Gladys Liner returned from Switzerland with new vision and vigor to press forward with the message of revival. The Higginses looked forward to strengthening the ad hoc fellowships that had become the hallmark of the revival; the Liners felt nudged by God to be more aggressive and create an organization to carry the revival forward in North America.

Bill Liner was beginning to see his ministry as part of the East Africa Revival. He and his wife Gladys had begun publishing a newsletter called *Living Water*, which they soon expanded into a small magazine carrying revival news and messages from fellowship conferences. This quality production effectively spread the message of revival. Bill was considering radio ministry as well. He held meetings in Virginia, Maryland, Pennsylvania, Manitoba, Alberta, and Saskatchewan, including a week at Evangelical Mennonite Church, Swift Current, Saskatchewan. The high point was a campout conference in August: "Around ninety gathered for the week from Alberta, Saskatchewan, Manitoba, Virginia, Pennsylvania, Kansas, and California."[5]

The question arose as to whether the Liners should try to create an organization with officers, staff, and budgets that would include all the fellowship teams in North America. The idea understandably brought confusion to the teams and contributed to some loosening of closeness among fellowships in North America. Some brothers and sisters saw the Liner vision as a good thing; others were not convinced. Chuck Higgins, pastor of the Church of the Nazarene in Pasadena, California, questioned Roy Hession about Liner's vision:

He seems to agree that we cannot organize anything to promote revival. . . . I do hope we can keep this vision very clear in our minds. We must not muddy the waters with organizations to promote the work of the Holy Spirit in renewal. . . . We do praise the Lord for the way God has led Bill and Gladys [Liner] in this ministry, and we want to be one in the Spirit with them. But we must maintain our freedom to work and minister in the place we have been found by the Spirit. We need no longer be in bondage to join one another's organization or denomination.[6]

The idea was dropped, and the Liners eventually found other outlets for their energies, always carrying the message of revival in their hearts and in their testimony. The North American tendency to organize things did not seem to fit with the free movement of revival through the decades.

Erma Maust persists with the revival message

Erma Maust moved freely among many groups, some of which had embraced the charismatic movement. She did not take part in planning these meetings; she was busy with her speaking ministry, her ministry of helps, and in great demand for women's retreats, particularly in Mennonite churches. Erma also began giving devotional talks at meetings of the charismatic group Women's Aglow. Herbert and Erma Maust found this schedule grueling but also invigorating:

It has been such a joy traveling over the country, sharing and seeing God bring souls out of prison to praise His name. Even though this has meant being on the road most of the time, living out of a suitcase, sleeping in strange beds, . . . we love Him for Who He is and what He is doing for us in giving us such joy and in making us a real team in this ministry of "helps."[7]

The Mausts kept up a large correspondence with revival brothers and sisters. They often visited friends to take over domestic chores in times of need. Erma wrote of a few hours spent in fellowship with John and Dottie Freed, whom she had first met as young mission workers in the South Bronx. She was encouraged by their time together: "Isn't it just wonderful to know and be *willing* and *believe* he dearly and tenderly loves us and only allows what is for our good! I don't know where I'd be if he had not undergirded me with this word while going through the trials he allowed these past eight years or so."[8]

Life had not been easy for the Mausts. Misunderstandings about new directions in Erma's ministry brought much stress. Herbert and Erma's letters reflected their confidence in the outcome: "All he asks is that we be willing to be honest about our need as we come to him. But how difficult this is, for it cuts right across our pride, self-will, and our love of the approval of others."[9]

So the journeys continued. Erma could not stay in one place very long. She wrote: "Praise the Lord for all the open doors in Alabama and Florida in women's retreats, small-group Bible classes, and personal counseling." Erma also reported:

> We had a most blessed fellowship with the brothers and sisters of St. Paul's Episcopal Church at Haymarket, Virginia, on our way north; especially in the fellowship with the ladies (and a half-dozen men) of the various Bible classes Thursday noon at a luncheon; Friday evening with the St. Paul's Episcopal Fellowship in the parish hall, and again in the eleven o'clock service Sunday morning. God blessed in our time together, souls were set free and a deacon born into the family of God—made a new creature in Jesus. All praise to our wonderful Lord![10]

This was probably Erma Maust's first invitation to the Haymarket church, but she would be asked to speak there six more times. The rector of St. Paul's was the Rev. Robert Crewdson, who was touched by the East Africa Revival when he heard Archbishop Erica Sabiti preach in Eastern Mennonite College chapel.[11]

Making use of international speakers

Rev. Ernie Wilson announced fellowship meetings for March 1971 at Memorial Baptist Church, Huntingdon Valley, Pennsylvania, and High Street Church of God in Philadelphia. The speakers were to be Festo Kivengere and Zeb Kabaza from Uganda, East Africa.[12]

Glenn Zeager and Paul Landis took the initiative to arrange a meeting with Kivengere and Kabaza as well. They hoped to revive the nearly stagnant revival fellowships:

> For some time we have been praying about having a meeting of brothers and sisters who might give some direction to developing further fellowship meetings here in the East. Glenn Zeager has

been in touch with Brother Ernest Wilson and those who are planning for Festo Kivengere's schedule. Brother Festo will be in the East and would be available to meet with some of us on Thursday, May 27. Brother Ernest Wilson has very graciously invited us to meet in his home in Philadelphia.[13]

Paul and Ann Landis helped organize conferences.

Paul Landis, Wayne Lawton, Catharine Leatherman, Elam Stauffer, Luke Stoltzfus, and Ernie Wilson met with Festo Kivengere and Zeb Kabaza as a team at the end of May of 1971. They had already begun planning for a Camp Hebron Fellowship Conference in July, with Bill Liner and Wayne Lawton as speakers. Paul Landis was in charge of arrangements.

The visits of East Africans certainly encouraged people in North America to reorganize themselves into regular meetings. Since African visitors were actually representing AEE, they had only limited time to spend with the brothers here. Nevertheless, their ministry was much appreciated.

Paul Landis and Wayne Lawton organized a conference held in 1972 at the Free Methodist Camp at Spencerville, Maryland.[14]

When John Wilson of AEE came to the United States in 1972, he was eager to meet with revival brethren in America. John L. Freed, pastor of Towamencin Mennonite Church near Harleysville, Pennsylvania, arranged a fellowship meeting at the church, with Paul Burkholder's help. Paul Landis sent out notices to the revival fellowship mailing list. "We hope to discern some directions for the later conference [Dec. 31–Jan. 1] at this time rather than have a formal team meeting."[15]

Up to this time the North American fellowships did not have regularly scheduled large meetings. The conferences that took place were often set up because a visiting speaker was passing through, but these were blessed times.

Meeting new challenges

Don and Anna Ruth Jacobs returned to the United States in 1973 after completing their term in Kenya, where Don directed the Mennonite mission activities and taught at the University of Nairobi. Back in America, he served as overseas secretary for Eastern Mennonite Board of Missions and Charities and as executive director of the Mennonite Christian Leadership Foundation. He found no ongoing revival fellowships like those that used to meet when he had last been in America. In his analysis, the charismatic movement may have overwhelmed the older renewal movement by this time; also, within the revival fellowships was some resistance to the leadership of Erma Maust, who was increasingly in demand as a speaker in Women's Aglow meetings and gave her time and energy to them.[16]

Herbert and Erma Maust maintained a busy round of meetings and their less-visible ministry of helps. In June 1973, for example, Erma spoke at the Mennonite House of Friendship in the Bronx, where John I. Smucker was pastor; spent a week in Philadelphia in meetings arranged by Ruth Graybill and Judy Moss; crossed the state to Mansfield, Pennsylvania, for three days of meetings; and came back to Philadelphia for ministry with the Jesus People.[17] Beginning among San Francisco "hippies," the Jesus People, or "Jesus Freaks," reached many young people in the streets and on campuses in the early 1970s. George and Dorothy Smoker wrote in 1972: "One glowing thing about this past year has been the joy of feeling ourselves one with some of the Jesus People we have met and shared with. God is surely at work here just as he was and is in East Africa."[18]

Erma and Herbert Maust, as they celebrate 50 years of marriage.

Doors opened wide for Erma Maust's ministry in 1973 and later. Even though she was not involved in leadership in the revival, she continued to carry its message, which changed her originally and formed her through the years. Her ministry, however, was in Bible conference settings and in Women's Aglow meetings, which she loved. Erma had a word of life and encouragement for all, whether they were Episcopalians, Lutherans, Baptists, or independent. Her message was essentially the revival message of walking with Jesus in close fellowship while deciding moment by moment to look to him for everything, even for the willingness to follow him! For her, the most obvious sign of the presence of the Holy Spirit in one's life was the broken, willing spirit, ready to follow Jesus no matter what.

Wayne Lawton, Ron Lofthouse, Paul Landis, and others carried the burden for revival conferences in the mid 1970s. Ron and Marge Lofthouse con-

Stanley and Doreen Voke, well-loved Bible teachers, home in the United Kingdom.

vened a retreat in March 1975 at Camp Kahquah near Mangetawan, Ontario. The announced theme was "How to Live the Abundant Christian Life." The speakers listed were "Rev. Wayne Lawton . . . and Mrs. Erma Maust."[19] Paul Landis organized two fellowship conferences at Camp Hebron, near Halifax, Pennsylvania, one in June 1976[20] and another in 1977, at which Stanley Voke of Britain was the speaker.[21] These two meetings marked the end of the fellowship meetings and conferences in eastern United States for some time.

Unlike East Africa, where regional teams developed and met on a regular basis, the fellowships in North America did not form such ongoing teams. Groups of people cooperated in sponsoring conferences, but no "team," in the East African sense of the word, developed at that time. When a noteworthy visiting revival speaker stopped in the area, some of the revived held ad hoc meetings to prepare. This lack of continuing structure is part of the reason the retreats came to an end. Erma Maust was the likely person to take initiatives, but she did not enjoy the support of some influential persons in the fellowships. Not until a decade later did a team emerge in eastern United States, with Erma and Herbert Maust as full participants.

A new voice from Tanzania: Titus Lwebandiza

The visit of a Tanzanian government official to southern California brought a new witness to God's work in East Africa. Fred and Lois Craven held a fellowship meeting at their home in Bellflower, California, "for those who can come to meet another African brother, Titus Lwebandiza," who was on official business for his government. Lwebandiza encountered Christ in 1945 through the East Africa Revival. Although he was brought up in the Lutheran church, he said that Christ found him a bitter, quarrelsome, alcoholic ex-polygamist. He trained at Makerere University to be a veterinary officer, and following Tanzania's independence, became director of all agricultural training institutes. In 1962, Lwebandiza was appointed

Titus Lwebandiza, Tanzanian government official who blessed many while in the United States.

director of veterinary services for the entire country; on the resignation of the last colonial director in 1969, he became the first Tanzanian director of agriculture. He later left that post to give himself to a ministry of evangelism as part of the AEE team.[22]

Methuselah Nyagwaswa joined the AEE team in 1977. The next year he went with Festo Kivengere and Don Jacobs to Egypt as part of a team preaching in Protestant churches there. Nyagwaswa came with John Wilson for a preaching mission in the United States soon afterward.[23]

Roy and Pam Hession received an official invitation to participate in the National Prayer Breakfast events in Washington, DC, in February 1977. The invitation gave them some hope that they would not just enjoy the event but also have ministry. Wayne Lawton recalled:

> In the fall of 1977, I sat down and typed a letter to Roy Hession. I told him that we had been pastoring this small Free Methodist congregation near Washington, DC, for five years, and we really needed his ministry. I realized [that] we were too small a congregation to invite someone as well-known as himself; I knew we couldn't afford his plane fare; but if he came to the United States again, would he consider coming to minister to us? I let that letter sit on my desk, gathering dust. I just didn't have the courage to send it.
>
> It sat there for several months until one day in February 1978 I answered the phone and couldn't believe my ears. It was Roy Hession—fairly obvious with that crisp British accent. He said that he was calling from a hotel room in Washington, DC. He further shared that he and Pam were repenting because they felt they had not really sought the Lord sufficiently in regards to coming to the United States again. They had been invited to the presidential prayer breakfast, and he feared it had simply appealed to their pride. They had been told that speaking engagements would be arranged in local churches, but alas, that had not happened.
>
> As they were sitting in that hotel room repenting, the thought

had come to give us a call. My response was, "I wrote you a letter a few months ago, but I didn't have the courage to mail it. Could I read it to you now?" Of course, he waited while I picked up that dusty letter and read it to him over the phone. In a matter of a few hours, I had contacted the board members, and while we didn't have funds for an unplanned special meeting, permission was granted to have meetings that week and give whatever came in the offering to the speaker. I'm sure he was underpaid, but Roy and Pam came and stayed with us, and he preached four nights at our little church. One night it snowed and only a few people made it to the meeting, but we recorded the messages each night. People were blessed and seed was sown and we experienced fruit in our own lives and saw fruit in others resulting from this series of meetings.[24]

The nature of the revival fellowship reveals itself in instances like this. Wherever brothers and sisters are in the world, they love to link with those who love Jesus. More important than huge crowds and dramatic happenings is the love bond that binds those who know one another as repentant, happy, saved, and fulfilled sinners.

Wayne and Mary Lou Lawton with Erma and Herbert Maust.

Stirrings in Canada

Simeon Hurst returned to his native Ontario after years of service in Tanganyika and accepted a call to pastor Hawkesville Mennonite Church, and later Bethel Mennonite Church, both near Elmira. Ron Lofthouse was the pastor of Rosebank Brethren in Christ Church at nearby Petersburg, Ontario, and from 1978 also pastor of Westheights Community Church of Kitchener. Together Hurst and Lofthouse planned to revive the eastern Ontario fellowship conferences with a conference at Kitchener. Erma Maust wrote of their plans in 1981:

Some of you will remember the fellowship conferences we used to have when Roy Hession, Festo Kivengere, or Stanley Voke would meet with us. You will remember the precious refreshing times we had as we met at the feet of Jesus. Many have been asking, "Why don't we have them anymore?"[25]

By 1980 changes were also occurring internationally. Festo Kivengere, who had carried the witness of the East Africa Revival to many different denominations during his years in America, was now back in Uganda. William Nagenda had died. Roy Hession was unable to pursue his phenomenally fruitful ministries of speaking and writing. John Leatherman had gone on to glory. For a time, the movement seemed rudderless.

—17—

Reflections on Revival: New Beginnings Beyond Africa

Many of the pioneers in the revival movement went to their reward after 1980. Elam Stauffer died in 1981 after a fruitful ministry in his native Lancaster County. Phebe Yoder also died in 1981. She left Tanzania in 1971 and spent a year with Glenn and Florence Zeager in the Bronx, teaching literacy and sharing her Lord. Because of failing health in 1973, she retired to Schowalter Villa in Hesston, Kansas.[1]

Notwithstanding the passing of these servants of the Lord, the revival message continued to spread and deepen in both Europe and North America.

Teams and conferences in Europe

One of the major differences between the revival in Europe and East Africa was that East Africa was dotted with hundreds of local fellowships that met on a regular basis, usually weekly, while in Europe and UK the center of activity was in the regional teams that met much less frequently. There were several reasons for this: One had to do with numbers; there were simply more saved ones in Africa, and they lived close to one another. They tended to be more scattered in Europe. Also, Africans knew that if they did not continue in fellowships of light on a regular basis, their spiritual zeal would flag. Westerners are probably less convinced of that because their culture is more individualistic.

This does not mean that the brothers and sisters in Europe did not have meaningful fellowship. They met casually for meals and prayer and fellowship when occasions arose. In addition, many of the brothers and sisters were involved in their local congregations and participated in groups there. Some of the groups were rather shallow, while others lent themselves to going deeper with Jesus on a more intimate level.

Over the years the European brothers and sisters provided ongoing fellowship and ministry by sponsoring regular regional conferences. Each of these overflowed with the grace the teams experienced in their life together and were scenes of great blessing.

In Europe, regional teams became the focal point for the planning of conferences to spread the good news of freedom in Jesus Christ. Annual conferences began in 1958 in Lesin, Switzerland, and were held annually there until 1977. The conference then moved to the picturesque Swiss village of Les Diablerets and continued annually until 2000. The Les Diablerets conference was conducted in French, German, and English, and became a hub of revival for Europe.

The major annual revival conferences in the United Kingdom took the form of family holidays that lasted for a month in the summer. They were held at camps where there were activities for all members of the family. These camps became popular and attracted many who had a deep hunger for the Lord, along with others who enjoyed the time together in a Christian setting with good preaching and teaching. Families usually came for one of the four weeks. Roy Hession along with John Collinson, Eric McLellan, Vincent Kidger-Preston, and others provided able leadership for the highly successful Southwold conferences, through which the blessing of God flowed. In addition to local speakers, the conferences often included speakers from Africa and North America.

The Southwold Family Holiday Conference enjoyed a fruitful ministry for about two decades. The last one was held in 1988. The team then discerned that the era for such a full-fledged family holiday camp was passing. They found that they were channeling an inordinate amount of energy and resources into providing meaningful family activities that detracted from the primary purpose of the conference: to experience life-changing revival in the Lord Jesus Christ. There were probably other reasons as well. But the camp organizers concluded that they should find more focused settings to spread the good news of freedom in Christ.

The British teams felt led to move forward with two venues, an annual weeklong conference in a hotel in Scarborough in Yorkshire, and a two-week camp at La Quinta Conference Center in North Wales. These two ministries proved to be appropriate for almost two decades.

The Scarborough weeklong conference served a discerned need to encourage those walking the Calvary Way and to bring others into the freedom of Christ. Blessings flowed from that conference. In due time its primary organizers, Vincent and Margaret Kidger-Preston, needed to curtail their workload because of health issues. The team felt that the weeklong hotel venue had served its purpose and should be phased out. The last conference, a blessed event, was held in 2002.

Meanwhile, a lively team sponsored a two-week conference at the well-known La Quinta Conference Center. This was a highly successful ministry, attracting both adults and young people. Leaders in that team included David and Alfie Wilson, and Ray and Vera Grout, all veterans of Southwold. La Quinta attracted many new people touched by the message of grace. They found new freedom in Christ and attended the conference to experience love and a nurturing community. The team purchased a property with modest acreage in a Welsh village called Pant-y-Dwr, which became the Grout's residence. It was large enough to accommodate a camp conference, so in 2002 the team shifted the ministry from La Quinta to the Grout's property. The team members responsible for this ministry had long histories in the revival fellowship, including the Wilsons and the Grouts, Herbert Osborn, Keith and Anne Jarvis, plus some energetic Jesus-loving younger people with a clear vision of the revival's future. Throughout Britain, clusters of believers continue to meet on an ad hoc basis for fellowship and mutual support.

In addition to providing conferences and retreats, the British teams encouraged and supported articulate men and women who wrote, spoke, and encouraged others, including Roy and Revel and (later) Pam Hession, Stanley and Doreen Voke, John and Muriel Collinson, Eric and Edith McLellan, Bert Osborne, David and Alfie Wilson, and Vincent and Margaret Kidger-Preston. More books and literature on the East Africa Revival have been published in Britain than in any other nation. In this way it has been a special blessing to the international revival fellowships.

While the continental European teams did not produce as much literature as the British ones did, they likewise encouraged exceptionally gifted believers, including Claire-Lise and Elizabeth de Benoit, Ernst Krebs, Leonard and Rudolph Brechet, Jean Marc and Bernadette Brechet, Elizabeth Aebi, Friedhelm and Irmgard Nusch, Hugo Zimmerman, Detmar Scheunemann, and many others. They channeled their energies into the conferences through the years. The conferences served marvelously to spread the message of freedom in the atoning work of Jesus.

Les Diablerets conference comes to an end

The last of the all-Europe conferences in Les Diablerets, Switzerland, took place in 2000. The conference was always conducted in German, French, and English, which contributed to its popularity and worth. The organizing team eventually discerned, however, that such multilingual weeklong conferences had served a vital need for several decades but were no longer the best vehicle for the future. The group was aging, and the venue where the conference was held was becoming prohibitively expensive for the younger generation with families. That did not mean the end of conferences in Europe, however. There were already strong conferences in Rehe in Germany, Aeschi in German-speaking Switzerland, and the new French team in Alsace. These regional conferences maintained the enthusiasm for ongoing meetings and have pressed forward. This is a transitional stage, in many ways, but the teams are enthusiastic and hopeful.

In France, the leaders of the mission society "France for Christ," notably Nicolas and Edith Kessley, and Alain and Martine Stamp, have been deeply affected by the message of revival and have adopted the core of the revival message in their mission theology and practice. Their Missions House in Drulingen, France, is a center for establishing churches that determine to follow the Calvary Way. This mission has established many evangelical churches in France in their twenty-five year history.

Britain was blessed with outstanding leaders and teachers in the revival. Some of them had roots in mission service in Rwanda and Uganda, while others, such as Roy Hession and Stanley Voke, served the Lord in Britain but were just as deeply touched by the message of grace as anyone. As these honored seniors in the faith aged or went on to be with the Lord, the mantle fell on younger shoulders. The Lord is proving faithful in raising up young people with a heart for revival.

A changing scene on the U.S. West Coast

Ed Bridgeford of California recalled:

My introduction to the East African revival came while I was a student at Biola in about 1961. I was meeting with a group of guys at Biola after classes for prayer. A man by the name of Don Widmark was putting on a weekend conference in the local mountains, and four of us decided to go. The speaker was an African by the name of William Nagenda. He spoke from the book of Nehemiah. I cannot tell you precisely what he said, but it was life-changing for me. This was what I had been searching for since my teen years.

That conference with William Nagenda was the first of many fellowship conferences on the West Coast. Dick Shirk and I

worked with Don [Widmark] in planning many fellowship conferences and meetings over the years. We enjoyed a long parade of
speakers that had been transformed by Jesus through the African
revival. We had the privilege of fellowshipping with Festo
Kivengere, Roy Hession, Stanley Voke, Methuselah Nyagwaswa,
Cory ten Boom, John Wilson, and many more.

When I reflect on those times I realize what a special time of
God's grace it was. After that first meeting with Don Widmark, I
called him and was amazed that he wanted to take the time to get
together with me. Out of that call a weekly fellowship meeting was
started in my parent's [Carl and Dorothy Bridgeford's] home that
continued for more than 15 years. Don and his mother, Maude,
and sometimes Aunt Bernie, drove each week from Glendale just to
share how Jesus was working in their lives. We came hungry and
left filled with the grace of God week after week.[2]

Jean and Carl Roberts were also in this fellowship. They graciously
helped many people to walk in humility with Jesus Christ. That fellowship
in Fullerton, California, was an oasis of blessings.

Roy and Revel Hession visited the Pacific Northwest in 1962. Their
ministry that year bore exceptional fruit. They shared in Seattle,
Washington, at a Christian conference camp called Miracle Ranch. Roy
spoke at King's Garden, and he and Revel traveled around the Pacific
Northwest and spoke at several small churches as well as some large ones.

Ted and Betty McJunkin, who were to play a significant role in Washington, recall that they first met the
Hessions at that conference at Miracle Ranch. A couple
from Olympia, Washington, whose hearts had been
touched by the East Africa Revival through Don
Widmark from California, had invited the McJunkins to
go along. Betty then wrote an article for *Family Life
Today* in 1979:

Betty and Ted
McJunkin, 1954

In 1962, the Lord in his mercy sent an English evangelist and his
wife to speak at a nearby conference grounds. As they shared
about how they had been spiritually revived by allowing the Holy
Spirit to deal with sin in their lives, we were convicted of the deep
hatred we had toward our adopted sons. We saw in a new way the
meaning of the blood of Christ and its availability to us whenever

we sin. We had been excusing sin and blaming circumstances and others for our attitudes. Verses such as 1 John 1:7 began to have new meaning for us: "If we walk in the light as he is in the light, we have fellowship with one another, and the blood of Jesus his son cleanses us from all sin." As we confessed to the Lord the many hidden resentments we had, even toward one another, our fellowship with Jesus and with one another became real and enjoyable. It was like being born again. That was the beginning of living in revival for us, walking with Jesus on a daily basis, walking in his light and beginning to understand what it means to "glory in the cross of our Lord Jesus Christ" [cf. Gal 6:14].[3]

Lyle Burden recalled: "In February 1963 or 1964, our church held a meeting for spiritual renewal with two Africans [who] would be speaking. The church was Lake Avenue Congregational Church in Pasadena, California. The Africans speaking were Festo Kivengere and William Nagenda, with Chuck and Marge Higgins ministering in music." Lyle and his wife were among those who embraced the message of grace in a new way and longed for more of the freedom of Christ in their own lives.

In 1963 Herbert and Erma Maust traveled to the West Coast. They touched the many people but perhaps none more profoundly than Ted and Betty McJunkin. Erma helped them to grow in their walk with Jesus and showed them how to live by dying to self. Her helpful, practical, and inspired sayings encouraged and challenged them, such as this one: "I am not willing to accept this hard situation, and I am not willing to thank you for it, but I choose to accept all with thanks. Praise for the blood to cleanse and for Jesus, who took the cup of our iniquity and gave thanks, so now as we repent deeply, He is also our enabling to take our cup and give thanks."

Stanley and Doreen Voke from England visited the Pacific Northwest many times in the 1960s, and even up to a year or so before Stanley's homegoing in 1997. Ted and Betty McJunkin wrote:

The message of their lives always pointed to the cross, and God used them over the years to keep us focused on Jesus Christ. Their wise and loving counsel through letters and face-to-face are an integral part of our spiritual growth. Calvary Chapel (our church affiliation) loved them very much, and Stanley was a featured speaker at their annual pastors' conference until he was no longer able to travel to the U.S.[4]

When Festo Kivengere and William Nagenda traveled in the United States in the 1960s and 1970s, there was neither a huge following nor signs of a great revival. But slowly and quietly the Holy Spirit was touching hearts. The McJunkins recalled:

We first heard Festo and William in 1963 at a Covenant church near Seattle where they were speaking. We will never forget how we hung on every word from their mouths. We were so hungry and thirsty for Jesus. We had tried for ten years to live the Christian life, but we had missed Jesus because of our self-righteousness. We were trying in ourselves to be good Christians and of course failed miserably! God had brought some very hard trials into our lives that brought us to the end of ourselves, and we had just felt like "throwing in the towel," so to speak. God knows the right time when we are ready to receive his grace, and he began sending one dear brother or sister after another to show us the way to walk with Jesus.

Festo had spoken at Prairie Bible Institute in Three Hills, Alberta, in about 1965, and several hearts were touched during that time: Les and Joan Simons, Bill and Gladys Liner, Alvin and Mary Doerksen, and Claudia Fureby, to name a few. The Liners began having fellowship campouts in the early 1970s, and they continued for at least ten years. During that time the Liners produced a little booklet bimonthly called *Living Water*, which included messages and testimonies of brothers and sisters who were walking the way of the cross. These continued until about 1986, when that fellowship in Canada no longer met for conferences.[5]

Methuselah "Matt" Nyagwaswa from Tanzania came to the United States in the 1960s for study and stayed with Jim and Jean Perry in Arizona for a while. Nyagwaswa graduated from Westmont College in Santa Barbara, California, with a degree in English literature, and then moved to Pasadena to pursue a master's degree in English at California State University, Los Angeles. By then the Smokers had returned to Tanzania but they made their upstairs room available to Nyagwaswa. That was near to the house of Lyle and Jan Burden, who recalled:

With Matt living across the street, we became very close, and it was natural to invite people to come to Pasadena for fellowship meetings because they wanted to come to see Matt. For quite a while—around two years—we met once a week in our home. It was there that we met Erica Sabiti. We also met Les and Joan Simons when they came to our home for fellowship. It was a rich and growing time in our lives.

Lyle was deeply moved as he listened to the conversation between Matt and Festo and was drawn to them because they were speaking about Jesus in such a refreshing way and a way in which both of us had recently been touched by Jesus.[6]

When the Smokers returned to Africa, Nyagwaswa moved in with Lyle and Jan Burden, further strengthening the bonds of fellowship.

The Lord used Nyagwaswa in many lives during those days. He spoke in Seattle several times, staying with the McJunkins. He was single then. His first wife had died, and his mother was caring for his five children back home in Tanzania. Nyagwaswa then married a Kenyan nurse, Josephine, in California. The couple stayed with Ted and Betty McJunkin in Seattle in 1968, encouraging them to keep focused on Jesus and to keep in fellowship with others who were walking in the light. The McJunkins maintained a close relationship with the Nyagwaswas. They wrote, "We were able to see Matt face-to-face at the East Africa Revival Convention in Kikuyu, Kenya, in 2000. It was such a joy to be reunited with him after so many years."[7] Lyle Burden remembered Nyagwaswa's influence:

The fellowship continued for a while in our home after Matt returned to Africa around 1965 and then later met in George and Dorothy Smoker's home after that, when they retired and returned home from Tanzania. . . . One thing that made us feel connected with this fellowship was the freshness of their walk with Jesus. We had the same experiences as many of them did, but had never been with others to share what Jesus was showing us about his grace.[8]

Revival conferences on the West Coast

The West Coast fellowship conferences that began in the early 1970s were held when revival speakers from abroad came through, as recalled by the McJunkins:

The first one we remember was at Mission Springs in Santa Cruz, California. Stanley Voke, Roy Hession, Chuck Higgins, Dorothy Smoker, Jim Perry, and Don Widmark are some we remember as being there. It was well attended, with around one hundred people. In the early 1980s, the conferences were held at Mt Shasta Conference Center near Redding, California. Festo, the Hessions, and the Vokes were there at various times.[9]

The Los Angeles fellowship was a lively group in the late 1970s and early 1980s. George and Dorothy lived in Pasadena and were active in the development of the fellowship, which often met in their home. For a while, newly converted Jesus People joined the regular times of fellowship and were established in their walk by the fellowship of love they encountered there.

Even though no formal fellowship continued in the Los Angeles area, the Bridgefords and Burdens have continued to meet on a regular basis for fellowship and prayer.

A small group from Northern California, Oregon, and Washington met at Lassen Pines Retreat Center in Viola, California, in 1987. Roy Hession and Festo Kivengere were present for that meeting, though Festo was not well. This group met again for two additional years at Lassen Pines, near the church that a brother, Stan Brown, was pastoring.

Betty McJunkin wrote:

The California group was rather inactive through the 1980s. Then Jim and Jean Perry, in fellowship with others, felt led to establish an annual conference in the vicinity of Ashland, Oregon. The meetings were held in a local hotel for a few years, then in a church of one of the pastors who was part of the fellowship. Les and Joan Simons, Chuck and Marge Higgins, Jim and Jean Perry, [and] Eric and Edith McLellan from England were some of the speakers in those days. Then in 1998 it was moved to St. Rita's Retreat Center in Gold Hill, Oregon.

In the Seattle area, since 1999, the fellowship group has met every Saturday evening at our home. There were only three of us at first, and at times it was discouraging, but because we believed the Lord had guided, we repented of worrying about "numbers" and remembered that Jesus said, "Where two or three are gathered together in my name, there I am in the midst of them" [Matt 18:20]. We now have about 8-10 who come quite regularly. We were encouraged by Zeb Kabaza to keep meeting for fellowship even if there were only two of us. That is a very important ingredient in the East African Revival and one of the reasons it continues today.[10]

The weekly fellowship in Seattle may be a strong indicator of the way the revival message will be propagated in the future—by fellowships of blood-bought, repentant, renewed disciples, meeting regularly to experience life together in Jesus Christ. It could well be that the message cannot be sustained without the experience of face-to-face fellow-

Jim and Jean Perry, lifelong revivalists.

ships of light in which Jesus speaks into the lives of all.

In the early 1990s a Pacific Northwest team began to meet. Jim and Jean Perry, and Dick and Barb Woodruff, and Mark Anderson met for fellowship in the Lord. Out of this fellowship sprang the Oregon fellowship retreat. The first meeting was held in 1992 at Buckhorn Falls near Ashland, Oregon, at a bed-and-breakfast. In 1994 they moved to Ashland Hills Inn, and then in 1998 they shifted to St. Rita's Retreat Center at Gold Hills, Oregon. The Lord blessed those who attended this rather small but powerful retreat. Speakers have included local persons such as Jim Perry and Dick Woodruff, together with John Garrick, Chuck and Marge Higgins, Don Jacobs, and Stephen Bamutingire of Uganda. A stalwart pillar was Dorothy Smoker, who managed to attend even as she began to suffer some memory loss. Her memory was as clear as crystal, however, when it came to walking with Jesus in daily blessed fellowship.

Dick Woodruff testified:

Some of the most powerful moments have come when the Lord has touched lives so deeply that inner wounds have surfaced and been healed with prayer and love from the fellowship at the direction of the Spirit. I'm not sure how many people remember the teachings and who said what, but those attending would surely remember the confessions of those in need of Jesus. Some needs were for attitude adjustments, for strength or direction, and some were for powerful cleansing and restoration by Jesus. It is the circled sharing time where the Lord seems to do his work amongst us. All the teaching time and meals and time together seem to culminate when we circle our wagons and face one another and the Lord with what he has placed in our hearts. St. Rita's has offered us a place of solitude, which adds to the fellowship time. There are few distractions, and the business of the world is more distant, forcing us to look deeper within.

I know I have returned from fellowship gatherings having been blessed by the Lord and with fresh testimony of the power of Christ in lives, both mine and others'. I've found too that hearing pastors from Africa or other denominations helps one see the church of Christ unbound by denominational distinctives. We pay no attention to who is "holier" or who has the most legalistic background or who is more charismatic. These labels fade as broken believers gladly fellowship around the Lord Jesus Christ.[11]

In his candid fashion, Dick confessed, "There were times when I honestly did not want to go to the conferences because of pressing issues, like projects at home or at the church that needed my attention. Yet, I have never been disappointed by foregoing the obvious to spend a weekend fellowshipping."[12]

Betty and Ted McJunkin, 1989, witnessed in the Pacific Northwest.

Ted and Betty McJunkin provided an invaluable service. They wrote:

The Lord led us in 1997 to take the messages given at the revival fellowship conferences and put them into a report that we mail to other brethren in the fellowship throughout the world. God is faithful, and we thank him for the dear brothers and sisters in East Africa, in England, in the U.S. who have faithfully held up the cross of Jesus and shared from their lives, some even unto death, that life only comes through the blood of Christ, through the atonement, and as we are willing to die to self and let Jesus be on the throne of our hearts. The light will grow brighter and brighter as we continue to obey the light, continue to be cleansed in his blood, and yield to the Holy Spirit working in us and through us. "But the path of the just is as the shining light, that shines more and more unto the perfect day" [Prov 4:18].

Twenty years of campouts in Alberta, 1967–1987

Bill and Gladys Liner, together with the team that met in their region, initiated a fellowship week to accommodate the people in their area, in the form of campouts. Those who were hungry for more of Jesus gathered in an area where they could park their trailers or pitch their tents for a week of fellowship and ministry of the Word. This proved to be one of the longest-lived annual conferences in North America, lasting twenty years. The grace of God flowed in these informal camp settings.

Mary Doerksen with her husband, Alvin, attended most of these campouts and commented:

> In 1969 my husband, Alvin, and I were pastoring a church in a small town in Saskatchewan. One Sunday Rev. Les Simons came to be the speaker in our church, and afterward came to our house for lunch. I had baked beans but they got burned, so I quickly had to try and find something else to serve. Les said, "Jesus knew that I could not eat beans." I was embarrassed that my lunch had not turned out, but to say that Jesus cared about that was a new thought for me. In fact, I thought that he was kind of weird. I was touched by his message, and it opened up a well of hunger and thirst for Jesus, but I couldn't quite get it.
>
> In 1970 we moved to Three Hills, Alberta, where Alvin was to be the accountant and business manager for Japan Evangelical Mission. Both the [Les and Joan] Simons and Bill and Gladys Liner were with the same mission. God used them in our lives to learn to see Jesus more clearly and to walk in brokenness with him. They introduced us to the campout conference that the Liners had started. This conference was held in the foothills of the Rockies one week every summer for people like us who were hungry and thirsty to get to know Jesus more intimately. For twelve years every summer, we would pack up our five children and our dog and pull our big, old camper, which the Lord had marvelously supplied for us, into the foothills to set up camp for conference. Our children looked forward to this annual conference as much as we did. People came from all four western provinces and western United States with their families to sit at the feet of Jesus for a week, and learn from him. We became like one big happy family. Our children made long-lasting friendships as well as we older folk. It was all around Jesus. One time my eight-year-old nephew said, "This is as close to heaven as we could get in this world."
>
> Every morning and evening we had an open-air service, which everyone attended. We had no children or youth classes. We all attended the meetings as families. We had various speakers from

other revival groups. At the end of the conference we all left refreshed and rejoicing for the time we had sitting at the feet of Jesus, looking forward to next summer, when we'd meet again. As one by one the campers pulled out of the campground, we would sing, "Reach out and touch the Lord / As he passes by. [You'll find he's not too busy / To hear your heart's cry. / He's passing by this moment / Your needs to supply. / Reach out and touch the Lord / As he passes by]" [author unknown]. And I learned that Jesus does care about the smallest details in our lives, even what we eat. And it's not weird.[13]

As the North American teams were seeking a sense of direction, Roy Hession felt called to visit and preach where invited, to bring others into the blessing of a daily walk with Jesus. Included in that visit was a meeting of interested brothers and sisters from across North America, held in Minneapolis, Minnesota. Roy called this group together to pray about the future of the revival fellowships. Could they move into the future with the clear message that Roy had so simply stated in his classic *Calvary Road* and subsequent books? That meeting proved to be extraordinarily fruitful.

The birthing of the Canada-East team, 1981

Simeon Hurst and Ron Lofthouse began to see the opportunity and the need to form a team in Ontario, Canada. God blessed the effort. A vigorous team developed that carried the work of revival forward for many years. Since 1981, they have held an annual fellowship conference, usually at Chesley Lake Camp near Lake Huron.

Darrell Jantzi reflected on the Canada-East revival fellowship since 1981:

Early April 1981, Simeon and Edna Hurst and Ron and Marjorie Lofthouse sent a prayer letter to a number of fellow pastors in the Kitchener-Waterloo area telling of a recent experience that deeply touched their hearts. They had just participated in a revival fellowship retreat in Minneapolis, where Roy and Pam Hession from England spoke on the theme "Jesus Satisfies." Thirty-six fellowship representatives from across USA and Canada had "spent five days together looking to Jesus, hearing what he had to say to us through our brothers and sisters as we opened our hearts to each other in repentance, confession, and praise. . . . It was truly a blessed time together as the love of Jesus filled our lives in a new way. . . . We felt the need to do this more often.

During this retreat, "there seemed to be a growing conviction that the Lord wants us together again here in the East later this summer." On May 22-24, fifteen persons met at the Emmanuel Bible College campus to pray and lay the groundwork for the first Canada-East Fellowship Conference, announced for September 11-13 at the Kitchener Holiday Inn. The speaking team included Roy and Pam Hession, Don Jacobs, Herbert and Erma Maust, and Bill and Gladys Liner.

The conference theme was Hebrews 12:2, "Looking unto Jesus, the author and finisher of our faith." Ron and Simeon co-chaired sessions. Without question, this was a retreat bathed in prayer, and the Spirit's presence was powerfully felt as each speaker lifted up Jesus and testimonies of God's grace were shared. The message of the cross and the way of brokenness and repentance was profoundly taught and modeled. Many hearts were touched and drawn to the foot of the cross in humility and repentance.

Tears flowed and relationships were restored. I recall how the East African song "Glory, glory, hallelujah, / Glory, glory to the Lamb, / For his cleansing blood has reached me, / Glory, glory to the Lamb" was led out in chorus as new victories were experienced and testified to. Jesus was speaking deep into my heart all day, and I just didn't want to leave that Saturday night session without coming to grips with what I was seeing. God's grace was magnified as I saw Jesus afresh, and my own sinfulness and pastoral pride was exposed, making me ashamed. A desire whelmed up within to come all the way to Jesus in open repentance.[14]

Darrell Jantzi further recalled: "In obedience, I began to experience a new freedom and joy in my life and ministry even as loud drumming from a ballroom next door was pounding out quite a different message. I sang 'Glory, glory to the Lamb.'"[15]

The Canada-East Fellowship Retreat was born. A local revival fellowship team emerged and met monthly to seek the Lord in continuing fellowship and for direction. They were Ron and Marjorie Lofthouse, Simeon and Edna Hurst, Amsey and Leona Martin, Darrell and Florence Jantzi, Nelson and Wilma Martin, Erwin and Marian Wiens, and Howard and Della Tyrrell. They prepared for the next conference at the Guelph Bible

Conference Center in Guelph, Ontario, in 1982. Later Samuel and Barbara Parker, a United Church pastor couple, together with John and Velma Young, were included on the team, which provided solid ongoing leadership in Canada-East fellowship.

Barbara and Sam Parker of Ontario, Canada.

When the Guelph Conference Grounds could no longer accommodate the growing numbers, they selected Chesley Lake Camp, in a beautiful lakeside setting 75 miles northwest of Guelph. Numbers attending have varied from 75 to 140 in that retreat setting.

The annual conference has met every year since 1981. People gathered in anticipation of clear practical teaching from Scripture and a fresh challenge for applying its truth to our daily lives. Participants have been blessed and enriched through the ministry of many excellent speakers from East Africa, Great Britain, Europe, and across North America. Each shares the message of the cross from their own spiritual and cultural perspective of learning to walk in the light with Jesus, by being broken and transparent with others and thus growing in the grace of our Lord. Sometimes a speaker's spouse shared testimony in response to the message, bringing a further clarity or practical dimension to what has been said. The uniqueness of these retreats is the openness and honesty in which Jesus' will and way is sought, God's word upheld, and his grace celebrated.

Victor and Viola Dorsch, who had revival roots in Somalia and Tanzania, settled in Canada in 1988 and came onto the team in that year. They served as a meaningful link between the Canada team and teams elsewhere.

Some members of the Canada-East team were privileged to share in the international conferences as speakers in their own right. The interaction has been mutually enriching. A special feature of the Canada-East conference was the professional recording services of David and Norma Kirby of Norday Communications. Their recordings spread the simple message of walking daily with Jesus to many hungry people. The team has also established a lending library containing all the cataloged tapes and many books available to interested persons.

Darrell Jantzi reported: "The Canada-East team meets at least quarter-

Marjorie and Ron Lofthouse, Florence and Daryl Jantzi, Viola and Victor Dorsch, of Canada-East team, 2005.

ly for prayer fellowship, evaluation, and planning. These times together are rich in fellowship, ministry to one another, and helping to keep [us] focused." In 2002 the team went through significant change. They polled the regular attendees to assess God's will for the future of the conference, and the response was a clear request to continue the annual conference at Chesley Lake. One person shared: "It is such a joy to watch and experience a group of people experience Jesus." The team incorporated Joram and Janiffer Kirundi, who were deeply involved with the Kenyan brothers and sisters before they recently migrated to Canada. Laverne and Marjorie

Leona and Amzie Martin, Velma and John Young, of Canada-East team, 2005.

Schwartzentruber also came onto the team. Darrell said, "It is our heart's desire that we might continue to flourish in fellowship and grow strong in Christ Jesus."[16]

Eastern United States in the 1980s and 1990s

Even though there was no formal team in eastern United States through the 1980s, Wayne Lawton and others often set up conferences when revival speakers came through, such as the one on May 13 and 14, 1982, at the Christian Retreat Center near Washington, DC, and another on March 1 and 2, 1984, at the same location, both with Stanley and Doreen Voke.

Folding newsletters announcing upcoming meetings.

As the team in eastern Canada grew, several people felt led to establish an Eastern U.S. team around 1988. It included Wayne and Mary Lou Lawton, Glenn and Florence Zeager, Henry and Florence Stauffer, Bill and Marion Scott, Rhoda Wenger, Catharine Leatherman, and Don and Anna Ruth Jacobs. The team was greatly encouraged when they met with the Canada-East team at Corning, New York, in May 1989. Later in 1989 they organized their first annual conference at the Salunga Mennonite Meetinghouse near Lancaster, and at the Bucher Meeting House on the campus of Elizabethtown (Pa.) College in April 1990. In 1991 they gathered at the Church of God in Bainbridge (Pa.), again at the Salunga Mennonite Meetinghouse in 1992, and then at the Elizabethtown Mennonite Church in 1993. The annual conferences took place there until 1998, when the group tried a setting at the Precious Blood Retreat Center near Columbia, Pennsylvania, where they met for two years but found the venue too confining. After that, they met at two Mennonite churches in the Harrisburg area, alternating between the Locust Lane Mennonite Chapel and Cedar Hill Mennonite Church.

Annual conferences proved to be a fruitful time for "cross-fertilization" of faith, as Roy Hession used to call it. Brothers and sisters from var-

Meeting of Canada-East and Eastern U.S. teams at Painted Post near Corning, N.Y., 1989.

ious cultures and nations gathered together to share and to walk the way of Calvary. The American conferences have been greatly enriched by the ministry of international guests, including John Gatu and Sam Gatere from Kenya, and Stephen and Stella Bamutingire and Joan Hall from Uganda.

In 2006 the Eastern U.S. team consisted of Wayne and Mary Lou Lawton, Tommy Hess, Lindsey and Myra Robinson, Simeon and Jean Hurst (Simeon married Jean after the death of his first wife, Edna), Jean Griswold,

Anna Ruth and Don Jacobs, Florence Stauffer, Mary Miller, C. Tom Hess. A team meeting at Jean Griswold's in Lititz, Pa.

Florence Saylor, Glenn (nephew of missionary Elam Stauffer) and Arlene Stauffer, Bill and Marian Scott, and Don and Anna Ruth Jacobs.

The fellowship between the Eastern U.S. team and the Canada-East team deepened during this period, and they attended one another's conferences as much as possible.

In 1996 the Eastern U.S. team felt led to establish a quarterly morning fellowship meeting in order to accommodate people who could not attend the larger conferences. They held the first one on Saturday, July 6, 1996, in the village of Bainbridge, Pennsylvania, near where the first revival fellowships were held in the 1960s. It proved to be a blessing as a time to enjoy a hearty breakfast in a restaurant setting and to hear the word of the Lord, share testimonies, pray, and encourage newcomers.

North America team meeting, June 1998

Three North American teams were meeting regularly by 1998—Pacific Northwest, Canada-East and Eastern U.S. They experienced a deepened relationship with the Lord and with one another. God was blessing their fellowships, and it seemed an appropriate time to convene a meeting of all the active teams in North America. An excited, eager group met in Kansas City, Missouri, in June 1998.

Zeb Kabaza attended the meeting in response to an invitation for East Africa fellowships to include a representative. Many in North America knew him, and the links between the Easterners and the Westerners were strengthened. Zeb's wisdom and insights into the Word of God encouraged all. The theme was taken from Hebrews 2:9: "We see Jesus. . . ." Chuck Higgins led the daily Bible studies based on the book of Hebrews.

The North American teams were aware of the importance of develop-

North American team meeting, Kansas City, 1998.

Typical Pennsylvania team meeting.

ing deeper fellowship among themselves. Unwittingly, some of the teams found themselves planning conferences instead of enjoying fellowship with one another, and they repented about that. They also recognized their obligation to use every means available to them to keep the message of God's grace before the world and the church.

Jim Perry articulated the spirit of conference:

> I want to close with this writing by A. W. Tozer. I think that brother really saw the Lord. He died in 1962. "'Saints with Holy Brightness.' I have met a few of God's saints that appear to have this holy brightness upon them, but they did not know it because of the humility and gentleness of spirit. I do not hesitate to confess that my fellowship with them has meant more to me than all the teaching I have ever received. I stand deeply indebted to every Bible teacher I have had through the years, but they did little but instruct my head. The [people] I have known who have had this strange and mysterious quality and awareness of God's Person and Presence instructed my heart."[17] That is what I have found here in this fellowship con-

ference, and that is why I will do anything to get here.

I remember Stanley Voke said to me one time, "Jim, there is something about the brethren." I asked him, "Yes, what is it?" He said, "They have a *live word* when they have something to say. There is something alive coming through them." I said, "That's it! They have a live word!" Praise the Lord! Amen.[18]

The Kansas City fellowship deepened the unity of the teams and recovered the vision of more and more people discovering the freeing power of the atoning work of Jesus Christ. They determined to stay on the message of the crucified, risen Lord and not become sidetracked by any of the popular winds that often detract from the centrality of Jesus Christ, in whom "dwells all the fullness of the Godhead bodily" (Col 2:9).

Herbert and Erma Maust filled their calendars with meetings in whirlwind trips, returning to old venues and venturing into new ones. In this way the simple message of revival appealed to open hearts and touched many. It was a season of great blessing in the ministry of the Mausts.

When regular revival gatherings occurred once again, Erma and Herbert were deeply involved in the fellowships. Their travels came to an end in October 1983. Returning from a revival conference in Ontario, they were involved in a one-car accident that sent their vehicle plummeting down an embankment. The injuries were serious and included internal ones. Herbert had ten broken ribs and Erma's jaw was badly broken. They were hospitalized in Rochester, New York, for three weeks. Their son, Jim, was one of the first to get there. He said, "Mother and Daddy didn't lose their sense of humor and they were on top spiritually even though terribly injured." Many Christian friends—some who they knew and others who had received word from people who knew them—came to visit and pray with them while they recuperated. When they returned to Pennsylvania they lived several weeks in the home of Henry and Florence Stauffer in Elizabethtown, where they received loving care.[19]

A year later, Erma was able to report:

It was just one year ago last month when we had our car accident. We are grateful to the Lord for the way he has restored health to us enabling us to be up and doing. Soon after the accident as I realized I was seriously hurt, I said to the Lord, "Lord, why didn't you take me home?" I'd turn to him in all my need and he would remind me, "I have a purpose in allowing all this."[20]

As they recovered, they became active again in Locust Lane Mennonite Church, an interracial congregation in Harrisburg, Pennsylvania. Friends in the revival fellowship helped them buy a mobile home in Elizabethtown, Pennsylvania, where they moved in October 1984. "We see him already opening more of a local ministry and people coming to see us instead of us going out as much as before."[21]

In 1992 Erma suffered a severe speech impairment that left her unable to communicate. Her speaking ministry was at an end. Herbert cared for his stricken wife until his death in 1994.

Betty Miller, who lived in the same retirement community and had early been touched by revival, was deeply appreciative for the ministry of helps she had received from Erma. So Betty came to feed, care for, and pray with Erma daily, as the prayers of many others surrounded them. We cannot be sure what was happening for the nine or more years Erma could not communicate freely. There was evidence that she was aware of what was happening around her. Betty and others strongly believed that Erma continued her prayer ministry even in those "silent" years. Erma Maust finally went to meet Jesus face-to-face on July 14, 2000, a day before her ninetieth birthday. Wayne Lawton said, "I took Zeb Kabaza to see Erma Maust when he was here in 1998. Zeb commented that he could feel the strong presence of Jesus in that room!"

Her memorial was a celebration of her faithful contribution to the revival. Messages and testimonies recapitulated the revival theme. Lawton reported that Don Jacobs mentioned "what at times seemed a mysterious ministry by a Mennonite woman. Don spoke lovingly of Erma and his appreciation for her and the fellowship they shared in the ministry of the cross."[22]

The testimony of Ahmed Kaloko at the funeral was quite impressive. He mentioned that for ten years people had been trying to get him to receive Christ, but he would not. Then the first day he met Erma at a picnic dinner at Locust Lane Chapel, she asked, "Have you ever received Christ as your personal Savior?" He replied, "No, I haven't." And she persisted, "Would you like to do that now?" and to his own surprise he said yes. A new life in Jesus began that day for him. Then he told how she would call him at work and he would say, "Why are you calling me? I'm saved now." She said, "But Ahmed, now you need to grow in Christ." He remarked, "For two years she had me driving from Harrisburg to their place in Elizabethtown [twenty miles] to have a Bible study every Thursday night." Ahmed has a PhD, but he admitted that until he met this woman with an eighth-grade education who helped him to Christ, he did not know how to live.

At Erma's funeral the refrain of "Glory, Glory, hallelujah" rang out as testimony after testimony was shared. Her long journey had ended, and she was home, face to face with the one who had redeemed her by his grace.[23]

The International revival conferences

International team meeting, Les Diablerets, Switzerland, 1991.

Twenty-one years had passed since representatives of teams in Africa, Europe, and North America had met. The time had come for another such meeting:

Seventy-two people representing three continents gathered from May 29 to June 3, 1991, in Les Diablerets, a Swiss village nestled in the majestic Alps. There they worshipped, prayed, studied, fellowshipped, and pondered anew the marvelous grace of Jesus Christ that flows so richly from Calvary.

The "revival message" has remained unaltered over the years. The enemy persists in his attempt to persuade those who have been saved by grace to either add to the message or take away from it. That struggle to maintain the cross of Jesus Christ as the central point of the vision never ceases. But through repentant faith the brothers and sisters have insisted on keeping Christ and him crucified as the focal point of their life together.

While at the present time there is no single issue [that] we face, the challenge is before us to return again and again to the vision that the apostle had when he entered Corinth, that is, to lift up only Jesus Christ and him crucified.

Every effort was made to keep Jesus Christ and him crucified and risen as the focus of attention. No attempt was made to judge and critique other movements of God's sovereign Spirit either past or current.

From the outset the Lord reminded us that revival is not an organized "movement" in the sense that it must have strong structures and offices and the such. Revival is simply Jesus at work in fellowships around the world. So there was no intention of creating an "international structure" for revival. The expanding family is held together by love and by the voluntary initiatives by individuals and fellowships. The life is in the fellowships that sprinkle the earth. The international network is simply to share what the Lord is doing in the local fellowships all over the world.

There was no attempt, therefore, to establish a structure at this meeting. The purpose was simply to let Jesus Christ speak and to respond to his word with obedience and joy. The theme was, "Let us fix our eyes on Jesus, the author and perfecter of our faith, who for the joy set before him endured the cross, scorning its shame, and sat down at the right hand of the throne of God. Consider him" (Heb 12:2-3 NIV). Here is a typical response: "What came through was the centrality and greatness of the cross of Christ, as a central point of all of God's activities and purposes in redemption and revival. As we again saw Jesus Christ and him crucified, our hearts were touched, our focus sharpened, our fellowship renewed, and our vision clarified. We were revived at the foot of the cross."[24]

In 1996 the East Africa team hosted the third International Revival Fellowship Team Meeting, the first one on African soil. It was held in Nairobi from June 16 to June 23. Ten people came from Canada, one from France, three from Germany, ten from Britain, six from Switzerland, and seven from the United States. Uganda was represented by six persons, and Kenya by eighteen.

The theme for this conference was 2 Timothy 2:15: "Do your best to present yourself to God as one approved, a workman who does not need to be ashamed and who correctly handles the word of truth" (NIV). Time and again the Holy Spirit brought the teams back to the central meeting place, the cross of Jesus Christ. In meetings like this, where cultures meet in open fellowship, opportunities arise to reexamine the heart of the gospel, which is the incarnate Jesus Christ doing good, dying as the sacrifice for our sins, raised from the dead, and now interceding for the world.

International team meeting, Nairobi, Kenya, 1996.

International guests scattered out in the vicinity of central Kenya, meeting with fellowships, attending conventions, staying in local homes, and enjoying the generous hospitality of dear brothers and sisters. This fellowship created bonds of love and friendship that will certainly endure. The conference recognized the need to have more fellowship across national, racial, and cultural lines.

At this meeting a note of joy was the good news that a few brothers and sisters from Rwanda and Burundi will be able to take part in the East Africa Revival team. Many of them survived the slaughter in Rwanda, but many others were martyred.

In 2001 Nicolas Keseley and the team directing the France for Christ mission invited representatives from the European teams to confer on the vision and hopes of that church-planting ministry. This pivotal May 2002 meeting, the first of teams from nations outside Africa, took place at the mission's headquarters in Drulingen, France.

As the teams fellowshipped in the Lord and shared what is happening in their lives and in their fellowships, it became evident that some, if not all, had taken their eyes off the goal of going deep in the Lord with one another. Instead, they organized conferences, and the teams were becoming, in effect, work teams instead of fellowships in which humble, forgiven sinners share their new lives in Christ and care deeply for one another as true brothers and sisters. This was clearly an anomaly. Team members were first and always glad disciples walking in light as repentant

Meeting of North American and European Teams, Drulingen, France, 2002.

ones, experiencing moment-by-moment freedom through the atoning merits of the Lord. Conferences must surely be the overflow of the love and light that the teams are experiencing as living fellowships.

All who attended left the conference were convicted of the shallow fellowship being experienced in the teams and determined to concentrate on true Calvary fellowship, not on pulling off successful conferences.

Revival literature

Literature has always been a vehicle for spreading the good news of revival in Jesus. The revival fellowships were blessed to have prolific writers such as Roy Hession, who near the end of his life produced several books that form a marvelous legacy for the life-giving message

A typical ministering team in 2002 at Locust Lane Chapel, Harrisburg, Pa. From left, Wayne Lawton, Marjorie and Chuck Higgins, John Gatu of Kenya, Joan Hall of Uganda, and Lindsay Robinson.

of new life in Christ. These include *My Calvary Road* (1978), *Not I but Christ* (1980), *Be Filled Now* (1989), *Good News for Bad People* (1990), *The Way of the Cross* (1991), *Forgotten Factors* (1992), *When I Saw Him* (1993), and *We Would See Jesus* (1997). The books found a wide audience in the English-speaking world and East Africa. They were instrumental in spelling out the delight of walking with Jesus and the challenges to that simple walk in everyday living.

Joe Church's insightful and widely read *Quest for His Highest* appeared in 1982. This was the most exhaustive story of revival written by one of the major players in the drama from its very beginning. It provided a definitive account of the joys and challenges in the East Africa Revival through the years as seen through the eyes of a participant.

Stanley Voke wrote two quite helpful books: *Personal Revival* (1997) and *Walking His Way* (2000). Both books and his pamphlets on revival themes were extremely popular.

Herbert H. Osborn played a significant role as historian and interpreter of the revival. His books *Fire in the Hills* (1991) and *Pioneers in the East African Revival* (2000) spread the news of the revival across the world.

Reflections on revival

What was so refreshingly new about the revival message? What made it so life-giving wherever it spread? And what was its universal appeal to all believers?

In pondering the life of Erma Maust, Mennonite bishop Enos Martin said, "The difference between the people in the revival fellowships and others is that they commit themselves to do without hesitation what the Spirit of Jesus Christ asks them to do." Erma Maust may not have absolutely agreed with those words, but she did live in the immediacy of God's Spirit. She never claimed to have a new message, just the old message embraced in its entirety, with a healthy freedom to follow the Lord in newness of life.

Almost from the beginning of the movement of the Spirit in Rwanda in the early 1930s, a variety of people found themselves at the cross together and discovered to their delight that they had the same walk with Jesus in spite of their races, cultures, and languages. Joe Church, for example, was a highly educated, meritorious medical doctor who was a shining example of the best in English culture. Simeon Nsibambi was of royal blood, a gifted health official, widely read in English literature, and a devoted Ugandan. William Nagenda was truly a child of two worlds, moving easily among Ugandans and Europeans. He communicated in both directions to people in his own culture and in other cultures. European audiences understood Festo Kivengere as well as his hometown. To be sure, many who entered into the way of revival were not as culturally ambidextrous, but a remarkable number of the early leaders were truly internationalists.

Not only that, but the movement also was a meeting place for all tribes and social classes in East Africa. Those who followed Jesus were considered brothers and sisters, and that is the way they viewed their new life together. The incidence of intertribal marriages was remarkably high. They did not put a premium on marrying into another tribe, but when it happened, they rejoiced and blessed such marriages.

Revival thrived in regular face-to-face fellowship; that was one of its essential features. Without such ongoing local fellowships, the spread of the message was stymied. The African brothers and sisters detected this early on and so reached out to enable every revived one to walk in meaningful fellowship, often with people who were different from them.

A recurrent theme in revival stated: "If one piece of wood is burning, it will soon go out; but if several are burning together, they will burn brightly and for a long time."

Revival did not lead to divisions but remained a movement within the churches. The theology stayed centered on Jesus Christ. While experiencing the fellowship of the Holy Spirit, believers acknowledged the reality and validity of signs and wonders. But they embraced these things without giving them prominence in their testimony or in public ministry. They did not deviate from their belief in the centrality of the atonement won by Jesus.

Many revival movements elsewhere rarely moved beyond the first culture. One thinks particularly of revivals in Indonesia in the 1960s, and another in Ethiopia a decade later. These revivals shook the cultures in which they occurred, but their impact did not spread much into other cultures. This is not to disparage those revivals, for through them many people received blessings. However, it does pose a question: Why do some revivals impact other cultures and some do not?

It was clearly not helpful to think of "exporting" the East Africa Revival into Western cultures. Some messengers had to present it in a way that people in the West could understand it. As it spread, it shed its African cultural rubric, and Western revivalists found that they were speaking of "their revival," not the revival of East Africa.

In East Africa regular meetings on the local level maintained the revival fires, as also happened in the homes of the Mausts and the Millers in eastern Pennsylvania. The meetings continued for several years but then dwindled until they no longer took place. The Mausts continued in ministry that blessed individuals, but ongoing fellowships did not emerge.

It is clear that fellowship is the God-appointed way, but doing that in every place was a challenge. One thing that worked and continues to work is through the use of teams. There are now three vibrant teams in North America meeting regularly on a fellowship level. Conferences often grow out of these experiences.

Obvious shortcomings

East Africa Revival swept from the Ruwenzori Mountains (Mountains of the Moon) of western Uganda to the Indian Ocean. Literally tens of thousands found salvation and hope in the simple though fresh message of revival. While the saved ones were never close to being a majority of the population, even in the areas where people received the message most eagerly, the numbers were substantial. Those numbers have persisted for the past sixty or so years.

This is unlike the situation in Europe and North America, where the numbers have been quite small. Of course, the religious landscape in East Africa was radically different from the Western world, which was on the verge of what might be called a post-Christian age. The question remains: Could the message of the East Africa Revival have had a greater impact on Christianity outside of East Africa? Probably so. The Pentecostal movement that sprang up in many places, particularly in California in the early twentieth century spread like wildfire. At the beginning it was contained mostly in independent churches, but then broke out into established denominations, Assemblies of God being one of the largest. The East Africa Revival stayed within the denominations as salt and light.

It is certainly true that the major themes of the revival are not alien to a large segment of evangelical Christianity. This may be one reason why the evangelical awakening has absorbed the East Africa Revival, as it has many others. For example, Stephen Olford, the renowned Bible expositor, freely expresses his debt to what he has learned of following Christ by his close association with Bishop Festo Kivengere, Roy Hession, and others.[25]

Some of the major flaws in the movement

At the beginning of the movement in East Africa, in the first blush of confession and testimony to the freeing power of the blood of Christ, some enthusiasts did not use much discretion in confessing past sins. In some cases this scandalized the movement, particularly when the repentant ones implicated others by name, causing great embarrassment. To an outsider, it could have appeared that the movement was more about repentance and confession than on walking in newness of life in Jesus. Unwise displays of public confession provided detractors with grist for their mill. As the movement matured, such public testimonies were discouraged. At times, if the leaders of a meeting felt that a public confession was becoming too graphic or that the testimony implicated others, they began to sing as a way to politely end it.

In the early years, some leveled the accusation that the movement was too subjective and too emotional. To be sure, there was an emotional aspect to the walk with Christ. Sometimes people had to restrain themselves when, for example, a notable person gave a testimony of salvation that absolutely thrilled the gathering. Such testimony represented a tremendous victory of the grace of God in Jesus that many in the meeting had experienced, and modest dancing sometimes broke out as people celebrated the triumph of the Lamb. The major denominations were uneasy with this, and some detractors labeled the movement one of excessive emotionalism. The critics failed to take into account that at every fellowship meeting the Scriptures were studied diligently and applied immediately. These people were truly "people of the Word."

Some felt that the fellowships excluded them because they could not testify to "getting saved" in the way others did. To be sure revival fellowships did "judge" others on the basis of whether they were truly contrite and repentant or whether they just wanted to belong. It must have been a struggle to discern whether confessions were authentic or not. Almost without exception, when a person first testified about meeting Jesus and what that meant, people listened politely and attentively. When the testifier was finished, the fellowship discerned if it was an authentic meeting with Jesus and a true confession. If they so discerned, they invariably sang their signature song: "Glory, glory, hallelujah, / Glory, glory to the Lamb, / For the cleansing blood has reached me, / Glory, glory to the Lamb." Furthermore, if a person truly repented, believers expected that one to join a local fellowship group and walk in light on a continual basis with those brothers and sisters. The fellowships did not have a doctrinal exam or list of beliefs to which adherents must subscribe, except for basic evangelical biblical doctrines.

Revival should have made a greater impact on the politics of East Africa

At the Kabale Convention in 1995, Festo Kivengere wondered if revival brothers and sisters should not be encouraged to enter politics. He was unsure in light of the fact that many politicians were corrupt. Many brothers and sisters did not feel called to enter politics, but they did influence the political direction in Uganda and Kenya through their martyrdoms. The Mau Mau martyrs and those who gave their lives after that uprising affected the politics of the day. Likewise, the death in Uganda of Archbishop Janani Luwum stunned the nation and impacted attitudes toward the brutal political regime in power. Within the past decade, however, people nurtured in revival began to enter politics in Uganda and Kenya.

Impact on the church

While revival brothers and sisters did not enter politics, they did impact the churches. Certainly the revival movement affected the general hue of Christianity in East Africa.

The revival had many opportunities to establish itself as a denomination. Nevertheless, early missionaries, mostly Anglicans, felt that the revival should flow freely into more and more denominations and not be institutionalized. Only time will tell if that was a wise judgment.

Ongoing Revival: Testimonies

Richard MacMaster

How did revival spread beyond the mission hospital at Gahini in the far-off country of Ruanda and a circle of prayer in Kampala? There was no plan, no agenda, no organization, only an agreement to pray together. Yet it did spread from place to place across East Africa, and not for a season or a year, but continues even today.

Could a revival continue for sixty or seventy years? I would not have thought so, but my friend Don Jacobs, a retired Mennonite bishop, shared with me what he observed on a trip to Africa in November 1998. Don and Anna Ruth Jacobs were in Kampala, the capital of Uganda. Their visit coincided with a miniconvention of saved ones, or *balokole*, as they are called in Luganda, the language of Uganda.

"The place was already jammed when we arrived, maybe 2,500 or 3,000 in attendance," Don said. "It is always a thrill to see hundreds of people together like this, for the sole purpose of moving closer to Christ and discovering what he wants them to do."

Zeb Kabaza, a respected elder, and the rest of the team planning the convention asked Don Jacobs to open the meeting. It did not matter to them that Don was a visitor from America. They knew him as a brother in Christ.

The meeting continued with personal testimony. A middle-aged man spoke first. He had been jailed for defrauding the government but came to Christ, repented, and put his life in order. Others spoke, too. Many responded, and each gave a personal witness.

I asked about follow-up and nurture for these young Christians who wanted to come to Jesus.

"All of those who came forward were referred to the groups that meet regularly where they live," said Don. "This is the beauty of the revival here;

people are not left dangling. All over Uganda groups meet. Each person is expected to join a group for fellowship so that one may grow in grace right there. Of course, they are encouraged to attend church, but that seldom meets the nurture needs of these new believers. That's the job of the little fellowship groups that dot the countryside and the cities."

"So these fellowship groups are important for the revival?" I asked.

Don answered thoughtfully: "If the people were to stop meeting, I suppose the fires would die down to embers in a year or so. Meetings continue in groups during the week, and on some Sundays groups from an area gather together. They also have these quarterly meetings. In addition they have several, maybe three or four, conventions a year. These are often organized by diocesan staff of the Church of Uganda with the help of the revival teams. All of these meetings are important in the total scheme of things."

That is true of Uganda, but what of North America? Does the message of revival have the same appeal now as it did in the beginning?

These questions are best answered through the witness of those moved by the revival. What follows are the testimonies of missionaries, revival team members, and others who witness to the grace of God revealed so compellingly through Jesus Christ.[1]

Dorothy Smoker, missionary to Tanzania and Kenya

I went to Wheaton College and while there I met a young man, George Smoker. We were both valedictorians. Now you would think we would be just great for the mission field but 'tain't so! We responded to the mission board's request and we were sent out to East Africa and to the mission that had been started at Musoma, Tanzania. We were so sure that we were going to be God's chosen people for Africa and everybody who heard the Word was going to believe.

When we got there, the church at our station had three members. After three years there was one! You know the letters missionaries are supposed to write home? "We baptized 20 this week and next month we will be baptizing 50." By the mercy of God, we didn't have any converts. There was no one who wanted what we had! Take that any way you want to. You can't make it worse than it was! We were absolutely finished! We knocked ourselves out. We traveled all over, we visited every village and talked to the people, but we were not getting anywhere. We decided to quit. It was against the rules in Mennonite missions to stop in the middle of a five-year term, but we were through.

Then Simeon Hurst came back from a visit into Uganda. He told us that something was happening over in Uganda. We were bound by the mission to go on a trip away from the station for a month anyway, so we decided to go Uganda. Actually, somebody booked us without our knowing it on the little island on Lake Bunyoni, way up on the border between Rwanda and Uganda. It sounded like an exciting journey to get there, and I like excitement! We took the Lake Victoria boat and got off at the first station in Uganda, and took a bus from the lake up to this hot elevated station on the western side of Uganda. On the boat were three Africans who had been sent as a team to share what God had done for them. When they heard we were going up there, they said, "Oh, good; you will be interested to hear what God has done for us." They began telling us the story of what God had done in saving them out of witchcraft and all sorts of things and had filled them with the Spirit.

They let people know on ahead that we were coming. They did this so well that we began to be met by Christians every time we stopped. We met people all along the way because of the word-of-mouth telegraph, which works so well there.

We went out in a little boat to this little island in Lake Bunyoni. The elderly missionaries on this station were friendly. They had been there most of their lives, but they were very discouraged and said, "We can't understand it. There is something strange happening these days. These people will sometimes shout and sing all night. They are so excited, and we think there is something wrong about it!" We settled into this little guesthouse, and every morning at six, when the sun rose, there arose a song all around the lake at a distance. All the families around the lake were singing "Tukutendereza, Yesu [We praise you, Jesus]": "Glory, glory, hallelujah, / Glory, glory to the Lamb, / For the cleansing blood has reached me, / Glory, glory to the Lamb." We said, "We don't know any group of Christians that wake up in the morning in America and sing praise to God." The missionaries told us not to pay any attention to that because they were sort of a wild group and think they have everything.

The doctor on the island with us had charge of the leper colony and asked us if we would like to go with him and see what was going on, and we told him yes. Today there is almost no leprosy left, but at that time the medication for leprosy had not been found, and lepers had terrible marks on their faces. We saw these people with fingers, toes, and noses gone. Many were blind. This one poor old leper said, "Oh, I just thank God that I have leprosy. I never would have heard about heaven and come to know Jesus if I hadn't gotten leprosy and was brought here. I'm on my way to heaven!" This shook us. Here were lepers in a worse condition than we had seen anybody, and they were praising God that they were so blessed.

We were there a week when a young man named Zeb Kabaza came to our door. He welcomed us and told us he just wanted to give his testimony to us for that day. He said, "The Lord convicted me of sin today of wanting the best piece of meat at the dinner table." He felt this was a great sin that he was able to repent of and give to the Lord. He asked George, "What's the Lord been doing for you today?" George cleared his throat and stumbled for words and then said, "Actually, I have something I need to say to Dorothy first." George broke down and cried and told me all the things from way back in his youth in his growing-up days, things he had done against God, things he had hidden that no one else knew. God convicted him of even the way he felt toward me. He repented of it, and the Lord convicted me, and I also opened my heart.

God also showed me things in my childhood that I never thought of having to repent of or even thought of these things. Both of us felt as if we had been saved for the first time. We felt free of any secrets we had had with each other. That was a wonderful night! I don't think we slept much that night, but we didn't need to!

We got up the next morning and went to this big church at Kabale. The archbishop of Canterbury had reproved the revival brethren because they had sung "Tukutendereza, Yesu" in church service, and it was prohibited. As soon as church was over, about three hundred were in a great circle outside, sharing what the Lord had done for them that week. Someone in charge leading this group said, "Now we can't all speak, so only those who have met the Lord this week can tell us, and we can rejoice with them." George said, "I think I am one of them, and we have something to say." We very stumblingly and awkwardly said, "We think that Jesus saved us last night, and we would like to learn how to walk with Jesus." The sky lifted up by the amount of singing and the hugs they gave us and by their accepting us as soul brothers and sisters in the Lord. They didn't care if we were black or white. They told us that it was wonderful that this happened, but this is a daily need. They told us it is not something that will last forever, but there will be a daily need to praise. They really gave us a teaching session in the afternoon.

The next day we went home. Our hearts were singing. We told the bus driver who was Muslim all about it, but we didn't care [that he was Muslim]. There was a line of people down the mountain to the coast of the sea, and they would all come out to greet us all the way down the mountainside. I don't know how they knew. The Muslim bus driver said, "I wish I had what you have!" We got hugged all the way from Kigali to Kampala. We began to learn the joy of brotherhood and sisterhood, of being a part of people based on the Lord, based on walking with the Lord, based on being committed to the Lord. I felt that this was the beginning of life for us—not the beginning of our "missionary service," but it was.

From then on, we had many apologies to make all over our tribe—people we had been cross with, people we had refused this or that. I remember an old man who once brought us milk that was curdled, and I had gotten so angry with him. I can't remember what I called him. I had to go all the way (five miles) to his home. I got down on my knees (he was a very old man in bed by then), and I said, "My dear father, I ask your forgiveness for the way I treated you about the milk, and I am very sorry I did that." In a short time it got all over the tribe, and we began to be able to share and to testify, to be received and loved as we would never have been if we didn't have that broken spirit and contrite heart."[2]

Catharine Leatherman, revivalist and missionary to Tanzania

I grew up in a Christian home. As a young girl I once boasted to my father, "I know everything in the Bible!" His reply was, "Then who was Melchizedek?" I didn't know!

I do not remember when I invited Jesus Christ into my heart, but I was very young. I thought about mission service and prayed, "Lord, send me to South America—those people seem more civilized than in Africa." Later I met John Leatherman at Eastern

Catharine Leatherman continued on the Eastern U.S. team for many years and was an effective Bible teacher.

Mennonite School in Virginia. He didn't say, "Will you marry me?" but "Will you go with me to Africa?"

Spiritually, I felt pretty good about myself. After all, there were several ministers in the family, and I made an A+ on the doctrinal exam for missionaries. I kept all of the rules and regulations of Lancaster Conference. But after getting to Africa, I was bothered that I lacked assurance of salvation. Somehow, crossing the ocean had not helped. I read my Bible and prayed.

Someone mentioned that God doesn't save Mennonites or good girls, but he saves sinners! I now was the mother of four children. We were busy. My husband baptized twelve new Christians. But it was apparent their lives were not changed. Then revival came, and I thought, "the Africans need it so much." Later I went to a weekend retreat at the African Inland Mission, and while there I received this assurance. The verses Colossians 1:21-22 were especially meaningful: "And you, that were sometimes alienated and enemies in your mind by wicked works, yet now hath he reconciled in the body of his flesh through death, to present you holy and unblameable and unreprovable in his sight." I came home rejoicing.

Later I was aware of impatience with my children and anger toward my husband and others. I felt that I had lost the "victorious Christian life" which had begun. I was getting nowhere. An African brother spoke to me: "Catharine, if you were carrying a load of bricks somewhere and one brick fell off, you wouldn't dump the entire load. You would just pick up the brick and move on." Catharine saw that through the blood of Jesus, I could do just that, and I began to walk in the light. Marriage is good when both partners focus on Jesus.

Hard times came. One of our children was wronged. How could I forgive? I couldn't—but I could repent of the unforgiveness—and God did the rest. The resentment left! One son was paralyzed as a young adult and died after years of inactivity. This required faith to accept. My husband died at age fifty-nine! This seemed too young to die. I read about John the Baptist. He was in his thirties when he was decapitated. Why? God answered, "His work was done." Then I could rest about [my husband] John dying at fifty-nine.

"The just shall live by faith." What has the Lord done? He has given me the ability to love people. He has also given me inner peace and the sure knowledge that I am loved. And in addition, he heals!

I feel like Cinderella when I read that I am unblameable and unreprovable in his sight! Now in my eighties, there is the downward physical slope—but there is the upward spiritual ascent. What is the greatest good in life? To be loved? NO. The greatest good is to hear the Lord's voice!

Rhoda Wenger, missionary to Tanzania, Somalia, Kenya, and the Caribbean

Rhoda Wenger, a lifelong sister in the revival.

I grew up on a farm in Chesapeake, Virginia, in a strict Mennonite home. They dressed very plain. The plain dress was very much a part of my religion, and I felt very pleased about it. I judged other people who claimed to be Christians but who were not plain. Then one day, about age twelve, I accepted Christ. The plain clothes had not kept me from needing salvation in Christ.

Then years later I went to Africa as a missionary; there I began to see the pride in my life, the sins of the spirit, especially as the revival spread and people walked in the light about their evil thoughts and motives. My life was transformed. I came home to tell what the Lord had done for me in Africa. I noticed that other missionaries were asked to speak in churches when they came home, but I didn't remember that I received any invitations. I resented that, but the Lord enabled me to repent. I have been given ample opportunity to share my love for Jesus. I still dress rather plain but one hardly notices that because it is the Lord who takes preeminence.

Mahlon Hess, missionary to Tanzania

I am reminded of Karl Barth's profound theological statement, "Jesus loves me! this I know, for the Bible tells me so" [from Anna B. Warner]. At age ten or twelve I began to feel the call to be a missionary in Africa. My first response was to take Jesus as my Savior. But it took two years until I was willing to confess stealing from father's change purse. During that time I dreamed of supporting myself by a poultry business because people had said "missionaries are lazy." So I wanted to be self-supporting. I taught Sunday

school. I attended EMC [Eastern Mennonite College]. Elam
Stauffer and John Mosemann came on furlough and nudged me in
the direction of missionary service. I was asked to help edit the
Missionary Messenger, I served on the mission board, and taught
at Lancaster Mennonite High School. I married Mabel Eshleman
in 1944. I also had a call to mission service. We went to Tanzania,
where God gave us five children.

It was in Africa that God taught me the simple way of humbling myself to my wife. It was there that I learned to fellowship
with Christians of other denominations. I went to a revival convention in Uganda. There were military people, women with bobbed
hair, sacramentalists, but all praising the Lord. Once my Catholic
counterpart in educational administration came to me and said,
"Mahlon, our church members in Kamageta are fighting. This must
not be; we serve the same Jesus." Within two weeks after arrival, a
senior missionary stopped to introduce us to some Seventh-Day
Adventist friends. I struggled whether to drink the orange juice
offered by "heretics." Later I learned to know this missionary as a
real brother in Christ. After planting a church in Dar es Salaam, we
returned to the U.S. to facilitate our children's education. In time
Mabel developed cancer and the Lord took her. We had moved to
Landis Homes. Then the Lord gave me Mary. We were in Tanzania
for two years. Now we are back at Landis Homes. A major concern
is the growing gap between rich and poor; people with money control our nation. Our nation depends on military solutions. Two
times Mabel and I withheld war taxes. Spiritually, I feel we are like
the story of the frog being slowly boiled to death. But personally,
I'm excited because Jesus is real! I keep myself accountable to my
wife and a spiritual mentor. It is difficult to fast and pray. But I see
a new awakening. The pastor's prayer meeting in western Lancaster
County is one evidence of that.

Simeon Hurst, missionary to Tanzania

I was born in Ontario, Canada, one of twelve children, in an Old
Order Mennonite home. They used horses and buggies. But my
father decided that they needed a truck on the farm, and he was
excommunicated. They found another church and continued serving the Lord. I accepted the Lord as a youth. My education was
through eighth grade, but at age twenty-three I went back to high

school and later attended Eastern Mennonite College. I met Edna Schmiedendorf, and I was preparing for missionary service. I loved her, so she began to prepare for missionary service, too. We were married in 1939 and went to Africa in 1940.

In 1943 we vacationed in Uganda at the Lee Wilson Farm. We met William Nagenda and many brothers and sisters who were "walking in the light." There was even Scripture for this (1 John 1:7). We returned to Tanzania more open and transparent with each other before the Lord. After we returned to this continent, Edna was diagnosed with Parkinson's disease and later died of a heart attack. Don Jacobs preached her funeral.

I found myself a lonely man. I was chaplain at Fairview Mennonite Retirement Home in Ontario. There were many widows there, and at times I felt some pressure. A sister in the fellowship, Marjorie Lofthouse, told me about Jean. I was open to meet her, but I wanted to be sure. We exchanged pictures and we prayed for God's will to be revealed.

Jean Hurst

I was raised in a Christian home. My mother was a spiritual Christian who influenced me greatly. I attended Messiah College in Grantham, Pennsylvania. There I met and later married David Kipe. We lived in Clarence Center, New York. After our two children were grown we prayed about the two empty bedrooms. God led them into a ministry of helping troubled people. One girl was filled with demons. David and I were not trained counselors, but in dependence upon God we ministered deliverance to quite a few persons. David was killed in an airplane accident. When the officer came to tell me, I said, "I know that he is with Jesus in heaven." The officer said, "You are a very courageous woman." I answered, "No, I am a Christian, and it is Christ who gives the power to say this."

I missed David and was lonely. One day as I was waiting on the Lord, and he spoke: "There is a widower who is going through the same thing you are, and I am preparing him for you." Jean was surprised. But like Mary, I said, "Yes, Lord, if you have a ministry for us, I'll accept that." Ronald and Marjorie Lofthouse had come to pastor the Brethren in Christ church. One day Ron told me about Simeon. I said, "Is he a Spirit-filled Christian?" Ron replied, "Oh, my, yes!" When Simeon came, I was assured that God was leading. Our wedding was scheduled for January 19, 1985. Don Jacobs was to preach the sermon. Don and Anna Ruth were bringing Herbert and Erma Maust, but the interstate was closed due to heavy snow. Ron performed the wedding. But now, fourteen years later, we continue to experience the fellowship of Jesus together and minister Christ's life to family and friends in the world and in the church!

Victor and Viola Dorsch, missionaries to Tanzania and Somalia

The Tanzanian Mennonite Church was considering sending teachers to southern Somalia, where there were people who spoke their language. So a team of four—including missionary Simeon Hurst and three Tanzanians: Ezekiel Muganda, Zedekia Kisare and Nashon Nyambok, all pastors—stayed at our place as they surveyed the area. They spent two weeks with us, traveling from village to village. The best thing that I remember of traveling with these brethren was the spiritual fellowship we could have. I began to understand for the first time what it meant to keep short accounts with your fellow workers and the Lord. These brethren were part of the East Africa Revival, which had touched each of them deeply.

I must confess that I was quite skeptical of them, as I observed their walk together as a team. In fact, I was watching for something in them that I could fault them with. Then it happened. After a long day on the rough roads and hot sun, as we neared home, two of the pastors got into a very fierce argument and very sharp words were exchanged. When we arrived home, each went to his room, only to come together for the evening meal, a short devotional period together, and then all of us retired. That night in bed I remember telling Viola that these brothers were no better than we were, as we too had our disagreements with fellow missionaries, and I related to her what had happened in the Land Rover earlier. I slept very well that night.

The next morning we were together again for breakfast at our house as usual. Then before we started our trek for the day, we again gathered in our living room for the reading of *Daily Light* and prayer. After the reading of the Scriptures and as the brother was ready to lead in prayer, one of the two pastors spoke up and said, "I have something to share. I did not sleep well last night, as I remembered the sharp words that I exchanged with my brother yesterday in the car." He then turned to his brother and asked for his forgiveness. The second brother then responded that he too did not sleep well because of what he had said the day before, and had asked the Lord to forgive him and for the other brother to forgive him. The two then forgave each other. We had prayer together for the day's work and were on our way. This was the aspect of revival that I did not like and was not willing to do with my fellow missionaries.

The Tanzania delegation ministered, then, at our annual missionary conference. The first morning of the conference the Spirit of God broke in among us, which continued on for the three-day conference. By the time the conference finished, the whole missionary team had been impacted by the revival message. This was the beginning for Viola and me to walk in the light with Jesus that continues on to this day. We were now seeking fellowship with the brethren whenever this was possible.

We returned to Canada in 1987 and eagerly joined the team there. This has not only given us the opportunity to fellowship with the brethren here in Canada, but has given us the privilege to fellowship with the two teams in the U.S., in Europe on several occasions, and back to Kenya and Tanzania several times. It has been such a joy to learn to walk in the light with Jesus and in fellowship with our brothers and sisters. It has brought such a joy and peace to our lives, and especially in our home. To walk in the way of repentance brings true peace and happiness that can only happen when we walk in the light with Jesus.[3]

Chuck Higgins, pastor in the Church of the Nazarene

Through the valley of shadows. A rigid legalistic holiness setting from my early years formed my unreal concept of God and my continuously fragile relationship with him. The community of believers in which I was raised, including my family, was very sincere and faithful. My life and conduct were regulated by a severe

Marge and Chuck Higgins, Church of the Nazarene pastor and highly influential Bible teacher.

list of ethical rules I could not even with the force of my will and best intentions perfectly meet. As a result, I lived a bipolar existence either in deep despair or euphoric pride, depending upon the degree of obedience I gave to these rules. It was a life of living in the "valley of shadows." My relationship with God was always measured by the degree to which I was able to meet those unbending rules. That life became a prison for me, with God serving as a jailer occasionally releasing me on good behavior only to incarcerate me again for the slightest infraction of a rule. I knew deep in my heart this was not the life Jesus died to give me. But how to come into the assurance and freedom that I desperately longed for and that was freely offered by grace through faith in Christ? I had no clue whatsoever. The only grace I knew anything about was the grace by which I was saved when I repented of my sins. I had very little understanding of grace beyond that. It seemed I was hopelessly consigned to this exercise in futility all my life.

I entered the ministry as a pastor loaded down with all this heaviness. I finally concluded after a few years as a pastor I could no longer preach this legalistic message to my people when it was impossible for me as a pastor to live by it. I was invited to attend a nearby ashram (spiritual retreat) led by E. Stanley Jones, a dear man of God and a missionary evangelist in India. It was there I was able to confess all my pretenses and forsake my futile efforts to live a holy life and stood naked before God, offering nothing but my sinful self to him. It was then I discovered, to my incredible relief and sheer joy, Jesus alone to be all I should ever need: my salvation, my wisdom, my holiness, my hope, my strength, my all for my everything. After having lived a life plagued with guilt and condemnation, I now felt guilty for no longer feeling guilty! (a new kind of guilt, which I soon learned was not real). I needed, however, to learn how to walk this glorious newly found way.

This opportunity occurred while I was pastor of a church in Fresno, California, and I met Roy Hession from England, who preached a "strange" message, strange to my ears at least. It was *the* message I had for so long hungered to hear that brought hope for one who was feebly learning to walk daily with Jesus. It was the message of God's stunning grace, allowing me to come in whatever condition, just as I was, to Jesus. I began to learn how to walk in the light, confessing the truth of what God was reveal-

ing to me to be sin. Then to repent of it with faith in the blood
Jesus shed on the cross for that sin, and to continue living in the
joy and freedom of God's forgiveness and cleansing from any and
all condemnation. It was simply the working of God's grace in
Jesus, who is grace and truth.

Later I moved to pastor a church in Glendale, California,
where Don Widmark was a member. Don used the Holy Spirit to
help me to "see" Jesus more clearly, the way of the cross, and the
fullness of God's grace for repenting sinners. I shall always be
grateful for Don's faithful ministry to me. Don was leading a fellowship in the Los Angeles area of those who had been deeply
touched by the message I had just discovered. This fellowship was
born out of visits by Roy and Revel Hession, William Nagenda,
Festo Kivengere, Stanley Voke, Erma Maust, Bishop Barham,
Matt Nyagwaswa, and others. Their visits were times of encouragement, teaching, challenging, with unforgettable times of deep
searching and glorious breakthroughs into a closer walk with
Jesus and one another.

Their messages were not sermons but rather humble testimonies from their own lives. After having failed they too were
brought again to the cross and delivered into victory. These not
only came to speak but also to sit with us, helping us back to the
cross, giving us hope from their own testimonies of their walk with
Jesus. This fellowship met regularly, sharing and growing together
in Jesus, confessing our dryness, our emptiness, and our failures,
and with great joy finding Jesus meeting us as we were with his forgiving grace. Marriages were strengthened, churches revived, families reunited, pastors [were] finding new life and hope, differences
reconciled. We were discovering the real meaning of fellowship as
we met in our homes, churches, retreat centers, and parks. The
clearest and most convincing evidence of God's working in and
among us was not found in our meetings together but in what was
happening in our homes, with our relatives, in our church relationships, on our jobs, among our neighbors. Only eternity will reveal
the real and abiding ministry of the Holy Spirit during those days.
Lives are still being changed in similar ways, breaking out in testimony of weak people made strong, filled with the joy of the Lord
by the exciting grace of God in Jesus.

As a guest of the brethren in Uganda many years ago, I

learned a profound truth about freedom in Christ. I will never forget the time at a tea plantation outside Kampala. There was a group of Africans and a few Americans and Europeans gathered under a big mango tree. They were giving testimonies, and everyone was singing "Tukutendereza, Yesu." One lady got up and gave a testimony, and nobody sang "Tukutendereza, Yesu." I thought to myself, "What's wrong with that? I thought it was a pretty good testimony." But they knew. About a half-hour later, she got up and said, "Will you please forgive me? I didn't have a testimony." As soon as she said that, she had one and they sang "Tukutendereza, Yesu." It is so easy for us to know the words and to know the Way and be empty.[4]

Later on I got a new twist on Hebrews 6:1: "Therefore let us leave the elementary teachings about Christ and go on to maturity, not laying again the foundation of repentance from acts that lead to death" (NIV). In other words, it's not having to be convinced over and over again that you need to repent. I have decided that this is what I need to do, and you don't have to convince me again because it has already been settled. I don't have to be convinced "You need to repent" each time. Repentance is the bedrock of our faith.

I find for myself as I progress in this life that the list of the things we call mistakes and shortcomings gets longer and longer, and the list of the things we call sin gets shorter and shorter. I try to convince myself and the Lord: "That was just hereditary. Oh, that was just a shortcoming and a mistake." But Jesus died for sin. In 1 John the proverbial person in the first chapter was having a controversy with God, saying, "That was not sin." But the conclusion was that if it is not called sin, we make God out to be a liar, and his word is not in us (1 John 1:10). Growth and maturity is not moving beyond repentance but growing more sensitive to sin and the need to repent because we are seeing Jesus.[5]

Les Simons, Baptist Pastor

Before I became a Christian, I sang in nightclubs and was in show business for about five years. I smoked pot for nine years and wound up at forty years old in a psychiatric ward for alcoholics. During that time in that ward, my wife, Joan, found the Lord.

When I was discharged from that psychiatric ward for alcoholics, I gave her a terrible time for nine months, but I began to see what happened in her life, and I became hungry for what she had. After nine months, I accepted Christ as my Lord and Savior at age forty-one. The day after I was saved, my old drinking buddies came around and said, "Come on; let's get drunk." I had an opportunity for my very first testimony as a Christian. I said, "I can't do that anymore. I was in church yesterday." "You were what, in church yesterday?" I said, "Yes I was, and I asked Jesus Christ to be my Lord and Savior, and I can't do this anymore." So for two hours they tried to argue me out of this and got nowhere. They finally said, "Okay. We'll see you in six months."

Well, it has been thirty-six years, and they haven't seen me since, and I praise God for that. In seven days everything dropped off—the drinking, the smoking pot, and then the last thing to go was smoking cigarettes. I had smoked since age fourteen and I lit up a cigarette on the seventh day, and I thought I was going to choke to death. I coughed and gagged; tears ran down my face. I said, "Hey, that's God speaking to me. He doesn't want me to smoke!" And I haven't since. Those were all the outward things. The inner things that caused me to do all these outward things, God needed to deal with, and he is still dealing with those inward things.

He loved me so much that when I was eight months old in the Lord, he sent various people to help me see him. I didn't recognize him because I was a cocky, brash guy from Brooklyn, and I was going to be the biggest soul-winner in California. I praise the Lord for Jean Roberts because when I was eight months old in the Lord, she invited me to her home. Joan couldn't go at that time. There in her home was Eric Sabiti and Lawrence Barham. Along with them was a guy by the name of Chuck Higgins, sitting there looking forlorn and very glum. I said to myself, "What kind of Christian is this guy? No joy there." And then I heard their testimonies.

Lawrence Barham shared about his wife, how he was jealous of her because she spoke the language better than he did and got along with the Africans better than he did. As he was coming from his church after preaching one Sunday morning, this new babe in Christ, an African brother, rode up on a bicycle and said, "Brother, that was a wonderful message you preached, but how are things in your home?" Before he could answer, the African brother said, "You are jealous of your wife." And he left, praising the Lord on his bicycle. By the time Lawrence got home, the Lord showed him he had been jealous of his wife for sixteen years. When he got home, he called his wife into the room and asked her forgiveness for being jealous of her.

That opened up Pandora's box in her life, and she began to share some things that had been on her heart, and they had a hallelujah meeting in that room. Jesus came, and they saw him afresh for the first time in quite awhile. The next Sunday he didn't share a message but gave a testimony as to what God had done in his life. Revival had not come to his church up to that point, but it came that Sunday. The Lord just broke in, and revival came to his church.

Eric Sabiti shared a testimony on how he had been cheating and taking money from the till while he was a canon. He admitted all of this. I thought to myself, "These guys are weird. What's wrong with these fellows?" I had never heard anything like that. That was the first time God was seeking me out. Nothing happened. I went to Prairie Bible Institute and brought all this baggage into the Bible school that I had carried around for years. I was a tyrant in the home and had a terrible temper. I was playing the role, pretending to be a wonderful Christian at the Bible school.

Finally we went on a vacation after two years to California during the summer months, and there was Jean Roberts, again inviting us to come to her home to meet Matt Nyagwaswa, a dear brother. He began to tell all of these things the Lord was doing in his life, how he sinned and God forgave him when he repented. I interrupted him in my brash Brooklyn way, "Hey, Brother, you mean to tell me that a guy as spiritual as you sin?" He said very lovingly, "Just wait! You will find out."

It wasn't until 1965, when I was hearing all of these wonderful messages at Prairie about the overcoming life, the abundant life, the victorious life, and I would cry in my heart, "Please tell me how you got there." I wanted to hear a testimony but never heard one. The Lord in his mercy and grace sent a brother to me, a fellow student who said to me, "I want you to check out the doctrine in this book. I am not too much in agreement with it." It was *Calvary Road* by Roy Hession. I was big on doctrine but not big on practicing it in my home. So I opened the book to the chapter "Revival in the Home." The thing that jumped out at me was that revival must begin in the home. It is the most difficult place to begin, but the most necessary place to begin. I didn't want any part of that book, and I put it on a shelf in a closet.

You know, the Lord loved me so much that he sent the author of that book, Roy Hession, and dear brother Stanley Voke, to Prairie Bible Institute, of all places, for a weekend of meetings. At the first meeting, Stanley shared a testimony. It was a precious testimony between him and Doreen. He said, "Boys, that broke me." Right there in my seat, the Lord broke me, and for the first time I bawled like a baby, walked all the way home, and gathered my family around me, still crying. I said to Joan, "Joan, please forgive me for being the husband I have been to you. You have never seen Jesus." To my dear children I said, "Please forgive me, Children, for the kind of father I have been to you. You have never seen Jesus in me." They were shocked—because I was always right and never wrong. I would never say that I was sorry or ask forgiveness. That was just the beginning, but praise God for the beginnings. Every day is a new beginning.

The following week after this wonderful thing happened to me, I was getting on Joan's case for forgetting things on the table. "You forgot the salt. Where's the salt?" For a whole week I got on her case for forgetting things. I didn't know the Lord was working in her heart, but she was bound and determined to have everything on that table. But on the fifth day, she forgot one thing, and I blasted her for that. Joan left weeping and went to her room. She came out five minutes later, still weeping, looked me full in the face and said, "Please forgive me, dear. The Lord has shown me that I was not willing to be a servant to you." That broke me, and we both were on our knees together at the cross at Jesus' feet, asking forgiveness from one another.

This morning in our room was another beginning when Joan asked me to change my pants. She said, "You don't want to go down there with those pants on." They are my favorite walking pants, and I began in my heart to say, "I'm a big boy now. Can't I wear my own pants?" It wasn't long before the Lord showed me my heart and my attitude of annoyance toward a woman who has stood by me when I was going through all this phase, even before I was saved and was an alcoholic, and even as a Christian who was pretending and playing a role. He is the God of the again, and the again, and the again, and I praise him for that.[6]

Bill Scott, pastor of Grace Bible Church in Zion, Maryland

Five years into the ministry I became a very discouraged person. I was disappointed in myself as a pastor, as a husband, as a parent. I felt I was failing in all of these areas. My thought was, "Get out of the ministry." And I might have done so—BUT GOD! God spoke to me from Jeremiah 29:11: "For I know the plans I have for you, says the LORD, plans for [your] welfare and not for evil, to give you a future and a hope" (RSV).

I had felt imprisoned in these areas of failure, but God opened the prison doors just as the psalmist had experienced in praying, "Bring my soul out of prison, that I may praise your name" (Ps 142:7). What did God do? God gave me a fresh glimpse of JESUS, as my Savior, as my all and in all! I realized that Jesus had not just come to "help" me in ministry, but to "displace" me so that he could minister through me. I heard about King Saul being dethroned and Samuel telling him that God would give the kingdom "to a neighbor . . . better than thou" (1 Sam 15:28). I heard about a conference at Keswick Grove, New Jersey, where Roy Hession, an evangelist from England, was speaking. Roy was preaching about Saul. He was a wonderful fellow and had a lot going for him, head and shoulders above others. People looked up to King Saul. But I had a lot going for me too, and people looked up to me.

I was a college and seminary graduate, a great Greek and Hebrew scholar; I had gifts of leadership and was chosen in high school and college for positions of leadership. As a pastor I worked very hard—70 to 75 hours a week: 3 sermons, visitation door to door. The church grew, my family grew (seven children were born), but tensions also grew in my life. Things surfaced like irritation, anger, criticism of my wife and children. This bothered me because I knew I was not fully following the Lord. In 1 Samuel 15:11, God says in the KJV: "It repenteth me that I have set up Saul to be king." But I was like Saul when confronted. I blamed others: "The people, they . . ." I would work harder to bring an acceptable sacrifice to God, but I heard God say, "To obey is better than sacrifice" (1 Sam 15:22).

God spoke through Samuel to Saul, "The LORD has rejected you from being king. . . . The LORD has torn the kingdom of Israel from you and has given it to a neighbor . . . better than you" (1 Sam 15:26-28 RSV). And I heard God saying to me, "I have rejected you as being pastor." So I wondered who the next pastor would be. Maybe one of the professors of Lancaster Bible College, or a young fellow out of seminary. But through Roy Hession's ministry I heard the Holy Spirit saying, "The neighbor better than you is JESUS! The pastor better than you is JESUS! The husband better than you is JESUS! The father better than you is JESUS!" Galatians 2:20 became a reality: "I am crucified with Christ: nevertheless I live; yet not I, but Christ liveth in me." Then I could say, "I will go back and let Jesus live in me."

The Lord introduced Marian and me to Herbert and Erma Maust, who were at that Keswick Conference where Roy Hession spoke on King Saul. Erma prayed for me. Erma and Herbert invited themselves to our home. Erma upholstered our living room furniture and Herbert did some painting. God showed us the "all" verses (giving thanks always in all things, and so on). God put us into the revival fellowship. God made us aware of the place of repentance and prayer and daily cleansing.

Marion Scott, pastor's wife

The Lord has been so faithful. Erma taught us: "For this, I have Jesus." I came to the Lord as a little girl but was not led to assurance. I was a chronic doubter, the Lord a chronic Lifter-upper! In Jeremiah (31:3) I read, "I have loved thee with an everlasting love." I read verses like John 6:37: "All that the Father giveth me shall come to me; and him that comes to me I will in no wise cast out." I realized that God had chosen me! I praise him!

And verses from Deuteronomy 33:27 also encouraged me: "The eternal God is thy refuge, and underneath are the everlasting arms; and he shall thrust out the enemy from before thee." And Song of Solomon 7:10: "I am my beloved's, and his desire is toward me." Don Jacobs once said, "The enemy wants us to deny the presence of Christ in our life, but he is a liar!" This Christmas I have been challenged with Mary's response: "Be it unto me according to thy word" (Luke 1:38). Her simplicity of faith spoke to me. Hannah cried for a child. Eli spoke, and Hannah took God at his word. The Syrophoenician woman accepted what Jesus said. Psalm 71:3 is my prayer, "Be thou my strong habitation, whereunto I may continually resort," and so is verse 18, "Now also when I am old and gray-headed, O God, forsake me not; until I have showed thy strength unto this generation, and thy power to every-one that is to come."

Paul and Miriam Burkholder, missionaries in New York City

Glenn and Florence Zeager (now Florence Saylor) were God's gift to us. We heard these people repenting and putting things right. This woman, Erma Maust, kept coming to see us and helping us walk with Jesus. Then we read *The Calvary Road*, by Roy Hession, and we had to put many things right with each other, our parents, and others.

Miriam shared the following: We were invited to come and work with the Jewish people in New York City. There Glenn and Florence Zeager shared with us about the revival in East Africa. Then Erma Maust came and taught me. I hadn't felt loved by Jesus. But at that time I saw the Lord and realized that he did love me. I started reading the Bible. John 5:44 really stood out: "How can you believe, who receive honor one of another, and seek not the honor that comes from God only?" Now when I had fear, there was trust in Jesus, instead of trusting in the fact that I wore plain clothes.

Lindsey Robinson, Mennonite Pastor in Pennsylvania

Myra and Lindsay Robinson, pastor couple in the Mennonite Church in Harrisburg, Pa., and active on the Eastern U.S. team.

I was born in Chicago. My parents sent me to Sunday school. It took! I recognized that there was a God. At age eleven I was baptized and joined the church. But there was no necessity of the new birth. I was active in church but didn't know Christ. I attended a liturgical church in my teen years. I trusted in works righteousness and taking the sacraments. I intellectually believed in God and in Jesus Christ, his Son. I attended college in the 1960s. Two things happened: I discovered that I was black (black consciousness), and I majored in revolution. I rebelled against my father and my family and lived my life according to what I wanted to do. But I never lost the sense of my need for God. In my senior year of college, I was searching for something

to give meaning and peace. I wasn't finding it in black consciousness and the antiwar movement. I was trying to promote peace,
but I didn't have peace.

The churches of South Chicago were having a crusade. The
speaker was an ex-gang member named Tom Skinner. I went to
hear him. It was the Holy Spirit that was drawing me. I may have
heard the gospel for the first time. For the first time I trusted
Christ for salvation.

Then I went to Bible college and met and fell in love with
Myra. There I was taught to seek the baptism of the Holy Spirit,
which I did—but afterward I seemed to spring a leak. I was not
the best person to get along with. There were problems with several issues in my life. I had the feeling that there must be more. I
talked to the cook at school, who referred me to books by
Watchman Nee (*The Normal Christian Life* and others). I wanted
the supernatural, death to self, brokenness, identification with
Christ. Later I read *The Calvary Road,* by Roy Hession, about
personal revival, brokenness, walking in the light, the power of the
blood of Christ. I also read Andrew Murray and books by A. B.
Simpson. I moved to Philadelphia in 1972. I had sensed a call from
God but had thought, "I cannot be a preacher, telling people how
to live. No, Myra would never marry a preacher." There at Fort
Washington we had contact with Worldwide Evangelization
Crusade (WEC) and the Christian Literature Crusade (CLC)
bookstore. We met missionaries who believed in the deeper life for
Christians.

We were married and were involved in church planting nearby. In 1983 we moved to Harrisburg. After speaking at a meeting
Don Jacobs said, "We are brothers." The Lord knew what he was
doing in bringing us here. Erma Maust had spoken at WEC.
Locust Lane is where she was a member. Glenn Zeager was the
pastor, and Mervin and Mary Miller were members there.

I want to tell you about two powers: the power of prayer and
the power of pride. In 1999, after we had become pastors at
Locust Lane, on Sunday afternoon I was thinking, "I have gotten
our son off to university, and I'm scheduled to go to Florida for a
meeting." I was looking forward to Florida. I went to bed feeling
fine. The next morning I was weak, but I went to the office in
Lancaster, as best as I could. But I was still weak. It was all I could

do to drive, I was so weak. I started to feel worse. A co-worker drove me home to the Polyclinic Hospital. Myra met me there. After tests and a CAT scan they found a cancerous tumor in my brain. Doctors felt that it wasn't safe to perform surgery. They recommended that I be taken to John Hopkins in Baltimore for radiation. We started praying. The congregation at Locust Lane prayed. The conference prayed. The fellowship prayed: "Healing, please." Jeff came from Asbury to pray for me. I was strengthened by the prayers of God's people. I began to feel, "I'm going to make it." Surgery was performed. They had to leave some of it, and radiation was performed on the rest. At my checkup they said, "You don't need any more radiation. Come back every six months." I'll be on medicine the rest of my life. They have since reduced the dosage. People ask, "Are you healed?" and I reply, "I am divinely helped." Jesus is my primary physician. The doctors are secondary. Thank you, JESUS.

Now I want to tell you about the power of pride. We have a son, age twenty-two, the pride of my life. We adopted him at six months, and he has brought us much joy. We invested a lot in him—church, Christian schools, summer camps. He attended our church university and graduated in April of this year. In February he had come home with a young woman. He told us she was pregnant with his baby. We were devastated. I can't tell you how hurt I was. All this investment for nothing! He had made a terrible mistake. I was angry. I tried to pray—nothing. People knew something was wrong. I told the elders and another couple in our church. I thought about resigning. I preached against this—now my son! My pride was hurt. I am the conference minister. What will people think? Being a black minister, the whites will say, "You know how they are." I called a friend in the fellowship and went to see him. He spoke to me about taking cleansing at the root. I began to experience a release. I went to my son and asked him to forgive me. At the revival fellowship conference (held at Locust Lane) in May, the Lord cleansed me. Chuck Higgins kept saying, "Everything that's happening is NOT EVERYTHING THAT'S HAPPENING." God's grace is working behind the scenes and is greater than all our sin.

Wayne Lawton, pastor and revivalist, Elizabethtown, Pennsylvania

The winds of the East Africa revival first blew in my life when I was thirteen years of age. Dan and Nancy Wegmueller, Free Methodist missionaries to Burundi, came to speak at the Oklahoma Conference camp meeting. I had not yet received Christ, but I remember the "stir" that Sunday, when several leaders

Wayne and Mary Lou Lawton, former pastor in Free Methodist church, now serving Mennonite church. Pillars in the Eastern U.S. team.

went forward for prayer. Our leaders professed to be "entirely sanctified," and I had never known them to admit failures in their lives. So this was a noteworthy occasion, when they stood, tears streaming down their faces as they gave testimony to fresh cleansing in their lives.

I accepted Christ as my Savior in 1951. Later I attended our church school in McPherson, Kansas. The president, G. Edgar Whiteman, had been touched by the message of *The Calvary Road*. He walked in true brokenness and humility, and his life brought conviction to me and many others. Once he took some students to Lake Geneva, Wisconsin, to hear Roy and Revel Hession. I remember people being very open at that meeting. In the next two years I heard the Hessions speak on several occasions. The Holy Spirit showed me that even though I was born again and seeking a Spirit-filled walk, I was a sinner who would need the atoning blood of Jesus for the rest of my days on earth.

Mary Lou and I were married in 1958 and went to serve at Olive Branch Mission in Chicago. While there, Dan and Nancy Wegmueller came and gave testimonies to the staff. This was a moving spiritual experience. Also, Roy Hession came to speak at Moody Bible Church. He brought Don Widmark from California, and Don stayed with us. When they learned that we were moving to Washington, DC, they told us about Erma Maust and the fellowship groups that were meeting in Pennsylvania. We connected with Herbert and Erma Maust and Mervin and Mary Miller when we moved in August 1959.

This was such a blessing. Not long after moving to Washington, Erma came bringing Emma Good. Later she came with William Nagenda and Clyde and Alta Shenk. We came to realize what real fellowship means as brothers and sisters surrounded us. Jesus was so real at a conference at Harmony Heart, near Jermyn, Pennsylvania. I will never forget it. There was such openness in sharing testimonies, and such joy expressed in worship and in hearing the Word, that when we came home I told Mary Lou, "I'm never going to go to church again—just fellowship conferences." Well, as a pastor I had to "swallow" those words quickly, but a desire had been planted to see the church really be the church as Jesus had planned it, where people could be real in praising, in repenting, in confessing, in sharing and caring.

While we lived in Washington, we began meeting East Africans who had come through the U.S. state department's program called Aiding Indigenous Development (AID). Those who called us said they had been given our name by Mahlon Hess. We didn't know Mahlon Hess at that time, but later we learned that he was part of the revival fellowship in Africa. These Africans came and shared testimonies of Jesus saving them. We learned so much from these brothers and sisters. Our two daughters who were born while we were there were loved by these African brethren. We were pastoring in an African-American neighborhood. William Nagenda and Festo Kivengere came to make contact with African Americans. We were blest to have them stay in our home.

We moved to Waynesboro, Virginia, in 1965, and later to Harrisonburg. Mary Lou worked in the business office at Eastern Mennonite College while I went to school. After graduating there, we moved to Silver Spring, Maryland. We pastored a Free Methodist Church there for nearly seventeen years. Mary Lou had begun to do licensed childcare in our home. The church was in a do-it-yourself building program. This took its toll on both of us. I broke under it and experienced failure of a nature needing professional help. This was a bitter pill to my pride. How could someone in the fellowship need such professional help? Wasn't Jesus enough? Don Jacobs referred me to a psychiatrist, Enos Martin. All I knew about him was that he was a Mennonite. But from being in the fellowship, I knew not all Mennonites were the same. As it turned out, he was a Spirit-filled man who accomplished more through love and prayer than through professional services, though his professional services were good. God brought a great healing to my life going way back into my childhood and clearing up much confusion. What a great Savior and sanctifier Jesus is!

Since 1989 we have lived in Elizabethtown. We have received so much love and care from Christians in this area. It has been our joy to share the gifts God has given us in support of the fellowship meetings and in ministering now in the Elizabethtown District of the Mennonite Church.

David Shenk, missionary, author, and teacher

Grace (my wife) grew up in Ephrata. I grew up in Shirati, Tanzania. I was born in 1937. I was ten when I came to the United States and saw snowflakes for the first time. I thought snow came down in chunks! We Shenk children talked about white people as if our parents were not white. While still a boy in Africa, revival came to Bumangi, where we lived as a family. There were early morning prayers. Revival fires were burning across the church. As a young boy of six, I came to Jesus in the night. I could not sleep—I opened my heart to the Savior—and then I could not sleep for joy! I went to church in the morning and covenanted to live my life for the Lord.

My brother and I asked our dad [J. Clyde Shenk] to have devotions with us. He shared from John 15 about the "true vine" and "the branches" and the importance of staying connected to Jesus, the vine. Nearby was a branch that had broken off a eucalyptus tree. We knew it would die. And Dad was telling us that we would die unless we stay connected to Jesus. Abiding in him, there is life. First John 1:7 and 1:9 were so much a part of my understanding, growing up in the revival.

As a child I read the Bible through each year, and I continue to do that. But when I first read about kings who started out right and then fell away, I became scared. What if that would happen to me? The word in Colossians 2:6, "As you have therefore received Christ Jesus the Lord, so walk ye in him," taught me to never graduate from that initial grace. I continue to see myself to be a sinner in a saving relationship to Jesus. Early in life God called me to serve and give special attention to those who don't know Jesus.

One couple whose marriage was performed by my father had married across clan lines, so they received curses from their pagan relatives. These relatives waited to see them die or their children die. But God blessed this couple with thirteen children, and at their fiftieth wedding anniversary (no couple in that area had ever remained married for fifty years because of polygamy) they sang, "There's not a friend like the lowly Jesus, / No, not one! No, not one!" (Johnson Oatman Jr.), to the seven-hundred-plus guests who gathered for the celebration.

At age fifteen I came to live in the United States and worshipped at Millersville Mennonite Church. The church at that time was taking a very conservative turn in matters of dress, etc. I had only seen my dad in a plain coat one time. Now to hear that if you don't wear one you are not saved came as a shock. But we had learned in the revival, if your church is a desert, you don't leave. How can you share the blessing you have in Christ, if you leave?

I asked Grace to marry me, and what a thrill it was when she said yes. We went to New York City, where I was studying and preparing for missionary service in Africa. Then I was told that the church would not send me because I was not in fellowship with my bishop. In New York I had been wearing a necktie. This rejection made me angry. At that time we were meeting for fellowship in the home of Glenn and Florence Zeager every week. When I expressed my outrage over this necktie issue, they said to me, "Your attitude is awful; you need to repent." The Lord enabled me to do that; and we returned to Millersville and submitted to the leadership there. On went the plain coat. It was then that I taught at Lancaster Mennonite High School for two years. Because we stayed in our church, we were able to bring blessings to our church.

While in Somalia, we were not allowed to teach or preach, so we learned to have a "presence-based ministry," manifesting the presence of the Lord in various ways and situations. From Somalia we moved to Kenya and had many engagements with Muslims. The Muslims said to us, "You believe the gospel, but you respect us." This gave us acceptance among them. Recently in Toronto, one imam responded to the teaching of the gospel by saying, "Glory cannot suffer." But in Christ glory does suffer! This is how I introduce Christ to Muslims: "Christ crucified for me." I recently spoke to seventy evangelists and pastors in Uzbekistan. I contrasted two journeys: Jesus going to the cross for crucifixion, and Mohammad going to Medina for military pursuit.

Arlene Hege, missionary to Ethiopia

I thought about God as long as I can remember. We had a radio in our home, and we were allowed to listen to sermons on Sunday. I enjoyed the Lutheran preacher. To become a Mennonite girl meant a complete change of outfit and appearance. But I was hungry for God. Hannah Whitall Smith's book *The Christian's Secret of a Happy Life* was on the shelf at home. I didn't want anyone to see me reading it, but I read it.

Then the letters began coming from the missionaries in Tanzania—not the snake-and-hunting stories but the message of new life in Jesus. These letters stirred my hunger for God. At age fifteen I went to Arbutus Camp, and there I rededicated my life to the Lord. He became Lord of my life. Then in my junior year of high school, Lancaster Mennonite School opened, and my father insisted I attend. Now I see that God was in this move (it followed my recommitment) even though I would have preferred staying in public school. In 1950 I was engaged to Nathan Hege. We then left for mission service in Ethiopia and were later married there.

We kept looking at Tanzania because God was at work there. We prayed for Ethiopia. Don Jacobs came, and we experienced new joy in the Lord. Our marriage improved at this time. Prayer and Bible reading took on new dimensions. God poured out his Spirit, and there was a charismatic move in the Ethiopian church. The churches became full.

Then in 1985 our son Peter was killed in an accident, leaving his wife and five children. In 1988 our son John was in a car accident that left him an invalid the rest of his life. We heard a brief confession of faith the night before he died. All of this was a test of my faith.

Nathan Hege, missionary to Ethiopia

I first learned about the East Africa Revival fellowship in 1946 when Clyde Shenk presented a message at our church about a closer walk with the Lord. He was so intense. He wanted us to understand. It was evident that his message about walking in the light

Nathan and Arlene Hege, missionaries to Ethiopia and active in promoting revival.

was much more important to him than relating the strange customs of Tanzanians (he was on furlough at the time) or a hunting trip to the Serengeti, or the hyena stories we had grown up with in the 1930s. Clyde was asking us to consider the call that God places on the life of every Christian, and he made it clear that Christ has much more for us than enduring the humdrum existence of religious tradition. I had a limited understanding of the life he was talking about, but I did understand that to be serious with the Lord meant that I needed to make myself available to the call of the church, which we understood in those days as the call of God to do whatever God was directing the church to do.

In the late 1940s we heard the stories about how Tanzanian missionaries were making the leaders in our denomination uneasy with their calls for repentance. In 1949 I graduated from Eastern Mennonite College. The speaker for the graduation ceremonies was to be John Leatherman. The grapevine had it that a closed-door meeting was held by the college administration to determine whether or not Leatherman would be allowed to give the commencement address. Something about his theology was apparently off-key. It was a puzzle to me that a missionary of the church would return from Africa with a theology that would somehow disqualify him from speaking in the college chapel. He was allowed to speak, but having heard the grapevine story, it appeared to me that he spoke under some constraint, as though he had to be careful about his choice of words, as though he was aware that the college faculty was checking on him. I could not detect error, nor could I sort out the problem he caused.

We went to Ethiopia in 1950, determined to be good missionaries, but we discovered that when we were put on a mission compound with several other families—where our work life, our social life, and our worship life were all with the same people—then the rough edges of our personalities caused conflict and ill feelings toward our fellow workers. We tried to patch up our relationships at our annual conferences, but those new commitments were short lived.

In 1954 we visited Tanzania, attended their conference and their afternoon or evening fellowships on their compounds, and began to experience what walking in the light meant to our brothers and sisters in that country. One evening as we shared around the Scriptures with a group at Bukiroba, on Lake Victoria, Sister

Catharine Leatherman gave her testimony. She had played the accordion during our singing time together earlier, and in her testimony she said: "As I was playing the accordion, I was thinking that Nathan and Arlene will certainly be impressed with how well I am doing. Those are proud thoughts, and I wish to confess them." Wow! Does walking in the light have to cut that close? Does it have to be that open? You can imagine how uncomfortable we felt about our proud thoughts, the thoughts that we had about not needing East Africa Revival in Ethiopia, thoughts much more serious than her pride.

Well, we plodded along for ten years. Elam Stauffer would make his visits and tell us about living in victory. We had Keswick meetings in Ethiopia. We heard Festo Kivengere. We listened to Elam and Festo with great interest.

But a time we remember is our annual conference of 1965. I came to that conference disgruntled, complaining about anything and everything. The mission policies were not right, and the mission directors did not consult adequately with the missionaries before making decisions. Don Jacobs was speaker that year. Don gave the story of Naaman, the leper. He embellished every possible detail of that story—the proud Naaman who had better rivers in his own country. The Naaman who finally went beneath the muddy waters of Jordan one time, two times, three times—each time checking his skin to see if his leprosy had gone. As Don went through those details, he made a Freudian slip. Instead of saying Naaman, he said Nathan. He did it several times. He usually corrected himself, but the damage was done. I had to go beneath the Jordan waters, actually plunge into the cleansing fountain to receive what my Tanzanian brothers and sisters were talking about. It was then that the song which has come out of our fellowship took on a new meaning: "For the cleansing blood has reached me, / Glory, glory to the Lamb!"

The whole mission group was renewed. We walked on air during the next week. Walking on air is the best way I can describe it, a feeling of lightness, of burdens rolled away. Our marital relationship was transformed. Our relationships with Ethiopians became loving and positive. They knew something had happened to us.

What about since then? I don't always have that sense of walking on air. But I do know there is a way back when I go astray. I remember the advice Don gave us after that conference, before he went back to Nairobi. He said, "Just remember to obey. The key word is obey. Obey what the Lord tells you to do."

Then we were stricken with tragedy: the death of our son in 1985, leaving his wife to raise five small children, and an accident in 1988 that completely disabled another son for ten years before he passed away in 1999. People ask us what such experiences do to our faith? And we reply, "Faith is all we have. Faith in a good God, the God who loved us and gave himself for us, the God of our Lord Jesus Christ, who stands ready to bring renewal the moment we admit our need." The counsel and prayers of brothers and sisters out of Africa have helped sustain us through these years. We still grieve, and I wonder sometimes whether we speak very well to that grief issue.

I believe that the East Africa Revival movement can be instructive for us today. The revival brothers and sisters brought renewal to churches in East Africa without setting up another denominational structure. I believe we could learn from this. Let us bring the message of revival and renewal wherever we go and not spend energy dividing and setting up more denominational structures. I praise the Lord for brothers and sisters out of Africa, who have shown me new ways of walking with the Lord. Praise God!

Jean Griswold, revivalist, Pennsylvania

I experienced salvation in 1951, but I was always hungry for more of Jesus, not just in my head but in my heart. The gospel song "Softly and tenderly, Jesus is calling" (Will L. Thompson) was very meaningful to me. I had not grown up in a Christian home—far from it. I was married and had two children, and then a son died in 1951. I sought the Lord.

In 1953 I attended a conference at Worldwide Evangelization Crusade in Fort Washington, Pennsylvania. Roy and Revel Hession were speaking, and also William Nagenda. William preached from Revelation (1:9), "I, John, who also am your brother," and he said, "If you have come to find revival in me, I am going back to Africa. Revival is only in Jesus." He printed a sign and put it up—JUST JESUS—and told us, "Everything is in Jesus."

Phebe Yoder, a missionary from Tanzania, asked me pertinent questions that no one else had ever asked me. I saw that Psalm

73:25 was God's word to me: "Whom have I in heaven but thee? There is none upon earth that I desire beside thee." In 1956 I met a lady in Lancaster County named Erma Maust. She was a plain (dressed in the so-called plain dress) Mennonite. After meeting her, I wanted to be "plain," too. I came to Mervin and Mary Miller's for fellowship meetings.

In 1959 I wanted to attend the retreat at Harmony Heart. I asked my husband, but he wanted me to be a "normal" Christian and thought fellowship was somehow "extreme." But I did attend the conference. I was twenty-nine at that time. I roomed with Erma Maust and Catharine Leatherman. I asked them, "How can I get to know Jesus the way you do? What's the matter with me?" I prayed, "Lord, I'm willing to be anything, even a person in an insane asylum, to get to know you better."

The Lord spoke to me through John 5:44, about the spirit of covetousness. I always wanted my mother to love me, my husband and my children to love me. But I was seeking the honor of people more than the honor of God. I confessed this to God and went to sleep that night. The Holy Spirit came in, and I was made new.

The next day I went to the meeting with joy. They always sang the "Glory" song when people repented. I had determined that they would never sing that over me—but this day I asked them to sing it over me! The song "Down at the cross" mentions that "Jesus so sweetly abides within" (Elisha A. Hoffman). That was my experience now!

I was divorced at age 43. I thought, "God has failed me." I stayed away from fellowship meetings. I didn't get in touch. I moved to Georgetown, Maryland. I intended to call Mary Lou and Wayne Lawton and visit them in Maryland but never did. There came a day when I couldn't run anymore. I was consumed by bitterness and anger. I cried to the Lord, who said, "Lancaster County." I have had thirty-two addresses in my life! The Lord said, "Go back to fellowship with your family of believers there." Praise God, he enabled me to repent of my waywardness and return not only to him but the fellowship of believers who loved me with great love.

Second Corinthians 5:21 is my life verse: "God made him who had no sin to be sin for us, so that in him we might become the righteousness of God" (NIV). Also Romans 6:14: "Sin shall not have dominion over you." I do not always feel God's presence, but I can choose faith. God's peace attends my soul. I am satisfied with his honor alone!

Anna Ruth Jacobs, missionary to East Africa

"Ebenezer, . . . hitherto hath the Lord helped us" (1 Sam 7:12). I praise God for the Christian heritage. My parents loved the Lord and modeled servanthood. At a young age I embraced the faith of my parents. At age ten I wondered if God might be calling me to Africa. I remember hearing preaching about sin at Lancaster Mennonite School and that you could be cleansed. But what do you do with sins that come after that cleansing? That's where hypocrisy came into my life. When Don and I went to Africa and experienced the people who were walking in the light, I thought

they were putting on a front. But the Holy Spirit broke me, and daily life in the Spirit became a reality that continues—and there is grace for grandparents!

Anna Ruth and Don Jacobs.

Don Jacobs, missionary to East Africa

I praise God for the unity Jesus gives Anna Ruth and me in marriage. Anna Ruth is my wife, but she is also my sister in Jesus. We walk together daily in the Spirit, and this just makes life so wonderful. I once thought how smart I was to get converted, then how clever I was to get a good wife. Later I pondered the words of Jesus in John 15:16: "You have not chosen me, but I have chosen you." I am humbled by the grace of God.

At age sixteen I was running, but the Lord grabbed me at Eastern Mennonite High School in Harrisonburg, Virginia. I determined to be a Mennonite of the Mennonites. And that is not a bad thing. Later we went to Africa—I did not feel a call to Africa—it was just a period of voluntary service to be done with and then return to getting on with life in America.

We studied in London and while there sat under the ministry of Martin Lloyd-Jones. His messages on the cross of Christ gripped me. I was held as in a vice when I pondered the love of God in Jesus dying for me. This vision of the cross was somehow different from the rather "bloodless" atonement that better suited my spiritual sensitivity.

When we got to Africa and saw people who "walk in the light," I said, "Is this possible?" But God had sent a brother to me, a Ugandan named Eliezer Mugimba, who came to Tanzania as a missionary from the revival brethren in Uganda. He later told me that God said, "That young missionary is your mission field." This man loved me and taught me how to deal with post-baptismal sin. We had read all the "victory books"—"Don't call it sin; just reckon yourself dead"—but now we were shown how to come to the mercy seat continually, every time we have a need.

My tendency is to wallow in problems, marinate in disappointment, get pickled in the brine of problems. I flip my problems like I'm frying fish, but Jesus says, "Bring them to me."

It is the little things that trip me up. We meet God in repentance at the prescribed place, the only place, at the mercy seat, where the blood of the eternal sacrifice was poured out once and forever.

Mark Whims

Mark Whims, a businessman living in Seattle, gave a testimony that was typical of many who found a way of walking with Jesus moment by moment, in fellowship with fellow pilgrims on the way.

I praise the Lord Jesus for what he has done in my life. I accepted Christ at the age of nineteen. Soon after graduating from Bible college, I accepted a position on the staff. I was married during my years on staff, and we had three beautiful children.

As time went on, I realized my marriage was suffering. It eventually ended in a divorce. It was the most difficult thing I have ever faced in my life. Throughout my Christian life, I always thought being a Christian meant you read your Bible daily, go to church at least once a week, pray often, witness to one person a week, etc. I always looked at sin in the past tense, never the present. As a result of this divorce, I began to cry out to God in a desperate way. I couldn't find comfort or peace in attempting to fall back on my theology, my years of study, or on working harder at the Christian life. I finally came to a point and asked the Lord, "If you are real, please meet me in this difficult time. Otherwise, I am ready to forget about this Christian life."

I am amazed at God's timing. I soon met an older couple who had been touched by the East Africa Revival. They would share about walking with Jesus in the "now," moment by moment, calling sin sin, and trusting that the blood of Jesus is more than sufficient to cleanse the sin. They would "walk in the light" with each other and those close to them, meaning they would be open as to how Jesus met them in little way's (such as irritations with each other, pride, lust, etc.), and they would be willing to share this with others. I was baffled as to this walk, this way.

I have learned to walk with Jesus moment by moment, quickly call sin sin, and let his blood cleanse the sin and share how Jesus is meeting me daily. I am amazed at how he has worked in my life and others close to me. He showed me clearly the bitterness and resentment I held toward my ex-wife and how I needed to be cleansed of the sin toward her (1 John 4:19-21). Even though she has gone on to remarry, Jesus has given me his love for her and her husband. I don't really understand these things. My walk with Jesus is so different than before. How he has so clearly unmessed a huge mess in my life and continues to bring good out of a difficult situation! I pray I will continue to keep Jesus at the center as I walk moment by moment with him.[7]

Dwight Clough, author and counselor, Sun Prairie, Wisconsin

The year was 1982, and I was drifting farther and farther from God. Not because I wanted to, I suppose, but rather because I didn't think I had any other choice. Evangelicalism had disappointed me. I was caught in a trap of bitterness that I didn't know how to escape. Sometime during that year, I went to visit my wife's family. I stumbled into my mother-in-law's kitchen, and there sat Roy Hession. It was suppertime, and we were both guests, but he was more of a guest than I. "Can you microwave a hamburger?" I asked, but Roy Hession didn't know. I didn't know either, but we decided to give it a try.

A few minutes later we were both eating microwaved hamburgers, just he and I. I looked him over and decided to ask him a question: "What do you spend your time doing?" I asked him. I already knew the answer, but I wanted to see what he would say. "I've been a preacher of the gospel for thirty-five years," he said matter-of-factly, between bites. But he seemed pleased with the accomplishment. "Do you enjoy that?" I asked, because I didn't know, and because seven years earlier I had set out to become just that—a preacher of the gospel. But somewhere along the line, I became sidetracked, derailed. Somewhere along the line I stopped enjoying church and the things that go with it. I went to church because I had to. God commanded it, and I didn't have a choice. I went every week. I sat through every service—Sunday after Sunday of boring ritual that had no relevance to my life. We sang those stale songs from the songbook. As we did, I looked around and realized that everybody was as bored as I was. The faces were the faces of the dead. They had died to church. They had died to church music. Just like me. Every Sunday I listened to a sermon that seemed to excite one person—the one giving it. Meanwhile, the clock ticked on, and if there was prayer, we were praying for noon to come.

I asked Roy Hession if he enjoyed being a preacher of the gospel. Did he like it? And what was it all about? I wanted to ask: "Are you building a kingdom—a kingdom of dead churches filled with dead people singing dead songs, all waiting and praying for the clock to strike twelve?" The preacher put down his fork. He looked up at me and his voice softened. "Yes," he said, "I enjoy it very much."

I don't suppose I'll ever be able to explain to you what it was that I heard in Roy Hession's voice that evening as we paused for a moment over our microwaved hamburgers. I doubt that he knew I was hearing it. And I don't know how I knew it, but I knew. My search to find something meaningful inside a church was over. I had found Christ. I had found him inside a man.

Tommy Hess, Eastern U.S. team

"The Spirit of the Lord is upon me, . . . to set the captives free" (cf. Luke 4:18). All of us are captives to sin until the Lord sets us free. Even persons out of prison are often still captive to enslaving habits and mind-sets. Jubilee Ministries [of Harrisburg, Pennsylvania] teaches that Jesus Christ transforms lives. I am a construction supervisor, which involves anything from repairing fences to building houses. The men who work with me learn the discipline of a seven a.m. to five p.m. job. God challenges me with the same things he is teaching the men. I was reluctant to testify here today, but God has shown me the way back to himself. . . . Can I be good enough on my own, by reading a little more, praying a little more, quoting Bible verses? But am I trusting Christ or myself? You have to realize that you can't do it on your own. Jesus said, "Blessed are the poor in spirit" (Matt 5:3). It's not enough to know that I'm bad, but I must also believe that God is good and able to change me. I believe God can change me. I have noticed that when we are truly grateful, we go on with Christ.

Tony Jordan, recovering addict, Harrisburg, Pennsylvania

I am Tony Jordan, age fifty-three (and six feet four inches tall). My father was a minister, and mother was a Sunday school teacher, but when I was five they divorced. I didn't smoke or drink but decided at age 17 that Christianity wasn't enough. During the Vietnam conflict I wanted to be a military police officer. In preparation, I studied the history of the United States. Why were we blacks so mistreated? I kept looking for some reason more complicated than just sin. Later I became a conscientious objector. When I was being forced to go and kill, I went AWOL. Of course I had to do time for that in the army. At one point my father appeared and told me that he was a conscientious objector during the Korean conflict. This was some comfort to me. But later I started shooting heroine. I was married two times. I was transferred from the VA hospital detox center to Lebanon Rescue Mission. Here I met Tommy Hess. He taught me how to use tools; but more than that, he taught me how to focus on Christ and be a wholesome person. I had seldom been around people like Tommy Hess. He doesn't mind asking me: "How does that bring glory to God?" I love him as a brother. Praise the Lord!

International relationships

This book has recorded interactions among the international revival fellowships. Here is an instance of the ongoing nature of that fellowship.

According to Wayne Lawton, someone at Church Missionary Society in London gave Wayne's address to Stephen Bamutingire of Uganda. Bamutingire wanted it because he was looking forward to an extended residence in the United States as an Anglican clergyman. Wayne comments, "I don't know anyone at CMS, so I don't know how that happened." When Bamutingire arrived in Maryland in February 2001, he wrote to Wayne: "My name is Stephen, and I wish to get in touch with you. I am Ugandan from Mbarara, born-again through the East Africa Revival fellowship. I am wondering whether you have any recorded voice of William Nagenda, a stalwart preacher from Uganda who used to come to the United States frequently. Please get back to me as soon as you are able." Wayne replied to Bamutingire:

> "Tukutendereza, Yesu!" We have such a wonderful Savior. Praise him for the great sacrifice of his life's blood to forgive and cleanse me. And I praise him for sending ambassadors to me from Uganda, Kenya, and Tanzania—to teach me that I am indeed a sinner (even though having been saved at age fourteen). I needed to continue to see the sins in my life and bring them to Jesus for cleansing. And now, thanks to William Nagenda, Festo Kivengere, John Henry Okullu, Titus Lwebandiza, John Wilson, Zeb Kabaza and many others, I am seeing the "way of the cross," which happens to be the way of "righteousness, and peace, and joy in the Holy Ghost" (Rom 14:17). Just today I found myself so tired (stayed up too late last night). Then I was irritable with my wife and spoke some angry words. She repents more quickly than I do, it seems, but I did choose to repent and to praise, and in this past hour I have been singing a song that I learned as a boy:
>
> The blood that Jesus once shed for me,
> As my Redeemer, upon the tree;
> The blood that setteth the pris'ner free,
> Will never lose its pow'r. (Civilla D. Martin)

So the gentle winds of God continue to blow. Lives are transformed, sin is exposed, Jesus remains the only answer. Joy replaces fear and dread, and walking with Jesus is not only a possibility but also a blessed reality. May these winds continue to bring blessing to needy people, through the witness of those touched by God in the revival that this book describes and through the testimony of all those who love Jesus dearly. Such people look to the Holy Spirit for constant guidance and love the Bible, which reveals God's good news to people everywhere.

Notes

Abbreviations Used in the Notes

AEE	Africa Evangelistic Enterprise
Africa Letters	bound volumes of mimeographed letters from Mennonite missionaries in Africa, with complete files at LMHS and AMC
AMC	Archives of the Mennonite Church, Goshen, Indiana
Bishop Board	Bishop Board of the Lancaster Mennonite Conference
ca.	circa, about, approximately
CLC	Christian Literature Crusade
CMS	Church Missionary Society of the Church of England (Anglican)
diss.	unpublished dissertation prepared for a doctoral degree
EMBMC	Eastern Mennonite Board of Missions and Charities, Salunga, Pennsylvania
EMM	Eastern Mennonite Missions, after name change from EMBMC in 1993
EMU	Eastern Mennonite University, Archives, Harrisonburg, Virginia
LMHS	Lancaster Mennonite Historical Society, Lancaster, Pennsylvania
n.d.	no date
SCM	Student Christian Movement

Preface

1. David W. Shenk, *Peace and Reconciliation in Africa* (Nairobi: Uzima, 1983), 129-30.

2. Z. Marwa Kisare and Joseph C. Shenk, *Kisare, a Mennonite of Kiseru* (Salunga, Pa.: EMBMC, 1984), 81.

3. Christopher Bryan, "Individualism," *Sewanee Theological Review* 41(1997): 3-9.

4. Anne Coomes, *Festo Kivengere: A Biography* (Eastbourne, UK: Monarch, 1990), 294.

Introduction

1. Don Jacobs, interview, August 2004.

2. Unpublished report of International Revival Team Fellowship, Les Diablerets, Switzerland, May 29–June 2, 1991, pp. 4-5.

3. Roy [and Revel] Hession, *The Calvary Road* (Fort Washington, Pa.: CLC, 1950, online: http://www.worldinvisible.com/library/hession/ calvary%20road/contents.htm; many reprints; rev. ed., Alresford, UK: CLC, 1995).

1. Praying for Revival, 1929–1932

1. The hospital at Gahini in what is now Rwanda was staffed by the Ruanda Mission of the Church of England. Rwanda, an independent nation since 1962, was called Ruanda while under Belgian colonial administration.

2. Don Jacobs, interview, August 2004.

3. Zabuloni Kabaza, interview; Patricia M. St. John, *Breath of Life: The Story of the Ruanda Mission* (London: Norfolk Press, 1971), 20.

4. Herbert H. Osborn, *Fire in the Hills* (Crowborough, UK: Highland, 1991), 52-53.

5. St. John, *Breath of Life*, 62-63.

6. John E. ["Joe"] Church, *Quest for the Highest: An Autobiographical Account of the East African Revival* (Exeter: Paternoster, 1981), 66.

7. *Muganda* means an individual of the Baganda or Ganda people.

8. Church, *Quest*, 66-68.

9. Herbert H. Osborn, *Pioneers in the East African Revival* (Winchester, UK: Apologia, 2000), 17-18.

10. Ibid., 15-16.

11. In an interview in 1952, Simeon Nsibambi told Zabuloni Kabaza how he was saved; Zeb Kabaza, diary, August 31, 1952.

12. Zabuloni Kabaza, interview; Catherine Ellen Robins, "Tukutendereza: A Study of Social Change and Sectarian Withdrawal in

the Balokole Revival of Uganda" (PhD diss., Columbia University, 1975), 98, with statements based on an interview with Simeon Nsibambi in 1970.

13. Zeb Kabaza, diary, August 31, 1952.

14. Osborn, *Pioneers*, 17.

15. Ibid., 19.

16. Ibid., 17.

17. Adrian Hastings, *The Church in Africa, 1450–1950* (Oxford: Clarendon, 1994), 376, 381-83; Jocelyn Murray, *Proclaim the Good News: A Short History of the Church Missionary Society* (London: Hodder & Stoughton, 1985), 121-26.

18. Gordon Hewitt, *The Problems of Success: A History of the Church Missionary Society, 1910-1942*, vol. 1, *In Tropical Africa . . .* (London: SCM, 1971), 221; Vincent Harlow and E. M. Chilver, eds., *History of East Africa* (Oxford: Clarendon, 1965), 2:116-77.

19. Hastings, *Church in Africa*, 468, 476-77; Murray, *Proclaim the Good News*, 130.

20. Stephen Neill, *A History of Christian Missions*, 2d ed. (Harmondsworth: Penguin, 1986), 221, 326-27.

21. Harlow and Chilver, *History of East Africa*, 2:81, 115.

22. William B. Anderson, *The Church in East Africa, 1840-1974* (Dodoma, Tanzania: Central Tanganyika Press, 1977), 123. For many years there was only one Protestant church in all of Uganda, part of the worldwide Anglican Communion, and one mission organization, the Church Missionary Society of the Church of England. When the nondenominational Africa Inland Mission began work in Uganda, they agreed to send only Anglican missionaries and to work under the Anglican bishop. Donald A. Low and Alison Smith, eds., *History of East Africa* (Oxford: Clarendon, 1976), 3:400.

23. Zabuloni Kabaza, interview; John V. Taylor, *The Growth of the Church in Buganda* (London: SCM, 1958), 98-99.

24. Zabuloni Kabaza, interview; Taylor, *Growth of the Church in Buganda*, 98-99.

25. Robins, "Tukutendereza," 62; Frederick B. Welbourn, *East African Rebels: A Study of Some Independent Churches* (London: SCM, 1961), 60-69, 190-91.

26. Church, *Quest*, 69-70.

27. That their father, a high government official, walked barefoot was difficult for his children to understand; Osborn, *Pioneers*, 21; Robins, "Tukutendereza," 62.

28. Zabuloni Kabaza, diary, August 31, 1952.

29. Church, *Quest*, 86.

30. Ibid., 74, 86-87.

31. Zabuloni Kabaza, interview.

32. Mark A. Noll, *A History of Christianity in the United States and Canada* (Grand Rapids: Eerdmans, 1992), 174-78, 181.

33. They were full brothers. The use of family surnames was not yet common. Both names were given names: Blasio was his baptismal name, and Kigozi his personal name from birth.

34. A. C. Stanley Smith, *Road to Revival: The Story of the Ruanda Mission* (London: CMS, 1946), 54-57.

35. Church, *Quest*, 79.

36. Stanley Smith, *Road to Revival*, 55.

37. Ibid., 57.

38. Church, *Quest*, 94.

39. Ibid., 86-87.

2. Blasio Kigosi: Beginnings in Ruanda and Urundi, 1932–1936

1. Neville Langford-Smith, "Revival in East Africa," *International Review of Missions* 43 (1954): 77.

2. Herbert H. Osborn, *Revival: Precious Heritage* (Winchester, UK: Apologia, 1995), 17-18.

3. Catherine Ellen Robins, "Tukutendereza: A Study of Social Change and Sectarian Withdrawal in the Balokole Revival of Uganda" (PhD diss., Columbia University, 1975), 135.

4. Church, *Quest,* 95.

5. Osborn, *Fire in the Hills*, 71.

6. Church, *Quest*, 98-99.

7. Coomes, *Festo Kivengere*, 63.

8. Katharine Makower, *The Coming of the Rain: The Life of Dr. Joe Church* (Carlisle: Paternoster, 1999), 107-8.

9. Osborn, *Pioneers*, 12-13.

10. Stanley Smith, *Road to Revival*, 72; Robins, "Tukutendereza," 133-34.

11. Quoted in Robins, "Tukutendereza," 136.

12. Joe Church, *Awake! An African Calling: The Story of Blasio Kigozi* (London: CMS, 1937), 21.

13. Osborn, *Revival*, 21.

14. Festo Kivengere with Dorothy Smoker, *Revolutionary Love* (Fort Washington, Pa.: CLC, 1983), 63-64.

15. Ibid., 64.

16. Coomes, *Festo Kivengere*, 72-73.

17. Church, *Awake!* 19.

18. Murray, *Proclaim the Good News*, 191; St. John, *Breath of Life*, 127.

19. Zabuloni Kabaza, interview.

20. Ibid.

21. Luganda is the language of Uganda; Church, *Awake!* 15-17. Sala Nagenda, Katharine Kigozi's sister, was also at his deathbed.

22. Osborn, *Fire in the Hills*, 80-81.

23. Church, *Quest*, 121-24; Stanley Smith, *Road to Revival*, 71-73.

24. Osborn, *Fire in the Hills*, 83.

25. Gerald Bates, *Soul Afire: The Life of J. W. Haley* (Winona Lake, Ind.: Light & Life, 1981), 30-34; Edna H. Chilson, *Ambassador of the King* (Wichita, Kan.: E. H. Chilson, 1943), 190-95; Stanley Smith, *Road to Revival*, 65-66.

26. Chilson, *Ambassador of the King*, 29, 166; Christina H. Jones, *American Friends in World Missions* (Elgin, Ill.: Brethren Publishing House, 1946), 188-91; Ane Marie Bak Rasmussen, *A History of the Quaker Movement in Africa* (London: British Academic Press, 1995), 16.

27. Chilson, *Ambassador of the King*, 211; Stanley Smith, *Road to Revival*, 80.

28. Osborn, *Fire in the Hills*, 75-76.

29. Ibid., 84.

30. Stanley Smith, *Road to Revival*, 74.

3. Expansion and Opposition, 1937–1942

1. Entebbe, near Kampala, was the headquarters of the British administration; Church, *Quest*, 125; Stanley Smith, *Road to Revival*, 73.

2. Kevin Ward, "'Obedient Rebels'—The Relationship Between the Early 'Balokole' and the Church of Uganda: The Mukono Crisis of 1941," *Journal of Religion in Africa* 19 (1989): 202; Osborn, *Pioneers*, 111-13.

3. Church, *Quest*, 138; Robins, "Tukutendereza," 150-51.

4. Osborn, *Pioneers*, 119.

5. InterVarsity Christian Fellowship, Urbana 54.

6. J. E. Church et al., *Forgive Them: The Story of an African Martyr* (London: Hodder & Stoughton, 1966), 26-27.

7. Jacobs, interview, August 2004.

8. Ward, "Obedient Rebels," 194-227.

9. Kevin Ward, "'Tukutendereza, Yesu': The Balokole Revival in Uganda," in *From Mission to Church: A Handbook of Christianity in East Africa*, ed. Zablon Nthamburi (Nairobi: Uzima, 1991), 118.

10. Bill Butler, *Hill Ablaze* (London: Hodder & Stoughton, 1976), 9-15.

11. Ibid., 55-59.

12. A detailed account of the Mukono crisis based on contemporary correspondence is in Robins, "Tukutendereza," 153ff.; Church, *Quest*, 180-86; Ward, "Obedient Rebels," 204-7.

13. Ward, "Obedient Rebels," 209.

14. Hewitt, *Problems of Success*, 1:240-41.

15. Malcolm Lea-Wilson, interview; Church, *Quest*, 186, 194-95.

16. Osborn, *Pioneers*, 232.

17. Ibid.; Church, *Quest*, 140.

18. Osborn, *Pioneers*, 233.

19. Ibid., 242-43.

20. Ibid., 243.

21. Langford-Smith, "Revival in East Africa," 78.

22. Dorothy W. Smoker, *Ambushed by Love: God's Triumph in Kenya's Terror* (Fort Washington, Pa.: CLC, 1994), 28-29.

23. Obadiah Kariuki, *A Bishop Facing Mount Kenya: An Autobiography, 1902-1978* (Nairobi: Uzima, 1985), 52-53.

24. Church, *Quest*, 145; St. John, *Breath of Life*, 133-55.

25. Langford-Smith, "Revival in East Africa," 79-80.

26. Harlow and Chilver, *History of East Africa*, 2:209-13; Kenneth Ingham, *History of East Africa*, 3d ed. (London: Longmans, 1965), 171.

27. Harlow and Childers, *History of East Africa*, 2:257, 340; Tabitha Kanogo, *Squatters and the Roots of Mau Mau* (London: Currey, 1987), 8-13.

28. Harlow and Childers, *History of East Africa*, 2:362-65.

29. Jocelyn M. Murray, "The Kikuyu Female Circumcision Controversy, with Special Reference to the Church Missionary Society Sphere of Influence," PhD diss., University of California, Los Angeles, 1974, is the basic work on this subject; D. W. Smoker, *Ambushed by Love*, 283; William Ochieng, ed. *A Modern History of Kenya, 1895–1980* (Nairobi: Evans Brothers, 1989), 131-32.

30. Ochieng, *Modern History of Kenya.*, 341-42; J. M. Lonsdale, "Political Associations in Western Kenya," in *Protest and Power in Black*

Africa, ed. Robert I. Rothberg and Ali A. Mazrui (New York: Oxford University Press, 1970), 618.

31. Church, *Quest*, 158.

32. D. W. Smoker, *Ambushed by Love*, 29; Kariuki, *A Bishop Facing Mount Kenya*, 53-57.

33. Church, *Quest*, 157.

34. Jacobs, interview, August 2004.

35. Church, *Quest*, 171.

36. Ibid., 171-72.

37. Osborn, *Fire in the Hills*, 86.

38. Church, *Quest*, 165-72; Stanley Smith, *Road to Revival*, 103-5.

39. Church, *Quest*, 189.

40. Ibid., 182; Osborn, *Pioneers*, 47.

4. Fresh Winds Blow Across Tanganyika, 1942

1. Mahlon M. Hess, *Pilgrimage of Faith of Tanzania Mennonite Church, 1934–83* (Salunga, Pa.: EMBMC, 1985), 25-28, 38-39, 45; John H. and Ruth H. Mosemann, *Mosemann Family Directory* (Baltimore: Gateway, 1987), 79.

2. Catharine Leatherman, interview; J. C. Wenger, *History of the Mennonites of Franconia Conference* (Telford, Pa.: Franconia Mennonite Historical Society, 1937), 198, 279-80.

3. Joseph C. Shenk, *Silver Thread: The Ups and Downs of a Mennonite Family in Mission (1895–1995)* (Intercourse, Pa.: Good Books, 1996), 25, 103; Hess, *Pilgrimage*, 25-27, 47-52.

4. Simeon W. Hurst, interview; Edna and Simeon Hurst, December 3, 1940, *Africa Letters* 50:9.

5. Jacobs, interview, August 2004.

6. Phebe Yoder, chapel talk, Lancaster Mennonite High School, October 13, 1969; tape recording in possession of Catharine Leatherman.

7. Catharine Leatherman, "Phebe—My Friend," *Missionary Messenger*, August 1982, 2.

8. Louise Stoltzfus, "A Planter of Trees: Phebe Ethel Yoder," *Pennsylvania Mennonite Heritage* 22 (July 1999): 16-23; Hess, *Pilgrimage*, 45.

9. Lillian E. Elliott, interview; Elam W. Stauffer, "The Holy Spirit's Working in East Africa," n.d. (ca. 1963-64), Stauffer Papers, LMHS; Hess, *Pilgrimage*, 56.

10. Simeon W. Hurst, interview.

11. Elam W. Stauffer, "The Holy Spirit's Working in East Africa."

12. Ibid.

13. Hess, *Pilgrimage*, 57-58.

14. Joseph Shenk, *Silver Thread*, 77-78.

15. Phebe Yoder, Ray and Miriam Wenger, May 29, 1942, *Africa Letters* 59:6; Joseph Shenk, *Silver Thread*, 77-78.

16. Simeon W. Hurst, interview; Elam W. Stauffer, "The Holy Spirit's Working in East Africa."

17. Elam W. Stauffer to Bishop Board, October 9, 1942, Stauffer Papers, LMHS.

18. Ibid.

19. John E. Leatherman, September 26, 1942, *Africa Letters* 60:3-4.

20. Elam W. Stauffer, "The Holy Spirit's Working in East Africa."

21. Kisare and Joseph Shenk, *Kisare*, 81-82.

22. Church, *Quest*, 244.

5. The Fellowship Deepens and Widens, 1942–1944

1. Kisare and Joseph Shenk, *Kisare*, 75.

2. *Kisare*, 82.

3. John E. Leatherman, October 2, 1943, *Africa Letters* 64:2-3.

4. C. Leatherman, "Phebe," 2.

5. Catharine Leatherman, "Missionaries Who Needed to Be Broken," in *My Personal Pentecost*, ed. Roy S. and Martha Koch (Scottdale, Pa.: Herald Press, 1977), 198-209; the quotations are from John E. Leatherman's letter of October 2, 1943.

6. John E. and Catharine Leatherman to Orie O. Miller, September 9, 1943, John H. Mosemann Jr. Collection, Hist. MSS 1-229, Box 7, AMC.

7. Eastern Mennonite Board of Missions and Charities, Executive Committee Minutes, November 9, 1943, EMM.

8. Simeon W. Hurst to Richard K. MacMaster, August 30, 1995; Simeon Hurst, interview.

9. J. Clyde Shenk, September 9, 1943, *Africa Letters* 64:4.

10. Hess, *Pilgrimage*, 82.

11. Simeon and Edna Hurst, December 13, 1943, *Africa Letters* 66:5; Joseph Shenk, *Silver Thread*, 76-77; Simeon W. Hurst, interview.

12. Phebe Yoder, April 4, 1943; May 25, 1943, *Africa Letters* 63:5-6; Church, *Quest*, 209-10.

13. Osborn, *Fire in the Hills*, 123.

14. H. Ray Wenger, September 27, 1944, *Africa Letters* 71:3; Catharine

Leatherman, January 26, 1945, *Africa Letters* 73:8; Church, *Quest*, 211-13; John E. Leatherman, diary, February 2, 1945; March 24, 1945; Catharine Leatherman, interview.

15. Ward, "Obedient Rebels," 210-13; Church, *Quest*, 202.

16. Osborn, *Pioneers*, 47.

17. Church, *Quest*, 202-3; Robins, "Tukutendereza," 174-75.

6. American Churches in Need of Revival, 1944–1946

1. A full discussion of these issues can be found in James C. Juhnke, *Vision, Doctrine, War: Mennonite Identity and Organization in America, 1890–1930* (Scottdale, Pa.: Herald Press, 1989), 112-19, 129-30; and Paul Toews, *Mennonites in American Society, 1930–1970: Modernity and the Persistence of Religious Community* (Scottdale, Pa.: Herald Press, 1996), 71-76.

2. Ruth N. Graybill, *Living Waters* (Morgantown, Pa.: Masthof, 1997), 12.

3. J. E. Leatherman, diary, April 15, 1945.

4. Elam W. Stauffer to Bishop Board, August 17, 1944, Stauffer Papers, LMHS.

5. For a thorough analysis of the changing emphasis of the Lancaster Conference Discipline, see Steven M. Nolt, "Church Discipline in the Lancaster Mennonite Conference: The Printed *Rules and Discipline*, 1881–1968," *Pennsylvania Mennonite Heritage* 15 (October 1992): 2-16.

6. J. E. Leatherman, diary, April 28, 1945.

7. Catharine Leatherman had been the first woman allowed to speak in the Mount Joy church on the eve of sailing for Africa in 1936, but she was told to speak from her pew; J. E. Leatherman, diary, April 25, 29, 1945; Catharine Leatherman, interview.

8. J. E. Leatherman, diary, May 6-12, 1945.

9. Graybill, *Living Waters*, 12.

10. Abner and Betty Miller, interview, June 25, 1996.

11. Mary K. Miller to Richard MacMaster, February 5, 1998.

12. John E. Leatherman was a member of the Franconia Conference, north of Philadelphia.

13. Leatherman, Diary, May 13-15, 1945.

14. Eastern Mennonite School, now Eastern Mennonite University, was recognized by the Commonwealth of Virginia as a junior college in 1930 and as a four-year college in 1947. The excerpts in this section are from the J. E. Leatherman, diary, May 13-15, 1945; and from letters from John L.

Stauffer to John E. Leatherman, May 19, 1945, and from John E. Leatherman to John L. Stauffer, May 31, 1945. Both letters are in the J. L. Stauffer Papers in the EMU archives.

15. John H. Mosemann Jr. to Bishop Board, n.d. [ca. May 1943], September 15, 1943, Henry Lutz Papers, LMHS.

16. The signers were ministers and deacons in the Elizabethtown, Gingrich, Marietta, Slate Hill, Stauffer, Steelton, Strickler, Vine Street, and York congregations. Marietta, Steelton, Vine Street, and York were home missions. Petition, John H. Mosemann Jr. et al., n.d. [read June 22, 1944], Henry Lutz Papers, LMHS; Bishop Board Minutes, June 22, 1944, LMHS; Russell R. Krabill, *John Shank Hiestand, 1909–1992: Mennonite Minister and Founder of the Congregational Bible Church* (Elkhart, Ind.: R. R. Krabill, 1992), 18-19.

17. John H. Mosemann Jr. to Dear Sharers of His Cross, July 3, 1944, Mosemann Papers, Box 7, AMC.

18. J. Kenneth Fisher, February 10, 1997.

19. Esther Mae Hiestand, n.d. [1997]. Simon Garber was the father of Henry Garber, chair of the Mission Board and Catharine Leatherman's grandfather.

20. Frank N. Hertzler was deacon at Steelton mission; J. E. Leatherman, diary, July 8, 1945.

21. The break in his diary until 1946 probably resulted from classes, reading assignments, papers, and sermon preparation during this busy time.

22. John H. Mosemann to Board of Bishops, September 15, 1945, Henry Lutz Papers, LMHS.

23. J. E. Leatherman, diary, March 11-13, 1946; April 21-22, 1946.

24. Bishop Board Minutes, April 4, 1946, LMHS; J. E. Leatherman, diary, April 4, 1946.

25. Elam W. Stauffer to the Mission and Bishop Boards of Lancaster Mennonite Conference, February 4, 1946, EMM.

26. Elam W. Stauffer to the Bishop Board, August 17, 1946, Stauffer Papers, LMHS.

27. Bishop Board Minutes, July 16, 1946; December 10, 1946; December 26, 1946; January 15, 1948; August 30, 1949; October 18, 1949, LMHS; Simeon W. Hurst, "Reactions on Foreign Missions Polity," n.d. [1949], LCMHS.

7. Growing Influence of Revival Following World War II

1. Hess, *Pilgrimage*, 83-84.

2. N. A. Kivuti, *A Church Comes of Age: Fifty Years of Revival in the CPK Diocese of Embu, 1942–1992* (Nairobi: Action, 1992).

3. John Karanja, *Founding an African Faith: Kikuyu Anglican Christianity, 1900–1945* (Nairobi: Uzima, 1999), 247-49.

4. Norman P. Grubb, "Introduction," in *The Calvary Road*, by Roy [and Revel] Hession (see note 3 for introduction, above); online: http://www.worldinvisible.com/library/hession/calvary%20road/preface.htm.

5. Robins, "Tukutendereza," 174; Coomes, *Festo Kivengere*, 131-34.

6. Elam W. Stauffer, "The Holy Spirit's Working in East Africa."

7. Coomes, *Festo Kivengere*, 111-12.

8. Church, *Quest*, 215.

9. Ward, "Obedient Rebels," 216.

10. J. E. Leatherman, diary, June 9, 1946.

11. Dorothy W. Smoker, "The East African Revival: How It Affected Us," n.d. (ca. 1996).

12. George and Dorothy Smoker, n.d., 1946, *Africa Letters* 82:7.

13. Ibid.

14. J. E. Leatherman, diary, July 17, 1946.

15. Ibid., July 21, 1946; August 5, 1946.

16. John E. Leatherman, diary, November 17-19, 1946.

17. Leatherman called them the Bugufi team. Murgwanza is in the former kingdom of Bugufi, in western Tanganyika/Tanzania and next to Urundi/Burundi. J. E. Leatherman, diary, November 17-19, 1946; December 5-8, 1946; Church, *Quest,* 139.

18. John E. Leatherman, December 1946, *Africa Letters,* 83:1-2.

19. Ibid.

20. Mahlon M. Hess, June 12, 1947, *Africa Letters* 86:2.

21. J. E. Leatherman, diary, February 21, March 21, April 8, and April 27, 1947.

22. John E. Leatherman, August 9, 1947, *Africa Letters* 87:4; Phebe Yoder, September 31, 1947, *Africa Letters* 88:1.

23. J. E. Leatherman, diary, June 30–July 8, 1947. The Church Missionary Society asked permission to distribute *Mjumbe wa Kristo* to all their stations in 1948; J. E. Leatherman, diary, March 5, 1948.

24. J. E. Leatherman, diary, June 30–July 8, 1947; John E. Leatherman, August 9, 1947, *Africa Letters* 87:2-4; Church, *Quest,* 172.

25. Dorothy Smoker, August 9, 1947, *Africa Letters* 87:2.

26. John Leatherman, August 9, 1947, *Africa Letters,* 87:2-4.

27. J. E. Leatherman, diary, July 21-29, 1947.

28. Ibid., July 28, 1947; Hess, *Pilgrimage,* 87.

29. John E. Leatherman, "Report of Mission Conference, Nyabasi, July 28-31, 1953," EMM; Dorothy Smoker and Merle W. Eshleman, *God Led Us to Tanzania* (Salunga, Pa.: EMBMC, 1956), 37-40; Hess, *Pilgrimage,* 93-95.

30. Hess, *Pilgrimage,* 84.

31. Stauffer, "The Holy Spirit's Working in East Africa," 3.

32. J. E. Leatherman, diary, December 16, 1947; August 7-12, 1949; Elam W. Stauffer, "The Holy Spirit's Working in East Africa"; Levi and Mary Hurst, December 5, 1947, *Africa Letters* 89:3; Hess, *Pilgrimage,* 84.

33. Hess, *Pilgrimage,* 86.

34. John E. Leatherman, August 9, 1947, *Africa Letters* 87:2-4.

8. Changing Lives in Europe and Abroad, 1946–1955

1. Osborn, *Fire in the Hills,* 127-28.

2. Church, *Quest,* 226-27.

3. Roy [and Revel] Hession, *The Calvary Road,* 8-9; Norman P. Grubb contributed the introduction to the original 1950 edition.

4. Church, *Quest,* 236; Norman P. Grubb, *Continuous Revival* (London: CLC, 1952), 46 pages; online: http://www.biblical-theology.com/revival/conrev.htm.

5. Roy Hession, *My Calvary Road* (Grand Rapids: Zondervan, 1978), 93.

6. Langford-Smith, "Revival in East Africa," 78.

7. Roy Hession, *My Calvary Road,* 85.

8. Ibid., 46ff., 80-82; Roy [and Revel] Hession, *The Calvary Road,* 13.

9. Roy Hession, *My Calvary Road,* 85-86.

10. Ibid., 19.

11. Ibid., 91; Roy [and Revel] Hession, *The Calvary Road,* 15.

12. Roy Hession, *My Calvary Road,* 95.

13. Osborn, *Fire in the Hills,* 127; Osborn, *Revival,* 108.

14. Makower, *Coming of the Rain,* 161.

15. Ibid.

16. Osborn, *Fire in the Hills,* 127-28.

17. Church, *Quest,* 231-34, 239; Makower, *Coming of the Rain,* 163; Osborn, *Revival,* 109.

18. Church, *Quest,* 244.

19. Lillian Elliott, interview.

20. Bishop Board Minutes, 775, May 19, 1949, LMHS.

21. Lillian Elliott, interview; Ruth Graybill, interview.

22. J. E. Leatherman, diary, February 13, 1946.

23. Lela R. Marzolf to James Maust, December 12, 1996.

24. Betty Miller, interview, June 25, 1996.

25. Ibid.

26. J. E. Leatherman, diary, March 8, 15-16, and 18, 1946.

27. Betty Miller, interview, June 25, 1996.

28. Paul M. Miller, interview.

29. In his seventieth year Samuel L. Longenecker was ordained in 1957 as minister to the Dauphin County penal institutions; Abner Miller, interview, June 25, 1996.

30. Abner and Betty Miller, interview; Mervin and Mary K. Miller, interview.

31. The Lancaster *Intelligencer Journal*, October 15, 1994.

32. Mervin and Mary K. Miller, interview; Paul M. Miller, interview; *Intelligencer Journal*, October 15, 1994.

33. Lela R. Marzolf to James Maust, December 12, 1996.

34. J. E. Leatherman, diary, October 23, 1947.

35. Erma Maust, form letter, June 1948: "Since I'd be writing part of this letter to several of you, I'm using this method in order to write to you all."

36. Ibid.

37. Erma Maust to unnamed correspondent, July 21, 1948.

38. Erma Maust, form letter, June 1948; Mary K. Miller, "A Life Testimony" (1988, unpublished, loaned to the author), 7; Mary K. and Mervin Miller, interview.

39. Mary K. Miller, "A Life Testimony," 5.

40. Ibid., 6.

41. Mervin and Mary K. Miller, interview; Mary K. Miller to Richard K. MacMaster, February 5, 1998.

42. Mary K. Miller, interview.

43. Erma Maust to Paul and Miriam Burkholder, September 1956.

44. Mary K. Miller, interview.

45. Ibid.

46. Florence Stauffer, interview.

47. Florence Good Zeager, interview.

48. Emma Ebersole, interview.

49. Thomas A. Hess, interview.

50. Mary K. Miller, interview; Florence Good Zeager, interview; Florence Stauffer, interview.

51. They dated this in 1951-52; John and Florence Miller, interview.

52. Mary K. Miller, interview; Abner and Betty Miller, interview.

53. Draft Minutes, July 14, 1948, Henry Lutz Papers, LMHS.

54. Abner Miller, interview.

55. Paul M. Miller, interview; Bishop Board Minutes, 765-766, 772, April 26, 1949, LMHS.

56. Bishop Board Minutes, 209, March 20, 1946, LMHS.

57. Harold Longenecker to James Maust, December 10, 1996.

58. Mervin and Mary K. Miller, Interview. Abner and Betty Miller, Interview.

59. Abram L. Gish, *Washing the Saints' Feet* (Elizabethtown, Pa.: Scofield Bible Class, n.d. [ca. 1948]), 6-9; Elaine Gish Huber, *Holding Forth the Word of Life, 1950–1990* (Bainbridge, Pa.: Word of Life Chapel, 1991), 18-19.

60. Bishop Board Minutes, 881, November 17, 1949; 894, December 20, 1949, LMHS.

61. Ibid., A114, July 19, 1951; A128, August 16, 1951; September 6, 1951, LMHS.

62. Ibid., 904, January 19, 1950; 929, February 16, 1950, LMHS.

63. Esther Mae Hiestand, *Through the Windows of Wickersham* (Elizabethtown, Pa.: Y/Z Printing, 1986), 154; Huber, *Holding Forth*, 21-23.

64. Abner and Betty Miller, interview.

65. Alvin and Ethel Miller to James Maust, December 19, 1996.

66. John H. Kraybill, "Before I Forget," 72ff., LMHS.

67. J. E. Leatherman, diary, July 4, 1951.

68. At Fort Washington, Pa., the CLC published *The Calvary Road* in several editions.

69. Roy Hession, *My Calvary Road*, 132-37.

70. Church, *Quest*, 244-45.

71. Jean Griswold, interview.

72. Osborn, *Fire in the Hills*, 162-63.

73. Hession, *My Calvary Road*, 138.

74. Church, *Quest*, 245.

75. William Nagenda's Urbana 54 sermon is on the InterVarsity Christian Fellowship Web site: http://www.urbana.org/_articles.cfm?RecordId=131.

76. Jean Griswold, interview.

77. Nagenda, Urbana 54.

9. Revival Takes Deeper Root in North America, 1955–1959

1. Amos S. Horst to Elam W. Stauffer, March 21, 1955, Stauffer Papers, LMHS.

2. *The Calvary Road* was first published in England in 1950 (see note 3 for the introduction, above); Mildred Plank to Wayne and Mary Lou Lawton, July 8, 1996.

3. Mildred Plank to James Maust, January 6, 1997. Letter loaned to the author.

4. He was uneasy about his job, "not wanting to join the union," and consulted Bishop Clarence E. Lutz about it. C. E. Lutz, Diary, November 21, 1952. LMHS. The quote is from Herbert Maust to Dear Ones in Jesus, July 11, 1960.

5. Herbert Maust to Dear Ones in Jesus, July 11, 1960.

6. Erma Maust to Paul and Miriam Burkholder, April 26, 1955.

7. Erma Maust to Dear Ones in Jesus, June 1955.

8. Ibid.

9. Herbert and Erma Maust to Paul and Miriam Burkholder, June 1955.

10. Erma Maust to Paul and Miriam Burkholder, September 1955.

11. Mildred Plank to James Maust, January 6, 1997.

12. Erma Maust to Paul and Miriam Burkholder, September 1955.

13. Mildred Plank to James Maust, January 6, 1997.

14. Erma Maust to Dear Ones in Jesus, September 1955.

15. Erma Maust to Paul and Miriam Burkholder, November 1955.

16. Erma Maust to Dear Ones in Jesus, September 1955; Mildred Plank to Wayne and Mary Lou Lawton, July 8, 1996.

17. Erma Maust to Paul and Miriam Burkholder, November 1955.

18. Erma Maust to Paul and Miriam Burkholder, February 1956; Erma Maust to Paul and Miriam Burkholder, April 1956.

19. Erma Maust to Dear Ones, April 1956; May 1956.

20. Erma Maust to Paul and Miriam Burkholder, October 5, 1957.

21. Erma Maust to Miriam Burkholder, July 9, 1958.

22. Jacobs, interview, August 2004.

23. Erma Maust to Paul and Miriam Burkholder, June 1956.

24. Erma Maust to Dear Ones, January 1957.

25. Erma Maust to Dear Ones in Jesus, May 26, 1957.

26. Jack Ludlam to Dear Friends in Christ, May 9, 1957.

27. Erma Maust to Dear Ones, July 1957.

28. Ronald and Marjorie Lofthouse, interview.

29. Erma Maust to Paul and Miriam Burkholder, October 5, 1957.

30. Ronald and Marjorie Lofthouse, interview.

31. Ronald Lofthouse, interview.

32. Erma Maust to Paul and Miriam Burkholder, November 11, 1957.

33. William and Marian Scott, interviews.

34. Marian Scott, interview.

35. Erma Maust to Paul and Miriam Burkholder, January 1958.

36. Erma Maust to Paul and Miriam Burkholder, January 1957.

37. Erma Maust to Paul and Miriam Burkholder, November 11, 1957.

38. Erma Maust to Paul and Miriam Burkholder, January 7, 1958.

39. Paul Burkholder, "Dedication and Fellowship Meeting," October 1959.

40. J. E. Leatherman, diary, March 10, 1958.

41. Ibid., April 21, 1958.

42. Ibid., August 3, 1958.

43. Ibid., March 24, 1958.

44. Erma Maust to Dear Ones, April 1958.

45. J. E. Leatherman, diary, May 16, 1958.

46. Ibid., May 17-18, 1958.

47. Ibid., May 29, 1958.

48. Erma Maust to Dear Ones, July 1958.

49. J. E. Leatherman, diary, October 11, 1958.

50. Ibid., November 12-16, 1958.

51. Robert Crewdson, interview.

52. Herbert and Erma Maust to Dear Ones in Jesus, December 26, 1958.

53. Fellowship Conference circular.

54. John I. Smucker, interview; J. E. Leatherman, diary, April 13, 1959.

55. Joe Church in *Revival*, by Osborn, 121-22 (see note 2 for chap. 2).

56. J. E. Leatherman, diary, March 3 and April 7, 1959.

57. Ibid., March 14, 1959.

58. Ibid., April 24-29, 1959.

59. Ibid., June 7-9, 1959.

60. Erma Maust to Dear Ones in Jesus, May 4, 1959; Jack Ludlam, "Fellowship Retreat," circular; J. E. Leatherman, diary, June 12-14, 1959.

61. Erma Maust to Paul and Miriam Burkholder, April 1958.

62. Jacobs, interview, August 2004.

63. Erma Maust to Dear Ones in Jesus, May 4, 1959.

64. Emma Good and Erma Maust to Paul and Miriam Burkholder, October 1959.

65. Erma Maust to Paul and Miriam Burkholder, January 17, 1960.

66. Erma Maust to Paul and Miriam Burkholder, January 25, 1960.

67. J. E. Leatherman, diary, September 9, 1959; Bishop Board Minutes, 563, August 20, 1959, LMHS.

68. Ibid., July 23 and 29, 1959.

69. Erma Maust to Dear Ones in Jesus, September 12, 1959.

70. J. E. Leatherman, diary, October 1-3, 1959.

71. Ibid., October 11-15, 1959.

10. The Revival Enables Relationships for the Life of the Church, 1954–1960

1. Donald R. Jacobs, *Pilgrimage in Mission* (Scottdale, Pa.: Herald Press, 1983), 91-92.

2. David J. Bosch, *Transforming Mission: Paradigm Shifts in Theology of Mission* (Maryknoll, NY: Orbis Books, 1991), 421.

3. Donald R. Jacobs, interview, December 27, 1996.

4. Stuart Murray Williams, "Unpacking the Core Convictions," *Anabaptism Today* 31 (October 2002): 30.

5. Donald R. Jacobs, "My Pilgrimage in Mission," *International Bulletin of Missionary Research* 42 (October 1992): 146.

6. On this renewal effort in the Mennonite Church, see Toews, *Mennonites in American Society*, 214-16; Jacobs, "My Pilgrimage in Mission," 146.

7. Jacobs, interview; Jacobs, "My Pilgrimage in Mission," 146.

8. Jacobs, interview; on Eliezer Mugimba, see Church, *Quest*, 186, 208; Ward, "Obedient Rebels," 218.

9. Jacobs, "My Pilgrimage in Mission," 147.

10. Jacobs, interview; Coomes, *Festo Kivengere*, 171.

11. The Church Army is a voluntary association of lay members of the Church of England and other churches of the Anglican Communion, organized like the Salvation Army, for evangelical and mission work and helping the needy; Jacobs, interview.

12. Orie O. Miller to John E. Leatherman, April 2, 1953; John E. Leatherman to Orie O. Miller, May 2, 1953, EMM; Bishop Board Minutes, A436, May 6, 1953, LMHS.

13. Jacobs, "My Pilgrimage in Mission," 146.

14. Hess, *Pilgrimage*, 88-89.

15. John E. Leatherman to Orie O. Miller, February 10, 1953; Orie O. Miller to John E. Leatherman, March 13, 1953, EMM.

16. Hess, *Pilgrimage,* 88-89.

17. John E. Leatherman, "Tanganyika Mission Annual Report for 1953," EMM.

18. Elam W. Stauffer, "Tanganyika Mission Annual Report for 1952," EMM.

19. John E. Leatherman to Orie O. Miller, May 9, 1953, EMM.

20. John E. Leatherman, "Tanganyika Mission Annual Report for 1953," EMM.

21. Ibid., "Report for 1954," EMM.

22. Hess, *Pilgrimage,* 104.

23. John E. Leatherman, "Tanganyika Mission Annual Report for 1955," February 13, 1956, EMM.

24. Elam W. Stauffer to Amos Horst, July 29, 1955, Stauffer Papers, LMHS.

25. Elam W. Stauffer to Simon Bucher, September 6, 1955, Stauffer Papers, LMHS.

26. Elam W. Stauffer, "Report July 1954–July 1955," EMM.

27. Elam W. Stauffer to Simon Bucher et al., March 14, 1956, EMM.

28. Dorothy Smoker, *Why Africa Now?* (Scottdale, Pa.: Herald Press, 1956), 7.

29. Ward, "Tukutendereza, Yesu," 134 (see note 9 for chap. 3).

30. D. W. Smoker, *Ambushed by Love,* 24; T. F. C. Bewes, *Kikuyu Conflict: Mau Mau and the Christian Witness* (London: Highway, 1953), 5-6.

31. D. W. Smoker, *Ambushed by Love,* 89-90, 128-29, 171.

32. S. S. Momseri, general secretary of the Christian Council of Kenya, to Orie O. Miller, November 3, 1954; Paul Kraybill to Elam W. Stauffer and John E. Leatherman, November 12, 1954; John E. Leatherman to Orie O. Miller, January 29, 1955; Orie O. Miller to John E. Leatherman, February 22, 1955, EMM.

33. Orie O. Miller to John E. Leatherman, March 12, 1956, EMM; Victor Dorsch, "How the East African Revival Impacted My Life," (unpublished, loaned to the author).

34. Hess, *Pilgrimage,* 104.

35. Amos Horst, "Report to Joint Boards on Deputation to East Africa and Europe, June–August 1956," EMM.

36. Elam W. Stauffer to Paul Kraybill, December 7, 1956, EMM.

37. Coomes, *Festo Kivengere,* 173-79.

38. Elam W. Stauffer to Hershey Leaman, n.d. [November 1957];

Stauffer is replying to Hershey Leaman to Elam W. Stauffer, October 8, 1957, Stauffer Papers, LMHS.

39. Hess, *Pilgrimage*, 100.

40. Coomes, *Festo Kivengere*, 183.

41. Ibid., 186-92.

42. Jacobs, "My Pilgrimage in Mission," 147.

43. Ibid.

44. Ibid., 148.

45. Jacobs, *Pilgrimage in Mission*, 47.

46. Elam W. Stauffer to Hershey Leaman, n.d. [November 1957], Stauffer Papers, LMHS.

47. Jacobs, interview.

11. Revival Message Clarified and Unity Promoted, 1959–1961

1. Kevin Ward, "Tukutendereza, Yesu," 134, 137.

2. Don Jacobs, interview, August 2004.

3. J. E. Leatherman, diary, March 15, 17, and 29, 1961; May 1, 1961.

4. Makower, *Coming of the Rain*, 181-90.

5. Osborn, *Fire in the Hills*, 221.

6. Don Jacobs, interview, August 2004.

7. Ibid.

8. Antoine Rutayisire, *Faith Under Fire* (Buckhurst Hill, UK: African Enterprise, 1995), 126 pages.

9. Ward, "Tukutendereza, Yesu," 135.

10. J. E. Leatherman, diary, August 19, 1961.

11. Coomes, *Festo Kivengere*, 208.

12. J. E. Leatherman, diary, August 20, 1961.

13. Don Jacobs, interview, 2004.

14. J. E. Leatherman, diary, September 9, 1959; Bishop Board Minutes, 563, August 20, 1959, LMHS.

15. Bishop Board Minutes, 604, 609, October 15, 1959, LMHS.

16. J. E. Leatherman, diary, October 16-20, 1959.

17. Ibid., October 23-24, 1959.

18. Ibid., December 29, 1959.

19. Ibid., November 23 and December 20, 1959; February 13-14, 1960.

20. Ibid., July 11-12, 1961.

21. Ibid., July 18, 1961.

22. Ibid., August 14, 1961.

23. Ibid., August 15, 1961.

24. Coomes, *Festo Kivengere*, 200-3.
25. J. E. Leatherman, diary, February 26 and March 1, 1960.
26. Ibid., October 21-22, 1959.
27. Coomes, *Festo Kivengere*, 204; Ward, "Tukutendereza, Yesu," 137.
28. Church, *Quest*, 256.
29. Ward, "Tukutendereza, Yesu," 137.
30. Osborn, *Pioneers*, 48-51.
31. Ward, "Tukutendereza, Yesu," 124-25.
32. J. E. Leatherman, diary, October 2-10, 1960.
33. Jacobs, interview, August 2004.
34. J. E. Leatherman, diary, November 7-9, 1960.
35. Ibid., November 10, 1960.
36. Ibid., November 11-12, 1960.
37. J. E. Leatherman, diary, December 10, 1960.
38. J. E. Leatherman, diary, December 8-11, 1960.
39. D. W. Smoker, *Why Africa Now?* 7-8.
40. J. E. Leatherman, diary, August 23-24, 1960; Hess, *Pilgrimage*, 110.
41. J. E. Leatherman, diary, January 27, 1961; Hess, *Pilgrimage*, 111.

12. Africans Strengthen Fellowship with Americans by Visits and Residence, 1960–1964

1. Erma Maust to Dear Ones in Jesus, January 5, 1960; Erma Maust to Dear Ones in Jesus, March 15, 1960.
2. Erma Maust to Paul and Miriam Burkholder, March 15, 1960.
3. Erma Maust to Dear Ones in Jesus, March 15, 1960.
4. Erma Maust to Dear Ones, July 11, 1960.
5. Paul and Miriam Burkholder to Erma Maust, April 13, 1960.
6. Erma Maust to Dear Ones in Jesus, July 11, 1960.
7. Quotations in this section are from Don Widmark, "Two Weeks with William Nagenda," May 1, 1960, (unpublished, loaned to the author).
8. Paul and Miriam Burkholder to Erma Maust, January 29, 1960.
9. Widmark, "Two Weeks."
10. Erma Maust to Dear Ones, July 11, 1960.
11. Erma Maust, diary, September 8, 1960. Erma did not usually keep a diary; this notebook included only their West Coast trip in September–November 1960. Erma Maust to Dear Brothers and Sisters, September 28, 1960.
12. Erma Maust to Dear Brothers and Sisters, September 28, 1960.
13. Erma Maust, diary, September 9, 1960.

14. Erma Maust, diary, September 21, 1960.

15. Erma Maust to Dear Brothers and Sisters, September 28, 1960.

16. Herbert and Erma Maust to Dear Brothers and Sisters, October 28, 1960.

17. Erma Maust to Paul and Miriam Burkholder, November 21, 1960.

18. Erma Maust to Dear Brothers and Sisters, September 28, 1960.

19. Yustasi Ruhindi, later Bishop of North Kigezi, was part of the revival fellowship in his years as a student in New Haven, CT; *African Enterprise Outlook* 11 (December 1974); 12 (February 1975).

20. Erma Maust to Dear Ones, December 1960; Erma Maust to Dear Ones in New York, n.d.

21. David W. Shenk to Richard K. MacMaster, August 30, 1995; David W. Shenk, interview.

22. Erma Maust to Paul and Miriam Burkholder, January 13, 1961.

23. Erma Maust to Dear Ones, February 20, 1961.

24. Herbert and Erma Maust to Paul and Miriam Burkholder, March 2, 1961.

25. Erma Maust to Dear Ones, June 1961.

26. Ibid., April 18, 1961.

27. Ibid.

28. Ibid.

29. Ibid., June 1961.

30. Marvin Plank in Erma Maust to Dear Ones, June 1961.

31. Erma Maust to Dear Ones, June 1961.

32. Erma Maust to Paul and Miriam Burkholder, August 24, 1961.

33. Erma Maust to Dear Brothers and Sisters in the Lord, September 7, 1961.

34. Erma Maust to Dear Marty, June 23, 1961.

35. Marvin Plank in Erma Maust to Dear Ones, June 1961.

36. Erma Maust to Dear Brothers and Sisters in the Lord, September 7, 1961.

37. Erma Maust to Dear Ones, October 1961.

38. Ibid.

39. Erma Maust to Paul and Miriam Burkholder, October 16, 1961.

40. Roy Hession, quoted in Erma Maust to Dear Ones, June 1961.

41. Betty Sanders Hendrick to Richard MacMaster, June 18, 2003.

42. Erma Maust to Dear Brothers and Sisters, January 12, 1962.

43. Coomes, *Festo Kivengere*, 215-16.

44. Erma Maust to Dear Ones, December 26, 1961; Erma Maust to Dear Brothers and Sisters, January 12, 1962.

45. Coomes, *Festo Kivengere*, 216-19.

46. Kivengere with Dorothy Smoker, *Revolutionary Love*, 70-72 (see note 14 for chap. 2).

47. Erma Maust to Mary K. Miller, January 15, 1962.

48. Erma Maust to Our Dear Friends, July 1962.

49. Erma Maust to Mary K. Miller, January 15, 1962.

50. Interview with Wayne Lawton, April 2006.

51. Herbert and Erma Maust, Announcement, n.d.

52. Charles and Pearl Bonner, Interview with Wayne D. Lawton.

53. Erma Maust to Dear Ones, February 14, 1962.

54. Ibid., March 29, 1962.

55. J. E. Leatherman, diary, June 1-8, 1962.

56. Erma Maust to Our Dear Friends, July 1962.

57. Erma Maust, Announcing Fellowship Conference, n.d., 1962.

58. Herbert and Erma Maust to Dear Marvin [Plank], August 17, 1962.

59. J. E. Leatherman, diary, June 1-4, 1965.

60. Erma Maust to Dear Ones, September 14, 1962.

61. Ibid., November 13, 1962.

62. Erma Maust to Dear Brethren, January 11, 1963.

63. Ibid.; Erma Maust to Our Dear Brothers and Sisters, March 14, 1963.

64. Erma Maust to Paul and Miriam Burkholder, March 14, 1963.

65. Wayne D. Lawton in unidentified newspaper clipping.

66. Erma Maust to Jean Griswold, May 6, 1963.

67. Erma Maust to Dear Brothers and Sisters, March 14, 1963.

68. Herbert and Erma Maust to Dear Ones, November 27, 1964.

69. Erma Maust to Jean Griswold, May 6, 1963.

70. Erma Maust to Paul and Miriam Burkholder, December 3, 1963.

71. Russell Krabill, diary, January 14, 1962.

72. Erma Maust to Paul and Miriam Burkholder, February 11, 1964.

73. Herbert and Erma Maust, Announcement, May 5, 1964.

74. Erma Maust to Dear Brothers and Sisters, July 1964.

75. Coomes, *Festo Kivengere*, 228-29.

76. Ward, "Tukutendereza, Yesu," 137.

77. Coomes, *Festo Kivengere*, 233-34.

78. Mildred Plank to Wayne and Mary Lou Lawton, July 8, 1996.

79. Herbert and Erma Maust to Dear Ones, November 27, 1964.

13. Transitions, 1964–1970

1. Hess, *Pilgrimage*, 115, 119.
2. J. E. Leatherman, diary, February 14, 1964.
3. Ibid., June 13, 1964.
4. "Farewell Meeting in Shirati, June 1964," Stauffer Papers, LMHS; J. E. Leatherman, diary, June 20-21, 1964.
5. J. E. Leatherman, diary, June 23, 1964.
6. Ibid., July 27-28, 1964.
7. Makower, *Coming of the Rain*, 196-97.
8. Leatherman, diary, July 17, 1965.
9. Hess, *Pilgrimage*, 113.
10. J. E. Leatherman, diary, March 18-20, 1964.
11. Ibid., March 21-24, 1964.
12. Hess, *Pilgrimage*, 119.
13. Kariuki, *A Bishop Facing Mount Kenya*, 6 (see note 23 for chap. 3).
14. Paul M. Miller, *Equipping for Ministry* (Dodoma, Tanzania: Central Tanganyika Press, 1969), 20.
15. George K. Mambo, "The Revival Fellowship (Brethren) in Kenya," in *Kenya Churches Handbook: The Development of Kenyan Christianity, 1498–1973*, ed. David B. Barrett and George K. Mambo (Kisumu, Kenya: Evangel Publishing House, 1973), 117.
16. Ibid., 114-15.
17. James B. Simpson and Edward M. Story, *The Long Shadows of Lambeth X* (New York: McGraw-Hill, 1969), 105.
18. Ibid., 106.
19. Ibid., 109.
20. Ibid., 217.
21. Mambo, "Revival Fellowship," 113.
22. J. E. Leatherman, diary, August 20-23, 1964.
23. Ibid., August 28, 1964.
24. Mambo, "Revival Fellowship," 115.
25. Robins, "Tukutendereza," 301-4.
26. David Shenk, *Peace and Reconciliation*, 93-100 (see note 1 to the preface).
27. Don Jacobs, interview, August 2004.
28. Ward, "Tukutendereza, Yesu," 137.
29. J. E. Leatherman, diary, September 21-24, 1964.
30. Ibid., April 18, 1965; Robins, "Tukutendereza," 306.
31. Jacobs, private interview.

32. Robins, "Tukutendereza," 304-5.

33. Osborn, *Pioneers*, 148.

34. J. E. Leatherman, diary, December 20, 1964.

35. Malcolm Lea-Wilson, interview.

36. Elam W. Stauffer, "The Holy Spirit's Working in East Africa."

14. International Teams Sharpen the Message of Revival, 1965–1969

1. Elam W. Stauffer, "The Holy Spirit's Working in East Africa."

2. Erma Maust to Dear Ones, February 10, 1965.

3. Erma Maust to Dear Brothers and Sisters, April 5, 1965: "There were only three carloads from the East at the Fellowship at Waynesburg. Mervin and Mary [Miller]; Virgie Keener; Joseph Ntabe, a student at Lincoln University; Wayne and Mary Lou Lawton; and two other young people from Washington, DC; and I went out Friday evening and had a precious time of fellowship at the home of Marvin Planks. Festo was there, as was Bob Hall. We all drove down to Waynesburg [PA] Saturday morning for the fellowship. Nancy Fry, Nancy Bruaw, Anna Stover, and Anna Hostetter drove out Saturday morning. Ernie Wilson was there, he was conducting meetings in Bob Jennings' churches for two weeks. Then there were those from the surrounding churches. Wayne opened it, and then Festo shared the word."

4. Erma Maust to Paul and Miriam Burkholder, February 16, 1965.

5. Paul G. Burkholder to Erma Maust, March 23, 1965.

6. Erma Maust to Paul G. Burkholder, March 30, 1965.

7. Methodist missionary E. Stanley Jones brought the Christian ashram movement from India; Erma Maust to Dear Brothers and Sisters, April 10, 1965.

8. Erma Maust and Mary K. Miller to Dear Brothers and Sisters, May 1965.

9. Announcement, n.d., 1965.

10. Erma Maust and Mary K. Miller to Dear Brothers and Sisters, May 1965.

11. Herbert and Erma Maust to Dear Brothers and Sisters, June 14, 1965: "We praise the Lord for the privilege of attending the Fellowship Conference at Washington, DC, the last Saturday of May. It was good to have Bill and Marian Scott with several from their area with us again, also Ted and Betty Grable and Bill Overholt. Then there was Betty Jennings and several others from their church; Marvin Plank and Festo Kivengere from the Pittsburgh area; Elam W. Stauffer, Clyde and Alta Shenk, Elmer Redcay,

Carl and Dorothy Burkholder from the Lancaster area; and Nancy Frey, Anna Stover, Nancy Bruaw, Kathryn Hertzler, Anna Hostetler, Mervin and Mary K. Miller, Henry and Florence Stauffer, Herbert and I from this area. Others came in from the Washington area, so we had about the usual number."

12. Herbert and Erma Maust to Brothers and Sisters, July 6, 1965.

13. Ibid., August 1965.

14. J. E. Leatherman, diary, September 5, 1965.

15. Ibid., September 7, 1965.

16. Herbert and Erma Maust to Brothers and Sisters, August 1965.

17. Erma Maust to Dear Brothers and Sisters, September 29, 1965.

18. J. E. Leatherman, diary, September 24-25, 1965.

19. Betty Shaeffer and Kathryn Hertzler to Brothers and Sisters, September 1965.

20. Herbert and Erma Maust to Brothers and Sisters, December 1965.

21. J. E. Leatherman, diary, December 30, 1965.

22. Ibid., December 31, 1965; January 1, 1966.

23. Ibid., January 21-22, 1966.

24. Ibid., February 26, 1966.

25. Herbert and Erma Maust to Brothers and Sisters, March 6, 1966.

26. Ibid.

27. Betty M. Shaffer to Brothers and Sisters, March 29, 1966.

28. Erma Maust to Brothers and Sisters, March 29, 1966.

29. Erma Maust to Brothers and Sisters, May 1966.

30. Mary K. Miller, "Report of the Fellowship Conference, April, 1966, Harrisonburg, Va."

31. J. E. Leatherman, diary, May 28, 1966.

32. Ibid., June 10-11, 1966.

33. Festo and Mera Kivengere, October 1966. This vision was more or less fulfilled a few years later when Festo brought a team into African Evangelistic Enterprise.

34. Erma Maust to Dear Brothers and Sisters, June 6, 1966.

35. J. E. Leatherman, diary, June 13, 1966.

36. Erma Maust to Dear Ones in Jesus, July 7, 1966.

37. J. E. Leatherman, diary, June 23, 1966.

38. Erma Maust to Dear Ones in Jesus, July 7, 1966.

39. J. E. Leatherman, diary, June 24, 1966.

40. Ibid., June 25, 1966.

41. Erma Maust to Brothers and Sisters, August 6, 1966.

42. Ibid., September 5, 1966.

43. Ibid., October 10, 1966.

44. Herbert and Erma Maust to Brothers and Sisters, December 3, 1966.

45. Erma Maust to Brothers and Sisters, November 1, 1966.

46. Coomes, *Festo Kivengere*, 239.

47. Herbert and Erma Maust to Brothers and Sisters, December 3, 1966.

48. Ibid., January 11, 1967.

49. J. E. Leatherman, diary, December 30, 1966.

50. Ibid., December 31, 1966.

51. Herbert and Erma Maust, January 11, 1967.

52. J. E. Leatherman, diary, February 4, 1967.

53. Erma Maust to Paul and Miriam Burkholder, January 11, 1967.

54. Paul Burkholder to Herbert and Erma Maust, January 21, 1967.

55. J. E. Leatherman, diary, February 25, 1967.

56. Herbert and Erma Maust to Brothers and Sisters, March 9, 1967.

57. J. E. Leatherman, diary, January 9, 1967.

58. Ibid., March 28, 1967; Herbert and Erma Maust to Brothers and Sisters, April 9, 1967.

59. Leatherman, diary, April 1, 1967.

60. Ibid., April 2, 1967.

61. Ibid., April 29, 1967.

62. Ibid., April 30, 1967.

63. Ibid., May 18, 1967.

64. Herbert and Erma Maust to Brothers and Sisters, May 12, 1967.

65. J. E. Leatherman, diary, June 19, 1967.

66. Ibid., July 23, 1967.

67. Shemaya Megati and Eliam Mauma were the others; Leatherman, diary, August 3, 1967.

68. J. E. Leatherman, diary, August 3, 5-6, 13, and 19, 1967.

69. Herbert and Erma Maust to Brothers and Sisters, September 27, 1967.

70. Ibid., November 23, 1967.

71. Ibid., March 1, 1968.

72. Ibid., July 10, 1968; Osborn, *Pioneers*, 150.

73. Herbert and Erma Maust to Brothers and Sisters, October 3, 1968.

74. Ibid., October 3, 1968.

75. John L. Freed, For the Team, to Dear Brethren, n.d. [April 29, 1969].

76. Erma Maust to Dear Brothers and Sisters, January 1970.

77. William E. Forges to Dear Brethren, July 9, 1969.

78. Coomes, *Festo Kivengere*, 269.

79. Ibid., 248, 260-61.

80. Ibid., 234-35, 255.

81. Ibid., 266-67.

82. Don Jacobs, interview with John Gatu, 1994.

83. Coomes, *Festo Kivengere*, 273.

15. Troubled Times in East Africa, 1970–2000

1. Gerald Anderson, "Moratorium on Missionaries?" in *Christian Century*, January 16, 1974.

2. Osborn, *Pioneers*, 247-48.

3. *African Enterprise Outlook* 17 (July 1980).

4. Coomes, *Festo Kivengere*, 285.

5. Ibid., 296-99.

6. Ibid., 304.

7. In 1974 Bishop Festo, Zebulon Kabaza, and Lillian Clarke were joined by Titus Lwebandiza and Metusaleh (Matt H.) Nyagwaswa, both based in Tanzania; John Wilson and James Katarikawe of Uganda; and Daniel Serwanga, based in Kenya. Coomes, *Festo Kivengere*, 319-20.

8. *African Enterprise Outlook* 11 (May 1974).

9. Wayne Lawton, promotional material, n.d. [April 1974].

10. *African Enterprise Outlook* 9 (August 1972).

11. *African Enterprise Outlook* 11 (September 1974); 11 (November 1974).

12. Wayne Lawton, promotional material, n.d. [April 1974].

13. *African Enterprise Outlook*, 12 (June 1975); 12 (July 1975).

14. Coomes, *Festo Kivengere*, 324.

15. Ibid., 331-32.

16. Ibid., 326-29.

17. *African Enterprise Outlook* 12 (March 1975).

18. Church, *Quest*, 219-20.

19. Coomes, *Festo Kivengere*, 335.

20. Makower, *Coming of the Rain*, 207.

21. *African Enterprise Outlook* 12 (October 1975).

22. John E. H. Wilson to Dear Friend, n.d. [ca. April 1974].

23. Osborn, *Pioneers*, 246-48.

24. Ugandamission.net, July 2005.

25. *African Enterprise Outlook* 14 (March 1977); 14 (May 1977); Coomes, *Festo Kivengere*, 355-67.

26. Bishop William Rukirande, interview.

27. Jacobs, interview, August 2004.

28. Coomes, *Festo Kivengere*, 372.

29. Jacobs, interview, November 2004.

30. Coomes, *Festo Kivengere*, 381.

31. Ibid., 378-79; *African Enterprise Outlook* 14 (July 1977).

32. Coomes, *Festo Kivengere*, 292.

33. Jacobs, interview, August 2004.

34. Ibid.

35. Ibid.

36. Michael Cassidy had published *African Enterprise Outlook* in South Africa for eight years before Festo Kivengere and Zebulon Kabaza (Zeb) became the East African team.

37. Festo Kivengere, *When God Moves in Revival* (rev. ed., Wheaton, Ill.: Tyndale, 1976); idem, *Love Unlimited* (Glendale, Calif.: G/L Regal Books, 1975).

38. *African Enterprise Outlook* 12 (September 1975); Coomes, *Festo Kivengere*, 336.

39. Kivengere with Dorothy Smoker, *Revolutionary Love* (Nairobi: AEE, 1981; Fort Washington, Pa.: CLC, 1983); Coomes, *Festo Kivengere*, 403.

40. *African Enterprise Outlook* 17 (May 1980); 17 (July 1980).

41. *African Enterprise Outlook* 18 (October 1981).

42. Coomes, *Festo Kivengere*, 446.

43. Osborn, *Pioneers*, 150.

44. William Nagenda spoke at Urbana 54, and he and Festo Kivengere both spoke at Urbana 61. The invitation from Billy Graham probably came after the 1961 conference.

45. George and Dorothy Smoker to Dear Friends of East Africa, January 9, 1973.

46. Coomes, *Festo Kivengere*, 310.

47. Osborn, *Pioneers*, 52.

48. Ibid., 260.

49. Coomes, *Festo Kivengere*, 445.

50. Don and Anna Ruth Jacobs, Europe and Africa Diary, May 13–June 2, 1988.

16. Challenges and New Opportunities in North America, 1970–1980

1. Don Jacobs, interview, August 2004.

2. Erma Maust's introduction to the charismatic movement came through Canon Dick Wooton and the Reverend Dennis J. Bennett of Seattle, who later told his story in the popular book *Nine O'Clock in the Morning* (Plainfield, NJL Logos International, 1970). Catharine Leatherman's testimony is in Koch, *My Personal Pentecost*, 198-209 (see note 5 for chap. 5).

3. Bill and Gladys Liner, n.d. [July 1970].

4. Elam W. Stauffer to Wayne Lawton, February 5, 1972.

5. *Living Water Newsletter*, April–September 1970.

6. Charles E. Higgins to Wayne D. Lawton, February 3, 1972.

7. Herbert and Erma Maust, December 1971.

8. Erma Maust to Paul and Miriam Burkholder, December 1971.

9. Herbert and Erma Maust, December 1971.

10. Herbert and Erma Maust to Brothers and Sisters, August 1972.

11. Rev. Robert Crewdson, interview.

12. Ernest Wilson, Fellowship Meetings, n.d. [March 1971].

13. Paul G. Landis to Dear Brothers and Sisters, May 13, 1971: The letter was sent to Rev. and Mrs. Eddie Young, Dixons Mills, Ala.; Rev. and Mrs. Ernest Wilson; Mr. and Mrs. Glenn Zeager; Rev. and Mrs. Ernest Gilmore, Moultrie, Ga.; Rev. and Mrs. Wayne Lawton; Rev. and Mrs. Elam W. Stauffer; Mrs. Catharine Leatherman; Rev. and Mrs. Luke Stoltzfus; and Festo Kivengere.

14. Elam W. Stauffer to Wayne Lawton, February 5, 1972.

15. John L. Freed to Wayne Lawton, October 20, 1972.

16. Don Jacobs, interview.

17. Herbert and Erma Maust to Dear Brothers and Sisters, August 1973; Graybill, *Living Waters*, 37.

18. George and Dorothy Smucker, March–April 1972.

19. Ron Lofthouse, Wainfleet, Ontario, to Brothers and Sisters, n.d. [1975].

20. Erma Maust, Retreat Schedule, 1976.

21. Herbert and Erma Maust to Brothers and Sisters, May 1977.

22. Bill and Vi Forges, Fellowship Letter, August 4, 1970.

23. *African Enterprise Outlook* 15 (May 1978).

24. Wayne Lawton, interview, December 2004.

25. Herbert and Erma Maust to Dear Ones in the Lord, June 1981.

17. Reflections on Revival: New Beginnings Beyond Africa

1. Louise Stolzfus, "A Planter of Trees: Phebe Ethel Yoder," *Pennsylvania Mennonite Heritage* 22 (July 1999): 23.

2. E-mail from Ed Bridgeford to Donald Jacobs, July 2003.

3. *Family Life Today*, April, 1979.

4. E-mail to Donald Jacobs, October 12, 2004.

5. E-mail to Donald Jacobs, October 12, 2004.

6. E-mail to Donald Jacobs, October 26, 2004.

7. E-mail to Donald Jacobs, October 12, 2004.

8. E-mail to Donald Jacobs, October 26, 2004.

9. E-mail to Donald Jacobs, October 12, 2004.

10. E-mail to Donald Jacobs, October 12, 2004.

11. E-mail to Donald Jacobs, 2004.

12. E-mail to Donald Jacobs, 2004.

13. E-mail to Donald Jacobs, 2004.

14. Letter from Darrell Jantzi to Donald Jacobs, October 2004.

15. Ibid.

16. Ibid.

17. A. W. Tozer, *I Call It Heresy!* compiled and edited by Gerald B. Smith (Camp Hill, Pa.: Christian Publications, 1991), chap. 5.

18. Unpublished report of the Kansas City North America Team Meeting, June 1998.

19. Interview with Wayne Lawton, April 11, 2006.

20. Unpublished report of the Kansas City North America Team Meeting, June 1998.

21. Herbert and Erma Maust to Dear Brothers and Sisters, November 1984.

22. Wayne Lawton report on Erma Maust Funeral, July 2000.

23. Wayne Lawton report on Erma Maust Funeral, July 2000.

24. Report of the International Revival Team Fellowship, 1991.

25. Jacobs, interview, August 2004.

18. Ongoing Revival: Testimonies

1. In these headings and testimonies "Tanzania" stands for Tanzania or Tanganyika (before October 1964). Likewise, "Burundi" and "Rwanda" may stand for "Urundi" and "Ruanda" (before 1962). Unless otherwise noted, these testimonies are taken from Quarterly Fellowship Meetings in Bainbridge, Pa., from 1998 through 2001.

2. North American Revival Team Fellowship, 1998, 13–15.

3. Undated 2004 e-mail to Donald Jacobs.

4. E-mail to Donald Jacobs, November 14, 2004.

5. Report of North American Revival Team Fellowship, 1998, 6.

6. Ibid., 22–24.

7. June 2004 e-mail to Donald Jacobs.

Annotated Bibliography

Roy [and Revel] Hession, *The Calvary Road* (Fort Washington, Pa.: CLC, 1950). This book has become a classic and has been translated into dozens of languages. It continues to be read by seekers around the world. It is a small volume, so readers quickly gain perspective on walking repentantly and in the light as people changed by the reviving power of God.

Roy Hession and Stanley Voke, *My Calvary Road* (Grand Rapids: Zondervan, 1978). In this book, Hession reviews his own life as a traveler on the Calvary Road. He shares many challenges he encountered and encourages readers to walk this way of joy, peace and hope.

Oswald Chambers, *My Utmost for His Highest*, (New York: Dodd, Mead & Co., 1935; recently published in updated formats by Barbour Publishing and Discovery House Publishers). This devotional classic was a formative book for many leaders of the East Africa Revival. Many of the themes in Chambers' book parallel those of the revival. That Chambers was a missionary in Egypt added credence to the book for many revivalists.

Norman Grubb, *Continuous Revival*, (Fort Washington, Pa.: CLC, 1997) Norman Grubb of World Evangelical Fellowship was deeply touched by the Lord through the message of the East Africa Revival. He became an advocate for the major emphases of revival.

Stanley Voke, *Personal Revival: Living the Christian Life in the Light of the Cross*, (Fort Washington, Pa.: CLC, Reprinted 1997) Stanley lays out in a very readable fashion the message of revival as he learned and experienced it.

Joseph E. Church, *Quest for the Highest*, (Exeter, UK: Paternoster Press, 1981) In his retirement, Church published an account of his life and involvement in revival in East Africa. Much of the book is in a highly detailed diary format. It recounts the exciting days when the Lord changed Church's life and the lives of those around him. This book is best appreciated by people who have an intimate acquaintance with the history and geography of East Africa, but for the persistent reader it yields a wealth of information about the work of God.

H. H. Osborn, *Pioneers in the East Africa Revival* (Winchester, UK: Apologia Publishers 2000) Osborn served for many years in Rwanda and Uganda as an Anglican missionary. In this book he profiles six couples who served as pioneers in revival: Simeon and Eva Nsibambi, Joe and Decie Church, William and Sala Nagenda, Lawrence and Julia Barham, Yosiah and Dorokasi Kinuka, and Erica and Geraldine Sabiti.

Festo Kivengere:

—*When God Moves, You Move Too*, (Pasadena, Calif.: African Enterprise, 1973) Kivengere lays out in a most winning and telling way what it means to move with God when He moves. This simple book contains the essential message of revival for all cultures.

—with Dorothy Smoker, *Revolutionary Love*, (Nairobi, Kenya: African Evangelistic Enterprise, 1981; Republished: Fort Washington, Pa.: CLC, 1983) This is essentially Kivengere's testimony of how he faced fierce hatred from a regime intent on crushing all foes. Festo reviewed and expanded his own understanding of Christ's cross and applied it to his own life. Christian love is truly revolutionary and stands in strong contrast to revolutionary hate.

Other Works

William B. Anderson, *The Church in East Africa 1840-1974* (Dodoma, Tanganyika: Central Tanganyika Press, 1977).

Bill Butler, *Hill Ablaze* (London: Hodder & Stoughton, 1976).

Joe Church, *Awake—An African Calling: The Story of Blasio Kigozi* (London: Church Missionary Society, 1937).

J. E. Church et al., *Forgive Them: The Story of an African Martyr* (London: Hodder & Stoughton, 1966).

Anne Coomes, *Festo Kivengere* (Eastbourne, Sussex: Monarch, 1990).

Adrian Hastings, *The Church in Africa 1450-1950* (Oxford: Oxford University Press, 1994).

Mahlon M. Hess, *Pilgrimage of Faith: Tanzania Mennonite Church 1934-1983* (Salunga, Pa.: Eastern Mennonite Board of Missions and Charities, 1985).

Gordon Hewitt, *The Problems of Success: A History of the Church Missionary Society 1910-1942* (London: SCM Press, 1971).

John Karanja, *Founding an African Faith: Kikuyu Anglican Christianity 1900-1945* (Nairobi: Uzima Press, 1999).

Obadiah Kariuki, *A Bishop Facing Mount Kenya: An Autobiography, 1902-1978* (Nairobi: Uzima Press, 1985).

N. A. Kivuti, *A Church Comes of Age: Fifty Years of Revival in the C.P.K. Diocese of Embu 1942-1992* (Nairobi: Uzima Press, 1992).

Neville Langford-Smith, "Revival in East Africa," *International Review of Missions,* 43 (1954).

Katharine Makower, *The Coming of the Rain: The Life of Dr. Joe Church* (Carlisle, Cumbria: Paternoster Press, 1999).

Jocelyn Murray, *Proclaim the Good News: A Short History of the Church Missionary Society* (London: Hodder & Stoughton, 1985).

H. H. Osborn, *Revival—A Precious Heritage* (Winchester, Hampshire: Apologia Publications, 1995).

Catherine Ellen Robins, *Tukutendereza: A Study of Social Change and Sectarian Withdrawal in the Balokole Revival of Uganda* (PhD diss., Columbia University, 1975).

Patricia St. John, *Breath of Life: The Story of the Ruanda Mission* (London: Norfolk Press, 1971).

Mark Shaw, "A Hunger for Holiness," *Christian History*, 79 (Spring 2003).

A. C. Stanley Smith, *Road to Revival: The Story of the Ruanda Mission* (London: Church Missionary Society, 1946).

Kevin Ward, "Obedient Rebels—The Relationship Between the Early 'Balokole' and the Church of Uganda: The Mukono Crisis of 1941" *Journal of Religion in Africa*, 194-227 (XIX 1989).

Kevin Ward, " 'Tukutendereza Yesu' The Balokole Revival in Uganda" in Zablon Nthamburi, ed., *From Mission to Church: A Handbook of Christianity in East Africa* (Nairobi: Uzima Press, 1995).

Photo Credits

Miriam Maust Achenbach, page 151.

African Enterprise, pages 240, 265, 285.

Paul Burkholder, page 145.

Eastern Mennonite Missions, pages 70, 114, 169, 269, 327.

Jean Griswold, pages 121, 140.

Nathan Hege, page 347.

Janice Hess, pages 130, 135, 220, 239.

Mahlon Hess, page 83.

Charles Higgins, page 331.

Simeon Hurst, page 70.

Don Jacobs, pages 71, 79, 165, 167, 170, 174, 177, 187, 206, 223, 226, 278,
   311, 313, 314, 352.

Paul Landis, page 282.

Wayne Lawton, pages 107, 115, 139, 144, 150, 155, 161, 201, 204, 205,
   209, 210, 211, 213, 215, 216, 218, 246, 252, 258, 284, 286, 305, 306,
   307, 308, 314, 343.

Andrew Leatherman, page 69.

Catharine Leatherman, page 325.

Bill Liner, page 278.

Herbert Maust, pages 126, 283.

Betty Miller, page 138.

James Miller, pages 131, 212.

Ted McJunkin, page 299.

Methusela Nyagwaswa, page 247.

Herbert Osborn pages 27, 28, 35, 36.

Sam Parker, page 303.

Jim Perry, page 298.

Mildred Plank, page 245.

Lindsay Robinson, page 340.

Dora Sabiti, page 228.
Bill Scott, page 152.
Grace Stauffer, page 68.
John Young, pages 151, 304.

Index

The Authors

Richard K. MacMaster taught American history at Western Carolina University, James Madison University, and Bluffton College. He is now retired and living in Gainesville, Florida, where he is a member of Emmanuel Mennonite Church. Richard's previous books include *Conscience in Crisis* (1979) and *Land, Piety, Peoplehood* (1989). He holds undergraduate degrees from Fordham University and a PhD from Georgetown University.

Donald R. Jacobs served as an African missionary from 1953 to 1973, when he founded the Mennonite Theological College in Tanzania and later served on the faculty at the University of Nairobi. After his African ministry, Don directed overseas programs for Eastern Mennonite Missions and then worked as director of the Mennonite Christian Leadership Foundation. He lives in Lancaster, Pennsylvania, and is a member of Chestnut Hill Mennonite Church. His previous books include *From Rubble to Rejoicing* (1991) and *Pilgrimage in Mission* (1983).